Latina/os and World War II

Latina/os and World War II

Mobility, Agency, and Ideology

EDITED BY MAGGIE RIVAS-RODRIGUEZ
AND B. V. OLGUÍN

University of Texas Press   *Austin*

First paperback edition, 2015

Requests for permission to reproduce material from this work should be sent to:
Permissions
University of Texas Press
P.O. Box 7819
Austin, TX 78713–7819
http://utpress.utexas.edu/index.php/rp-form

♾ The paper used in this book meets the minimum requirements of ANSI/NISO
Z39.48–1992 (R1997) (Permanence of Paper).

Library of Congress Cataloging-in-Publication Data
Latina/os and World War II : mobility, agency, and ideology / edited by Maggie
Rivas-Rodriguez and B.V. Olguín. — First edition.
    pages cm
    Includes bibliographical references and index.
    ISBN 978-0-292-75625-0 (cloth : alk. paper)
    ISBN 978-1-4773-0762-5 (paperback)
    1. World War, 1939–1945—Participation, Hispanic American.   2. World War,
1939–1945—Social aspects—United States.   3. United States—Armed Forces—
Hispanic Americans—History—20th century.   4. Hispanic American soldiers—
History—20th century.   5. Hispanic Americans—Social conditions—20th century.
I. Rivas-Rodriguez, Maggie, author, editor of compilation.   II. Olguín, B. V.,
1965–   author, editor of compilation.   III. Title: Latinas and World War II.
IV. Title: Latinos and World War II.
    D769.8.H58U7   2014
    940.54′0468—dc23
                                                                                    2013028732

doi:10.7560/756250

In memory of Maggie Rivas–Rodriguez and B. V. Olguín family members who served in World War II:

Army Pvt. Secundino Silva (Philippines)
Army Cpl. Adán Valdez (North Africa Campaign)
Army Pvt. Victor M. Ledesma (Normandy Invasion, KIA)
Army Pvt. Ramón Martín Rivas (Dutch Harbor, Aleutian Islands)

Contents

PREFACE

Navigating Bureaucratic Imprecision in the Search for an Accurate Count of Latino/a Military Service in World War II

KARL ESCHBACH AND MAGGIE RIVAS-RODRIGUEZ

When twenty-five-year-old Trinidad Botello, from the small central Texas community of San Saba, was discharged from the U.S. Army in fall 1945, a clerk recorded his particulars: brown eyes, black hair, 5 feet, 5 inches, 145 pounds, U.S. citizen. Under "Race," where only three choices were offered—"White," "Negro," and "Other (specify)"—the clerk typed "Mexican."

The following year, his younger brother, Crisantos D. Botello, was discharged from the U.S. Army. His particulars were almost identical: brown eyes, black hair, 5 feet, 5 inches, 140 pounds, U.S. citizen. But under "Race," this clerk typed "White."[1]

In fact, there were five Botello brothers who served in World War II. Besides Trinidad and Crisantos there was John, who was inducted in summer 1943 and discharged in November 1945; Simon, sworn in November 1942 and discharged in summer 1946; and Gregorio, who joined the navy and was discharged in 1945. Simon was categorized as "White," John as "Mexican," and Gregorio as "White." So three of the five brothers were considered white and two, Mexican.

The Botello brothers' discharge papers illustrate the capriciousness of Latina/o racial categorization in that period. Because of a bureaucratic idiosyncrasy, the racial assignments of Mexican Americans and other Latina/os were inconsistent throughout World War II and to this day continue to bedevil demographers, public policy makers, historians, and even family members.[2] The irony of fluid racial assignments got the attention of World War II veterans. For instance, in one interview in 2000 a veteran from West Texas recalled being prodded by a drill instructor to answer whether he was Spanish or Mexican. Aniceto "Cheto" Nuñez recalled, "I told him, 'I was Mexican, but when the war started I became a white man.'" The instructor persisted, *Mexican*? "No, I was not born in Mexico," replied Nuñez. "I

Figure 0.1. Trinidad D. Botello, one of five Botello brothers from San Saba, Texas, was identified as "Mexican" by U.S. Army officials. Voces Oral History Project, Nettie Lee Benson Latin American Collection, University of Texas at Austin.

Figure 0.2. Simon D. Botello was classified as "white" on his discharge papers. Voces Oral History Project, Nettie Lee Benson Latin American Collection, University of Texas at Austin.

Figure 0.3. John D. Botello was listed as "Mexican" on his discharge papers. Voces Oral History Project, Nettie Lee Benson Latin American Collection, University of Texas at Austin.

Figure 0.4. Crisantos D. Botello was categorized as "white." Voces Oral History Project, Nettie Lee Benson Latin American Collection, University of Texas at Austin.

Figure 0.5. Gregorio D. Botello was considered "white" by navy officials. Voces Oral History Project, Nettie Lee Benson Latin American Collection, University of Texas at Austin.

was born in Fort Stockton, but they called me Mexican. And when the war started, I became a white man."[3]

Because of the unreliability of racial categorization, the question of Latino participation in the military during World War II has long been a matter of debate and conjecture. The total number of servicemen in World War II was well established: 16.1 million. That number was easily accessible from the federal government. It is known, for instance, that Americans categorized as "Negro" made up nearly one million military personnel during World War II, serving in segregated units.[4] But in fact those "Negro units" included some Hispanics.[5] Native Americans in the military totaled 21,767. Bernstein notes:

Indeed because the Indian soldiers did not serve in segregated units like their black counterparts, it is even difficult to trace the pattern of participation. Nevertheless, the involvement of thousands of young Indians in the military during World War II signaled a major break with the past for Indians and whites alike. It represented the first large-scale exodus of Indian men from the reservations since the defeat of their ancestors, and an unparalleled opportunity to compete in the white world in an arena where their talents and reputation as fighters inspired respect.[6]

Japanese Americans numbered 33,000 in World War II,[7] Chinese Americans around 13,000.[8] Although the numbers may suffer similarly from inaccuracy, it is likely that these soldiers were entered as Indian, Native American, or Japanese or Chinese Americans on their enlistment and discharge papers. Latina/os were another matter, as shown in the example of Mexican American soldiers. The situation was even more complicated for other Latinos. Puerto Ricans, U.S. citizens since 1917, were drafted and often assigned to the segregated Third Battalion of the 65th Infantry Regiment and the National Guard unit of the 295th Infantry Regiment. As Silvia Álvarez Curbelo has noted, the disconnect between the island's and the mainland's interpretation of race emerged: "The 'White' category handled by the Puerto Rican boards did not always conform with the popular version of the term in the United States. It included Puerto Ricans who were considered 'White' on the island but who would be seen as 'colored' elsewhere."[9] On the mainland, Latinos in general were not as easily identified: there were no clear demarcations between "Whites" and "Mexicans."[10]

Some public and scholarly estimates of Latina/o participation in World War II reported figures without providing their provenance, making it impossible to determine their validity.[11] Yet it is important to pursue the question of an accurate number as it conveys in general terms the participation of Latina/os among the 16 million men and women who served in the armed forces during World War II. For academics and the media, the numbers are crucial for assessing the extent to which the war effort included Latina/os—beyond the anecdotal. Research that includes statistical information is deemed more legitimate, more credible; enumeration may reveal a problem or show areas that require greater attention.[12]

To tackle the question of the number of Latina/os who served in the U.S. military during the war, we turned to information from the U.S. Census. But we immediately recognized some of the limitations and potential for under- or even overreporting. Among the challenges were changes in how the Census Bureau counts residents of Hispanic/Latina/o descent and migration of Latina/os from the mainland or Puerto Rico or other countries. Still the census is a good starting point: over the course of more than two hundred years of data collection, it has gathered information on military service sporadically. In 1950, four years after the end of World War II, the census included a question about service in the U.S. military and period of service in a sample count; that is, not all households were asked this question. In the censuses of 1960 through 2000 the veteran status question has been included on the so-called long form of the census, which collects detailed socioeconomic data from persons in a large sample of U.S. households.

In 1980 the census asked the following question about veteran status: "Is this person a veteran of active-duty military service in the Armed Forces of the United States?" Those who responded yes were asked, "Was active duty military service during . . . " Among the response categories were "World War II (September 1940–July 1947)," "May 1975 or later," "Vietnam Era," "February 1955–July 1964," "Korean Conflict," "World War I," and "Any other time." More recent censuses have included a similarly worded question.[13]

This question implements a classification of veteran status and period of service by self-identification. It is not validated by cross-checking against administrative service records, though errors introduced by self-report are likely small. It is a general measurement: the question does not include information about service in a combat unit, overseas deployment, or actual combat experience. Nonetheless, it provides a reasonable basis for a count of veterans on active duty for each service period and is used by the Veteran's Administration as the basis for its population model of the demographic characteristics of the veteran population of the United States.[14]

But a breakdown of the racial demographics of the veteran population using the 1950 and 1960 censuses still did not enable a determination of the Latina/o component. In 1930 the Census Bureau created the category "Mexican" but then discontinued it and did not include a question about membership in a Latina/o-descent population for forty years. In 1970 a sample of the population was asked a question about "origin or descent," with response categories focused on Latina/o origins. And in the following decennial census and subsequently, all respondents to both the short form and long form census schedule have been asked to report "Spanish/Hispanic" origin.[15]

In 1980 respondents were asked to classify themselves and their household members in response to the question, "Is this person of Spanish/Hispanic origin or descent?" Response categories included "Mexican, Mexican-Amer., Chicano," "Puerto Rican," "Cuban," "other Spanish/Hispanic," and "No, not Spanish/Hispanic." Since 1980 this question or minor variations of it have been used to identify the "Hispanic" population of the United States in the federal statistical system. It implements the system of using

Table 0.1. Latino World War II Veteran Population Counted in the United States Census, 1970–2000

Year	Men	Women	Total	95% Confidence Interval
1970	289,000	NA	289,000[†]	283,951–294,049[†]
1980	262,960	6,020	268,980	263,666–274,294
1990	201,881	4,941	206,822	200,996–212,648
2000	134,987	4,469	139,456	132,758–146,154

[†]Males only.
Source: Integrated Public-Use Microdata Project at the University of Minnesota, relying on U.S. censuses.

self-identification as the preferred way to classify persons in relation to racial and ethnic category membership.[16]

Thus each census from 1970 through 2000 gives a full, large sample estimate of the population that lived in the United States (including Puerto Rico), identified themselves as "Spanish or Hispanic," and reported active duty service in the U.S. military in the World War II era. But those counts had limitations similar to those of any census or survey: sampling error, undercount, and out-migration of the target population from the coverage area of the census. Moreover, the 1970 census did not include women in its count of veterans. It is also known that the wording of the question in the 1970 sample produced a smaller estimate of the U.S. Hispanic population than would have been the case with the wording used at the later censuses and in particular undercounted Mexican Americans.[17]

Table 0.1 shows these estimates, as reported from data in the Integrated Public-Use Microdata Project at the University of Minnesota, a probability sample of records from each census. Confidence intervals are reported based on information about item-specific design effects on standard errors reported at the time each data set was prepared.

How do these counts relate to an estimate of the number of Latina/o veterans who served in the U.S. military? We were lacking a key variable: how many Latina/o service personnel died between their entry into service and the day the census was taken? We needed to produce two numbers: (1) how many military personnel died during the period of service itself and (2) how many died from the end of the war until the date of the census—a period of approximately twenty-five years, reckoning from August 1945 (VJ Day) to April 1970 (the reference day for the U.S. Census in 1970), and then fifty-five years, to April 2000, the reference day for the final census.

The number of deaths in the postwar period may be estimated with some precision from information produced by the National Center for Health Statistics (NCHS) and predecessor agencies over the entire period. Each decade the NCHS produces a life table for the U.S. population by sex and for the white and black populations. These tables use registered deaths for the three years centered on each census, together with counts of population from the census, to calculate age- and sex-specific schedules of death rates for each population.[18] With this information, it is possible to produce estimates of deaths occurring in the intervals between the end of hostilities in 1945 and subsequent censuses, applying across each decade the mortality schedule derived for each period.

Some uncertainty is introduced because the age-specific death rates of the U.S. population as a whole may not apply directly to the population of Latina/o veterans. Other studies had shown that specific service experiences—such as exposure to combat and service in particular theaters—was linked to increased mortality among veterans after the war. But active duty status per se was not predictive of subsequent mortality, which we determined after we considered the countervailing effects of health selection in the veteran population and the negative effects of service.[19] Analyses of Hispanic mortality patterns have also shown that, with some differences in age patterns of mortality, Hispanic mortality rates are similar to or slightly lower than those of non-Hispanic whites.[20] It may be necessary to be sensitive to departures from average mortality schedules for the U.S. population. However, given what is known about Hispanic mortality and veteran mortality, we may make corrections of plausible magnitudes and still arrive at only modest increases in uncertainty about the size of the serving Latina/o population. That is to say, our estimates, after allowing for differences in both Hispanic and veteran mortality, should have only a nominal effect on our certainty.

Data suggest that the number of deaths from both combat and noncombat causes of active duty personnel during World War II was 2.5 percent of all active duty personnel.[21] Because records of deaths are not available for Latina/o servicemen and servicewomen, additional uncertainty is introduced about the exact size of the serving population. However, it is the case here as well that plausible increases or decreases in the active duty death rate for Latina/os compared to other groups would lead to a correction in the estimate of the total serving population in the range of a few thousand persons. One issue that cannot be ascertained at this time is whether those active duty death rates were higher in certain units and whether Latina/os were overrepresented in those units.

Table 0.2. Estimates of the Number of Latinos Who Served on Active Duty during World War II Derived from Census Counts of Veterans, 1970–2000

Estimate Based on Census of Year	Point Estimate of Veteran Population Alive in 1945	Adjustment for Deaths during Active Service	95% Confidence Interval
1970	328,000[†]	336,500[†]	330,600–342,300[†]
1980	363,000	372,400	365,000–379,700
1990	359,000	368,300	358,900–378,600
2000	351,000	360,100	342,800–377,400

[†]Males only.
Source: Census figures, authors' estimates, after weighing mortality rates for general military serviceman population.

Estimates of the number of Latina/os who served in World War II derived by these methods from subsequent census counts are presented in Table 0.2. These estimates are remarkably concordant over time, suggesting a Latina/o World War II service population in the range of 340,000 to 380,000.

Further adjustment of these estimates may be warranted, though the size of the adjustment is speculative. An adjustment for census undercount may be warranted. The 1970 count of Latina/os was certainly low, primarily because of question wording. The size of the correction is not known.[22] The Census Bureau estimated a net undercount of Hispanics in 1990 of approximately 5 percent and a net undercount in 2000 of 0.71 percent, the latter not significantly different from 0 percent.[23] It is likely that much of the apparent reduction in undercount between 1990 and 2000 was attributable to the change in the Census Bureau methodology for estimating undercount. In any case, the undercount of Hispanics in recent U.S. censuses has been attributed to the presence of the hard to enumerate undocumented immigrant population as part of the Hispanic population.[24] However, the World War II veteran population was overwhelmingly a citizen population by birth or naturalization by the time of the census counts. It is unlikely that this population was undercounted to the same degree as were younger immigrants.

A second source of underestimation would result from substantial emigration of Latina/o veterans from the United States and Puerto Rico between the end of the war and the census. We know from each census itself that approximately 1 percent of Latina/o World War II veterans reported living outside of the enumeration area five years before the census was taken. The largest proportion (1.5 percent) report this in 1970, when the number may have been elevated by World War II veterans who were career soldiers on active duty status in Vietnam or in other overseas deployment in 1965.

It is likely that at least a few Latina/o U.S. military veterans migrated to another country. This would have been most likely for foreign-born servicemen who chose to return to a country of origin in the years immediately after the war. As the cohort aged, retirement to areas with cheaper costs of living and more favorable climates, such as Mexico or elsewhere in Latin America, may have been seen as attractive, which is a choice made by some Americans of all racial and ethnic backgrounds. For the many Latina/o veterans who were near-border residents, such relocations may be minimally disruptive. Nonetheless, it should be recognized that net migration flows between Mexico, Latin America, and the United States in the postwar period were overwhelmingly from south to north. A substantial majority of Latina/os serving in active duty during World War II were born in the United States. An overwhelming majority of Latina/o veterans were U.S. citizens in the years after the war. These considerations suggest that outmigration of World War II veterans from the United States has had small effects on these estimates.

Probably the most important source of potential underestimation comes from changing self-definitions of ethnicity over time. For example, Alba and Islam estimated that approximately 10 to 15 percent of the Mexican-origin population disappeared from census counts between 1980 and 2000 because of changing self-definition of ethnicity.[25] This decrease may partly account for the slightly lower estimates of the size of the Latina/o veteran population derived from the 2000 census compared to the 1980 census as presented here. But it is also possible that similar attrition would have occurred between the war and the census counts used to make these estimates. From the point of view of census enumerations, this is a hypothetical question, because Latina/o identity choices were not available on census counts before 1970. In other words, an unknown portion of the Latina/o veteran population may have chosen not to report its ethnicity when filling out the census, even after the choice became available in 1970 and thereafter. The reasons for this are personal and may not reflect the complexity of feelings about ethnic identity of the individuals who make this choice. If Alba and Islam's estimates are correct, underreporting by individuals themselves of an identity as a Latina/o is likely the largest source of uncertainty about the size of the population of Latina/o World War II veterans. Depending on how the analyst interprets the ethnicity of persons who choose not to

Table 0.3. Percentage of Surviving Cohorts of Men Who Reported Service in the World War II Era: Pooled Censuses of 1980, 1990, and 2000

	Hispanics				Ratio to Non-Hispanics		
Age in 1940	U.S.-Born	Puerto Rico– Born	Immi- grated to U.S. before 1940*	Non- Hispanic, U.S.- Born	U.S.-Born	Puerto Rico– Born	Immi- grated to U.S. before 1940
10–15	38	11	46	51	0.75	0.22	0.90
16–22	60	26	53	73	0.82	0.36	0.73
23–27	39	16	41	46	0.85	0.35	0.89
28–35	21	7	20	25	0.84	0.28	0.80

*Data for immigrants are from Census 2000 only. Margin of error for immigrants varies from ±5 to ±8.
Source: U.S. Censuses of 1980, 1990, and 2000.

identify their Latino ancestry on a government form, an upward adjustment of the estimate presented here in the range of 10 to 20 percent may be warranted.

A second question that the census data can help us answer concerns the share of the World War II cohorts of Latinos who saw military service. Using the census data, we can calculate the percentage of Hispanic men from the age groups that provided the majority of service members during the World War II era and compare these to non-Hispanics. (Active duty service rates for women were approximately 1 to 2 percent of each age group, and group differences cannot be analyzed with much precision because of the small number of respondents who reported service.)

One's age at the start of the war is an important predictor of whether a man was called to active duty. The highest rates of service for all groups were for men between ages 16 and 22 in 1940 and thus (approximately) between ages 21 and 27 at the end of the war. Sixty percent of the Hispanic men who were natives of the U.S. mainland in this cohort reported World War II–era service at later censuses. This figure is approximately 20 percent lower than the service rate of non-Hispanic U.S. citizens in the same age cohort. This relationship between Hispanic and non-Hispanic service rates is similar across all cohorts.

As Table 0.3 shows, service rates were substantially lower for Puerto Rican men who were born in Puerto Rico than they were for mainland-born Hispanics. We do not have information from the censuses to fully explore this relationship; specifically, we do not have information about where the respondents lived during the wartime mobilization. However, the data appear to show that the key variable is geography, not ethnic origins. Puerto Rican men who were born on the U.S. mainland—and who likely lived on the U.S. mainland on Pearl Harbor day—served at a rate similar to Mexican Americans. It would appear that mobilization efforts in Puerto Rico, which did not yet have the Commonwealth status it would be granted in 1950, were less aggressive than the same efforts on the U.S. mainland.

Interestingly, we have no evidence that immigrant Hispanics who were already living in the United States at the start of the war served their country at lower rates than their native-born brethren. Service rates for immigrants are estimated with much less precision than for other groups because of the relatively small sample in the available census files, but these rates (see Table 0.3) are quite close to those of U.S.-born Hispanics. Of course, later years would see large new immigrant flows from Mexico, elsewhere in Central America, South America, and Cuba. These new postwar immigrants had not had the opportunity for active duty service in the U.S. military during the war.

The Latina/o population of the United States has both grown and diversified tremendously since the end of World War II. Latina/os—those who count themselves as such in responding to the census—in 2013 number more than 51 million and are the largest minority population in the United States. The largely Mexican American and Puerto Rican population of the period of the war has now been augmented by migration from throughout Latin America and by a high birthrate. The population has spread geographically throughout the United States, as well as throughout the U.S. social and economic structure. Knowing about the honorable service and sacrifices of as many as 400,000 Latina/o men and women in World War II helps us to understand the contributions of Latina/os to their country during a time of grave peril. Understanding the demographic parameters of this population helps us to know more about who they were and what they did.

Acknowledgments

This book seeks to pay a debt to Latina and Latino wartime soldiers and defense industry workers that of course can never be paid. They joined the millions of people in the United States and throughout the world to fight many bloody battles, as well as continuing postwar struggles, that have enabled small but crucial spaces for the interrogation of profound issues confronting humanity. The editors of and contributors to this book also wish to acknowledge a debt of gratitude to the families and friends of these soldiers and workers, in addition to the many supporters, volunteers, and staff members who have made this project possible.

This book is the fourth volume based in large measure on an oral history project, the U.S. Latino & Latina World War II Oral History Project, now the Voces Oral History Project, that began in 1999 in the School of Journalism of the University of Texas at Austin. Voces has conducted nearly one thousand interviews, and these are the basis for most of the chapters in this volume. Voces has also made sure that those interviews are mined for their richness by organizing workshops, conferences, and symposia to attract scholars with similar interests and to disseminate findings to the broader public.

This volume was conceived as a collective enterprise, and the goal was to enable participants to learn from one another in the workshops and conferences mentioned in the introduction. Some of the contributors to this volume participated in a weeklong workshop held from July 29 to August 2, 2002, at the University of Texas at Austin. Others joined us later, in a 2010 workshop at the Benson Latin American Collection at the University of Texas at Austin, when the U.S. Latino & Latina World War II Oral History Project celebrated its tenth anniversary and changed its name to the Voces Oral History Project to reflect the growth of the project beyond World War II. We followed these workshops with a contributor workshop and community symposium in April 29–30, 2011, at the University of Texas at San Antonio, which enabled us to refine the penultimate drafts of the individual chapters. We are gratified that this volume includes senior scholars such as Félix Gutiérrez, Gary Mormino, and Gerald Poyo, as well as graduate students who are completing their Ph.D.s, such as Jordan Beltrán Gonzales. During the writing process, one of our young scholars, Patricia Portales, earned her Ph.D. at the University of Texas at San Antonio, and the collaborative workshop model used to develop this book was instrumental to her successful dissertation work.

Some time ago, as we put a budget together for a major grant proposal, we were astonished to learn how many in-kind donations the Voces project has garnered, including those from our home and partner institutions. When we tallied what we received from volunteers, who conduct interviews, write stories, organize interview sessions, and conduct many other services, Voces had enjoyed over $3 million in volunteer support over the years. Quite simply, the interviews that form a substantial part of this volume and the workshops organized through the offices of the Voces Oral History Project have been possible in large part because of the men and women who have given freely of their time and expertise to conduct interviews. They are too numerous to list here. But they deserve a large measure of gratitude from all of us who benefit from their time and efforts collecting the many voices of Latina/os of the World War II era.

That in-kind support also extends to the administrators and staff at various universities, colleges, and research centers that have, since 1999, provided the infrastructure that enabled us to complete this fourth volume of the series. At the University of Texas at Austin, the Voces Oral History Project has received invaluable logistical support from the College of Communication, the School of Journalism, the Center for Mexican American Studies (CMAS), and the University of Texas Libraries and its Nettie Lee Benson Latin American Collection. The School of Journalism support staff includes Janice Henderson (journalism office manager), Sonia Reyes-Krempin (former journalism accountant), and Lourdes G. Jones (current journalism accountant). The College of Communications technical staff keep us up and running: Charles Soto, Scott Calhoun, Rod Edwards, Jeff Fromme, Kamran Hooshman, Larry Horvat, Josh Kinney, Brian Parrett, Mark Rogers, Alicia Vogel, and Dave Wiginton. We appreciate the College of Communication's administrative staff who have consistently supported us: Dean Rod Hart; Assistant Dean Janice Daman; Jeff

Toreki, finance manager; Rod Fehlhafer, human resource manager; and Jay Whitman, grant manager. At the University of Texas Libraries, we want to thank Fred Heath, vice provost and director; Doug Barnett, chief of staff; Casey Hunt and Dustin Younse, web developers; and Aaron Choate, who helped guide the entire process. At the Benson Latin American Collection, we have had a longtime and strong relationship with Mexican American Studies librarian Margo Gutierrez and archivist Christian Kelleher, as well as former Benson head librarian Ann Hartness. The Center for Mexican American Studies over the years has been one of our staunchest supporters, and we acknowledge the strong support of current director Dominó Perez and former director José Limón. The entire CMAS staff, in particular program manager Luis Guevara, has been helpful at various times.

This project is indebted to Voces Oral History Project staff members and volunteers, past and present, who helped on this volume in various ways: Erika Martinez Rizo, Violeta Dominguez Mehl, Liliana Velasquez Rodriguez, Valentín (Tino) Mauricio, Marc Hamel, Raquel Garza, Manuel Aviles-Santiago, Laura Barberena, and Paepin Goff.

At the University of Texas at San Antonio, the English Department and College of Liberal and Fine Arts provided generous and crucial funding, in addition to institutional support, for the aforementioned spring 2011 workshop that both enabled the contributors to collaboratively rework their drafts and disseminate those early findings to the broader public at a corresponding community symposium. We are especially thankful to U.S. Air Force Colonel (Ret.) Lisa Firmin for her keynote address at this public symposium. English Department Chair Bridget Drinka deserves special recognition. Work-study student Patrick Collins produced superb promotional materials responsible for the wide public participation in the event. English Department staff members Maureen A. Carroll and Peggy Garner provided the logistical expertise to make the event a success. University of Texas at San Antonio Downtown Campus staff also ensured the smooth operation of this project, and we are especially grateful to Sylvia Rodriguez and Rachel Jennings, Ph.D., whose additional expertise as a research scholar, author, and community organizer also contributed to the conceptual design of the final workshop that culminated in the chapters that comprise this book.

Above all else, this book, and the overall Voces Oral History Project, continues to be supported by grassroots community people who recognize that the main impetus behind this book is essentially to partner with them as they tell their own stories and develop the primary sources essential to ensuring that Latina/o perspectives are included and understood in the nation's discourse. Whether their particular stories appear in this volume or not, those interviews help us conceptualize themes and provide a depth of understanding we could not otherwise have gained.

Finally, Theresa J. May, editor in chief at the University of Texas Press, has been responsible for the cultivation of the most dynamic list in Latina/o Studies, of which this installment of the Voces Oral History Project is part. She quite literally has helped shape the field while simultaneously enabling productive interrogations of its operative paradigms. *Muchísimas gracias.*

Mapping Latina/o Mobility, Agency, and Ideology in the World War II Era

MAGGIE RIVAS-RODRIGUEZ AND B. V. OLGUÍN

In the academy it is often said that all research is a reflection of the scholar's own values, concerns, and obsessions. This certainly is true for this anthology, as most of the writers have a personal link to the topic: they are the sons and daughters, nieces and nephews, or grandchildren of Latina/o World War II–era military veterans and defense department workers. Yet beyond this shared legacy, the origination and inspiration for the essays in this book are as varied as the individual writers, whose case studies come from the family stories passed on through generations, boxes of family photos, and archived newspapers, as well as ongoing research projects for graduate school and monographs.

One of those starting points was the 2002 weeklong workshop in Austin, Texas, where the U.S. Latino & Latina World War II Oral History Project at the University of Texas at Austin brought together scholars from across the country. The goal of the workshop was to provide a foundation for research into Latina/os and World War II, as well as to stimulate scholarly use of the primary source materials that have been gathered by the oral history project since its foundation in 1999. A palpable excitement pervaded the fifth floor conference room on the University of Texas at Austin campus where we met daily for a week. The presenters, all experts on World War II–related matters, recognized the tremendous potential of investigating the Latina/o experience during World War II. They also knew that the interviews being recorded by the U.S. Latino & Latina World War II Oral History Project would provide the primary source material for future research projects. Presenters were assigned topics such as California and World War II or Latinas in World War II. Some of the presenters—Richard Griswold del Castillo, Dionicio Valdés, Joanne Rao Sánchez, Emilio Zamora,

Silvia Álvarez Curbelo, Rea Ann Trotter, and Ricardo Ainslie—later wrote chapters for a 2009 book, *Beyond the Latino World War II Hero: The Social and Political Legacy of a Generation*.[1] Others—Naomi Quiñonez and Erasmo Gamboa—contributed to the project's first book, *Mexican Americans and World War II*,[2] which got its start from the inaugural two-day conference in Austin in 2000. Two of this anthology's writers, both senior scholars, Félix Gutiérrez and Gary Mormino, also took part in that workshop. The complicated process of meditation and dialogue among intersecting networks of interlocutors illustrates the long-term conceptualization and planning required to bring to fruition a project such as this one. We thank all of those 2002 workshop presenters for their help in shaping this book.

Latina/os, World War II, and Beyond: The Past, Present, and Future of the Voces Oral History Project

This book marks another accomplishment: the evolution of the oral history work that is based on U.S. Latinas and Latinos. When the project was inaugurated in 1999, it focused exclusively on the World War II period, and we immediately were asked when we would include the Vietnam War. From the start, we conducted several Korean War–era interviews; there was a remarkable overlap between World War II and the Korean War since many interview subjects were veterans of both wars. The Vietnam War would require a major refocus that required resources beyond our means at that time. But in 2009 a major grant from the Institute for Museum and Library Services allowed us to expand the scope. As we finish this book, we are thinking ahead to similar research into Latina/os in the Korean and Vietnam War eras. With our expanded scope, the project has changed its name to the Voces Oral History Project (vocesoralhistoryproject.org). For consistency, in this book, all interviews from our collection, including those before the name change, are listed under the project's new name.

Since its start in 1999 the project's mission has been to create greater awareness of Latina/o participation during wartime, in the military as well as on the homefront. In addition to the nearly one thousand interviews it has recorded across the country (and which are housed at the University of Texas's renowned Nettie Lee Benson Latin American Collection), it has digitized over six thousand photographs at high resolution, dating from the early 1900s to the present. But it is not enough to collect the archival material. In order to promote the archive's use, the Voces Oral History Project has held symposia and conferences for both academic audiences and the general public, including one in Washington, DC, in 2004, and another in Tempe, Arizona, in 2006. It also has mounted photo exhibits; created educational materials; helped produce an original two-act play, *Voices of Valor*, written by Phoenix-based playwright James E. Garcia; and sponsored a video editing contest using World War II–era interviews with Latina/os as the basis. Its representatives have served on academic panels, have made speeches, and have engaged in numerous other related activities. This initiative has been the subject of stories that have appeared in local, national, and international newspapers, magazines, radio, and television newscasts, in addition to the web. It has become a resource that book publishers,[3] journalists, and documentarians seek out for material to support their own work. In addition, when various entities are looking for World War II-, Korean-, or Vietnam-era participants for panel discussions, commemorations, or observances, we are often consulted. We are very happy to oblige.

In 2007 we were thrust into the spotlight. In late 2006 we learned that in nine months PBS documentarian Ken Burns was scheduled to present a fourteen-and-a-half-hour documentary on World War II that included no Latina/os. We responded by sending dozens of emails to supporters across the country, beseeching them to help address what to us was a deplorable example of the deliberate effacement of Latina/os in the epochal moments of this nation's history. That effort became a national, grassroots campaign, Defend the Honor (see DefendtheHonor.org), that sent out weekly updates and staged pickets in various cities, as well as a teach-in in Austin. Burns eventually recorded additional interviews with two Latino World War II veterans and one Native American veteran and inserted them at the end of three of the seven parts of his series. But that addition is not included in the boxed set available for sale, nor was the additional footage shown in all markets. And in the accompanying coffee table book, there are no Latina/o voices. Burns's and PBS's omission resonated with Latina/os for a simple reason: we all had parents, grandparents, aunts, uncles, cousins, and friends who served in World War II, with little public recognition. Many never returned from battle. It was a sore spot for us that we had repeatedly been left out, and this time with public funds—our taxpayer dollars—so we demanded our due recognition.

But the issue was larger than World War II or Ken Burns, PBS, or television. It was emblematic of the continuing omission of Latina/os in the U.S.'s broader historical narrative. This is the reason that our oral history project came into being and continues to expand. This is not to say that we will be afraid to address some of the contradictions, problems, and tensions among the Latina/o population. Our aim is to present an honest and full understanding of our complex role in U.S. history.

Recovering the Multiethnic and Multiracial Latina/o Experiences during World War II

This anthology addresses several topics that either have not been addressed or have not been addressed in depth in extant scholarship on Latina/os and World War II. They all, in one way or another, examine how the war affected Latina and Latino geographic and social mobility and agency or the ability to make changes in their own lives. We also address the broader issue of ideology, that is, the range of personal and political beliefs that are found among U.S. Latinas and Latinos. Indeed, the book's contributors illustrate a healthy diversity of opinions, methods, disciplines, and analyses that will add to the ongoing debates about Latina/os and World War II. The book pays particular attention to Latina/os of different ethnicities and different races. Demographer Karl Eschbach and coeditor and journalist Maggie Rivas-Rodriguez have teamed up to explore the complexities of trying to determine the extent of U.S. Latina/o participation in World War II. In addition to recovering the most accurate estimate of Latino participation in World War II to date, Eschbach provides an innovative and groundbreaking methodology for extrapolating the numbers of Latina/os who served in the U.S. military during the war. His overview of the demographic profile of Latina/os in the war also extends to the present and provides new strategies for uncovering the effacement of Latina/os by institutions of power, specifically, various government agencies. Eschbach relied on census figures, weighing them to provide a measure of Latina military participation. Rivas-Rodriguez offers the human side of the equation, as discharged servicemen were labeled "White" in some cases, "N/A" in others, and "Mexican" in still others. As one West Texas World War II veteran put it, "When the war started I became a white man."[4] For him, segregation targeting Mexican Americans took a backseat to the U.S. need for front-line soldiers. Rivas-Rodriguez recovers important testimonial evidence in the Voces archive that dramatically illustrates the inconsistent, contradictory, and often baffling use of racial classifications for Mexican American soldiers.

Historian Gary Mormino introduces the book with a discussion of Ybor City's self-identified "Latin" communities, which included Spaniards, Cubans, and Italians. Mormino, who has conducted and published foundational research on Ybor City, examines the support system and interactions between the three ethnic and racial groups, and he also writes about various generations of Spanish Americans who are integral to this unique community even though they are often excluded from Latina/o research.

The history of Spanish and U.S. colonization figures prominently in other chapters, particularly that of Jordan Beltrán Gonzalez, who writes about the Filipino and Mexican American experiences in the Bataan Death March. Ironically, even in the Philippines, New Mexicans, who claim "Hispano" heritage, are mistaken for Mexicans—a confusion that continues to this day. The intersecting Spanish and U.S. colonial legacies in the Philippines and Caribbean cast a long shadow that informs additional research by other scholars. Journalism professor Félix Gutiérrez examines the World War II era, Los Angeles-based Mexican American newspaper and magazine, the *Mexican Voice*. He notes that readers were exhorted to claim their "Mexicanness" rather than try to pass as "Spanish" or Latin. The deliberate—and given the context of segregation, defiant—use of the word *Mexican* signifies a larger transformation of the men and women journalists who contributed to this youth publication. It reflected their refusal to efface their ethnic and racial identity even as they insisted on their claim to civil rights. This small yet profound media intervention presages the more comprehensive interventions that ensued after the war.

The issue of Latina/o ethnic and racial difference, and identity in general, is woven throughout the Voces Oral History Project archive, and this anthology includes several intersecting chapters on the compelling story of Cuban American Evelio Grillo, a World War II veteran whose African roots led to his identification with, and embrace by, African American soldiers. He is renowned for requesting a transfer out of a white army unit in favor of a black one, which scholars Frank Guridy, Gary Mormino, and Luis Alvarez explore further in their respective chapters. Guridy analyzes the complex ethnic, racial, and ideological negotiations of Afro-Latino World War II soldiers, some of whom embraced the mobility that military service enabled and another who likened service in the segregated U.S. Army of World War II to slavery.

Significantly, historian Luis Alvarez observes how many Latina/o World War II veterans engaged in a multiplicity of identifications in the United States and abroad, including Americans of different races and ethnicities, Muslim Moroccans, as well as various European and Asian nationalities. These negotiations, which were occasioned by their military service, anticipated what later generations of scholars have identified as transnational subjectivity. Alvarez's research underscores that the Voces Oral History Project archive provides evidence that these transnational models of Latinidad were already well under way before subsequent generations embraced and began theorizing transnationalism as an operative term in Chicana/o, Latina/o, and general American Studies. B. V. Olguín uses the Voces archive and other materials to complicate the ideological dimensions of Latino World War II transnationalism in his case studies of Latino-Japanese and Latino-white cross-cultural exchanges. The Voces Oral History Project archive, that is, reveals its potential to transform the field of Latina/o Studies.

Gerald Poyo extends the transnational dimensions of Latina/o mobility during the World War II era with an intimate family portrait of his father's and uncle's migration from Cuba to the United States and throughout Latin America before, during, and after the war. His account adds new insights into the social and economic spheres of Latina/o immigrants in this era outside of the usual focus on Mexican braceros or economic refugees from various Latin American and Caribbean countries. He thereby inaugurates a new avenue for mapping the class mobility of Latina/os in this era.

Painful Reflections: Dis-Covering Old Wounds and Introducing New Critiques of Latina/os in World War II

Having collected a large archive of interviews with Latina/o military veterans and civilians from World War II and most recently from the Korean and Vietnam War eras, the present challenge of the Voces Oral History Project is to continue collecting key interviews about unique experiences but also to continue theorizing this growing archive. This is both an exciting and a sobering venture. While new and productive discoveries have been made regarding Afro-Latina/o heritage, complex shifting transracial alliances, and even more convoluted transnational and supranational identities, other issues have emerged that require scholarly maturity, honesty, and bravery.

Much of the work related to the Voces Oral History Project has dutifully, and masterfully, recovered, honored, and contextualized World War II era Latina/o agency, and this anthology continues to participate in this important intervention. The jointly authored study by Angélica Aguilar Rodríguez, Julian Vasquez, and Allison Prochnow, for instance, features three new discoveries of Latina/o World War II soldier-scholars, with particular attention to the role of the GI Bill in promoting educational attainment for Latino veterans and their families.

Marianne Bueno brings new insights in her historiography of Carlos

Castañeda's complex negotiations of ideology and institutional politics in his role as head of the Fair Employment Practice Committee during World War II. Her study involves the use of new archival materials, in addition to contrapuntal arguments that help us complicate reductive assessments of the Latina/o World War II generation as assimilationist and accommodationist. Instead, Bueno maps Castañeda's strategic negotiations of identity, institutional power, and ideology as part of a civil rights agenda that preceded the postwar generation, which is often credited as the instigator of Latina/o civil rights struggles.

Sexism is an issue that continues to be effaced despite its persistence, and this anthology deliberately seeks to expose the depths of this issue and especially Latina agency in challenging it during the World War II era. It is important to note that sexism during the period also involves Latino veterans, who were discriminated against for their ethnicity and race but were also party to gender discrimination. Patricia Portales demonstrates the complexity of working on this topic using an archive that involves family members. Her nimble weaving of the *testimonio* she collected from her aunt—a defense industry welder of bomb parts—with contemporary theatrical explorations of gender relations among Latina/os during the World War II era both honors the people whose voices make up the archive and illustrates the responsibilities of intellectuals to appraise and critique the archival materials. Significantly, she reads the archive's utterances and silences, as well as theater's immediacy and subtlety, to make new discoveries and analyses that sometimes extend beyond what is immediately apparent or intended by the interviewees or authors. In an illustration of the surprises that research sometimes present, Portales's interview with her aunt actually began with questions about her uncle's service in the war. But on hearing her aunt's story about working as a welder in the Friedrich bomb factory in San Antonio, Texas, and Portales's closer examination of her aunt's scarred skin resulting from welding torch sparks, her research took an immediate turn toward recovering the story of Latinas in World War II, which has been even more effaced than male Latino service in the era.

Jordan Beltrán Gonzales introduces a similarly complex relationship to the archive and models a brave participant-observer methodology that is both respectful—after all, his Filipino grandfather was a survivor of the Bataan Death March—and critical. Beltrán Gonzales brings a scholarly responsibility in his critical interrogations of the macabre commodification of Latino soldiering through his discussion of the Bataan Death March Commemoration events in New Mexico. Moreover, he explores the even more controversial issue of ideology in the complex roles that Latino and Filipino soldiers have played both as subjects and as agents of U.S. empire. It is difficult to consider the issue of Latina/o and Filipina/o colonization, but these are historical facts: the United States invaded and colonized the Philippines and the U.S. Southwest in brutal and illegal imperialist wars of expansion. The subsequent inclusion of Latina/os in the United States is—still incomplete as well as unacknowledged—forever undergirded by these interrelated historical crimes.

War, in fact, often involves crimes, and even if combat and killing are contextualized in the laws of warfare, other disturbing issues emerge that the scholar and reader are compelled to consider. B. V. Olguín, coeditor of this anthology and also the grandson, nephew, and cousin of World War II veterans—including Victor Montez Ledesma from the Chalmers Courts Housing Project in East Austin, who was killed in combat in the Normandy invasion—ventures into the painful area of Latino death and dying, as well as combat and killing, in war. This is the elephant in the room that community members and scholars sometimes cannot see, or choose not to see, but which combat veterans and family members of soldiers killed in combat can never forget. It is even more difficult to process when we consider that some veterans have represented their military service and combat activities in ways that raise serious ethical and legal issues. In his treatment of Guy Gabaldon's memoir of combat in Saipan and in a theatrical treatment of post-traumatic stress disorder in a Latino World War II veteran, Olguín allows the record and texts to speak for themselves, however painful and disturbing they may be. Many topics and taboos emerge in his subsequent attempts to theorize the significance of these texts, from the issue of war crimes and Latino racial bigotries and fetishes to different performances of gender and sexuality. The Voces Oral History Project would do a disservice to the legacy of Latina/os in World War II and other U.S. wars if it did not address the many different roles that Latina/os have played in these conflicts, from combatants to conscientious objectors, as well as everything between and beyond.

Pete Haney complicates conventional accounts of Latino World War II soldiering, and especially overcelebratory discourses on "bravery," in his archival work on the Latina/o *carpa* and popular theater tradition in San Antonio. His research adds to the understanding of Latina/o agency during World War II by introducing the many ways Latina/os symbolically critiqued as well as participated in the wartime patriotic fervor. His recovery of the rich tapestry of Latina/o popular theater during and after this era is significant for the case study of this city's Latina/o community responses to the war, as well as for his extended explication of the role of *carpa* performances in parodying discourses on Latino hypermasculinity. Equally important, he reminds the audience of the real cost of war through references to blood and other body fluids.

This anthology thus seeks to continue recovering and featuring new stories, adding complexity to known figures, and raising difficult questions about the overall nature of the Latina/o experience in the United States. It is important to recognize that this stage of the project has introduced the phenomenon of metacritical inquiry and dialogue, in which scholars use the same or similar archives and texts to debate and theorize the potential significance in a variety of ways. However contentious and controversial this may sometimes be, this metacriticism signals the maturity of the Voces Oral History Project and Latina/o military studies in general. This metacritical inquiry is interdisciplinary and involves scholars from education, history, literature, journalism, sociology, anthropology, and numerous intersecting, as well as diverging, methodologies. This involves different modes of discourse and vocabulary and concepts that do not translate easily across disciplines or to the general public. The Voces Oral History Project, after all, prides itself on successfully bridging the "town and gown" divide with publications and activities that fully integrate laypeople and veterans from the community with university students and scholars in a broad-based dialogue of discovery. While we have endeavored to keep the writing in the chapters accessible to a general audience, we recognize that the authors' use of discipline-specific theoretical tools is appropriate and has an important function. Sometimes a hammer is the right tool for the job; other times a scalpel is required.

The metacritical nature of these chapters, and the scholarly attempt to recover legacies while challenging conveniently celebratory accounts, undoubtedly will be controversial. This is what scholars in Latina/o Studies, as well as intersecting fields and research projects, are charged with doing. We must recover and reassess, continually, honestly, and courageously. The veterans interviewed in the Voces Oral History Project deserve this; the ones who were killed in combat, or died before the project was inaugurated have earned it; and all their loved ones demand it.

A Note on Volume Design and the Enduring Legacy

We have organized this volume in two parts, one that explores ideological mobility and one that demonstrates cultural agency. The preface by Karl Eschbach and Maggie Rivas-Rodriguez has presented the broad context for our exploration of the scope of Latina/o participation in World War II. The book also is framed by a coda written by Gerald Poyo, who adds yet another newly recovered story about Latina/os and the World War II era. He presents it in an innovative first-person *testimonio* format about his own family. While we have endeavored to bring uniformity to the overall project, we also respect the unique disciplinary conventions and individual scholar's choice of nomenclature. At the same time, several copyediting decisions were made regarding capitalization, accents, and italics that provide stylistic uniformity. For instance, we generally followed standard editorial practices for capitalization, which means that nouns such as *pachuca* and *pachuco* are lowercased. Regarding accents, we respected individuals' decisions to use or to omit accents in their own names; the reader will therefore find inconsistent use of accents. We use "Latina/o" as the norm except in cases in which interviews, citations, or unique context determined the use of alternate terms.

Each contributor demonstrates and extends the legacy of Latina/os during World War II and the Voces Oral History Project in general: with each layer of documents, narratives, and cultural production that we pull back, ever new and more complex discoveries emerge. Indeed, this anthology seeks to challenge conventional understanding about Latina/os and the war and invites further theorizing about Latina/os in other wartime eras, from the nineteenth century to the present. We know from the small but growing amount of scholarship on Latina/os and war that Latina/os have participated in every one of this nation's wars, from the Indian Wars, American Revolution, U.S.-Mexico War, U.S. Civil War, and Spanish American War to World Wars I and II and the Korean and Vietnam Wars, as well as more recent ones, from the Bay of Pigs to counterinsurgency operations in Latin America to the Gulf War to the ongoing "war on terror." Significantly, Latina/os have participated in these wars in a variety of roles, from U.S. allies to U.S. enemies, as well as everything between and beyond. The research on Latina/o mobility, agency, and ideology that undergirds the essays in this volume promises to open new avenues for research on the broader legacy of Latina/o soldiering and citizenship.

I

IDEOLOGICAL MOBILITY

Ybor City Goes to War: The Evolution and Transformation of a "Latin" Community in Florida, 1886–1950

GARY R. MORMINO

On the morning of December 7, 1941, the 110,000 residents of Tampa, Florida, awakened with a sense of optimism and hope that the long decade of the Great Depression was over. The city's cigar industries and shipyards were booming once again. Home construction and tourism showed healthy signs of growth. By that evening, however, Americans everywhere realized that their lives had changed dramatically. The U.S. entry into World War II following the Japanese attack on Pearl Harbor profoundly altered the future of the ethnic enclave of immigrants and second-generation Cubans and Spaniards.

But war and revolution had already shaped the lives of Tampeños for three quarters of a century; indeed, domestic and international unrest was the reason so many lived there. In 1868 an uprising known as the Ten Years' War scoured the island of Cuba. Cubans—white and black—rebelled against oppressive Spanish rule. The bloody, unsuccessful struggle resulted in thousands of émigrés seeking sanctuary abroad. By 1870 over a thousand Cubans had migrated to Key West, Florida; by 1873 Cuban immigrants constituted a majority of the city's population, numbers that grew to almost five thousand by 1885.[1]

Christened "Cayo Hueso" (Bone Key) by Juan Ponce de León in 1513, Key West boomed and became a center of Cuban culture and cigar manufacturing by the end of the nineteenth century. In 1886 Vicente Martínez Ybor, unhappy with his laborers' attachment to radical labor causes and agitation for "Cuba Libre," relocated his cigar factories from Havana, Cuba, to Tampa, Florida. Located on the Gulf Coast, Tampa lies about 240 nautical miles from Key West. A feverish traffic between Key West and Tampa continued for decades, as Cubans floated easily between Florida and Cuba.

Thousands of Cubans (white and black), Spaniards (mostly Gallegos, from the Galicia region, and Asturianos, from Asturias), and later Italians (predominantly Sicilians) immigrated to Tampa, which soon succeeded Key West as the leading center for the manufacture of quality American cigars. The three groups—Cubans, Spaniards, and Italians—collectively referred to themselves as "Latins" in the local vernacular. Tampa was literally and figuratively an ethnic, industrial island in the Deep South.[2]

The history of Ybor City, however, deviates sharply from the narrative of Latina/os in the American West and Southwest.[3] Ybor City's Hispanics (a category that includes the aforementioned Spaniards as well as Cubans) and Italians used the transracial term *Latin* to identify themselves. Significantly, despite the South's biracial hierarchy, Spanish and Cuban immigrants—including Afro-Cubans—never occupied the bottom rungs of the social order. That was reserved for African Americans. Indeed, during the formative decades of Ybor City, Afro-Cubans and white Cubans worked and struggled together as "Latins" in the labor movement. From the moment they arrived, Tampeños (Sicilians excepted) rarely worked as day laborers or agricultural peons; rather, they moved into positions as relatively well paid artisans. Moreover, Tampa, unlike most industrial towns with an immigrant workforce, lacked competing and established white ethnic groups, such as the Irish. Ybor City is not only unique in Latina/o history and the broader history of Hispanic America; the community is unique in American and immigrant history because of the precise ethnic and racial groups brought together in Tampa and the Hispanic alliances forged with Italian immigrants, which included intermarriage.

Ybor City's reputation and prosperity were founded on cigars. Tobacco leaf arrived from Cuba, and in ornate factories and storefronts *tabaqueros* fashioned millions of *puro Habana* cigars. "The cigar industry is to this city," heralded the *Tampa Morning Tribune* in 1895, "what the iron industry is to Pittsburgh." Rolling cigars required skills acquired through long apprenticeships, and the workers were rewarded handsomely. A hierarchy of skills and trades characterized the cigar industry. Cigar manufacturers—many of them owned by Spanish and Cuban *patrones*—soon established factories in new communities or old neighborhoods: Ybor City, West Tampa, Palmetto Beach, Roberts City, and Gary. By 1930 over eleven thousand Spanish, Cuban, and Italian immigrants resided in Tampa, although the population fluctuated wildly during periods of labor conflict and economic depression.[4]

The case of West Tampa also exemplifies Latin pluck and success in Florida. The residents of West Tampa, which is located about five miles west of Ybor City, could easily intermingle with their Latin relatives via the urban streetcar. From its founding in the 1890s, West Tampa was largely popu-

Figure 1.1. Cigar workers ply their trade making premium Cuban cigars at the Corral, Wodiska and Company factory in 1929. Note the *lector* (reader) reading to the assembled workers from a raised platform, called *la tribuna*, in the upper right-hand corner. Courtesy Tampa-Hillsborough County Library System.

lated and governed by Latins. In 1910 only 626 of West Tampa's 8,258 inhabitants were native whites of Euro-American parentage. In 1925 West Tampa's last mayor, Enrique Henríquez, handed over the keys of the city to Tampa when the latter incorporated the former.[5]

One cannot overestimate the importance of the cigar industry when comparing and contrasting Tampa's Hispanic population with Mexicans in the American Southwest. Ybor City's Spanish-language press and vibrant theater were hardly unique; San Antonio, Los Angeles, and Santa Fe supported impressive numbers of writers and artists, many of them exiles from the Mexican Revolution. Similarly, Cuban and Spanish immigrants arrived in Tampa with relatively high rates of literacy. However, less than half of Tampa's immigrant Italians could read and write, compared to almost 100 percent of the city's Spanish and Cuban immigrants.[6] In Tampa the reverence for intellectuals—men (and occasionally women) who possessed oratorical and literary skills—was as impressive as it was revealing.

Figure 1.2. The cantina of El Centro Español in Ybor City. A mutual aid society, El Centro Español in Tampa opened the same day as its sister building in West Tampa, January 1, 1912. Courtesy Tampa-Hillsborough County Library System.

No occupation was as revered as that of *el lector*, the reader, who was elected by his fellow cigar workers to read Spanish-language newspapers, novels, *novelas*, and tracts of radical literature. Contemporary Spanish authors such as Benito Pérez-Galdos enjoyed popularity, but a special passion was reserved for Victor Hugo, whose novels about corrupt bishops and social justice appealed to Latin cigar makers. *Tabaqueros* also listened to readings of revolutionary writers, such as Peter Kropotkin, Michael Bakunin, Leo Tolstoy, Enrico Malatesta, and Karl Marx.[7]

The cigar factories also offered Cuban and Spanish immigrants an accelerated gateway to the respectable working and middle classes. Cigar factory paydays created and supported a remarkable social and economic infrastructure. Every immigrant group in American history has organized societies of mutual aid, but rarely has an immigrant community dedicated such elaborate structures as those dedicated in Tampa and West Tampa: El Centro Español, El Centro Asturiano, El Círculo Cubano, L'Unione Italiana, and La Unión Martí-Maceo. "They were wonderfully active cultural centers," remembered the writer and native Jose Yglesias,[8] "for those cigar makers knew how to organize more than trade unions, and two of them [Spanish societies] built hospitals for their members, the best in Tampa at that time." Moreover, he added, "these social clubs all had libraries, auditoriums, gyms, dance halls, and canteens. . . . All the clubs were organized and run by the cigar makers." By the 1920s Spanish and Cuban clubhouses bore the appearance of Greek temples: granite columns, imported tile, cast-iron balustrades with marble staircases. Each mutual aid society building also featured an elaborate stage where weekly entertainment included Spanish-language theater, concerts, and dances.[9]

In addition to these secular cathedrals, West Tampa and Ybor City became a self-contained community boasting restaurants and coffee shops, department stores and haberdasheries, banks and construction companies, newspapers and radio stations, establishments so vital to their lives that residents felt little need to shop downtown. And besides, the clerks and wait-

Figure 1.3. Looking more like a cathedral than an immigrant social club, El Centro Asturiano ministered to the social, cultural, and medical interests of its Spanish membership. This photo is from 1926. Courtesy Tampa-Hillsborough County Library System.

resses downtown most likely did not speak Spanish or approve of Ybor City folkways, such as the Latins' disdain for puritanical Blue Laws or their fondness for gambling. Native Ferdie Pacheco recalls:

> By the 1930s . . . an immigrant arriving from Spain could spend the rest of his life in Ybor City without having to learn the English language, nor change his life in any way, because Ybor City *was* Spain.[10]

The 1920s and 1930s—the decades of coming-of-age for the men and women who would experience World War II—profoundly influenced young Tampeños. Tampa remained a city deeply divided along issues of race, ethnicity, and class. Most Latin elites, dominated by the cigar manufacturers, lived in predominantly (non-Latin) white neighborhoods.[11] Working- and middle-class Spanish, Cuban, and Italian families still resided in the traditional Latin neighborhoods. Extraordinarily, many Afro-Cubans lived and worked in integrated quarters. Immigrant parents allowed children, who earlier were seen as workers, to remain in school longer. Schools served as powerful engines of Americanization. New heroes replaced the role models *los lectores* had lionized: labor leaders, revolutionaries, and writers. The popularity of automobiles, radios, and movies appealed especially to youth. Athletics also gripped the attention of young Latin males. "We rooted for teams that had Ybor City boys playing for them," remembered Ferdie Pacheco. Young Latin males admired new heroes: Al López, Tampa's first professional baseball player; Cuba's Kid Chocolate, a popular boxer; *boliteros*, professional bookies who collected vast sums from *bolita* (Tampa's version of the numbers game based on the throwing of the *bolita* ball); and moonshiners who drove fast cars and made fortunes supplying Prohibition liquor to whites. Meanwhile, Ybor City was acquiring an unsavory reputation among the English-language newspapers for its perceived lawlessness and gangland slayings.[12]

If *bolita* and bathtub gin flourished during the Great Depression, the same cannot be said of hand-rolled cigars. Consumers began to surrender their Tampa-made cigars for less expensive Durham machine-rolled cigarettes. As if the 1930s economic malaise was not bad enough, Ybor City's Spanish community watched in horror as Spain descended into a terrible civil war. Not since the 1890s Cuban War of Independence morphed into the Spanish-American War had Ybor City's Spanish community felt so hopeless and vulnerable. Not surprisingly, considering Ybor City's historic support of leftist causes, local residents passionately embraced Spain's Republican experiment in 1931 following its overthrow of the decaying monarchy. But the Republican government splintered, leading to social and economic tumult. In 1936 Spaniards elected a government under the banner of the Popular Front. By July 1936 Spain was engulfed in a civil war as army-backed Nationalists, a coalition of conservatives, monarchists, and fascists, clashed with the "red rule" of anarchists, socialists, and unionists.[13]

Tampa's Spanish community faithfully and vigorously supported the Popular Front, raising $200,000 for the Republic and purchasing four ambulances for the Spanish Red Cross. Latin women collected clothing and milk for war-torn Spain; children organized paper drives and joined the Juventud Democrática Antifascistas de West Tampa, singing lusty verses of "¡No pasarán!" (They shall not pass!). "Everybody gave 10 percent of their pay for the Republic," remembered Jose Yglesias. "I remember during this time my mother was very active in collecting and sending supplies to aid the less fortunate," recollected Braulio Alonso. "I remember thinking that someday I want to be like my parents and help others whenever I can." Frank Lastra, a young boy during the crisis, recalled listening to *La Voz de Madrid* on the radio to hear news from the front lines. The Spanish-language press became even more vital, as many Latins criticized the *Tampa Tribune* for its biased coverage of the conflict. Those who supported the rebels' Generalissimo Franco, who was supported by the hierarchy of Spain's Catholic Church, paid a price. On Sunday mornings, names of those attending Mass were recorded by critical observers. Boycotts and personal snubs followed. When General Franco triumphed in 1938, most Tampeños wept.[14]

But on the morning of December 7, 1941, the bombing of Guernica seemed far away. The front pages of the Sunday newspapers predicted a banner tourist season. The United States had instituted its first peacetime draft, and many Latins were already in uniform. Many more young Latins, the fruit of large immigrant families, could not have imagined how Pearl Harbor would transform their lives.

Remembering Pearl Harbor: Personal Reflections by Latins in Ybor City and Tampa

Maria Leto Pasetti, the daughter of Sicilian immigrants, was a teenager in 1941. She married a World War II veteran and traveled the world. She devoted a great deal of her life to the preservation of music and dance traditions in Ybor City. She recounted how she heard about Pearl Harbor.

> Sunday was the most exciting day of the week for us. We would spend all morning getting ready for the Sunday Tea Dance at the Centro Español. I laid out my favorite all-white dress. My aunt Pauline came along to chap-

erone my sister Phyllis and me. It was absolutely forbidden to have a boy-friend! As we approached the Centro, there was an excitement. We would go up the stairs and you'd hear the music of Don Francisco. I'd dance every dance. . . . Then Don Francisco stopped the music and told us the Japanese had bombed Pearl Harbor. There was a tremendous amount of screaming and crying. Some of the women fainted at the announcement. Many of the young men at the dance were in uniform. They were instructed to go down-stairs and wait for the military transport buses. As they drove away to war, we girls sobbed from the balcony.[15]

Braulio Alonso was born in Tampa in 1916, the son of a Spanish fa-ther and a mother born in Tampa to Spanish parents. His cigar-maker par-ents encouraged Braulio to acquire an education. His life story mirrors the profile of George Bailey, the character in the movie *It's a Wonderful Life*, who dreamed of an exciting life beyond Bedford Falls but remained there because of loyalty and circumstances. The valedictorian of his 1935 high school class, Alonso had always wanted to attend the University of Flor-ida and study to become a doctor. He explained why he chose to remain in his hometown and attend the University of Tampa: "I was making $15 a week at the Information News Stand in Ybor City. The Information News Stand is a misnomer. It was across the street from one of the largest gam-bling places in Tampa. The $15 was a good sum at the time and helped me

Figure 1.4. Braulio Alonso, the son of a Spanish father and a Spanish American mother, received gift packages of hand-rolled cigars from a factory back home while he served in Africa and Italy. "Even the regimental colonel would come by occasionally and say, 'Captain, do you have any extra cigars?'" recalled Alonso. Courtesy of Barbara Alonso Byars.

get through college." Alonso excelled at the University of Tampa, graduating as valedictorian in 1939. Although he was admitted to medical school, he chose to defer attending for one year to accept a position teaching high school physics and chemistry. The following year, eager to depart for medical school, he was again diverted, this time by a draft notice. He decided to marry his beloved, Adelfa Díaz, before entering the army. And then came Pearl Harbor.

> I remember well where I was on December 7, 1941. The Congress of the United States had narrowly passed that year a conscription law providing for the drafting of men for military training for a period of six months. All eligible men were to register, and a lottery was established to determine the order in which men would be drafted. I was one of the early "winners" of the lottery! . . . I reported to Camp Blanding, Florida . . . and then reported for basic training to Fort Bragg, North Carolina. I was at Fort Bragg on December 7, 1941. I was in the camp library with many other draftees when a first lieutenant entered the library and announced to all present that the Japanese had bombed Pearl Harbor. . . . Two days later I was called into our unit commander's office and informed that due to my present progress and my test scores, I would be sent to the officers' training at Fort Sill, Oklahoma. Those six months extended into over four years![16]

Alonso's experience typified the trajectory of many of Tampa's upwardly mobile sons whose college training and social skills propelled them to officer candidate school and the officer corps.

Latin women, too, benefited from Tampa's fluid social structure and opportunities. Few Hispanic women in the 1930s attended public universities located hundreds of miles from home. Josephine Acosta Pizzo was born in Ybor City in 1914, the daughter of Spanish immigrants. Her father, José Acosta, was a chef at the legendary Las Novedades Restaurant. Josephine was one of the first women in Ybor City to go away to college. On graduation from Florida State College for Women in 1936, she returned to Tampa to teach school and marry Anthony Pizzo. She recalls:

> Oh yes, I remember December 7, 1941. We were going to Our Lady of Perpetual Help Church, as we were going to be godparents to Tony's sister's son. Tony came in very excited and angry [and] . . . soon volunteered.[17]

Josephine Beiro Agliano was born in Tampa. Her father, Manuel Beiro, was a Spanish immigrant who founded Valencia Gardens, a fashionable

Spanish restaurant. In 1940, her parents were in charge of the restaurant in the Florida pavilion at the World's Fair in New York.

> Sunday, December 7, 1941, started out as a very quiet day for us. I was a high school student enjoying my Sunday making a pie. A friend of ours came running down the street very excited and yelling that the Japanese had bombed Pearl Harbor. We were not aware of the location but knew it was serious.[18]

Mario García was born in Ybor City, the son of Spanish and Mexican parents. He offers another dimension of the day:

> On December 7, 1941, I was enjoying a friendly game of dominoes at Rubio's, a small newsstand that sold sodas, candy, and, of course, *bolita*. That night, my fiancée, Mary González, and I attended a wedding. The mood of those attending was more like a funeral.[19]

Willie García, the son of Spanish immigrants, was born at the Centro Asturiano Hospital in 1931. He became an accomplished lawyer and devoted endless hours to the preservation of Ybor City and the Centro Asturiano. Several years before his death in 2008, he shared his memories of December 7, 1941:

> My brother Max was drafted in October 1941. Another brother, Manuel, had a restaurant downtown, El Madrillón. Another brother, Joe, worked at the shipyard. Every Sunday, I'd walk over to Joe's house and ride with him to our brother's restaurant. . . . Then we turned on the radio. . . . When I came out of the theater at 5 o'clock, I remember the newsboys with their "Xtras! Xtras!" The next day at A. L. Cuesta School, all the classes gathered to hear FDR. I cried like hell.[20]

Born in Tampa in 1927, Ferdie Pacheco has chronicled his youth in *Ybor City Chronicles*. His Spanish immigrant grandparents left revolutionary Mexico in 1910, settling in Tampa. His grandfather Gustavo Jiménez served as Spanish consul and his uncle John was a powerful city alderman. Pacheco became a physician, a television celebrity, and a noted painter, but he is perhaps best remembered as Muhammad Ali's "fight doctor." He recalled youthful Sunday afternoons observing the leaders of Ybor City huddled in front of a giant map of Spain, charting the course of the Spanish Civil War. On the afternoon of December 7, Pacheco recalls that he was playing baseball with neighborhood boys:

"The Japs just bombed Pearl Harbor! The Japs just bombed Pearl Harbor!"
I yelled at the Dawkins boys, relaying the news, and headed for my parlor.
We huddled around the Philco console, trying to hear the announcer.
It was not a drill. It was real. The nervous voice on the radio made us
feel like the Japs were in Sulphur Springs [a notoriously tough Tampa
neighborhood].[21]

The grandson of Spanish and Cuban immigrants, René González was
born in 1937. In 2000 he was honored as Tampa's Hispanic Man of the Year
for his lifelong dedication to Tampa's Spanish-language theater. Recollect-
ing the events of December 1941, he explained:

We were living at our building on Seventh Avenue and my cousins had
gone to the tea dance at the Centro Español. We were putting up our
Christmas tree. All of a sudden, my cousins came in and were crying. We
gathered around a big, old RCA radio to listen to the news. . . . That was
the last year we were able to do a Christmas tree—all of the ornaments
came from Germany or Japan. We used to paint light bulbs to make facsim-
iles. . . . There was an old lady behind Our Lady of Perpetual Help Church.
She insisted she would not take her Christmas tree down until her son came
back. He did and she did.[22]

The only good news in early December 1941 came in a telegram from
Ensign Richard Rodríguez of West Tampa. He was stationed at Pearl Harbor. A phone call informed his parents that he was safe.

The Ybor City Home Front War: Negotiating Ethnicity and Patriotism

Tampa may have been unique in its transracial setting and the use of the
term *Latin*, but Tampeños faced many of the same issues that Italian, Jewish, and Slavic immigrants and their children faced during the war years:
the pressures of assimilation in a climate of intense patriotism and the negotiation of a new American racial and ethnic identity while facing military
enemies bent on eradicating ethnic and racial minorities. The war crystal-
lized the meaning of Cuban and Spanish American ethnicity (which Latins sought to preserve) and the duties of American citizenship (which Latins sought to exercise). The war would also bring these two poles of Latin
identity into harmony and conflict.

Victoriano Manteiga, the fiery Cuban *lector* and immigrant editor of the
Spanish-language daily *La Gaceta*, warned readers, "Every man, just as ev-

ery city, should be prepared to face the horror of war."[23] Manteiga's son, Roland, enlisted in the military and engaged in fierce combat in the Solomon Islands and the Philippines. Only later in his life did Manteiga, who became a liberal newspaper publisher and activist, realize the profound irony of the American government sending a Cuban American to fight the imperial Japanese in the Philippines, a real and symbolic battleground in the Spanish-American War, which had culminated in the U.S. possession of these countries.[24]

The mutual aid societies reacted immediately to America's state of war. Many white Tampans remained suspicious of the city's Spaniards for their support of the Soviet Union–backed side in the Spanish Civil War. The Italian Club walked an especially perilous tightrope, considering that America was at war against Italy and that many of its members were now classified as "enemy aliens." Suddenly vulnerable, Latins were forced to pledge allegiance to their adopted country. The Centro Asturiano pledged "to throw the force of its eight thousand members behind the call to unity and bring this unhappy conflict to a quick and vigorous end." The president of the society emphasized, "This organization is 100 per cent American, contrary to the conception of some who think it is a foreign institution." Ramón Fernández Rey, president of the 6,000-member Centro Español, proclaimed, "This organization is a 100 percent American organization." A *Tampa Morning Tribune* editorial proclaimed, "Latin Americans are true Americans." The Afro-Cuban Martí-Maceo Club exhorted its members, "Buy defense bonds and stamps."[25]

Ybor City was suddenly swept into the vortex of the war. Since the New Deal, the federal government had played a prominent role in the lives of Americans far removed from Washington, DC. The war projected Uncle Sam into almost every sphere of American life. Tampeños thus enlisted in the armed services, volunteered for the Red Cross, and purchased war bonds as *both* patriotic Americans and citizens who were proud to be Spanish, Cuban, and Italian Americans. The war tested and reinforced, as well as defined and divided, ethnic loyalties. In an environment where everything from food to religion was regimented, one's memories of food (*moros y cristianos, pan cubano y café con leche, helado de coco*) and ethnicity became powerful motivators to return.

Ybor City and West Tampa fought and filtered the war though the elaborate network of voluntary associations. Centro Español, Centro Asturiano, and El Círculo Cubano dedicated walls and galleries to recognizing members who were fighting overseas. Clubs often circulated mimeographed newsletters to servicemen. Boy Scout and Girl Scout troops in Ybor City and West Tampa engaged in endless paper, scrap, and aluminum drives. A poster reminded residents, "Aluminio Usado Aquí!" (Used Aluminum Here!). Bob Martínez, son of Cubans Ida and Serafín Martínez and future governor of Florida (1987–1991), recalled the war as a young boy in West Tampa: "I was a student at Tampa Bay Elementary during the war. Every Friday at school, we were shown war movies. Every Friday, you took in all the twine and aluminum foil for scrap drives. We lived with airplanes day and night. We kids played war."[26]

The story of Mrs. T. Arenas typified the wartime sacrifices. Mrs. Arenas had lost her son, Sgt. Vernon Arenas, in a B-25 crash, yet Tampans read that she insisted on buying war bonds "to make sure he had not died in vain."[27]

The Salcines General Store on the corner of Howard Avenue and Main Street was the heart of West Tampa. Emiliano and Juanita Salcines were Spanish immigrants from Santander and Asturias. Emiliano served as the director of the war bond drive in Ybor City and West Tampa. War bond posters were plastered on walls and boards, recalled their son Emiliano José ("E. J.") Salcines Jr., who became a lawyer, state attorney, and judge. "My father cut out the *Tampa Tribune* and *Tampa Times*, the pictures of the young men from the Latin community. He placed the posters in the window of his store. People gathered around those posters. My parents made the rounds of the Ybor and West Tampa theaters and set up bond sales tables at intermission. They dressed me up like a little soldier or sailor," E. J. Salcines said later. The war's seemingly contradictory forces of patriotic nationalism and ethnic localism thus played out in the Salcines family as they did in so many other Latin families.[28]

War, Mobility, and Prosperity

The war also brought something that Americans and Tampeños had not seen in over a decade: prosperity. Headlines such as "2,000 Workers Sought For Shipyards Here" were commonplace. The shipyards paid handsome wages with union benefits. Angel Rañon, a Spanish immigrant, described how the war changed his life:

> In 1940, I had just graduated from Hillsborough High and was making 40 cents an hour as an apprentice carpenter. I went to work at Tampa Marine starting at 57 cents an hour. By the end of the war, I was a full-fledged mechanic in the mold loft making $1.40 an hour.

Armando Piñero, a son of Cuban immigrants, had been rejected by the military for medical reasons. He found a job at the McCloskey Shipyards working as a pipe fitter. His beginning pay was 66 cents an hour, which in his words "had been a pay hike as I had been working for Franquiz Distributors for 30 cents an hour, and, of course, no overtime pay for Saturdays." By the end of the war his pay rose to $1.20 an hour. Ferdie Pacheco observed the impact of "new money" and rationing on the old neighborhoods: "Quietly, families bought big bags of sugar. Fifty-five-gallon drums of gasoline and kerosene were hidden in the garages."[29]

A labor shortage allowed Pacheco to become a waiter at the famed Columbia Restaurant at age thirteen, with assistance from his aunt Lola, a Columbia cashier. "Ybor City was jumping," remembered Pacheco. "The Columbia, Las Novedades, the Spanish Park, Valencia Gardens, the Barcelona, and the many cafes overflowed. The dances were packed."[30]

Solidarity and ingenuity triumphed over the inconveniences created by war. Manuel García operated the Atlanta Restaurant next to the Cuesta-Rey cigar factory. During the Spanish Civil War, he sold churros door-to-door to raise funds for the Popular Front. His wife, Ramona, became the cook at the restaurant when the chef took a better-paying job. She cooked all of the meals over a coal stove. Manuel also served as el cafetero (the coffee man) to the factory's five hundred workers. Three times a day he and his staff brought huge pots of Cuban-roasted coffee and scalded milk to the cigar makers, who were almost certainly the nation's only factory workers allowed to drink café con leche on the job. William "Willie" García was ten years old at the time of the Pearl Harbor attack. He explained his father's challenge: "We were allotted a certain amount of sugar each month. At the end of the month, we would run low. My father explained the situation, 'The coffee at the end of the month is not going to be as sweet.' So the next day the workers brought in their ration coupons. My father filled up a storeroom with 25-pound bags of sugar!"[31]

The home front's single-minded purpose was to support the boys in uniform so they could win the war and return home. In this sense Ybor City and West Tampa were no different from Kalamazoo or Kokomo, albeit with a Latin twist. While Anglo-Americans stuffed ginger cookies and wool socks into their love letters, Tampeños stuffed cans of boliche (roasted eye of round stuffed with chorizo) and caldo gallego (a Galician soup of white beans, ham hock, kale, potatoes, and chorizos) into their care packages. Frank Lastra, the son of Spanish and Italian parents, left the Georgia Institute of Technology to enlist in the Signal Corps. On the remote Alaska island of Adak, he fondly recalled receiving packages of homemade delicacies: "I had told Mom the food was so bad the tables had jars of peanut butter and jam so the men would not starve." His mother proceeded "to send me four cans of garbanzo bean soup and some *pignolata*, an Italian dessert [fried dough lathered in caramelized, orange-blossom honey], a pastry Mom knew I loved." Beaming at the memories, Braulio Alonso recounted, "At the García & Vega cigar factory, 'Pancho' González, the owner, sent me beautiful packages of hand-rolled cigars. I never had less than three cigars a day when I was overseas in Africa and Italy." He added, "Even the regimental colonel would come by occasionally and say, 'Captain, do you have any extra cigars?'" Care packages went both ways. A September 1944 *Tribune* headline announced, "Mother Breaks into Tears at Gifts from Son in Pacific." Mrs. Consuelo Estévez was ecstatic that her son Benny, who was stationed in the South Pacific, had asked a reporter at the newspaper to buy his mother a birthday present with the $30 he enclosed. A weeping Mrs. Estévez could only mutter the words, "*gracias, gracias.*"[32]

Latin mothers and daughters faithfully wrote letters and shipped packages of Spanish delicacies to the boys overseas, but they also donned welding masks and work pants. As opportunities waned in Tampa's cigar factories, Latin women took advantage of the myriad opportunities in the city's shipyards and businesses. The 1942 headlines "City's First Lady Butcher" and "War Is Putting Women Back on Old Jobs of Turning out Bread" noted Inez Pecorino's and Peggy Lopez's new occupations.[33]

If Ybor City had a home front rallying point, it was the Columbia Restaurant. The establishment served as a refuge and mirror of the war. It attracted lovesick soldiers proposing to would-be brides as well as *boliteros* and underworld figures. The restaurant also served as a crossroads between Ybor City and the bustling shipyards, and was available by streetcar. The Columbia had become all things to all people by the early 1940s: to WASPs, it was an exotic evening in Old Spain; to soldiers stationed at MacDill Air Field, it was a dream location for a first date; for businessmen, it was a place to conduct business; to shipyard workers, it was a place to cash your check (providing you purchased a pint of liquor) and affirmation of your newfound status as a wage-earning U.S. soldier.[34]

The Military, Masculinity, and Mobility

The war meant mobility. Not since the peak years of immigration or the dislocation resulting from labor unrest had so many young Tampeños been on the move. Raised in insular neighborhoods, inculcated with a combustible upbringing of patriotism, machismo, and invincibility, Latin males entered the military services in large numbers. They marched off to war with a collective chip on their shoulders, eager to show the public that they were as American as the twelfth-generation descendant from the Plymouth Plantation.

To be sure, Tampa's Spaniards, Cubans, and Italians clashed and competed. Each was certain that the other groups possessed unattractive and undesirable qualities: Spaniards were considered arrogant and condescending; Cubans were spendthrift and rootless; Italians were hopelessly old world and frugal. Outsiders, however, made other ethnic and racial distinctions, such as when they hurled the epithet "Cuban nigger." But fifty years of racist rhetoric and nativist violence had created a palpable "us" versus "them" camaraderie: the internal and external forces that shaped a Latin identity and brotherhood were far greater than factors that separated the groups. Manuel Alfonso, an Afro-Cuban, offered an example. "We used to get along good," he explained. "When my grandmommy died [1923], she was buried on Noche Buena—Christmas Eve—which in Cuban houses always had big celebrations. The only black family on that block was my family. And when she died, nobody celebrated Nocha Buena on that block out of respect for her." Fights between young Latin teenagers and "Anglos" were commonplace. But as they marched off to basic training, Latins were encountering a strange new world.[35]

"We pre-Army-age kids," writes Ferdie Pacheco, "lived a wonderful life. All the excitement of war and none of the dangers or inconveniences." He and an entire generation quickly realized the reality of war. Daily, Tampa's English- and Spanish-language newspapers contained stories of local soldiers and their deeds, mundane and heroic. The *Tampa Morning Tribune*, perhaps the most influential newspaper in the state, featured a daily column, "Armed Forces Parade," followed in the afternoon by a *Tampa Daily Times* column, "With Our Boys on All Fronts." *La Gaceta*'s "Sirviendo La Nación" (Serving the Nation) kept its readers informed. On July 16, 1942, the paper profiled ninety-four local boys who were drafted. The stories of working-class Latins intersected with those of the sons of Anglo bankers and lawyers. For instance, readers learned that George M. Alvarez had worked as a "catcher" for the Zacchini Flying Trapeze Trio, or that Marine Herbert Meza had served as the president of the Ybor City Presbyterian Mission, or that Hector Gutiérrez had been designated a qualified radio operator.[36]

Americans enlisted and went to war for myriad reasons. Some enlisted because they held strong opinions about the geopolitical conflict; others genuinely embraced American patriotism; but most simply enlisted for the same reasons young men have always volunteered: communal and group approval and adventure. Many veterans compared the public mood after Pearl Harbor to a swift and powerful current that swept everything and everyone in its path into the maelstrom. Jose Yglesias, the son of a Gallego immigrant who had settled in Cuba, understood the discrimination his family and community had suffered. His uncle, the mayor of West Tampa and a reader at the Bustillo Bros. & Díaz cigar factory, had been kidnapped by labor vigilantes in 1902. "This [Ybor City] was our place," he once remarked. Yglesias had been profoundly influenced by the intellectual ferment of the 1930s. The Ybor City native joined the navy in 1942. "The draft board had classified me 3A [extreme hardship deferment] because I was my mother's support, but I volunteered anyway because I believed in the war, in the popular front against fascism, in the New Deal, in socialism and the brotherhood of man," he wrote in his memoir, *One German Dead*. He added, "It made me unique in the aviation unit, the entire cruiser."[37]

As American troops battled to take Tarawa and Iwo Jima, Anzio and Market Garden, Tampans read of stories of heroism and tragedy. By 1944 it seemed that almost every day Tampans learned of still another hero or casualty. That year two Tampa cousins, Pvt. Sergio García and Pfc. Oscar Alvarez, who had entered the army together and trained together, were wounded in Germany, just twenty-four hours apart. Mostly, news traveled from household to mailman to neighbor. "Perhaps one of the most popular personalities of the wartime years was the mailman," observed veteran Frank Lastra. "'Creo que tienes noticia del varón'" (I think you have news from the boy), the mailman would say, as he handed the mail to mothers. The moment was one of rejoicing!" One such letter brought extraordinary happiness to the parents of Marine Cpl. Miguel Serra, who had been captured on December 7, 1941, in the Philippines. A letter written in August 1944 and delivered in 1945 at last told the family that he was alive and in a prison camp at Osaka, Japan.[38]

Even the vaunted Columbia was not immune to the exigencies of war. Waiters, cooks, and dishwashers, too, enlisted in the military. Casimiro Yanez Jr. had begun work as a waiter in 1939; by 1942 he was hauling a different cargo, piloting C-47 transport planes and B-25 bombers to North Africa. A favorite story tells how Yanez ran into Eddie Díaz in Casablanca, Morocco. Díaz had worked making Cuban sandwiches at the Columbia. The two men proceeded to raid the mess hall, finding enough chicken, rice, pimientos, and onions to prepare *arroz con pollo* for their friends. They even procured precious strands of Spanish saffron in the Casbah.[39]

During the war, Tampa's American Legion posts served a vital role. Nick Palveda Sr. was the director of the Tampa post. A veteran of World War I, Palveda understood the problems World War II veterans would face, especially since his four sons had volunteered for the army, army air corps, marine corps, and navy.[40]

Arsenio Sánchez was one of thousands of Tampeños whose lives were uprooted by war. The son of Cuban and Spanish cigar workers, he finished high school in 1937 and found a job in the Tampa shipyards. He was making $45 a week when he was drafted. He joined the navy's Construction Battalion (CB-Seabees). Sánchez, who had never traveled, was sent to Adak Island, Alaska, where he helped construct a navy base. Later, in March 1945, he participated in the epic battle at Iwo Jima. Among his diary entries: "March 13: About 11, we sight Iwo—and Mount Suribachi." On March 30, he became a grave digger. "Most of the boys buried are 19 and 20 years old. I hope they have not died in vane [*sic*]. . . . Today we buried 21 new ones." One of the graves may have been for Infantryman Gilbert A. Salas, a Tampeño who died on Iwo Jima on March 27. Salas was a graduate of Hillsborough High and was attending aviation mechanics school before his induction into the army.[41]

The military recognized talent and leadership among the Tampeño soldiers. As a captain of the 85th Infantry Division, Braulio Alonso led his men through some of the war's toughest fighting in North Africa and Italy. On June 5, 1944, one of the happiest days in the European theater, Allied troops marched into Rome after many months of costly advances. He described the moment:

> I was with my Jeep, my driver and in battle gear. . . . The liberation of Rome had brought a delirious holiday to the people of the city. Never before or after have I seen such a demonstration of joy and elation as exhibited by the people of Rome that day. Thousands lined the streets and it was almost impossible to proceed. The people offered wine, laughed, danced, and sang and they showered us with flowers and kisses.

Avoiding the women of Rome, Alonso made his way to the Vatican, where he discovered four Jeeps. Five officers and five enlisted men, all in combat garb, approached a Swiss Guard and asked if it were possible to see the Holy Father. The guard gratefully accepted cigarettes and chocolate bars. "A short time later," wrote Alonso, "an Irish priest appeared and asked us to wait. About twenty minutes later, we were ushered into a small room where we disposed of our weapons. A frail man appeared—His Holiness

Pope Pius XII. He spoke to us in understandable English. . . . He blessed us and gave us each a medal. I still treasure mine."[42]

For Alonso, the war held little romance. "War is unpleasant, vicious, bloody and sacrificial . . . ," he wrote. Earning a Bronze Star and a Purple Heart with Oak Leaf Cluster for his courage, Alonso took pride in how the war ended:

> The surrender of the German troops in our division's sector of the Dolomite Alps was a humiliating experience for the troops of the master race. . . . Instead of surrendering to high officers as they expected, they were in for a great surprise. . . . Led by their high-ranking officers, the Germans had to surrender to our Black troops, who ordered them where to place their arms and escorted them to the place of internment.[43]

Denver Blanco, born in Tampa in 1920, was drafted in 1942. His Cuban parents named him Denver because they fled Tampa during the 1920 cigar strike and found work picking onions in Colorado. The army trained Denver to operate heavy machinery. He trained for six months in preparation for the D-day landings at Normandy. Nervously, he drove bulldozers and trucks on Omaha Beach and later participated in the Battle of the Bulge.[44]

Capt. Joe Benito served in the 112th Army Air Force. The son of Mr. and Mrs. Luis Benito, Benito flew ninety-three missions over Italy, France, and Germany in a P-47 Thunderbolt fighter. Benito received the Distinguished Flying Cross for "courageously pressing his attack in the face of intense anti-aircraft fire which heavily damaged his airplane" but still managing to destroy the targeted bridges.[45]

In August 1943 Tampans read in their morning newspaper the headline, "Tampan Lands on Sicily and Meets His Kin." Such a headline was not unusual following the U.S. invasions of Sicily and Italy. An Italian American visiting his family's village of origin made for a sentimental story. But in the case of Capt. Reinardo Pérez, the soldier was born in Ybor City, the son of Cuban and Sicilian parents. Trilingual and a graduate of the University of Florida, Pérez spoke the Sicilian dialect with his relatives. He wrote his mother, Catalina, "In a few minutes, the place was full with relatives and everybody wanted to kiss me. I have never been kissed so much in all my life." A fellow Tampeño, Oscar Rámos, died in Italy. He had just been awarded the Bronze Star for bravery.[46]

Western Union messengers or postmen delivered too many telegrams that began, "We regret to inform you that your son . . . " Emiliano José Salcines Jr. explained that the Western Union office stood just across the street

from his family's West Tampa store. As soon as Western Union had received the dreaded letter, an agent yelled to Juanita Salcines. The Salcines
family alerted neighbors to be prepared to comfort the soon-to-be gold star
mother. Salcines recalled the sight of "hollering, screaming, crying, weep-
ing—as neighbors tried to console mothers." That scene was reenacted
countless times. Pvt. Sandolio C. Alvarez died in July 1944 in Burma while
serving with Merrill's Marauders. Pfc. Harry Hernández, of the 36th Armored Infantry, was killed in action in France following the breakout after
D-day. He was serving as a tank gunner. The Orden Caballero Lodge No. 5
honored his sacrifice at a memorial service.[47]

The last weeks of World War II brought cascades of tears, as even more
telegrams sped the bad news. Henry B. Fernández Jr. was inducted into
the army in 1940 and assigned to the 466th Parachute Artillery, 17th Airborne Division. He died in late March 1945 while participating in Operation Varsity on the Rhine River, one of the largest single airborne operations of the war. Pfc. Juanito C. Menéndez and Pvt. William D. Rodríguez
both died in the Italian campaign in April 1945, some of the last combat
deaths in the European theater. Parents of Pfc. Alfonso Díaz, Pvt. Louis
Estévez, Pfc. Eugene A. Fernández, Vicente A. Fernández, 2nd Lt. Louis
Fueyo, Clarion Gárcia, José González Jr., Cilio Guerriere, Felix Andrew
Manríquez, Albert Rodríguez, Evelio Pedero Jr., Elio Posada, Anselmo
Quian, Sergio Sánchez, and Emilio C. Santos also received telegrams, but
they never found out any details about their sons' deaths. Roy Govantes
was killed in action in the Pacific theater while serving in the navy. Salva-
dor M. Ybor Jr., grandson of the namesake founder, died of wounds in the
Pacific campaign. Louis Guerra was killed in action over the Pacific while
flying with the 394th Bomb Squadron bombardier. Staff Sgt. C. L. Arnie-
lla had survived some of the war's bloodiest engagements. A veteran of D-
day, Market Garden, and the Battle of the Bulge, he died in Germany in
July 1945 of noncombat injuries following the end of the war in Europe.[48]

Tragedy and heroism transcended class, racial, or ethnic distinctions
among Tampa's Latins. Sgt. Roy P. Parra had completed only grammar
school and enlisted in the army in 1937. He was assigned to the 702nd Tank
Destroyer Battalion when he was killed in November 1944 in Germany.
William David Rodríguez had completed one year of high school and was
earning $18 a week as a truck driver when he enlisted in Battery A, 116th
Field Artillery, in September 1940. The place and time of death of Private
1st Class Rodríguez remain unknown. Joe Manuel Domínguez, an assistant
cook in the marine corps, died in the South Pacific. Second Lt. Louis Ori-
huela, twenty-four, was killed in action in the Pacific. The newspaper noted

that he was "an outstanding Tampa student and had joined a fraternity at the University of Florida." His four brothers were all serving in the armed forces. Lt. Joe Aizpuru was awarded the Bronze Star for heroism aboard the USS *Franklin*. A recipient of American Legion medals as a student at Hillsborough High, Aizpuru was a graduate of Georgia Tech and president of his college fraternity.[49]

The fate of some soldiers was not known for months, even years, after the war ended. Ybor City family and neighbors of Ambrosio Del Pino were notified in October 1945 that his son Antonio survived his ordeal in a notorious Japanese prisoner-of-war camp. The family had not heard from their son for nearly four years. Captured in the Philippines, Del Pino was forced to work in the coal mines of the notorious Fukoka prison camp. He, along with Tampa physician Frank Adamo, survived the Bataan Death March. Tampeños gasped when they read that the neighborhood's most celebrated veteran, Sgt. Tommy Gómez, survived the bloody crossing of the Roer River in Germany, barely. While convalescing from wounds, Gómez wrote friends, "Well, here I am back in England, full of holes and flat on my back. They almost got me this time. . . . I have holes the size of a quarter in both arms and four or five in my buttocks, in addition to one through my right leg." Gómez recovered and resumed his illustrious boxing career. Ranked as one of the top ten heavyweights after the war, he walked away from the sport in 1946, remarking, "I don't know whether it was the sixteen shrapnel wounds I received in the war or the long layoff of six years in the army . . . but I'm calling it quits."[50]

Frank Lastra illustrates how intensely local a world war can be:

> Among the officers from Ybor City serving gallantly were Captain Augustine "Chunchi" Fernández; Captain Joe Benito; Lt. Julian Fernandez; Captain Marcelino Huerta; Naval officer Tony Fernández and brother Buck Fernández; Colonel and West Pointer Joe Aizpuru. All these lived within a three-block radius of Centro Asturiano Hospital, an indication of the heavy participation of the area's sons and daughters in the armed forces.

The three blocks described by Lastra indeed produced some extraordinary war tales. Marcelino Huerta, a football star and B-24 pilot, was shot down over Yugoslavia and rescued by partisans. Capt. "Chunchi" Fernández served as a bombardier on a B-17. In a 1943 raid over Germany, his plane was badly shot up, and Fernández saved several crew members before parachuting. Captured, he spent several years in a German stalag.[51]

Tampa's most famous military address may be the Vila family's residence on Palmetto Street in West Tampa. Seven brothers served in the military. Three weeks after Pearl Harbor, Willie and Joe Vila tried to enlist at the Marine Corps Recruiting Station in Tampa but were turned down because they were only sixteen and seventeen, respectively. Undaunted—they were pumping gas on December 7 and vowed to become marines—they simply traveled to Orlando, lied about their ages, and signed up. Willie and Joe saw combat at Guadalcanal and Okinawa. Another brother served with the 82nd Airborne, while four younger brothers served in later wars. Carmen Vila, the mother of fourteen sons and daughters, vowed not to eat another crumb of her beloved Cuban bread—her husband worked as a baker—if God protected her boys. They all returned.[52]

Ironically, Tampa's most famous veteran of World War II would become famous in the next war. Baldomero "Baldy" López Jr., the son of an Asturian father and Sicilian mother, grew up in Ybor City and enlisted in the navy in 1943. His discipline and intelligence impressed superiors, and he received a Fleet appointment to the U.S. Naval Academy. The Class of 1947 had over a thousand midshipmen and included fewer than a dozen Hispanic surnames. On graduation in 1947, he became a 2nd lieutenant in the marine corps. In September 1950 1st Lieutenant López died at the Inchon invasion in Korea, and was awarded the Medal of Honor for falling on a hand grenade to save his comrades. The citation commended Lieutenant López "for conspicuous gallantry and intrepidity at the risk of his life above and beyond the call of duty." His parents had just received a letter from him written on the eve of the invasion. He had asked his father to send a box of good Tampa cigars "to replace these cigarettes we've been smoking." This last letter cautioned, "Knowing that my profession of arms calls for many hardships and many risks I feel that you all are now prepared for any eventuality."[53]

The End of War: VJ Day and Postwar Transformations

VJ Day, August 15, 1945, was one of the most deliriously joyous days in American history. Americans understood that the long ordeal was over, the boys were coming home, and soon cars and new homes would appear. In Tampa, citizens did not need to be told where to celebrate. Along prescribed and proscribed tenets, Anglos, African Americans, and Latins each celebrated in their own way and on their own turf. In Ybor City, pandemonium erupted when firemen began blowing sirens. Eighty-year-old René González reminisced years later, "All the lights returned to Ybor City! No one was collecting fares! Food! They dragged dummies of Hirohito behind cars. Everyone was asking, 'What will happen to the emperor's white horse?'" "Within a short time," noted a reporter, "residents of the area formed a parade which wandered up and down the streets. Headed by a group of youngsters waving flags, the procession was showered with traditional paper scraps." Another reporter observed, "Young and old joined in the kissing contests. Acquaintance was not necessary, although some girls insisted in kissing only sailors and some servicemen preferred blondes." The churches of Ybor City and West Tampa were filled as mothers, wives, and sisters crowded the pews, thanking Santa Bárbara, Santa Rosalia, and Our Lady of Caridad del Cobre.[54]

As soldiers poured into Tampa on VJ day, a local reporter camped out at the busiest intersection in the city, Union Station, where hordes of GIs were leaving and returning. "Every day," wrote the reporter, "more and more families gather at the railroad station hoping for the arrival of the menfolk—and some are disappointed." Such was not the case for the parents of Ruben Piñera, a twenty-year-old veteran who had joined the navy on December 7, 1942. The August 19, 1945, edition of the *Tampa Morning Tribune* reported:

> The whole Piñera family of father, mother, grandmothers, aunts and a small niece turned out to welcome the veteran from long weeks spent in a convalescent hospital in Seagate, N.Y. Finally the train pulled in, and baggage in hand, Piñera stepped off. When he saw his folks, he speeded up. As he neared the group, his mother shoved forward and he dropped his bags. Wordlessly, the two embraced, their eyes closed. The mother clutched her son as if she could never let him go again. . . . There was a big celebration at the Piñera home last night.[55]

Not everyone harbored nostalgic memories of VJ Day. Evelio Grillo, an Afro-Cuban who grew up in Ybor City during the 1920s and 1930s did not treasure his memories of his military service: "When I write that I do not remember VJ Day and VE Day, I do so with complete candor. My amnesia is total. I did not feel Germany and Japan as palpably as I felt the United States Army. The Army's oppression was direct, immediate, constant."[56]

When Juanito Came Marching Home:
Race, Class, and Mobility in Postwar Ybor City

In 1942 the pollster George Gallup asked Americans a rather indiscreet question: "Taking into account all the qualities possessed by the different people or races of the world, how would you rate the people listed below, in comparison with the people of the United States?" The findings of the "Confidential Report" serve as a 1942 ethnic and racial benchmark. Not surprisingly, Americans expressed admiration for Canadians, the English, and Scandinavians. Most shocking—certainly to students of the nineteenth century—were the high marks afforded the Irish. Americans may have hated Hitler in 1942, but citizens embraced Germans. Three groups ranking near the bottom—Spaniards, Italians, and Mexicans—suggested lingering fears of Catholicism and Latin customs. Predictably, the Japanese ranked as the least desirable group in 1942.[57]

In American history the military offers individuals, races, and ethnic groups opportunities to demonstrate their virtues and earn respect. Chevrons on freedmen's sleeves, argued Frederick Douglass, would advance the opportunities of former slaves. Certainly the heroic conduct of Irish Americans in the Civil War and World War I, most notably the Fighting 69th Infantry of New York, helped redeem the reputation of the Irish, who were arguably the most hated white ethnic group in nineteenth-century America. African Americans, however, found that their patriotic sacrifices and hopes for a less rigid racial line collided with the harsh realities of the 1920s.[58]

World War II, for Tampeños, affirmed their sense of belonging and status. To Braulio Alonso, the great lesson of the war was simple: "A group of persons of different backgrounds, ethnicity and religions can work together to achieve objectives in which they believe." The war and the threat of fascism and totalitarianism challenged democracies, but to Alonso and others the fight was just. "It is sometimes necessary to rise and to sacrifice to combat evil," philosophized Alonso. In his memoir Frank Lastra explained, "This was home. . . . There was a land to defend. Patriotism was real and it ran deep, though at times it carried a Latin flavor. . . . These new soldiers [Ybor citizens] . . . were as American as apple pie." The war also deeply affected Jose Yglesias, who served in the navy as an aviator-radioman-gunner and saw action in the Mediterranean campaigns. Proud of his Spanish past, he wrote about his father's native Galicia in the book, *The Goodbye Land*. Curiously, for a writer who took passionate pride in his culture, he never accented his name. When asked about it, he replied that he considered himself an American of Latin descent, and explained: "Assimilation does not mean abandoning our past, but enriching an already very rich mix. To me, assimilation has meant that in all my work as a writer I had tried to make American readers aware of the existence of Ybor City and its Latin cigarmakers."[59]

Not everyone agreed that the war had been a triumph of democracy, including the same Tampeños who had been singled out for praise and promotion. "I will never forget the time when I returned to Tampa from New York, on leave from my ship in the Navy during World War II," wrote Yglesias. "I stayed talking in the club car with two other servicemen. Believing that I was a New Yorker, they praised the virtues of Tampa. The only warning they gave me was about Ybor City: 'Don't go, it's a dangerous place. Full of "spics."'" Insults notwithstanding, most Tampeños felt the war had brought a new sense of acceptance and that their future was bright.[60]

But for Tampa's Afro-Cubans, the resentment toward the military was palpable. Francisco Rodríguez Jr. exemplifies the frustrations of being black and Cuban in the Jim Crow South. Born in 1916, he was a brilliant student, graduating from the state's only public black college, Florida Agricultural and Mechanical University. Francisco Rodríguez Sr. was a labor activist and a beloved leader of the Martí-Maceo Society. In 1943 young Francisco, his brother, Manuel, and sister, Myrtle, all worked as teachers in Tampa—the only three Afro-Cuban teachers in the county. Myrtle became Tampa's first Afro-Cuban female to earn a college degree. The seeds of Florida's modern civil rights revolution were sown during World War II, and the Rodríguezes helped steer the movement. The family assisted Harry T. Moore and Thurgood Marshall, the NAACP's Florida field secretary and legal counsel respectively, in filing lawsuits challenging teacher salaries based on race. The NAACP won several cases, including Hillsborough County's.[61] Francisco promptly quit his teaching job and joined the marine corps, which before Pearl Harbor had not accepted blacks. "I almost got into trouble one time," he confessed, "almost got court-martialed, because I wrote something about segregation in the military." An emboldened Francisco Rodríguez Jr. entered Howard Law School following military service. In 1948, as a law student at Howard, he wrote an angry letter to Tampa's black newspaper regarding discrimination he had experienced aboard a southbound train. He returned to a city and neighborhood that had changed. Ybor City had once been one of the South's most fluid multiracial societies, a place where Afro-Cubans lived and worked together. But any vestige of racial solidarity had seemingly vanished by 1945. Rodríguez later became the first Afro-Cuban to lead an NAACP chapter.[62]

For many of Ybor City's Latins, World War II represented a milestone and a coming-of-age. For the most part, Cubans, Spaniards, and Italians moved from the margins of social acceptance to the mainstream. Their military experience, in spite of encounters with Spam in a can, insensitive drill instructors, and ethnic jokes, was overwhelmingly positive. "The Army in World War II was an Americanization success," insisted Braulio Alonso.

"The 85th Infantry Division, the artillery battalion to which I belonged during the North African and Italian campaigns, [was] composed of men of many walks of life, of education, of different nationality backgrounds. One soon realized that the place of origin or ethnicity or religion of an individual made little difference." Ethnic tensions, which had polarized the city for half a century, began to diminish during and after the 1940s. In 1944 the Hillsborough County School Board announced that Latin students who spoke Spanish in school would "no longer be whipped." A 1943 newspaper headline, "West Tampans Have No Worries about Zoot-Suit Hoodlums," described the success of the local boys' clubs in directing youthful energies into athletics, noting that eighty members were serving in the armed forces. By the 1950s Tampa had elected its first Latin mayor (the first of four). Young Latin veterans largely abandoned the old neighborhoods and moved into the more anglicized suburbs. For the first time, significant numbers of young Latins married outside their ethnic groups. Attending Catholic Mass and joining (or rejoining) the Catholic Church became an important part of postwar life for some veterans as religious affiliation reached modern all-time highs.[63]

The GI Bill, which established housing, medical, and education programs for veterans, wrought far-reaching consequences for Tampa and America. For the first time many of Tampa's youth had traveled and ventured far beyond their old enclaves. More than a few brought back brides they had met at USO dances on distant bases. They returned to neighborhoods that offered veterans and wives substandard housing on narrow lots. Little new housing had been built since the 1920s, and the old cigar makers' wooden, shotgun cottages, which once conferred the American Dream to their immigrant parents, now seemed threadbare and inadequate. And besides, the generous GI Bill subsidized and encouraged *new* construction. Whether intended or unintended, the GI Bill devastated older immigrant neighborhoods across America.[64]

A resurgent federal government also flexed its muscle in the field of education. The GI Bill offered generous benefits to veterans who wished to enter or continue higher education as well as to former servicemen who wished to enroll in trade school. Judging by the rosters of Tampa war veterans who became teachers, lawyers, and physicians, as well as air conditioner repairmen and plumbing contractors, the GI Bill deserves its reputation as one of the federal government's most efficacious and inspiring programs. It may well have saved the faltering University of Tampa. By 1947 eight hundred veterans crowded the university's corridors, so many that former GIs outnumbered traditional students two to one. Tampeños played an active role in the university's postwar years. Latins constituted about 20 percent of the student body in the late 1940s, serving as class and club officers. Gloria González was homecoming queen in 1951, and Rudy Rodríguez served as president of the alumni association.[65]

"There was a time in our country," reminded Jose Yglesias, "when the children of the workers did not go to college." Yglesias now joined millions of such children at institutions of higher education. He chose Black Mountain College, an iconoclastic institution that became famous as an incubator for radicals and dissenters. On a North Carolina mountaintop, Yglesias decided to become a writer. He left after one year, but published his first short story, "Un Buen Obrero," in *New Masses* in 1946.[66]

But a resurgent federal government that had the power to subsidize education and build hospitals also had the power to bulldoze neighborhoods that bureaucrats deemed undesirable. Ybor City reached its zenith in the late 1930s or early 1940s. By the late 1940s Ybor City had begun to fray. Since the 1890s trolley cars had crisscrossed Ybor City and West Tampa, but in 1946 the streetcar era ended, the result of private greed and public love for the automobile. More serious problems exacerbated the conditions in Ybor City: housing was deteriorating, and businesses and younger families were fleeing to the new suburbs. The new freedoms that Tampeños embraced—mobility, intermarriage, and the popularity of the postwar automobiles—began to empty Ybor City of its Latin inhabitants. The cigar factories, once the oxygen of the town, turned to machines and non-union labor. Cigar workers listened to the 1947 World Series on radio; *lectores* had been banished in the fiery strike of 1931, Ybor City's last great labor uprising.

Ybor City's demise was West Tampa's gain. West Tampa served as Ybor City's halfway house to suburbia, offering young veterans and their growing families inexpensive housing, room for new developments, and a Latin infrastructure of Spanish-Cuban–Italian stores, cafés, mutual aid societies, and butcher shops. Rev. Walter Passiglia stood at the center of the maelstrom. He had built up such a faithful following at the Ybor City Presbyterian Mission that he established St. John's Presbyterian Church in West Tampa. "All 130 persons from the mission transferred over here," he exulted. Jorge García explained that "the young Latins and their families had become Americanized to a point, but they still had this strong feeling of heritage and community. The only place in town that offered them a chance to buy good property in a suburban environment *and* still hold onto some of their culture and language was West Tampa." He added, "It was like a mass migration from the inner city to the suburbs of West Tampa. It was the thing to do among the members of my generation."[67]

Tampa eagerly used federal funds to demolish some of the city's most notorious African American slums, and increasing numbers of the displaced residents found cheap housing in Ybor City. By July 1955 the situation alarmed Victoriano Manteiga. The liberal political lion of Ybor City, Manteiga had witnessed its rise and fall. A Cuban immigrant, he had served as a vaunted *lector*, founded the Spanish-language newspaper *La Gaceta*, championed the Loyalist, or Republican, cause in the Spanish Civil War, and cheered the Allied cause during World War II while his son fought in the jungles of the Pacific. He now confronted an imperiled Ybor City. Calling for an emergency meeting of Ybor City business leaders, he condemned realtors for "exploitation," criticized the "influx of Negroes" into the enclave, and vowed to preserve the area's "Latin" culture. Once the beacon of racial harmony in the Deep South, Ybor City, too, was changing.[68]

But Ybor City remained a near-mythological place in Cuban history. A 1953 newspaper headline announced, "Ybor City Begins to Look Spanish Again." At the very moment Ybor City began to wane, private and public efforts attempted to impose architecture to match the past. Cuban tourists continued to flock to a home on Eighth Avenue, where Afro-Cuban *patriota* Paulina Pedroso nursed the Apostle of Cuban Liberty, José Martí, to health after Spanish agents had poisoned his wine. It would not be the last time Cuban revolutionaries came to Ybor City seeking disciples and money. In November 1955 an exiled Cuban revolutionary requested a meeting hall to raise money for his cause. Fidel Castro was still unfamiliar to most Tampeños; he had only recently been freed from prison following his July 26, 1953, attack on the army barracks at Moncada. Victoriano Manteiga headed the Club 26th of July in Tampa. But the Cuban Club and the Italian Club denied Fidel Castro a forum. The CIO Hall finally provided him with a space to speak. When Tampeños heard the news of *los barbudos'* triumph on New Year's Eve, 1958, jubilation followed. After all, Fulgencio Batista was a dictator, and Ybor City had always championed revolutions and revolutionaries. But quickly many Latins expressed uncertainty, followed by doubt and hostility. Times had changed. Most Latin veterans were too busy with their new lives and families, or now were too uncomfortable with leftist causes to get involved in what the U.S. government came to represent as another Caribbean coup d'état. But the Cuban Revolution's nationalization of industry and overt espousal of socialism, which eventually led to the U.S. embargo, meant that Ybor City's already struggling cigar factories now had to look elsewhere for tobacco leaf. Worse, a community that had passionately embraced Spanish and Cuban culture now felt politically estranged from Franco's Spain and diplomatically isolated from Cuba.[69]

In the 1960s the Great Society also left its imprint on Ybor City. Two interstate highways bisected Ybor City and West Tampa in the early 1960s. Then, in a misguided effort at social engineering and urban renewal, Great Society bureaucrats and local politicians flattened thousands of Ybor City homes and businesses, leaving seventy acres barren. "They tore down old homes and never rebuilt new ones," accused Francisco Rodríguez Jr. Then the federal government simply walked away from the shattered community. Since the 1980s Ybor City has been on a roller-coaster boom-and-bust cycle. The magnificent monuments to the cigar workers and Latin immigrants have survived amid tattoo parlors, Irish pubs, and the venerable Columbia Restaurant. The V. M. Ybor cigar factory, dedicated in 1886, is now home to the Church of Scientology. One may still enter the ornate portals of Centro Asturiano and the Cuban Club and discover memorials to club members who served in World War II.[70]

World War II transformed the lives of Tampeños, ending the Great Depression, breaking open their insular lives, regimenting the lives of military-age males, bringing them into contact with men and women in faraway places. The war-fueled economy provided work on the home front. The war affirmed the place and position of Cuban and Spanish Americans while stigmatizing and accentuating the increasingly segregated status of Afro-Cubans. The home-front war punctuated Ybor City's apogee; the war's end marked the demise of this unique ethnic enclave.

CHAPTER 2

Pvt. Evelio Grillo and Sgt. Norberto González: Afro-Latino Experiences of War and Segregation

FRANK ANDRÉ GURIDY

Norberto González found himself in a peculiar situation. He had recently arrived in the United States from the small town of Puerto Padre, Cuba, in August 1944 to pursue a better life for himself and his family. A few months later he enlisted in the U.S. Army to fight in World War II, where he experienced his first encounters with legalized racial segregation. Although of African descent, "since I was a Cuban," he recalled, "they considered me a white person" and placed him in the "white" regiment. However, González never felt comfortable in the battalion, due to the differential treatment he received from white soldiers. Thus, he requested a transfer to the "colored" regiment. His reasoning was simple. "My background is more or less similar to the background of Afro-Americans," he insisted. "Their [whites'] origins are from Anglo-Saxons, and Africans and us Cubans are descendants of Africans and Spaniards, but . . . our background is African." During the remainder of his tenure in the U.S. Army González served in the "colored" 1315th Engineering Construction Battalion. His change to the black regiment made him feel more comfortable in an ostensibly foreign environment. This was the first of a lifetime of negotiations González made, which were similar to negotiations made by other Latina/os of African descent. African-descended Latina/os have deployed multiple strategies to carve out lives for themselves as actors who experienced particular forms of social, cultural, and political exclusion. Rather than result in a path to assimilation as "Americans," for black Latina/os, military service cemented a racial awareness born out of forms of racialization that are akin to, yet distinct from, those experienced by African Americans.

Norberto González's encounters with the color line in the U.S. military during the Second World War illustrate the ways African descendants, regardless of their national origin, were forced to contend with Jim Crow

Figure 2.1. Norberto González, center, with his two sisters and his parents in Cuba in 1931; as a young man, he came to the United States to pursue a "better life." González enlisted in the army in 1944, and because he was Cuban, he was assigned to a "white" regiment. But González soon requested a transfer to a "colored" regiment where he felt a greater kinship with the other soldiers. Voces Oral History Project, Nettie Lee Benson Latin American Collection, University of Texas at Austin.

racism in the United States. His experience resonates with what scholars and activists now call "Afro-Latina/os," persons of African descent from Iberian backgrounds who have a unique experience and identity that has been profoundly shaped by racism both in their homelands and in the United States.[1] González's request to be transferred to a black battalion shows how he, as an Afro-Cuban, perceived the similarities between himself and African Americans. Rather than dis-identify with African Americans, González, like many Afro-Latinos in this period, preferred to carve out a life among African Americans. Thus rather than construct his self-identity against blackness, González embraced it, even if for strategic purposes, thereby highlighting a key part of the Afro-Latina/o experience in the United States that is not as uncommon as many Latina/o immigrant narratives have often suggested.

This chapter draws from the interviews of González and Evelio Grillo, an Afro-Cuban veteran born in Ybor City, Florida, conducted by the U.S. Latino & Latina World War II Oral History Project to explore the making of Afro-Latina/o identifications during the 1940s.[2] Despite their distinct backgrounds, González's and Grillo's experiences illustrate the complicated ways African-descent Latinos negotiated life in the Jim Crow-era United States. Their encounters with racialization parallel those of other black and brown Latina/os: from baseball players to intellectuals, including Arturo "Arthur" Schomburg, the Afro–Puerto Rican bibliophile, historian, and writer whose personal collection formed the basis of the New York Public Library's Schomburg Center for Research in Black Culture in Harlem. While a common language and Iberian cultural heritage provided the bases for commonality among Latinos, an attentiveness to Afro-Latino experiences illuminates the ways racialization created fault lines among Latinos, which in turn necessitated negotiation strategies that were distinct from those developed by Latinos racialized as "mestizo" or "Spanish."[3] Afro-Latina/os often had little choice but to cast their lot with African Americans, often relying on black institutions for their survival in the United States. However, their cultural heritage enabled them to stand out from their African American peers, making them "black" and "Latina/o" at the same time.[4]

"I have a hybrid identity that can't be torn apart": Evelio Grillo's Multiple Migrations

Evelio Grillo was born in Ybor City, Florida, on June 4, 1919. His story is well known thanks to his memoir, *Black Cuban, Black American*.[5] Grillo writes of his struggle against discrimination while growing up in the segregated worlds of Tampa, Washington, and New Orleans. Grillo spent his childhood in Ybor City, the so-called Latin Quarter of the Tampa region. Ybor City became home to a transcultural, multiethnic/multiracial community settled by Spaniards, Italians, and Cubans drawn to the region by the emerging cigar industry.[6] Although historians have clearly illustrated the cultural distinctiveness of the community, which facilitated cross-cultural interaction unseen in most parts of the U.S. South, recent scholarship shows that the town was also profoundly shaped by the implementation of legalized racial segregation in the late nineteenth and early twentieth century. Thanks to Grillo's narrative, we have a greater awareness of the complexities of the Cuban American experience in general, and the Afro-Latina/o experience in particular. Moreover, Grillo's experience in the U.S. military during the Second World War underscores the peculiar racial dimensions of U.S. Latina/os of African descent, who as citizens and not as "foreigners," as many Latinos are often categorized in popular conceptions of U.S. identity, are subject to unique forms of racial exclusion analogous to those experienced by African Americans.[7]

Grillo's 2003 interview with Mario Barrera in the U.S. Latina/os and World War II Oral History Project covers much of the same ground as his 2002 memoir, *Black Cuban, Black American* but with some important new information. His parents arrived in Ybor City as part of the larger wave of Cuban migration to the Tampa Bay area during the late nineteenth century. Indeed, it was Tampa and Key West, not Miami, that was the center of the early Cuban American community in the United States. After the outbreak of the Ten Years' War in 1868, cigar manufacturers, most notably Vicente Martínez Ybor, relocated their operations to Key West and then Tampa, attracting thousands of workers who developed small colonies in Florida and other parts of the United States. These multiracial Cuban communities, though small, were visible and deeply connected with affairs in Cuba. With the outbreak of the Cuban Wars for Independence in the 1860s, Key West and Tampa, like New York City, housed active exile communities agitating for Cuban independence. Ybor City was a key site of Cuban separatist activity, which was buoyed by the support of Cuban cigar workers. Prominent Cuban independence movement leaders like José Martí, as well as Afro-Cuban independence leaders including Rafael Serra, rallied Cuban exiles to the cause of "Cuba Libre" (Free Cuba) during the 1890s. Cubans of African descent, as historians have shown, forcefully linked the independence movement to their own desires for true social and political equality.[8]

Grillo's biography is a small part of a larger story of Afro-Cuban interactions with African Americans in Ybor City. Racial segregation compelled Afro-Cubans to interact with U.S.-born blacks. For example, as the Grillo story illustrates, Afro-Cubans who sought to pursue an education were forced to accept the segregated Jim Crow educational system. Moreover, at the turn of the twentieth century, African American educators like Booker T. Washington sought to recruit Afro-Cuban students from Tampa and Key West to his Tuskegee Institute, the well-known school he founded for African Americans in 1881. Although he failed to recruit students from Tampa and Key West, he did manage to attract Afro-Cuban students from the island during the first two decades of the twentieth century. Afro-Cubans, who themselves were still less than two decades removed from slavery, found Washington's message of industrial education appealing. Indeed, a number of Afro-Cuban figures corresponded with and were admirers of Washington and his school. Figures like Rafael Serra, the Afro-Cuban patriot, moved between Florida, Cuba, and New York to found *sociedades de instrucción y recreo* (instructional and recreational societies), which were designed to educate illiterate people of African descent. Thus Grillo was one of many Afro-Cubans who were educated in black schools in this period. Grillo recalled in his memoir that he "did not know any black Cuban college graduate of my generation, and all the generations preceding desegregation who is not a graduate of a historically black college."[9]

The particularities of the Afro-Cuban Tampeño experience evident in Grillo's story are rooted in the overlapping worlds that converged in Ybor City. The cigar-making center was settled by Cuban, Spanish, and Italian immigrants, along with the native African American and white American population. In his interview with Barrera, one can note Grillo's transcultural background in his somewhat unusual accent, which is closer to that of a U.S.-born black man from the South than to a "Cuban" or "Latin" accent. Grillo highlights the ways racial segregation permeated every aspect of his youth spent in Jim Crow Florida. In his memoir and his interview with Barrera, Grillo insists that the racial logic of Jim Crow cut across national lines: "I never played with a white child, not one," he recalled emphatically to illustrate the ways racial segregation shaped their lives, except for an "Italian boy who played with us." He had very "fond memories" of this "Italian."[10] As a result, Grillo became closely integrated into the city's African American community: "We became culturally African-Americans," he insisted. "There were differences and slight tensions," Grillo continued. "But all in all, [we] were fully integrated into the social life of African-Americans except that we did not go to the churches because we were Catholics and it was a sin to go to Protestant churches." Jim Crow also shaped the intimate lives of Afro-Cubans in Tampa. "Most of the black Cuban girls sought African-American men," he remembered. "And most black Cuban men sought African American women. . . . There were some black Cuban-black Cuban marriages, but very few." (Grillo's references to the romantic relationships of himself and his peers underscore the ways such unions shaped racial and ethnic identifications, a theme that also emerges in Norberto González's narrative and that I discuss further below.)[11]

Grillo's recollections of the dynamics of racial segregation in Tampa certainly illustrate the impact of U.S. racial norms on Cubans in the United States. Yet he stopped short of pinning racial exclusion solely on the American segregation system. When Barrera asked him to what extent racial "attitudes between black Cubans and white Cubans" were brought from Cuba or a product of mainland racial ideas, Grillo recalled, "Some of it was brought over from Cuba." But he added that "the white Cubans are white, and they are Spanish, they are descendants of Spanish." "Now there is a lot of integration of Spaniards and white Cubans, but make no mistake about it," he said, as he emphatically smacked his hands together, "the power and the money is in the hands of Spaniards." Here Grillo's comments about the whiteness of Spaniards highlights their power in Cuba and in all Latin American societies, where the colonial social structures enabled them to benefit from racialized social hierarchies even with the histories of racial mixture.

Grillo's evolving identity as a black person in the United States was concretized by his migration to Washington, DC, a city with a large and diverse black population. In the 1930s Grillo found himself in one of the more distinguished African American communities in the country in Washington after Nicholas Martin, a black acquaintance, took him north to continue his education. As he recalled with a laugh in his interview, Martin told him, "Now boy, you go up there and show them what a Southern Colored boy can do." In Martin's view, Grillo was not a Cuban but a "Southern Colored boy" who had the chance to pursue an educational path similar to other "Colored boys" in the segregated worlds of the United States. Yet Grillo took Martin's admonition as a source of motivation: "That is one of the piercing memories, and I went up there and I showed them!" He wound up enrolling in prestigious Dunbar High, formerly M Street High School, which was the leading African American educational institution in the country. Moreover, he was taken in by Sue Bailey and her husband, Howard Thurman, dean of Howard University's Rankin Chapel, the center of cultural and religious life on campus, which put him in contact with African American intellectual luminaries, including historian Rayford Logan, political scientist Ralph Bunche, and philosopher Alain Locke. It was this experience in Washington that led him to feel "free to be unambiguously black."[12]

After graduating from Dunbar, he attended Xavier University, the black Catholic school in New Orleans. Soon after graduating from Xavier, he was drafted into the U.S. Army. He was placed in the 823rd Engineer Aviation "Colored" Battalion. In his interview, as in his memoir, Grillo recounted the struggles of himself and other African Americans soldiers in the battalion. The brutal conditions, products of being in war and also in separate and unequal conditions, felt like a war not only against a foreign enemy, he said, but also against the segregationist "enemy" within the U.S. military. For these reasons, Grillo told Barrera that the title "engineer" was a euphemism because it was "a slave labor battalion." Eating segregated meals, suffering through squalid conditions onboard the USS *Santa Paula* en route to India, and general mistreatment by white superior officers were constant reminders of the second-class citizenship of Grillo and his fellow black soldiers.

Significantly, Grillo's military experience profoundly affected his postwar career path. He and his fellow soldiers filed a protest against their unequal treatment. While stationed in India, he became head recreational sergeant, in charge of entertaining the troops with movies, music, and sporting activities. By the time the Germans surrendered in September 1945, Grillo says he felt no need to celebrate the U.S. victory because he was "too drained from [his] experience in India."[13] His other war was still not over.

While Grillo's experience of the war was painful and frustrating, he managed to draw on it to create a remarkably productive postwar career. Indeed, one of the values of Grillo's interview is his elaborate discussion of his life after the war, which receives only a few pages in his memoir. In 1949 he enrolled at Columbia University to pursue a Ph.D. in Latin American history. His decision to study Latin America was based on his belief that he was "a possible bridge between English-speaking and Spanish-speaking peoples," he recalled. "But especially between English-speaking blacks and what are now referred to as 'Latinos' which are the Spanish-speaking African-Americans, which is what I am. . . . Somewhere in my ancestry there is some Spanish blood, but the most relevant piece of genealogy is I am African-American, I am an African in derivation, so I pursued Latin American history." However, after two and a half years at Columbia, he left, disenchanted with the program, particularly with one historian who Grillo stridently characterized as a "racist of the first order." Grillo's challenges at Columbia are not surprising, given that U.S. mainstream academic institutions were far from hospitable places for young scholars of African descent in this period.

After his less than satisfying experience at Columbia, Grillo's path was once again profoundly shaped by Howard and Sue Bailey Thurman. Sometime after living in New York, he followed the Thurmans to the San Francisco Bay Area, where Thurman was founding the Church of the Fellowship of All Peoples, the first integrated, interfaith congregation in the United States. Grillo eventually settled in Oakland, where he began a long career in social work. In 1953 he obtained an advanced degree in social welfare at the University of California, Berkeley, and he became active in local politics and social welfare agencies. Like other black immigrants to Oakland, Grillo successfully pursued career possibilities rarely available in the Jim Crow South. "Oakland is a mecca for ambitious blacks who come here seeking a place to be and a place to express," he told Barrera. "And by osmosis they hear that Oakland is a pretty good place to be a black and so they come. And that is the legacy I had a hand in developing."

Grillo's interview, while enlightening, could not cover all the significant details of his years in Oakland, where he continued to reside long after his retirement. Oakland's black population, which consisted mostly of descendants of migrants from the South, spearheaded the region's civil rights and Black Power activism during the 1960s and 1970s. It was propelled in part by the founding of the Black Panther Party in the city. Left unclear in his conversation with Barrera is his relationship with the Panthers and the younger generation of black activists in Oakland, as well as a discussion of his effectiveness as a cultural "bridge" between the city's Mexican American and African American communities. From his professional experiences in social welfare institutions and his active role in the local branches of the Democratic Party, one can conclude that Grillo did not embark on a radical political trajectory along the lines of the sixties cohort of Black Power activists. Instead, he seemed to prefer to work within state institutions to improve the conditions of people of color in the East Bay.[14]

Evelio Grillo's story seems to easily lend itself to an assimilationist narrative, but it is far more complex. It is tempting to insert him in a linear narrative of the immigrant child who left his Cuban background to become a (black) American. Yet I would suggest that his and his family's experiences actually highlight the process of transculturation, the making of a proto-Afro-Latino culture and identification from two or more preexisting cultures. The Grillos' encounters with African Americans widen a notion of blackness that transcends the confines of an English-speaking "African American" construction. Because of his deep roots in Cuban and African American communities, he became a cultural broker between them. Evelio Grillo, along with his siblings, Sergio and Sylvia, who also attended black schools in Florida and Washington, became transcultural subjects whose experiences elude the conceptual frame of race and nation. To Grillo, this was a transcultural understanding of blackness that was rooted in both his Cuban and his American experience. "I have a hybrid identity that can't be torn apart," he recalls. "It's not this, that, or that. I can't be [just] Afro-Cuban. I have to be both at the same time all the time."[15]

This multiple identification-making process is also clear in the life of Norberto González, a Cuban-born U.S. Latino whose encounters with Jim Crow segregation in the military also compelled navigation strategies that produced a unique Afro-Latina/o experience that became increasingly common after the Second World War.

Sgt. Norberto González: From Puerto Padre to Manila and Beyond

Norberto González's life story in many ways parallels Grillo's; but it has some significant differences. González was born only a few months after Grillo, on September 4, 1919, in Puerto Padre, Cuba, a small port town on the northeastern coast. In the early twentieth century Puerto Padre was a main port for two of the largest sugar mills in Cuba: the Central Chaparra and Central Delicias, both owned by the Cuban-American Sugar Company (Cubanaco). Cubanaco was owned by Texas congressman Robert Hawley and managed by Mario García Menocal, a veteran of the Cuban independence wars, a Cornell University graduate, and eventual president of Cuba (1913–1921).[16] As historian Gillian McGillivray has shown, the influence of the Chaparra and Delicias sugar mills extended to Puerto Padre, converting it, for all intents and purposes, into a company town. The emergence of the town was in many ways tied to the rise of these sugar mills.[17]

Curiously, González did not mention Chaparra and Delicias in his interview. When asked about his family background, he described his father as a "shoemaker," "public employee," and "clerk."[18] Not once does he mention anyone in his family working in the region's sugar fields. Indeed, cane cutting was perhaps the likeliest occupation for the region's working poor. This curious omission could be due to the fact that the González family belonged to the town's artisan class, which may mean that his family was not as humble as he suggests in his interview. Or, it is possible, but perhaps unlikely, that González actively silenced the family's ties to sugarcane because of the negative connotation that cane cutting occupation has had in Cuban history. To be a cane cutter is to work in conditions analogous to slavery. Indeed, the vast majority of enslaved Africans in Cuba worked on the

Figure 2.2. Norberto González and his first wife, Lucila Mustelier Miranda, in 1945. The couple married in Cuba on González's first furlough. After her death, González married another Cuban woman and later would have relationships with Latina women of other ethnic groups, including a Puerto Rican and a Dominican. Voces Oral History Project. Nettie Lee Benson Latin American Collection, University of Texas at Austin.

island's sugar plantations.[19] Regardless of the precise reasons for the absence of sugar in González's life history, his silence on this subject is part of a larger reticence that permeates much of his interview. It is also suggestive of the ways class and race can shape immigrant experiences and memories of home, a marked contrast to Grillo's more forthright reflections of his hometown, Ybor City.

Although the González family's relationship to the dominant force in the region's political economy is less than clear, Norberto's recollections of his youth in Puerto Padre resonate with our understanding of the history of the region and the island during the 1920s, 1930s, and 1940s. While Grillo was eventually reared among educated African Americans, albeit in a Jim Crow context, González emerged from the impoverished conditions of the Cuban working class on the island. Like many Cubans living in isolated sugar towns during this period, Norberto and his family seem to have suffered from the limited opportunities available to the island's laboring majority. "I come from a family with a humble background," González told his interviewer in the U.S. Latino & Latina World War II Oral History Project in 2002. "The majority of the time my father was unemployed. Those years, the '30s and '40s . . . were terrible in my country. There was a lot of poverty and misery. My family came from that group."

González's recollections were no doubt shaped by his experience growing up in Cuba during the Great Depression, which devastated the island's economy and spun its politics into almost complete disarray. When asked about his memories of major events from the period, he immediately re-called the fall of President Gerardo Machado, an event that capped more than a decade of economic, social, and political turmoil in Cuba. The late 1910s was a boom period for towns like Puerto Padre, which benefited from the rise of sugar prices during the First World War as Cuban sugar pro-ducers, like the Cuban-American Sugar Company, profited from the dis-ruption of the European sugar market by the war. However, after the war the sugar industry began a period of steady decline that continued through-out the 1920s, gradually crippling the Cuban economy. At the same time, new political forces, including middle-class political organizations, the stu-dent movement, the Communist Party, and organized labor presented ma-jor challenges to a corrupt Cuban political order. Much of this mobilization concentrated on contesting the repressive regime of Machado, an initially popular president who manipulated the Cuban constitution to engineer his reelection in 1928 and who became increasingly authoritarian in subsequent years. Machado's second term in office (1929–1933) was a period of eco-nomic dislocation and political violence as his government resorted to force to eliminate his political opponents. As the Cuban economy was brought to near-collapse by the stock market crash of 1929, which crippled the island's sugar industry, the movement against Machado used retaliatory violence. In August 1933 a general strike initiated by Havana transit workers led to the collapse of the Machado government, and a period of greater political up-heaval and economic turmoil ensued. It was not until the adoption of a new Cuban constitution in 1940 that the island began to emerge from the dark-ness of the Machado era. It is for these reasons that González recalled the "misery" of the period.[20]

If the influence of the Cuban-American Sugar Company is not evident in González's memories of his hometown, his encounters with U.S. Ameri-can culture in Cuba show up periodically in his story. He informs the inter-viewer of his desire to learn English due to his father's learning of the lan-guage from U.S. soldiers who were in his hometown, most likely during the U.S. military occupations of the island (1898–1902 or 1906–1909). More-over, González identifies his religious background as Protestant instead of Catholic. His religious affiliation might very well be a manifestation of the impact of U.S. Protestant missionaries throughout the island, particularly in company towns dominated by U.S. sugar companies. Thus one can detect the dominant influence of the United States in Cuba in González's indirect references to it in his recollections of life in Puerto Padre.[21]

It was these circumstances, combined with the limited educational op-

Figure 2.3. Evelio Grillo in Washington, DC, 1945. Grillo, an Afro-Cuban born in Ybor City, Florida, attended segregated schools. As part of that segregation, he recalled in an interview, "we become culturally African Americans. . . . We were fully integrated into the social life of African Americans except that we did not go to the churches because we were Catholics and it was a sin to go to Protestant churches." Voces Oral History Project, Nettie Lee Benson Latin American Collection, University of Texas at Austin.

portunities available to working-class Cubans, that prompted González to migrate to the United States. Like many Cuban migrants to the United States in this period, González settled, not in Miami, but in New York City, arriving in New York as a twenty-five-year-old in 1944. When asked what his family thought about his decision to migrate to the United States, he revealingly recalled that people in his hometown were afraid of the United States because they heard about the "lynching" of blacks. González's comments here highlight the ways Cubans became familiar with Jim Crow racism in this period. Despite the González family's anxieties about his decision to relocate to the United States, he seems to have quickly adapted to his environment. His ability to adapt was surely facilitated by the presence of the city's Latino, particularly Puerto Rican, population, which was beginning its rapid growth in New York City during the 1940s. Although he does not directly discuss his interactions with other Latinos in New York during this period, one can infer his relationships with them in his brief references to his work as a musician in the Latin music scene as well as in the ethnic/national identifications of his romantic partners over the years. In fact, when his interviewer asked about the latter, González replied that he had maintained relationships with women from other Latino groups after the death of his first wife, Lucila Mustelier Miranda, including a Puerto Rican and a Dominican. Thus, as was the case in Grillo's narrative of Jim Crow life in Ybor City, González's recollections of his romantic relationships illustrate the ways such relationships could facilitate a cross-national, Latina/o cultural awareness, one that emerged in pan-Latino contexts like New York City.[22]

It was soon after his arrival in New York that González decided to enlist in the U.S. military. His decision to enlist was, like his decision to migrate to the United States, a means to a better life for himself, his parents, and his spouse. In his interview he plainly stated that his motivations for enlisting were to learn English and to provide money for his family in Cuba. During his term of service, the army sent his mother, Juana, and his wife, Lucila, $50 a month, "which at that time was a small fortune," he recalled. Military service also gave him a path to U.S. citizenship, which he received in 1947.

González's recollections of his service during the war are similar to his memories of his childhood and early adulthood in Cuba. González portrays his experience of the war in frank and unromantic terms. For much of his stint in the service, he was stationed in the Philippines. As a member of the 1315th Engineering Construction Battalion, he built new roads and guarded Japanese war prisoners. Like Grillo, González was not directly involved in the main battles of the war. His memories are helped by a photo album he keeps from his time in the service. "Manila had been totally destroyed," he recalled. "There was a lot of poverty and misery." Even his recollections of his encounters with racial discrimination in the military are portrayed matter-of-factly and without the specific details provided by Grillo. When asked how he was treated when he was placed in the "white" battalion, he replied simply that he was treated differently on account of his racial and national background. Once González's request to switch to a "black" battalion was granted, he seems to have thrived. In fact at no point in his interview does he refer to the squalid conditions that Grillo compared to slave labor. When asked how he got along with his fellow black soldiers, he replied, "Very well, because they were very modest and humble. I felt more in common with them and I was able to advance more." His recollections are backed up by the service awards he received, including the Asiatic-Pacific Campaign Medal, the World War II Victory Medal, and the Philippine Liberation Ribbon.

Although González portrayed his time in the service in grim and somewhat unremarkable terms, he nonetheless acknowledged the ways his life improved after his migration and his enlistment. Unlike Grillo, he did not participate in civil rights activism, preferring to live an apolitical life as a working-class Latino in the United States. When asked how the Second World War changed his life, he responded, "Significantly . . . I was able to learn English, something I had always wanted to do." González's ability to acquire a second language, which he links to his military experience, underscores the ways he ties his bilingualism to his eventual upward mobility from an impoverished family in Cuba to a seemingly more financially stable working-class life in the United States during the postwar era. During his time in the military he was able to send money to his family in Cuba. Indeed, he insists that he "never suffered the same level of poverty" that he had experienced in Cuba. Thus, for González, military service served a specific purpose: to improve the material circumstances of himself and his family. To a large extent, González achieved this goal. Serving in the military during the Second World War, despite its clear practices of racism, became a viable path to upward mobility for González, as it has been for other working-class people of color.

Conclusion: Afro-Latina/os and Latinidad in the Postwar United States

The experiences of Evelio Grillo and Norberto González, while unique in their own ways, represent a larger reservoir of experiences of Latina/os of African descent. Like all Latina/os, they share the common Iberian colonial heritage and the struggles of living in an English-speaking country. However, as people of African descent, they stand apart due to their experiences of racism in the United States and in the Americas at large. Moreover, both Grillo and González belong to the generation of Afro-Latina/os who lived under legalized segregation during the Jim Crow era, which made their experiences similar to those of African Americans. Their encounters with racial segregation in the military and in other spheres of life decisively shaped their outlook on Latinidad. These racial and generational differences are clear in their comments about Latina/o identity and politics in the United States at the turn of the twenty-first century. In his interview González distanced himself from the politics of prominent Cuban American leaders in the Miami area. In his later years health issues prompted González to relocate to Miami, where he could be closer to his family. Instead of feeling comfortable in a city that houses one of the most robust Cuban communities in the United States, González tellingly found Miami a less than hospitable place. "Here the Cubans consider themselves superior to other Hispanos," he said. "The majority of the Cubans here are powerful people and I don't like their attitude."[23]

González echoed similar feelings about Cuban American politics in Miami. Although his interview was conducted in Spanish, when asked about his feelings about sending remittances to Cuba, he chose to say the following in English:

> There are Cubans here who don't want to send money. Don't send money; don't send money because it helps Castro [they say]. But you have to send money. If you have a mother or sister there, will you not send money? I send it. I don't care about Castro. If it helps them buy food to eat or whatever, if the money then goes to Castro, I don't care![24]

Here González expresses an explicit dis-identification with the dominant Cuban American political culture in Miami. His concern with his family's well-being, rather than the political line of the Cuban American political elite is in many ways a courageous act that sets him apart from the core anti-Castroite political positioning that has been central to Cuban American identity and politics since the triumph of the Cuban Revolution in 1959. Here we can note the generational, class, and, to some extent, racial differences between González and more dominant understandings of Cuban Americanness. González's criticism of Cuban American politics widens our understanding of Cuban Americans beyond the still-dominant stereotype of the Cuban American as a white, anti-Castro subject.

These racial and generational differences between González and Miami Cuban politics are also clear in Evelio Grillo's strident assessments of contemporary Latina/o identity:

> Latino is a reality and Latino identity has caught on like wildfire. But the term does violence to the fundamental identity of the person. Because it doesn't tell you a thing except that they have some Spanish in the background. And it is very convenient. So by using the term Latino, they can be done with any implication that they are somehow Africans, but the fact of the matter is that most Latinos have African in their background, and Latino gives them a rubric that can take out any discussion of any African-American antecedent, so they have a new . . . they come from a country called [laughs] *Latinoland*. So I permit myself to be called Latino, but other people call me Latino, I call myself a *Black Cuban*. Because that refers to my Cuban roots and my black roots and that is what I am comfortable with.[25]

Grillo's critical comments about the anti-blackness embedded in some constructions of "Latinoland" reveal the gap between his understanding of Latino-ness and more recent iterations of Latinidad. While his assertions are based on the assumption that national identifications are somehow more concrete than ethnic categories, they nonetheless provide a useful critique of the historic invisibility of Afro-Latina/os. His life history, like the history of Norberto González, widens our understanding of the Latina/o experience in the United States by highlighting the different ways Latina/os across the racial spectrum have been shaped by racializing processes in the past and the present.

Higher Education, the GI Bill, and the Postwar Lives of Latino Veterans and Their Families

ANGÉLICA AGUILAR RODRÍGUEZ,
JULIAN VASQUEZ HEILIG, AND ALLISON PROCHNOW

In 1897 a federal district court declared that the Treaty of Guadalupe Hidalgo, and subsequent federal policies, conferred on Mexican Americans a "white" racial status for naturalization and classification purposes.[1] Thus, despite the "separate but equal" decision in *Plessy v. Ferguson*,[2] Latina/os should have had equal access to the same public schools as whites. However, racial bias was pervasive. Mexican Americans, often referred to as "greasers," faced cultural prejudices analogous to the racial animus suffered by African Americans. Indeed, Mexican Americans in this era endured several high-profile lynchings, and during the Great Depression city governments like that of Houston actively encouraged their repatriation to Mexico.[3] Professor E. E. Davis of the University of Texas asserted in a 1923 publication that white American children did not want to attend school with "the dirty 'greaser' type of Mexican child," and should not be required to do so. Instead Davis advocated that Mexican children be placed in separate schools until they were able to contribute positively to society.[4] It is in this context that we explore the experiences of Latino World War II veterans in U.S. schools before and after the war.

We begin with a brief review of established scholarship on the structural racism that Latina/os faced in the U.S. educational system. We then describe the elementary and secondary educational experiences of several Latino veterans who participated in the U.S. Latino and Latina World War II Oral History Project, later the Voces Oral History Project, at the University of Texas at Austin. We conclude with profiles of three Latino veterans derived from follow-up interviews that focused specifically on their higher education experiences before and after the war. Little has been written about the lived experiences of Latino veterans who returned from service to enter the academy. We ultimately show the survival heuristics and pathways that several Latino veterans used to achieve success despite racism in the broader society.

Latino Education in the World War II Era

The highly racialized educational contexts that denigrated the culture, heritage, and language of Mexican Americans were evident throughout the school systems in Texas, California, and other states where large concentrations of Latinos were living. World War II ushered in a new era of opportunity in American society, one with increased economic prosperity and new educational possibilities for some Latina/os who previously would not have had the opportunity to attend secondary schools and go on to higher education.[5] In 1944 President Franklin D. Roosevelt signed into law the Servicemen's Readjustment Act, known colloquially as the GI Bill (P.L. 78-346, 58 Stat. 284m). This act provided a path for World War II veterans to access higher education, an opportunity once reserved for the rich.[6] Created as a measure to inoculate the United States from another financial disaster, as when World War I veterans rebelled after returning to the home front with only a "$60 allowance and a train ticket,"[7] the GI Bill, unexpectedly, helped create a highly educated citizenry and a powerful economic and technologically advanced society.[8]

The GI Bill had a positive impact on African American, Latino, and low-income military men and women in general. Provisions of the GI Bill called for the U.S. government to give financial assistance for tuition, fees, books, and supplies, as well as a stipend. For World War II veterans,[9] this reduced the "opportunity costs" of attending higher education.[10] Research has demonstrated that the African American veteran participation in higher education due to the GI Bill helped create a black middle class[11] and increased civil participation, including civil rights–era activism.[12]

Early Education Experiences of World War II Veterans

Many Latinas and Latinos of the World War II generation attended segregated schools where they faced prejudice and limited educational opportunities. Several veterans recounted the difficult environments in which their elementary school classes took place and how they struggled to attain an education. Many obstacles kept Latina/o students from completing their education. Ramón Rivas, an army veteran from Charlotte, Texas (located

50 miles south of San Antonio), described the obstacles Latina/o students faced to simply advance to the next grade level. He explained that in Charlotte, Latina/o students remained in separate Mexican schools until the fourth grade, after which Mexican and Anglo students attended the same school. However, he said that Mexican students never made it to the integrated school because Mexican students "would start 1st grade, stay there two or three years, and then go to 2nd grade, then stay there like that . . .".[13] The decision to repeat a grade was given solely to the teacher; parental involvement was limited. This story is similar to another Voces project respondent, Nicanór Aguilar of Big Spring, Texas. He told UT-Austin researchers it was only because of a white teacher's intervention that his younger sister, Maria, went on to the eighth grade. This practice of retaining Latina/o students greatly affected their ability to complete elementary school, because they were kept in the same grades for several years depite their potential.[14] Even when students were able to advance, family circumstances, or the need to work, often obstructed the pathway to graduation. Raymon Elizondo, an army veteran from Salt Lake City, Utah, spoke of the difficulties he and his family faced completing school. Although he greatly desired to graduate and break the cycle of low levels of educational attainment in his family, he was only able to finish the ninth grade, when at the age of seventeen financial difficulties forced him to take a job with the Union Pacific Railroad. In his family of twelve children, only one sister completed high school.[15]

Other veterans offered specific memories about the discrimination and racism faced by Latina/os in schools. Julian L. Gonzalez, an army veteran raised in Chapin, Texas (about 60 miles east of Dallas), remembered being called into the principal's office after writing "Viva Mexico" on the playground. The principal told him, "You like Mexico so much, why don't you go on the next train."[16] Adam Gastelum, a veteran from Tucson, Arizona, described a school coach's harsh treatment of students caught speaking Spanish. He stated that the coach would punish the students by picking them up by their sideburns or squeezing their legs to the point of bruising.[17] Paul Gil, an army veteran from Gonzales County, Texas (about 60 miles east of San Antonio), recounted that the teachers hated him for being a "smart Mexican" after he advanced from kindergarten to second grade on his first day of school because of his reading and writing skills, which he had obtained at home.[18] Lorenza Lujano, a family member of a veteran from Newton, Kansas, related that she made the decision in the tenth grade to withdraw from school because the "racially prejudiced" environment she and her family faced in school was "too much to bear." Lujano felt that this environment even led to the false accusation that her sister Esperanza had stolen a cheerleading skirt from the school.[19] Despite these barriers, some Latina/o students were able to develop strategies for success.

Strategic Interventions: The GI Bill, Latino Veterans, and Class Mobility

Of the estimated hundreds, and perhaps thousands, of Latino veterans who benefited from the GI Bill, three men from Texas illuminate the impact this legislation had on transforming the racist landscape of higher education for Mexican Americans: Virgilio Roel, A. D. Azios, and Julian L. Gonzalez. They gained access to higher education and thus access to powerful positions and increased social capital in American society. All three of these individuals came from impoverished homes, and most were successful students before the war. The funds and entrée provided by the GI Bill gave them not only an education but also the opportunity to pursue their dreams of becoming engineers, lawyers, judges, and community activists. One interviewee described the GI Bill as an "education revolution," one that made it possible not only for him but also other Latinos around the country to pursue their educational and career objectives.

In these profiles, we define success as social and class mobility, acquisition of positions of authority in the public sphere, increased agency to advocate for social minorities, and the creation of an educational pathway for their children and grandchildren. Though these stories describe obstacles, perseverance, and success, it is important to note that they are more complex and nuanced than mere progress narratives. The veterans negotiated their identities, as Latinos, men, and working-class subjects, in the war, in higher education, and in the professional class. Their responses were varied, from purposefully integrating their past identities into their new ones or returning to their former identities with little desire to change. Significantly, two of these veterans became judges, having an impact on their communities in the legal sphere.

Virgilio Roel: Leadership, the Law, and the UT Laredo Club as a Catalyst for Educational Desegregation

For Virgilio Roel, the GI Bill was not only a ticket to higher education but also the opportunity to stand up to racial oppression. This profile will chronicle how the GI Bill facilitated the work of a Mexican American to question the authority of the state in regard to Mexican American children in public education, as well as battle for equal representation of women and racial minorities in government positions. This is not a hero story, though. It is the story of a man provided with the means to educate himself, a story of a man whose agency and self-efficacy merged with the emerging civil rights movement. Still, these successes occurred in positions of power, where he was able to shape the lives of those who are not in positions of power. For Roel, the effect of the GI Bill can be seen far beyond his career and the lives of his children and grandchildren. Indeed, individuals as different as residents of the rural towns of Three Rivers and Victoria, Texas, and indigenous peoples of American Samoa inadvertently were affected by Roel's use of the GI Bill.

As a young boy growing up in Laredo, Texas, on the U.S.-Mexico border, Virgilio Roel was undaunted in his dream to attend college after high school. His friends' shared interest in attending college would propel him to study at the University of Texas at Austin after the war. Also, he had a deep desire to "help his fellow man and woman, and the best path was education."[20] During his high school years, he prepared himself for admission into college, but the U.S. entry into World War II abruptly changed his plans. Instead of going straight to college after graduation, in 1942 he was one of 16 million men and women who joined the military. He spent the next three years in the army, first with the 84th Infantry Division and then with the 2nd Battalion, 517th Parachute Infantry Regiment. During his time in the military, Roel trained as a paratrooper and even studied at the Ohio State University with the Army Specialized Training Program (ASTP), studying languages and geopolitics.[21]

Although both of Roel's parents were teachers, he did not see himself as automatically seeking a post–high school education. He notes, "If it hadn't been for my military service, I probably would never have gone to college, I would have stayed in Laredo working for $37 a week [as a railroad surveyor]."[22] The GI Bill had great sway over his ability to even access higher education. "The GI Bill of Rights, which I think is the biggest piece of legislation that I think Congress ever passed, was the one that really started . . . the 'education revolution,'" Roel explained. "It made [higher education] possible."[23] The funding for his tuition and other educational expenses, as well as a stipend, provided him leverage to attend UT Austin. Still, Roel had to work to supplement what he received through the GI Bill. He worked thirty-five hours a week at the Texas Bookstore and at the Triple XXX, a drive-in restaurant, that kept him well fed.

While in college, Roel publicly pursued his passion: organizing against and confronting racism and oppression. For example, initially he and other Latina/os were not allowed to live on campus in the university's residence

Figure 3.1. Virgilio G. Roel, a native of Laredo, Texas, was able to use the GI Bill to attend the University of Texas at Austin, where he began finding ways to combat racism and oppression. One target was Texas Attorney General Price Daniel's opinion that provided for legally segregating schoolchildren based on language. Critics recognized that the opinion left a gaping loophole for segregationists. Roel would go on to graduate from Georgetown Law School. Voces Oral History Project, Nettie Lee Benson Latin American Collection, University of Texas at Austin.

halls. He lived off campus with five other students, three from Laredo and two from Mexico, in one room. He and other Latina/os successfully pushed the university administration into allowing them live in the residence halls. Roel utilized a column called the "Firing Line" in the campus newspaper, the *Daily Texan*, to accuse the university, its president, Theophilus Shickel Painter, and high-level administrators of discrimination. Through a series of letters to the "Firing Line," Roel said, "we raised some Cain [and] we finally got [rooms in campus residence halls] the next semester."[24]

Roel founded the UT Laredo Club to organize fellow Laredoans on campus. In addition to being a social club, the group spread activism to small towns like Three Rivers,[25] educating residents on their rights, specifically, the educational rights of children. "We used to go on the weekends to organize people in the small towns in [Texas] . . . to fight discrimination . . . so they knew their rights as citizens,"[26] Roel recalls. The UT Laredo Club also challenged discriminatory actions, including Texas Attorney General Marion Price Daniel's opinion regarding segregation of children based on language.[27] This opinion was drafted after the 1946 decision in *Mendez v. Westminster*, a case that found that Mexican students could not be segregated in different classrooms and different buildings due to language.[28] Daniel countered that Mexican children could be segregated if they had language deficiencies.[29] After rebuffing the invitations from the

Laredo Club several times, Daniel finally attended one of its meetings to hear the group's case. Influential educator George I. Sánchez also attended the meeting, and Sánchez, Roel, and other members of the Laredo Club challenged Daniel's opinion. According to Roel, the attorney general left the meeting with a change of heart.

Roel excelled at UT Austin, studying history and government and graduating magnum cum laude in February 1948, having finished his college career in two and a half years with the help of transfer credits from the Ohio State University. After a short summer stint as a railroad surveyor, he hitchhiked his way to Washington, DC, to attend Georgetown University School of Law, getting caught in rainstorms, sleeping on the sides of mountains, and taking buses and trains when he could. When he arrived, he slept on the streets because he "didn't have any other place to go."[30] Roel attended Georgetown Law at night, spending his days as a public liaison with the U.S. Department of State and the United Nations. Later Roel did something no other Latina/o had done or has done since: he became an associate justice on the High Court of American Samoa.

American Samoa, a former colony of several European powers and ultimately a U.S. territory, has a large indigenous population, and one that lacked real authority immediately after the war. Members of its High Court are appointed by the U.S. Department of the Interior rather than by the local government. American Samoans had little power affecting their own judiciary.[31] Roel's position gave him tremendous influence in the lives of American Samoans, and he took his position seriously. During his term as associate judge, he advocated for an increase in Native American Samoan judges, prosecutors, and public defenders.

After Roel's tenure in Samoa, he returned to the U.S. mainland. He was a general attorney and a member of the Board of Appeals and Review of the U.S. Postal Service. He recalls, "On one of my trips to [the U.S.] I went and talked to the head of the Democratic National Committee, and he offered me [a legal position at the] U.S. Postal Service."[32] This was to demonstrate that the Johnson administration was aiding in the cause of Mexican American rights.

Roel did use his time at the U.S. Postal Service to improve the position of Mexican Americans and other minorities. He recruited women and Latina/os to positions of authority and sought to change the culture of the agency. Roel notes one of his conditions for accepting the position: I would go around the country to recruit Mexican Americans and minorities for supervisory positions because they were outwardly discriminated [against]." He adds, "Not only that, women were completely discriminated [against] and it was my condition for accepting the position."[33]

After serving in the U.S. Postal Service, he was appointed national director for conciliation for the U.S. Department of Housing and Urban Development to end discriminatory housing practices. Roel noted that even the "regional directors of the Agency, they themselves did not want to implement the Equal Housing rules and the Equal Rights regulations."[34] He had to focus on dismantling a culture in which there had been "bias for so long."[35] After many years in Washington, DC, and abroad, Roel and his wife yearned to return to Texas.

For Roel, his education at UT Austin and then at Georgetown Law not only afforded him an exciting and varied career in which he was able to help provide opportunities for other minorities, but it also gave his children and grandchildren the impetus to pursue higher education as well. His four children attended college; two are physicians, and two are certified public accountants. He states, "I was in the first wave of veterans that benefited from [the GI Bill], but once our generation of veterans . . . had university degrees, it was taken for granted that our children [and our grandchildren] were going to go to the university."[36]

Virgilio Roel's trajectory, from a precocious boy in a small border town to his time in Washington, DC, and back, is a testament to the impact of his college education, an education he recognizes would have been difficult to obtain without the GI Bill. He not only excelled academically, but he was politically active, a trait also seen in African American veterans who went on to higher education after the war.[37]

For Roel, his personal, economic, and financial success rested on education and the "educational revolution" created by the passage of the GI Bill. He believes that the GI Bill created a "golden era" for Mexican Americans, as they had the opportunity to pursue higher education. He continued to stress that his greatest success was graduating from UT Austin. His education provided him with the resources, choices, and opportunities to pursue his dreams and aid others. Education for Roel is an act of citizenship. As Dr. Hector P. Garcia, founder of the GI Forum has noted, "Education is our freedom, and freedom is everybody's business."

A. D. Azios: Translingual Citizenship, Military Service, and Social Mobility

The benefits of bilingualism and multilingualism have been extensively detailed,[38] but in the case of A. D. Azios, it was a matter of life and death. His childhood bilingualism and adult trilingualism facilitated his and his men's safe return from war. It also informed his decision to act as a mentor to young Latina/os and propelled him to pursue higher education and a career in the law. Azios's story is the story of a man who chose to empower himself through education, before, during, and after World War II, and this was facilitated by his unique bilingual identity as a Latino.

Arnulfo "A. D." Azios was born in Laredo, Texas, one of six sons of Mexican parents. His parents had been refugees from the Mexican Revolution and moved their family to several different cities on the U.S.-Mexico border. Azios's childhood was filled with other Latina/o children and families like his, speaking mostly Spanish. Although he knew little English when he began school, he soon became proficient, mastering the language by the second grade.

A gifted student, Azios graduated from high school in 1939 excited about pursuing higher education. Many of his Mexican American friends from Laredo were heading off to college, and this peer influence acted as a strong inducement. Azios was motivated to be a role model to other Latina/o children in his community. He delayed his entrance into college for two years, working as a customs broker for an import-export company, until he hitchhiked to Austin to start school at the University of Texas in 1941.

That December, on the radio, he heard reports about the bombing of Pearl Harbor while he was studying with a former roommate. On hearing about this act of war on the United States he made a prediction to his roommate: "We'll whip 'em in 90 days."[39] He hitchhiked to San Antonio, with 60 cents in his pocket, and enlisted in the Army Enlisted Reserve Corps. Azios continued his studies at UT Austin until 1943, when his unit was called to active duty as the UT Austin tower bells played "You're in the Army Now."

Azios's ability to learn languages quickly became an asset for him in the military. He scored high on the army's entrance exam, and he and other high scorers were sent to universities around the country to cultivate their skills. Already proficient in English and Spanish, he was sent to the University of Nebraska from September 1943 to December 1943 to study German. (This new skill would become more important than he ever imagined.) After his three-month German training, he returned to his unit at Camp Maxey in Paris, Texas, for basic training, and then shipped out with the 9th Armored Division to the European theater.

During his time in Europe, Azios participated in the Battle of the Bulge, and his German proficiency would save both his life and the lives of other American soldiers. During the battle, Azios was wounded, his eyesight damaged temporarily by shrapnel. He escaped to a neighboring building

Figure 3.2. A. D. Azios, June 1945. Azios heard about the attack on Pearl Harbor while studying at the University of Texas at Austin, and he predicted that "we'll whip 'em in 90 days." Azios enlisted in the reserves and was called to active duty in 1943. He studied German in the military and later, during the Battle of the Bulge, was taken prisoner by German forces. His German-speaking skills helped him lead ten men to escape from the camp. This photo was taken on the porch steps of his mother's (Petra Azios) home in Laredo, Texas. Voces Oral History Project, Nettie Lee Benson Latin American Collection, University of Texas at Austin.

to hide, but on hearing German soldiers closing in on his location he called out to them in German and was captured.

While in a German POW camp, Azios used his German to barter with the guards and civilians, helping his men trade cigarettes for bread and potatoes. During his four months as a POW, he gained the guards' trust, which emboldened him to escape. While the POWs were being moved to a new location, away from approaching Allied forces, Azios hatched a plan with a corporal to pretend that he and his ten men were resting. During the escape a German officer confronted the group. On the pretext that he and his men were injured, Azios convinced the German officer that his group was heading to the nearby hospital but had become separated from the rest of the prisoners.

Once they were out of sight of German soldiers they made their way to a dairy farm where they hid in haystacks. The dairy farmers were also prisoners and provided the men with soup and allowed them to hide out on the land. That night they slept outside and were bombarded by heavy artillery.

The next day, an American lieutenant arrived, and Azios, as the leader of his group, came out of hiding to salute his superior officer. The group of ten escapees was saved.

After being rescued, Azios returned to the United States, recuperating and preparing to return to war, this time in the Pacific theater. But the war ended before he could be redeployed. Instead of returning to war, he returned to school. Azios took the long train ride from Boston to San Antonio, was discharged, and returned to Austin to complete his studies in pre-law.

After the war, the campus was filled with veterans. Azios recounted, "If you weren't a veteran, people would look down and said, 'Well, where were you? Where were you during the Long War?'"[40] Although Azios did not discuss the social pressure to participate in the military during the war, it is obvious that young men were expected to have fought, and instead of accolades for veterans it was men who did not fight who were singled out.

He also noticed an increase in Latina/os on campus that he believed was due to increased knowledge about college and its benefits. He recalls, "When I was in high school very few people went to college, very few, so when we GIs came back and went in waves the rest of the kids said 'Hey, I guess I'll go to school too.' . . . We set an example for other kids."[41] For Azios, military experience provided more than access to financial resources for college. The army had instilled a sense of discipline in him for both college and civilian life. He was taught to be more dedicated to his work and not to put off tasks until later. Azios insisted that the military changed his attitude from "I'll do it mañana [to] 'No no, you'll do it now.'"[42] As an individual who taught himself English by the second grade, it is difficult to imagine that he was a procrastinator prior to his army experience.

Unlike other servicemen who attended college because of the financial opportunities provided by the GI Bill, Azios had already spent two years in college without the benefit and would have gone to college with or without it. But, he notes, "it helped me because it paid for my books, my tuition, and $75 a month to live."[43] The GI Bill helped him specifically by providing him financial resources to attend college, but he still worked grueling hours to afford to go. During his time at UT Austin, he worked as a janitor, a night watchman at the campus gymnasium, and an elevator operator in the UT Austin tower. Azios would work a full eight-hour day and then spend the night studying. It was a lifestyle that he considered "rough, rough, rough."[44]

After he graduated from UT Austin, he attended the South Texas College of Law in Houston. His law career took off after law school; he became first an attorney and then a state judge. His time after school was difficult for him and his family. As a young lawyer, Azios made just enough money to provide for his family. But he ascended from a firm attorney to his own practice. Then he became a justice of the peace and ended his career as a district judge in the 232nd Judicial District Court of Harris County. Azios retired at the end of 1993 and began serving as a visiting judge.

Azios's time as a judge is compelling. He influenced the lives of local citizens while sitting on the criminal court bench. Latina/os make up a small percentage of judges at all levels of government, often due to a lack of an influential Latina/o voice and lack of unity of Latino special interests.[45] Azios was able to galvanize support and be elected to the bench. Importantly, when Latina/os are represented on the bench, their approval of the judiciary increases, as does their political awareness, as was the case with the appointment of Supreme Court Justice Sonia Sotomayor.[46] Azios, by his presence on the bench, likely had an impact on his community's perception of the local judiciary and the lives of minority defendants, who are overrepresented in criminal justice systems due to the confluence of a number of social ills: poverty, lack of education, and sentencing policies, among others.[47]

The experience of attending college had a profound effect on Azios. He fulfilled the goal of completing college, which was sparked when he was still a child in Laredo. He focused on being a role model to younger Latina/o children and encouraged them to attend college. In addition, his three children and grandchildren have continued his legacy by pursing their own college careers. Decades after he completed his undergraduate education, college still has a strong appeal to Azios: "If I was a young guy I would go [back again]."[48]

Julian L. Gonzalez: Nontraditional Students, Labor, and Political Consciousness

When Julian L. Gonzalez was approached to participate in the writing of this chapter, he wondered if he would add any value because he did not have "the traditional college experience."[49] Yet his is a common story of part-time students and many World War II veterans.[50] In 1959, the first year in which statistics on the subject are available, part-time students made up approximately a third of all college students.[51] Unlike Azios's and Roel's stories, Gonzalez was not an officer, nor did he have educational mentors. He, like the majority of Latina/os then and now, sought to improve his life through work. He remained a member of the working class, moving through the ranks not through higher education but by his hard work and seniority.

Figure 3.3. Julian L. Gonzalez was drafted in 1944 when he was a high school student in San Antonio. Gonzalez appealed and was allowed to finish high school. He rose to the rank of sergeant in the war and later attended San Antonio College and St. Mary's University. It would take thirteen years and his wife's insistence for him to get his bachelor's degree in sociology, with a minor in history. This photo of Gonzalez was taken in San Antonio in 1945. Voces Oral History Project, Nettie Lee Benson Latin American Collection, University of Texas at Austin.

Julian Gonzalez grew up in San Antonio, Texas, the child of Mexican immigrants. His father worked at a cement factory, and his mother picked cotton around the Austin area. School did not come easily to Gonzalez because he did not speak English well; he failed several grade levels. Yet he continued his education, moving through high school, up to his senior year. In 1944 he was drafted into the army. He appealed his draft order to finish high school and was allowed to enter the service immediately after graduating. Unlike Roel and Azios, whose education was facilitated by the military, Gonzalez had to persuade the military to let him finish high school. Having defended his desire to remain in school, he put himself in a position to take advantage of the GI Bill. Shortly after graduating from high school a semester early, he was sent to Fort Sam Houston in San Antonio.

At Fort Sam Houston, Gonzalez was trained as a combat medic and then sent to Camp Beale in California to prepare for his deployment to the Pacific theater. In late 1944 he sailed to New Guinea, where he helped build schools and hospitals. Gonzalez also worked with civilians as a member of the Philippines Civil Affairs Unit #10 to construct a government unit. During this time he waited to see action, as talks of an atomic bomb began to circulate. He was never to see battle; the war ended after atomic bombs were dropped on Hiroshima and Nagasaki.

After being discharged from the military in April 1946, he returned to San Antonio. Gonzalez had not graduated with his class, as he had already begun his time in the service. When he returned he had no job and no money. In essence, his only alternative was higher education. He also wanted to take advantage of the GI Bill. Without the "privilege" of the GI Bill, Gonzalez questioned if he would have been able to attend college because of the lack of funds. He did believe, though, that he was more mature and focused on the "urgency . . . to get that piece of white paper."[52]

Gonzalez began his career in higher education at San Antonio College (SAC), a community college that is now a branch of the Alamo Community College system.[53] After two years at SAC, he transferred to St. Mary's University in San Antonio. While he was still in high school he had dreamed of being a social worker to "help the poor people."[54] This dream is in sharp contrast to Roel's and Azios's work to facilitate change through hierarchical institutions. Gonzalez desired to meet with individuals in grassroots contexts. These differing strategies demonstrate the complexity of differing tracks to fight social injustice and how social hierarchies influence people's movements. To fulfill this goal, Gonzalez chose to pursue a degree in sociology, with a minor in history. Though he was motivated to become formally educated and realize his civic ambition, life responsibilities interfered.

Gonzalez worked full-time while he completed his degree. He first worked as an assistant timekeeper for the San Antonio Portland Cement Company. As he advanced slowly in his coursework, he also advanced at his job, taking on positions of greater authority and responsibility. Consequently, he was limited to taking two night classes each semester. Gonzalez generally stayed at school late into the night, which left little time for making connections with other students. He explained, "I went to night school . . . you leave there at 9:30 or 10:00 and you're anxious to get home, so there's no time for socializing. . . . I didn't have the [traditional] college education."[55] As is the case with many part-time students, social issues such as housing, transportation, and lack of child care can interfere with the path to college completion. These socially created barriers continue to reinforce social stratification and can cement a perpetual underclass. Gonzalez was able to escape this, at least partially. Unfortunately, he had already had a history of disrupted education.

By the time Gonzalez received his diploma, he had spent thirteen years pursuing his degree. Five years into his degree he had spent all the money provided by the GI Bill and paid the rest out of pocket. Fortunately, his wife, who had attended SAC to receive her nursing degree, "pushed, enticed, and dragged"[56] him to finish his degree. Though he never pursued a career in social work, his degree earned him a position as a manager at his plant, counseling employees on retirement, personal issues, income tax returns, and Social Security benefits.

Another area where his military service and higher education benefited Gonzalez was his civic and political engagement. Roach has described the increased civic engagement of African American World War II veterans who utilized the GI Bill, particularly during the civil rights movement, versus the lower civic engagement of those who did not utilize the educational resources provided by the legislation.[57] Although Gonzalez was not a member of civil rights organizations, he was active in the civic sphere, particularly in Democratic precincts.

His degree also affected his family members. His wife and one daughter became nurses, but his other children and some grandchildren were unable to finish their degrees. Gonzalez cited a lack of financial resources as the reason that his other two children and grandchildren were unable to finish college. Though Gonzalez did not directly use his degree professionally, the pursuit of education had an impact on his personal, civic, and professional development. It is important to note that his wife, possibly even more than the GI Bill, had a strong and direct impact on his pursuit and completion of his college degree.

Gonzalez's story demonstrates how the GI Bill created a pathway and incentive to attend college while also illustrating how social pressures and obstacles can disrupt and curtail a veteran's educational career. His story of being a part-time student and a full-time employee is a common one for many Latina/os. The path to higher education for these students is often community college rather than a four-year research university. These institutions often lack resources, their transfer and completion rates are often low, and the time it takes to graduate is often extended. Factors beyond financial aid, such as advocates, support structures, and agency, have an influence on one's ability to graduate. With the GI Bill it still took Gonzalez fifteen years. Even with other "success" stories, it is important to note the shortcomings of the policy and the systemic and institutional structures that impede educational careers and stratify those who do not have these opportunities or family legacies.

Education, Agency, and Mobility

For these three veterans, experience in the military had a direct impact on their higher education experience. First and foremost, the ability to use the GI Bill to access, fund, and complete a college degree was paramount.

Though two stated that attending college was a given regardless of the GI Bill, they both also recognized that it provided increased opportunities. Gonzalez, on the other hand, may not have pursued a college degree without the funding and inducements of the GI Bill.

The pursuit of higher education by the three men created a legacy of education for their families. Their children and grandchildren went on to pursue higher education at different levels. Unsurprisingly, the two veterans who went on to postgraduate studies also had children who pursued postgraduate education, demonstrating how educational pathways can become normalized and solidified. Grandchildren also benefited indirectly, as they also participated in higher education, from community colleges to graduate programs.

Finally, the men became more engaged in their communities. Whether it was pursuing a career in public service, participating in local political party organizations, or being more aware of the trials of underrepresented groups, the three veterans profiled here demonstrate how higher education, as well as their veteran status, propelled them to be more engaged in politics. Similar to Roach's (1997) assessment, participation in World War II along with higher education helped to create a civically engaged, educated cohort of middle-class professionals who would militate within existing political structures for economic and social mobility. In this case, although outliers, these three Latino veterans were able to incorporate themselves into the broader American society. Our respondents used three tactics—the law, interpretation of the law, and grassroots or at least working-class alliances and organizing efforts—to expand the benefits to others. These and other veterans' profiles illuminate their success and survival in an otherwise unfriendly higher education and societal environment. Although World War II was costly for the United States, including Latina/os, new educational opportunities for some Latina/os did emerge from the conflict.[58]

Transnational Latino Soldiering: Military Service and Ethnic Politics during World War II

LUIS ALVAREZ

Rudy Acosta learned most of what he knew about World War II from newsreels shown in theaters around the Lincoln Heights neighborhood of East Los Angeles where he grew up. The son of Mexican immigrants, Acosta loved the movies and was always eager to hear the latest on the escalating conflict in Europe and the Pacific, in part because his older brother, Bill, had been drafted just prior to Pearl Harbor. Acosta recalled that people in the theaters and around the city were "gung ho" for the war, but he never dreamed that he would later fly in the B-17 bombers he saw on screen. He was drafted into the army in late December 1942, however, and served in the 719th Bomber Squadron, a largely white unit that flew missions from North Africa to Italy and across Europe. When asked many years later about how the war changed him, Acosta thoughtfully reflected that he "aged ten years in knowledge in those three years" of service because of all the places, people, and combat he experienced. "I would have never been able to learn," he said, "if I stayed home, in a little closed environment, or shell you might call it."[1]

Acosta's recollection hints at the formative and long-lasting impact of military duty on Latina/os who served during World War II. Though much has been made about military service as evidence of Latina/o patriotism and leverage in postwar calls for political inclusion on the home front, the actual experiences and practices of Latino soldiering remain relatively unexamined. This chapter, consequently, asks two central questions: What did military duty entail that so dramatically shaped the lives of soldiers like Rudy Acosta? And what might closer inspection of Latino soldiering tell us about ethnic politics during World War II? I thus begin with the proposition that there is much to learn about both the experience of Latinos in the armed forces and how their stories complicate our understanding of what it

Figure 4.1. Rudy Acosta receiving his air medal, Italy, 1944. Acosta, who was born in El Paso and grew up in California, would say that his three years in the war had aged him "ten years in knowledge.... All the places I was stationed at and all the things I witnessed and the things I saw, I would never have been able to learn if I had just stayed home." Voces Oral History Project, Nettie Lee Benson Latin American Collection, University of Texas at Austin.

meant to be Americans of Mexican, Puerto Rican, or Cuban descent during World War II.

My objective is not so much to detail heroic or tragic stories of Latino servicemen as it is to consider how their many geographic and racial crossings complicate our understanding of wartime ethnic politics. My argument is twofold. First, I propose that Latina/o struggles for inclusion and belonging did not happen only in civilian circles on the home front, but that those struggles also unfolded as part of soldiers' daily routines during training and combat. Second, I suggest that Latino soldiering encompassed a range of multiracial and transnational experiences that foreshadowed the diverse theories of Latinidad in more recent decades. Latino servicemen embodied ethnic identities that were at least partially produced outside of the territorial boundaries of the United States and in relation to a range of non-American people and cultures, in the context of total war that served American imperialism.[2]

To make sense of Latino soldiering and the range of ethnic politics it fostered, it is important to note that Latinos and other racialized groups in the United States during World War II faced the uneven shift from an exclusionary to a more inclusionary brand of U.S. racism and race relations. While Latinos continued to face long-standing patterns of economic exploitation, racial discrimination, and segregation, as well as political marginalization, they were expected to serve the war effort and conform to popular demands for wartime consensus. Latino soldiers thus faced the challenges of second-class citizenship at the same time they fulfilled, often with great enthusiasm, their "patriotic duty" to fight overseas. Pursuing what Ana Ramos Zayas has called the "politics of worthiness," many Latino soldiers "proved their deservingness" of full U.S. citizenship, civil rights, and social benefits in the face of popular rhetoric and policy that viewed them as unworthy and outside the bounds of U.S. national identity.[3] In such instances, their military service represented the ultimate sacrifice for nation and, in some cases, enhanced attempts to be viewed as white.[4] Animated by a military brotherhood based on the shared masculine behavior and performance common in basic training, combat, and everyday life in the armed forces, many of these same Latino soldiers simultaneously drew on multiracial or transnational affinities to survive the perilous conditions of the war. Because of the extensive travel and cross-racial encounters that came with toiling in the service of the American military, soldiers were among those who most clearly demonstrated the multiracial and transnational character of Latino ethnic politics and identities during World War II. Latino soldiers' politics of worthiness and their diverse ethnic politics were not mutually exclusive: their multiracial and transnational practices of ethnicity were as "true blue" American as was their service to country.

This chapter draws from select oral histories by Latino World War II veterans to illustrate how the practices and experiences of Latino soldiering during the war enabled this wide range of geographic, racial, and ideological mobility.[5] The first two sections highlight the geographic mobility and multiracial encounters inherent in Latino soldiering during stateside training and overseas duty, both patterns that were profoundly informed by performances of wartime masculinity. The goal of these sections is to explore what Latino soldiering entailed and how Latino soldiers' own sense of U.S. identity and the American imaginary was stretched to include their many multiracial and transnational experiences with the people and places they came to know in the course of their service. The chapter concludes by briefly reconsidering what we might learn from the long historical range of transnational and multiracial ethnic politics evident in Latino soldiering in the World War II era. Though this chapter only offers a preliminary sketch of Latino soldiering during one war, it nonetheless proposes that Latino soldiering is a viable object of study and generative force of ethnic politics.

Boot Camp, Stateside Travel, and the Multiracial Military

Soon after they enlisted or were drafted, thousands of Mexican Americans from the Southwest, Puerto Ricans from the island, smaller but still substantial numbers of Puerto Ricans and Cuban Americans from the eastern seaboard, and Mexican nationals who fought as part of U.S. forces were all shipped to points across the country for basic training. Well before they were shipped overseas, Latino soldiers entered into contact zones where they crossed paths, shared barracks, and joined forces with other enlistees that more than likely had very different historical, geographic, or cultural experiences.[6] Stationed for weeks or months in areas that had negligible Latino populations, and sharing close quarters with fellow soldiers and officers unfamiliar with Latinos, Latino GIs found ways to make the best of new, strange, and often difficult conditions. If civilian life presented challenges for Latinos seeking equality and the benefits of wartime democracy, so too did life in the military. Most seized basic training as an opportunity to prove they belonged in their units and were as American as anyone else despite their racial, ethnic, or cultural difference. For many Latino soldiers who were away from home for the first time and pumped up from boot camp, moreover, gender quickly became the terrain on which they discovered a sense of belonging, collectivity, and camaraderie. Fueled in part by the idea that their service made them better, stronger, and more complete men, most Latino soldiers cultivated a military brotherhood based on masculine behavior and male bravado with Latinos and non-Latinos alike as a way to adjust to life in uniform.

From the moment they stopped being civilians, Latino GIs encountered new places, people, and experiences at a phenomenally fast rate, setting in motion a military experience in which their evolving sense of ethnic identity was fundamentally shaped by their extensive travel and multiracial encounters. Almost immediately, most were sent to basic training in distant locations such as Fort Benning, Georgia; Camp Pendleton, California; and Camp Wolters, Texas—often on the other side of the country from where they grew up. Inducted right behind New York Yankees pitcher Red Ruffin in 1943, for example, Rudy Acosta embarked on what was not an atypical journey. He was initially shipped to Atlantic City, New Jersey, which was a far cry from his East L.A. home. After just a few days of being housed with other GIs in the hotel rooms of the city's big casinos and conducting training runs along the boardwalk every morning, Acosta was shipped to Kansas City for radio school, back to Fresno, California, to learn Japanese code, and, finally, to Las Vegas, Nevada, where he learned to calibrate machine guns as part of a B-17 "flying fortress" crew, all in the span of a few short months.[7]

Like Acosta and thousands of others, Edward Prado, a Mexican American from San Antonio, crisscrossed the country as part of his stateside training for his eventual assignment to the 131st Field Artillery Battalion in the Texas-based 36th Infantry Division. Though he was ultimately shipped to North Africa in April 1943 to prepare for the Salerno invasion into Italy against Mussolini's forces, Prado traveled to Brownsville, Texas; Cape Cod, Massachusetts; Newport News, Virginia; and North Carolina before he even left the United States.

Fred Gomez also served in North Africa and Italy as part of the 45th Infantry Division but similarly saw much of the United States before he got there. Born of Mexican parents who eventually settled in Chicago, Gomez began his stateside training at Fort Sheridan, Illinois, soon moved to Arkansas and Pennsylvania for basic training, and then shipped out from New York across the Atlantic. As much as their initial weeks and months in uniform enabled Acosta, Prado, Gomez, and other Latino soldiers to see much of the country, it also forced them to rapidly learn how to lean on fellow GIs to make sense of the dramatic changes in their lives.

It is no surprise that once inducted, most Latino soldiers quickly began to foster a pan-ethnic or multiracial military brotherhood that helped them adjust to unfamiliar surroundings and the daunting specter of war. Stationed in regions with few Latino civilians, and also bunking, socializing, and readying for war with whites and, in some cases, African Americans, Latinos bonded with fellow soldiers from similar working-class backgrounds through a shared sense of manhood, male bravado, and brotherly devotion to one another. As historian Allison Varzally shows in her study of nonwhite soldiers from California during World War II, gender often functioned as the meeting ground for soldiers from different backgrounds to collectively navigate the disorienting newness of basic training and build friendships with others in their unit.[8] Based in part on class, regional, or ethnic similarities, this military brotherhood was also born from the demands of their daily routine. Summarizing his boot camp experience, for example, Raul Morin underscored that the physical and gendered nature of combat training brought soldiers together. He noted:

> Rich or poor, light or dark, the educated and the ignorant—all were thrown together to accomplish the same objective, mainly that of learning military skills; and all were subjected to the same rude Army discipline. . . . What mattered most, was that you had to be rough, tough and alert of mind.[9]

Boyle Heights–born Richard Dominguez agreed that one's boot camp experience was determined by the macho, manly realities of training for war. Thinking back to the mentality instilled by the military, he recalled that "they really pumped you up through training!"[10] As they put their physical bodies on the line for U.S. victory in the war, Latino soldiers also seemed to implicitly understand that their masculine performance and physical prowess would serve as shortcuts to the camaraderie that made life in the military bearable.

In leisure time, just as in actual training, Latino soldiers forged common ground with fellow GIs through shared ideas about masculinity and sexuality. Off-duty carousing, drinking, and womanizing brought men together across lines of racial and ethnic difference as much as it may have sparked competition between them. Rudy Acosta remembered "having a ball" and a "grand time" with his friends and fellow soldiers on leave, especially in Kansas City, where the nightclubs and roadside inns had great jukeboxes filled with the likes of Glen Miller; they met plenty of girls and drank lots of beer.[11] Guy Gabaldon, a Mexican American marine from Los Angeles who later garnered great fame for his combat exploits in Saipan, fondly remembered that his favorite pastime during training in Oklahoma and Texas was to make a game out of how many women he could hook up with at bars, not just for sex, but to say, "I'm better than you!" to the other men in his unit. To listen to Gabaldon, he made his reputation as a man's man on the beer joint circuits of middle America as much as the battlefields in the Far East.[12] Along with drinking and women, athletics generated male camaraderie and competition among Latino soldiers and others. Edward Prado remembered boxing as one of the most popular hobbies during training, especially among the few Mexicans in his largely white company. Prado and the other Mexicans saw the sport as a way to gain respect for themselves and other Mexicans in uniform and also from their white counterparts.[13] For Acosta, Gabaldon, Prado, and many other Latino soldiers, daily interactions with the other men in their units determined how easy or difficult their adjustment to military life would be. Given that their fellow soldiers were often not Latinos, male bonding and bravado surfaced as the easiest way to face up to basic training. Leaning on manliness as a tactic for survival and relationship building, moreover, was made that much easier in the context of basic training and the military's goal of producing effective and efficient fighting men.

While military brotherhood was by no means limited to Latinos, it did help them face unique ethnic and racial challenges. Unlike African American soldiers, most Latinos were not segregated in the armed forces but served alongside their white and, in some cases, black American counterparts. Though there were a number of primarily Latino outfits, most were part of predominantly white units or, in the case of some Afro-Latinos, segregated black units. In both cases, Latino GIs trained, lived, and battled alongside white and black soldiers, making their experience in the military

Figure 4.2. Richard Dominguez, 1944. Dominguez was selected as one of Gen. Douglas MacArthur's Honor Guard and had the privilege of escorting him aboard the battleship USS *Missouri* to sign the peace treaty with the Japanese on September 9, 1945. Voces Oral History Project, Nettie Lee Benson Latin American Collection, University of Texas at Austin.

dependent on relationships with non-Latinos. Their participation in military brotherhood was thus incumbent on their aptitude for traversing racial and ethnic differences. Once in the service, Latino soldiers quickly learned that their soldiering experience and their own identity as Mexicans, Puerto Ricans, Cubans, and Americans more generally was shaped by their interaction with Anglos, Jews, ethnic whites, African Americans, Filipinos, Japanese, and others, both as allies and as enemies. Latino soldiers implicitly understood that their very survival in the military and place in its racial order was dependent on their relationships with and positioning vis-à-vis non-Latinos.[14]

For many, the demands of navigating the multiracial military were an extension of their prewar lives. Those who had come of age in Los Angeles, New York, Chicago, Florida, and elsewhere were used to diverse environments and spent much of their youth navigating the color lines between black, white, and brown. In Los Angeles, for example, thousands of future soldiers were born and bred on the city's eastside, an area that was a Mexican American enclave for decades but also made up of barrios where multiracial living was a way of life in housing, employment, education, and social patterns.[15] Mexican American soldiers Rudy Acosta, Richard Dominguez, and Guy Gabaldon, for instance, noted that everyday interaction with African Americans, Japanese Americans (before internment), Filipino Americans, and ethnic white immigrants in school, at work, or around the city at dances and nightclubs was common. Acosta recalled his Lincoln Heights neighborhood as being largely Mexican and Italian, with Japanese, Chinese, a few blacks, and a "sprinkling" of Russians and running across even greater racial mixing at downtown entertainment centers like the Orpheum and Paramount Theaters. Dominguez and Gabaldon had similar memories of Boyle Heights. Dominguez recalled the area as populated by Armenians, Russians, Mexicans, Jews, Anglos, and Japanese Americans.[16] After his own family situation became untenable, Gabaldon was even taken in by a Japanese American foster family.[17] Though perhaps shaded by romanticism for their younger days and a bygone era, all three remember "little racial separation," life being "not segregated," and few racial antagonisms.[18]

Though smaller in number than Mexican American soldiers, Afro-Latino GIs from Florida, where black Cubans made up much of the cigar industry labor, or New York City, where Cuban and Puerto Rican diasporas took root following U.S. occupation of the two islands, experienced very different prewar multiracial lives that nevertheless prepared them for their time in the military.[19] Evelio Grillo, for instance, hailed from the Ybor City community of Tampa, where his parents settled as part of the large migration of Cubans seeking cigar work. Grillo noted Ybor City was "a mixture of white Cubans, Italians, black Cubans, black Americans, Spaniards, and a not very visible number of white Americans of European extraction."[20] Though most ethnic groups maintained their own communities, Grillo noted how young black Cubans regularly interfaced with others, especially black Americans. In his memoir he wrote that, despite the prejudices of some older community members, "as children we had intensive interaction with black Americans in school. We became good friends. We studied with them, we played with them and, as we grew older, we married them. Our feelings toward them were very positive and we were sensitive to remarks critical of them. Reciprocally, they considered us part of the black community, for that was the way we were perceived by the larger American society."[21] Grillo also remembered the prevalence of what he called racial "permutations," or mixing and overlap between black Cubans, black Americans, and others while growing up in Florida. The prewar lives of Afro-Latino soldiers like Grillo remind us that Latino soldiers brought a wide range of experience with multiracial living to the military, including identifying as black and sharing affinities with African Americans.

For many Latino soldiers, military service brought them even closer to those different from themselves at the same time others were kept at a distance through the legal and informal segregation of the armed forces. Negotiating racial and ethnic lines was a necessity from the initial days of boot camp if Latino soldiers wished to secure a sense of belonging, comfort, and access to the military brotherhood. These negotiations also took different forms. Those assigned to largely white units often simultaneously pursued both multiracial and more ethnically parochial approaches. Some Mexican Americans, especially those who were lighter skinned, understood they could thrive more easily in white units. Fred Gomez and Guy Gabaldon, for example, remembered being in battalions and combat units as the "only Chicano" or with "no other Latinos." Richard Dominguez recalled that in the air and tank corps he was friendly with GIs from a number of ethnic backgrounds since he was one of only a handful of Latinos. Most in similar situations became "good buddies" with lots of whites, "never had any problems," and worked with them to always "help each other out." After being reassigned to a paratrooper unit that had several other Mexican Americans and Latinos, however, Dominguez emphasized, "We associated with them," and routinely spoke Spanish during training and while on leave.

Similarly, Edward Prado was assigned to share a tent with the four other Mexicans in his company, a situation he happily accepted and that led them to actively discuss their segregated conditions. And though he and many others claimed to never experience any discrimination, Dominguez admitted, "I happened to be lighter complected than many other Mexicans . . . maybe that made a difference." Scores of black Cubans and Puerto Ricans, like Norberto González and Evelio Grillo, could not say the same, as they were assigned, or, as in González's case, requested a transfer to, segregated black units.[22]

Latino soldiers responded to new places and people they encountered in basic training by drawing on their multiracial pasts at the same time they associated with those with whom they were most comfortable. Raul Morin argued that multiracial prewar lives were an advantage once they joined the military:

> For many there was nothing too unusual about living, working and playing together with groups of many different races. We had been doing it back home; in school, where we worked and in the daily social and recreational activities. But there were many who came from various and different types of sectors in the United States where minority groups were kept segregated, or where minority groups were small in number. Here for the first time in their lives they became acquainted and really got to know their fellow countryman of a different nationality and racial background. . . . We *Mejicanos* sought the companionship of each other [because we felt a keen familiarity with one another and were] like brothers. . . . Mexican Americans

in our own group sought out each other for tentmates. You just couldn't keep us apart. Every morning, even those who were camped in another area would come over to us, to be together and partake of the delicious hot coffee that Joe Nevrios had brewing.[23]

Later, when they faced the "uncomfortable and bleak" battle conditions of war on the front lines, Latino soldiers continued to draw on their multiracial sensibilities and growing transnational affinities.[24]

Combat, Transnationalism, and Overseas Duty

Despite the violence and horror of the war, Latino soldiers described their overseas journeys in positive terms: "beautiful to see;"[25] of "all the things I witnessed . . . I would have never been able to learn if I just stayed home;"[26] and "I was not a world traveler [before the army]; I was brought up in the barrio, but it opened my eyes to a lot of things."[27] Once stationed overseas, engagement with new places, people, and difficult circumstances only intensified, producing a range of transnational experiences and affinities that affected Latino soldiers' senses of identity and nationalism.[28] Sent to locations from Europe to the Pacific to North Africa as part of racially and ethnically diverse units, they found ways to feel like they belonged and make sense of their surroundings. As they traveled to front lines in faraway countries and experienced combat for the first time, many leaned on their shared military brotherhood, multiracial affinities, and emerging relations with their new surroundings to both adjust to their new conditions and prove their worthiness as equal members of their units. Their ethnic politics and identity came to be dramatically informed by being outside the borders of the United States and their encounters with spaces where distinct national identities were linked by the circumstances of war. Latino GIs often underwent transnational experiences in which they articulated an alternative understanding of ethnic and national identity that transcended boundaries and conventional wartime thinking about what constituted being American or Latino.[29] Despite being the agents of U.S. imperial force and military might, or perhaps because they were part of it, Latino soldiers crafted the beginnings of a more worldly ethnic politics that interlaced with their patriotism and dedication to country. The Latino experience in World War II thus included an extensive range of ideological mobility that encompassed ethnic nationalism, multiracial identifications, and patriotism.

The extensive travel associated with overseas duty began with the trip abroad, which immediately forced Latino soldiers to rely on their fellow soldiers to help cope with being so far from home. In one typical journey, Rudy Acosta departed the United States after months of training with his fellow GIs from San Francisco by traveling through Phoenix; Midland, Texas; Memphis; West Palm Beach, Florida; Trinidad; Brazil; Dakar, Africa; French Morocco; Tunisia; and finally Italy. Many others took similarly long journeys and, when they looked back on the experience, noted the impact such travel had on their lives. Fred Gomez, who served in the 45th Infantry Division, noted that military travel was "an experience definitely that you can never buy. The trip that I took to go overseas, being in different countries, I don't think I would be able to do that if I was just a civilian."[30] Richard Dominguez argued that "getting to know people from other parts of the country, getting to know other cultures" was the biggest advantage of serving. "I learned a lot in the military. I got to meet a lot of people from other cultures that I felt were of interest to me and informative. I got to travel; first time I'd been on a train," Dominguez said. "I went mostly in the South and the Southwest and, of course, overseas a couple of times. And that was a learning experience."[31]

What Latino soldiers learned from military travel surely depended on where they went, what they did, who they met, and their individual experiences, but it is evident that their encounters with racial, cultural, and geographic difference shaped their own evolving senses of self and ethnic politics.

Like other nonwhite soldiers, Latinos understood that there was much at stake in their service. Military duty was a means to demonstrate their patriotism, manhood, and equality with white soldiers at the same time it enabled a salient ethnic nationalism that was often predicated on hypermasculine performance and competition. Voicing what many others must have felt, Edward Prado stressed that his service was important to him because it made others

> appreciate the fact what we, as Mexican Americans are; we struggled and we worked hard to try and make the Mexican American be recognized for what they are as human beings, as anybody else, and equal, equal as anybody else. That's what I think that they should look up to us and remember that we have accomplished. If in 100 years they accomplished that, that we were a part of it, of that struggle.

Prado's sentiment was echoed by many others, including Raul Morin, who argued that he and other Latino soldiers "became Americans" in their "living and thinking" through their service, as "all we wanted was a chance to prove how loyal and American we were."[32] And, to be sure, the masculine heroics of combat were often the vehicle for Latino soldiers to prove their worthiness. Stories abound of Latino soldiers' heroism on the battlefield, so much so that Morin and others were buoyed by rumors that General Mac-Arthur himself was known to have said, "Send us more of those Mexican boys; they make good jungle fighters."[33]

Guy Gabaldon embodied the manly, heroic Latino soldier. His combat exploits in Saipan garnered him respect, celebrity, and, in his own words, the reputation of a "flag waver" because "I love the red, white, and blue." Known as the "Maverick Marine," Gabaldon was famous for death-defying solo missions into enemy Japanese territory on which he, against orders, single-handedly captured hundreds of prisoners by using his prewar knowledge of Japanese language and culture. He had a willingness to put his own neck on the line, a willingness that some labeled a "death wish." Other soldiers viewed him as "a one-man Marine Corps and a legend," even placing bets on how many prisoners he would bring back on any given mission.[34] Gabaldon, who further described himself as "Dracula" because he was always "out for blood," claimed to bring in more prisoners than any other marine in the entire war. Proving his manhood and patriotism to his mostly white unit was important to Gabaldon. "Maybe I was saying," he later observed, "'I'm a tough son of a bitch who's going to kill more than any other Marine.'"

As much as he was one of a kind, Gabaldon described all Mexican American soldiers as "fighting bastards." In the middle of one heated gunfire exchange, for example, he remembered meeting three other marines, including a fellow Mexican American named Alfredo from the Maravilla neighborhood of East Los Angeles. Pinned down by enemy fire, Alfredo read a passage from his Bible before turning to the others and saying, "Okay, let's fight!" He then jumped up, got drilled by a grenade and hundreds of rounds, only to have his head blown to bits. "This," recalled Gabaldon, "was the way the Chicano Marine fought!" Unlike Alfredo and other Latino soldiers, Gabaldon became an American icon whose story was retold in his postwar memoir, *Saipan: Suicide Island*, and the Hollywood film version of his life, *Hell to Eternity: The Guts! Glory! Gallantry of America's Hell-Bent for Victory Marines!* Although Gabaldon was a particularly compelling figure, he was one of countless Latino soldiers who sought to prove their worthiness by demonstrating masculine strength and virility. In an ironic twist that underscored the limits of such efforts in the military and U.S. society at large after the war, the main character based on Gabaldon in *Hell to*

Eternity was transformed into an Italian American: The short, dark, Mexican American from East L.A. was played by tall, blond, blue-eyed actor Jeffrey Hunter.[35]

As they proved themselves on the battlefield, Latino soldiers intuitively understood that their experience in the military was fundamentally shaped by the racial composition of their units. Mirroring the experience of many others, Rudy Acosta, Edward Prado, and Fred Gomez recalled that their units consisted of almost all whites and fondly remembered the camaraderie they felt with ethnic whites during the war. Prado noted that his white peers "liked me pretty well" and that he often hung out, frequented beer joints, and had a lot of fun in Naples, Italy, whenever they were able to secure a pass. In many cases there was an especially strong connection with Polish American, Italian American, and other ethnic whites on working-class or religious grounds. Acosta, for example, noted that while there were no other Latinos in his air gunnery unit, there were three other Catholics with European immigrant backgrounds. Though some Mexican Americans and other Latinos were able to cross the color line with relative ease, there were constant reminders that they weren't quite as white as others.[36] Fred Gomez underscored this point when he observed that his infantry division was home to a few other Latinos besides himself but that "the officers were all white," suggesting that few Latinos were promoted beyond the lower ranks.[37]

There were also Afro-Cubans and Afro–Puerto Ricans who were identified by the military as "black" and who served in segregated units; others were assigned to white units, but some later asked for transfers to "colored" units. For these Latino soldiers, being in the military and serving overseas meant negotiating a different color line. Their blackness made it difficult, if not impossible, to comfortably serve in white units, and some found it easier in black battalions. Cuban-born Norberto González, for example, joined the army in 1944 after migrating to New York City because sending his military salary home would help support his mother and wife still in Cuba. Revealing the uncertainty with which the military and wider U.S. society viewed the racial identity of most Latinos, González was initially assigned to an all-white unit. After experiencing some discrimination and feeling uncomfortable, however, he requested a transfer to a black unit and was assigned to the "colored" 1315th Engineer Construction Battalion. Though he didn't speak much English at the time and the largely African American unit initially viewed him as a foreigner, it didn't take long for González to feel at home: "My relationship with the soldiers in my battalion was good; they were down to earth people. I felt good. I felt like I could progress with them." Though he was one of only two Afro-Latinos in the entire unit, González's sense of belonging stemmed from both his own sense of blackness and his shared experience with his African American comrades as black men living in the United States. If he had continued to serve in his white unit, González was convinced, he would not have been promoted, have developed close-knit friendships, or have been nearly as comfortable.[38]

Serving in black units also taught Afro-Latinos lessons in both injustice and identity politics. Cuban American Evelio Grillo was assigned to the segregated 823rd Engineer Aviator Battalion and remembered the stark inequality of serving in a "colored" unit. He recalled that the "all-black outfit [was] led by all-white officers, just like slaves and slave masters." As one of the more educated men in his unit, Grillo was a key figure in addressing grievances to superior officers because he knew how to do so in ways that did not "invite retribution." While aboard the USS *Santa Paula*, for instance, Grillo led a petition against the poor treatment of black troops, which had included sleeping in tents on the muddy ground during monsoon season while white officers slept on elevated bamboo pallets. Facing such conditions was a constant reminder for Grillo and others like him that he was both black and Latino. Grillo astutely described his identity as "a hybrid identity that can't be torn apart," because "I have to be both all the time." The experiences of Grillo, González, and other Afro-Latinos remind us that as much as the desire to prove their Americanness may have inspired soldiers, their daily lives included struggles to negotiate race in the military and ensure their own belonging.

As much as their military duty was shaped by the immediacy of their units, Latino soldiers were also deeply affected by the places and people they encountered around the world. Despite the asymmetrical relations of power with many of the civilians they met, Latino GIs often related to them through shared interlocking experiences of war and cultural exchange. They developed transnational cultural, class, and political connections with those they met in the Philippines, North Africa, and Europe. In spite of, or more likely because of, the challenges they faced as nonwhite servicemen, many Latino soldiers thus crafted multiracial and transnational ethnic politics at the same time they sought to fit into their military units, claim whiteness, or prove their patriotism.

Latino soldiers serving in the Philippines especially felt a kinship and solidarity with Filipinos based on shared culture, skin color, and recognition of one another's historical struggle with Spanish colonialism. Rudolph Tovar, for example, was a U.S. soldier born in Juárez, Mexico. He was

Figure 4.3. Bertha and Edward Prado on their wedding day, December 9, 1942. Prado returned to his assignment in Massachusetts a few days later. While serving in Oral, Algeria, he was surprised to learn that many Algerians spoke Spanish because of their colonial link to Spain. One young boy he befriended "was like me—brown! . . . He looked like a Mexican, but they were Arabs." Voces Oral History Project, Nettie Lee Benson Latin American Collection, University of Texas at Austin.

Figure 4.4. Rudolph Tovar with Romie Lopez, April 1, 1944, Club Babalu, Los Angeles, California. Tovar would say of his war experience that he had not been a "world traveler before" his years in the military but that his time abroad had "opened up his eyes to a lot of things." Voces Oral History Project, Nettie Lee Benson Latin American Collection, University of Texas at Austin.

Figure 4.5. Leopold Moreno, Camp Roberts, 1943. Moreno said he felt comfortable with the Filipinos he met while stationed in the Philippines because many spoke Spanish and had Spanish surnames. Voces Oral History Project, Nettie Lee Benson Latin American Collection, University of Texas at Austin.

drafted only after his attempt to join the marines the day after Pearl Harbor was denied based on his Mexican citizenship. Tovar recalled that his time in the Philippines was marked by a real affinity for the local population. "Most of us Latino soldiers got along fine with the Filipinos. . . . We could relate to them more because of our skin color, our history, and because we could communicate with them in Spanish."[39] Norberto González remembered being impressed by the hardship suffered by the Filipinos and thinking, "How was it possible for us to have too much when these people had nothing?" While in Manila, González was reminded how Filipinos were not unlike most folks he had known back home in Cuba, noting that they were "very poor" and "didn't have anything." As noted, González, in fact, joined the army in part to help his mother and wife back in Cuba, to whom he sent a good chunk of his monthly salary.[40] He observed further that "there were many Filipinos who spoke Spanish" and that a shared history with struggling for independence from Spain helped build relationships with Latino soldiers. He ultimately concluded that the Filipinos were "very good people" and "very intelligent."[41] Like González, Leo Moreno similarly recalled that he "met a lot of nice Filipino people" and that it was not difficult to become friends with them because many spoke Spanish and had Spanish surnames.[42]

Edward Prado also identified with the people who lived in the areas where he served in North Africa and Italy. On top of memories of breaking bread with Arab merchants and Italian farmers, Prado recalled a young Arab boy he met shortly after arriving in Oran, Algeria, where his unit was stationed. One morning when he got up, "there was an Arab boy standing over there. I looked at him and I said to him in Spanish, '¿*Cómo estás?*'" The boy responded, "*Estoy bien. ¿Y tú?*" "That surprised the heck out of me!" Prado recalled, but he soon learned that a number of Arabs spoke Spanish because of their historical links with Spanish Morocco. Prado concluded that the boy "was like me, brown!" and that "he looked like a Mexican, but they were Arabs."[43]

Though they were sent overseas to win a war, Latino soldiers crafted ethnic and American identities, at least in part, from their engagement with non-Latino people and places around the world. Most soon realized, however, that the military and U.S. society more broadly were not nearly as inclusive in their notions of race and national belonging.

Lessons of Latino Soldiering

Just as the home front was the scene of intense struggles by Mexican, Cuban, and Puerto Rican Americans for equality during World War II, so too was the military. Latino GIs struggled through boot camp and overseas duty to ensure inclusion and belonging in their units, if for no other reason than to make their service bearable and to maintain a sense of dignity. In doing so, however, they also crafted a diverse range of ethnic politics that was often multiracial and transnational in its daily routine and outlook. In the process of encountering so many new people and places, their commitment to country was intertwined with an ethnic and American identity that was increasingly fueled by experiences, identifications, and influences that crossed racial and national boundaries. If home front rhetoric demanded consensus and homogeneity, Latino soldiering revealed the diverse, multiracial, and transnational ethnic politics of the Latino World War II generation. Identifying the practices and experiences of Latino soldiering reveals how the U.S. war machine produced a diverse range of Latino ethnic politics that, even if only in embryonic form, nonetheless enabled one group of men to make sense of, and work through, their relationship to the broader American imaginary. Rather than merely considering it ironic that this set of experiences unfolded within the military, we might be better served to observe that these particular Latinos had such experiences *because* they were in the military.

Though there is still much to be learned about Latino soldiering, including how it varied across branches of the service, what its impact was on those soldiers who returned, and how World War II was different from other wars, this preliminary sketch enhances our understanding of the complex negotiations of race and place by members of the Latino World War II generation. Yet several issues remain to be discussed and debated. First and foremost, it is imperative that scholars of World War II consider the actual practices and experiences of Latino soldiering. As important as veterans were to the postwar struggle for civil rights, no longer should their service be considered only relative to home front campaigns for assimilation. Their extensive travel and race relations while in the military were equally important sites in Latino battles for inclusion and belonging during World War II and should be analyzed on their own terms.

Second, Latino soldiering underscored how the United States managed its own racialized populations during World War II and the different ways those groups stretched the American racial and national imaginary. If U.S. dependence on Latino and other nonwhite soldiers indicated a shift from an exclusionary to a more inclusionary brand of race relations, Latino soldiers showed that inclusion was not always easy, to be taken at face value, or even what it was cracked up to be. Belonging, respect, and dignity in their units did not come automatically because of a shared uniform but was fostered at least in part by their multiracial and transnational relationships and negotiations.

Third, Latino soldiering complicates the periodization of Chicana/o and Latina/o history. Much of the literature underscores the discontinuity between the World War II and 1960s and 1970s eras, emphasizing generational and political rupture between earlier efforts for accommodation and assimilation and the militancy and radicalism of the later period. Rather than assume Latino soldiering produced a single narrative that reinforced such an interpretation, we can see the ways its multiple narratives and diverse experiences highlighted the transnational, multiracial, and gendered character of Latino identity that surfaced more forcefully by the 1960s. Far from suggesting the World War II generation was as militant as the next, or that its politics were not often driven by desires to assimilate and embrace a fully American identity, I do think we have too quickly dismissed the complexity of Latino soldiering, especially during World War II, and its anticipation of ethnic political struggles of future generations.

Fourth, and finally, the oral histories of Latino war veterans sampled herein strike a poignant chord with more recent articulations of Latinidad. Though I have used "Latino" throughout this chapter for shorthand and clarity of argument, none of the soldiers used it as a self-referent during the war, for it had yet to enter popular usage. Nonetheless, without overstating the case, Mexican American, Cuban American, and Puerto Rican soldiers during World War II practiced what we might call a proto-Latino identity and politics. Juan Flores notes that the contemporary construction of a relational Latino identity and politics radiates in at least three directions: the "cross" (as in cross-ethnically and cross-racially), the "intra" (as in intra-ethnic relations of citizenship, gender, class, and sexuality), and the "trans" (as in the transnational reach of the Chicana/o, Puerto Rican, or Cuban experiences).[44] Latino GIs during World War II did much of the same, and much earlier than has been acknowledged.

"Intellectually He Was Courageous; in Public Action He Was Cautious and Prudent": A Reassessment of Carlos E. Castañeda's Wartime Service

MARIANNE M. BUENO

On August 23, 1943, in Dallas, Texas, Carlos E. Castañeda, librarian and professor at the University of Texas at Austin, took an oath to become the first senior examiner for Region X of the Fair Employment Practice Commission (FEPC), a federal agency within the executive branch charged by President Franklin D. Roosevelt to ensure fair and equal employment opportunities for workers in the mobilization industry during World War II.[1] In Castañeda's quest to support his country's effort to defeat fascism abroad he also contributed to advancing the social and economic rights of Mexican Americans in the United States, first as a senior examiner, later as Region X's regional director, and finally as the special assistant to the FEPC chairman for Latin American Problems. In fact, Castañeda actively pursued a position with the FEPC as a means to fulfill his long-term goal of effecting positive social change for people of Mexican descent.

Born and raised along the South Texas–Mexico border at the turn of the twentieth century, Castañeda not only witnessed the political and social implications of the Mexican Revolution for Mexicans on both sides of the border but also the economic and structural changes in the state, initiated by the onset of the Texas Modern in 1880, whereby white dominance was predicated on the subjugation of Mexican Americans.[2] For people of Mexican descent in South Texas, the Texas Modern instigated a race war that left Mexican American communities terrorized and resulted in an unprecedented number of Mexican American deaths due to white vigilante violence and lynchings.[3] In the context of such indiscriminate and unchecked brutality, and long before his appointment to the president's commission, Castañeda and his Mexican American contemporaries developed a new, less violent strategy of resistance. Their collective effort manifested in a number of civil rights organizations aimed to combat the rise of severe racial discrimination in Texas. Of special importance was a strategic decision to predicate their fight for Mexican American civil rights on their status as U.S. citizens and not on their racial or ethnic background.[4] Castañeda and his generation's reliance on their citizenship status to gain equal rights also reflects an understanding that doing so meant they would need to work within the U.S. power structure, in particular with whites in power. Castañeda's work with the FEPC is a clear reflection of this newfound strategy of demanding equitable rights and privileges of first-class citizenship for Mexican Americans.

In his biography of Castañeda, historian Félix D. Almaráz Jr. describes Castañeda's public life in early-twentieth-century Texas as overwhelmingly "apolitical." Almaráz explains that because Castañeda was a Mexican national who became a U.S. citizen in 1936 and was employed by the state of Texas, he made only intermittent forays into the Mexican American political scene. Almaráz claims that Castañeda remained on the periphery at best and instead used his role as a librarian, professor, and historian of the Spanish borderlands to communicate his opinion on public affairs on a hemispheric level. Mario T. García's short biography of Castañeda, like Almaráz's, also foregrounds Castañeda's intellectual work as his most meaningful contribution to the advancement of Mexican American political rights.[5]

Through his unpublished writings, Castañeda indicts racist and classist structures of oppression for the contemporary and historical condition of Mexican Americans in the United States and advocates for a pan-American pluralistic society to alleviate white–Mexican American conflict. His academic record of "eighteen books and nearly fifty articles" clearly reflects an intellectual genealogy concerned with Texas history in general and with foregrounding the positive contributions of Mexican Americans to that history in particular. Much of Castañeda's work, as evident in the seven-volume work, *Our Catholic Heritage of Texas, 1519–1936*, is firmly rooted in his Catholic faith and reflects a positivist understanding of history. Castañeda, in other words, adhered to a Eurocentric and Catholic worldview wherein progress is marked by the expansion of a "European-Christian civilization."[6] Nonetheless, according to Almaráz and García, Castañeda's writings underscored his belief that history should and could be used as a means to mend cultural and racial animosities between whites and Mexican Americans. Hence Almaraz's characterization of Castañeda's academic work as "courageous" and his public action as "cautious," and García's contention that it "predated the efforts by the larger number of Chicano intellectuals a generation later to link the world of scholarship to the social realities of the Mexican American community."[7]

On the other hand, in his study of Mexican American workers in Texas during World War II Emilio Zamora argues that "Castañeda contributed more than well-written statements against discrimination and the second-class status of Mexicans."[8] Through his investigation of Castañeda's appointment to the FEPC, his affiliation with LULAC and Mexican consulates, and his strategic use of the Good Neighbor Policy, Zamora demonstrates how Castañeda's wartime service enabled him to shore up his fight against the discriminatory treatment of Mexican Americans in Texas. Following Zamora's lead, this chapter asserts that through his work during World War II, Carlos E. Castañeda did indeed take bold public action on behalf of people of Mexican descent and thus supports García's and Zamora's assertions that Castañeda and his generation's political work represents more than that of mere middle-class accommodationists.[9] I argue that in his various roles with the FEPC, Castañeda consistently worked to disrupt the country's prevailing black-white racial paradigm while he demanded, often to the chagrin of his superiors, the rights and privileges of first-class citizenship for workers of Mexican descent. I argue, moreover, that during Castañeda's tenure with the FEPC he also managed to consolidate a Texas-originated Mexican American historical bloc that ultimately coalesced with other historical blocs in an attempt to permanently alter racial and civil rights discourses in the United States.

The Rise and Demise of the Fair Employment Practice Commission

Unhappy with the New Deal, African Americans launched an attack to end racial discrimination in the growing U.S. defense industry and also to desegregate the armed forces. A. Philip Randolph, founder of the March on Washington Movement and the Brotherhood of Sleeping Car Porters, threatened President Roosevelt with a massive "March on Washington" in July 1941 of at least 100,000 African Americans if he did not take immediate action to rectify the Jim Crow conditions of the war industries and the military.[10] More specifically, Randolph informed Roosevelt that African Americans would not accept anything less than an executive order that mandated industry employers to hire African Americans. Only when President Roosevelt signed Executive Order 8802 (EO 8802) to prohibit discrimination in the defense industry and establish the FEPC on June 25, 1941, did Randolph call off the march. Roosevelt charged the FEPC with reaffirming the state's policy of "full participation in the defense program by all persons regardless of race, creed, color, or national origin."[11] While EO 8802 ostensibly granted the commission the duty of ensuring that no discrimination took place in the defense industries, the executive order lacked any mechanism to effectively police, reverse, and enforce nondiscriminatory practices. Staff, allies, and advocates of the FEPC nonetheless spent the next year staging a series of public hearings in different parts of the country to not only assess, and when possible correct, discriminatory practices but also publicize the commission's role on the home front.

After a series of hearings in Los Angeles, Chicago, New York, Washington, and Birmingham, where the commission's work successfully publicized its existence and in some cases actually secured the "voluntary compliance" of offending parties, Roosevelt transferred the FEPC from the War Production Board and established it as an "organizational entity" of the War Manpower Commission (WMC).[12] Roosevelt transferred the FEPC to the WMC at the behest of Paul V. McNutt, WMC chair, who viewed the FEPC as encroaching on his administrative oversight of manpower issues and who in spite of being a New Dealer did not necessarily support racial equality.[13] As a result, life for the FEPC at the WMC indeed proved to be quite difficult. While under the auspices of the War Production Board the FEPC functioned as an autonomous agency and secured its operating budget directly from Roosevelt himself. On reassignment the commission fell under the direct supervision of McNutt, and the southern-controlled Congress had complete discretion over the FEPC's budget. That is, it was a southern-controlled Congress that represented a political constituency antagonistic to the idea of government-imposed equal employment opportunities.[14]

Proponents of the FEPC, in fact, spent the better part of 1942 and 1943 battling enemies from both within and outside the agency. McNutt proved very quickly to be unsupportive of the commission's work. He seemingly undermined the FEPC with his nominal integration of the agency into the WMC and his unexpected cancellation of a long-anticipated commission hearing on discrimination against African American railroad workers on southern lines and carriers. U.S. business owners and lobbyists and advocates of business vehemently opposed the mandates outlined in EO 8802. This faction generally sought to destabilize the FEPC for one of three reasons:

1) they saw the work of the FEPC as government intervention into the business sector;

2) they feared the reaction of white workers; or

3) they themselves held prejudices against ethnic and racial minorities.[15]

Individual business owners, business associations, and chambers of commerce wrote letters, saturated communities with fliers, and also aggressively campaigned to dismantle any and all state and federal legislation that imposed fair and equitable hiring and promotion practices in their respective industries. Unions and union members in the North and South repeatedly employed hate and wildcat strikes as a means to reinforce racist ideology and practices in the workplace.[16] But southern white business owners, politicians, female workers, newspapers, and the general public represented the FEPC's biggest obstacle to maintaining full and equitable employment in the war industries. Southern newspapers wrote inflammatory articles about the FEPC, officers of southern courts made public statements in support of white supremacy, and still other southerners threatened violence to prevent the FEPC from implementing equal employment opportunities for African American workers that might disrupt the racial order in the South.[17]

In a concerted effort FEPC supporters, including the March on Washington Movement and numerous African American civil rights groups, staged their own multifront offensive in an attempt to reinstate the FEPC's autonomy, secure an increase in its operating budget, and strengthen the political and social efficacy of the commission in general. Allies wrote letters and sent telegrams to President Roosevelt, the black press wrote articles and editorialized on Jim Crow's presence outside of the South, and Randolph and his supporters threatened another march on Washington.

Between the FEPC's precarious position in the WMC, McNutt's sabotage, the aggressive tactics of unions and business, the political and social wrangling of white southerners, and the mass mobilization of FEPC supporters, the commission's work reached a virtual standstill in January 1943. On February 3, President Roosevelt, apparently vacillating under pressure, publicly ordered McNutt to call a meeting between civil rights leaders and WMC representatives to discuss the reorganization of the FEPC. Roosevelt and McNutt, ostensibly unwilling to acquiesce to recommendations made by community members and FEPC officials at the mid-February meeting, retreated and proceeded to reconstitute the commission in private. Friends of the commission waited impatiently, and after a month and a half of silence, Earl Dickerson, a prominent African American attorney and civil rights leader and acting chair of the FEPC, soon thereafter announced hearings in Detroit on May 24 and 25, 1943, and then in St. Louis, Cleveland, Philadelphia, and Baltimore.[18]

Figure 5.1. Carlos E. Castañeda served as a part-time associate professor of history at the University of Texas at Austin from 1936 to 1946, when he was named professor of Latin American history, a position he held until his death in 1958. Castañeda's wartime statements demanded equal rights and privileges for Mexican American workers. Nettie Lee Benson Latin American Collection, the University of Texas at Austin.

Whether Roosevelt felt pushed into action by Dickerson's announcement or whether he really intended to reconstitute the commission on May 27, 1943, he issued EO 9346, and therein created a new, independent FEPC housed within the Office of Production Management, which fell under the sole purview of the president himself.[19] Even when it was under the direct control of the executive branch, the FEPC continued to sustain political, social, and even judicial attacks for the next two years. The political influence of southern politicians, lobbyists, and business owners, needless to say, proved to be far-reaching because after numerous congressional battles over its budget, southern Democrats eventually underfunded the FEPC into obliteration in 1945.[20]

Race, Citizenship, and the Making of a Historical Bloc

Castañeda's reputation as a historian of the U.S.-Mexico borderlands, his prolific scholarly record, and his unfailing commitment to the fight for Mexican American civil rights undoubtedly made him an outstanding candidate to serve on Roosevelt's Commission on Fair Employment Practice, as he and a number of key political allies believed. As such, within days of the announcement of EO 9346, Castañeda mobilized a diverse support base for his bid for an appointment to the president's commission. Castañeda promptly secured letters of support from religious, civil rights and political leaders at the local, state and national levels. He appealed to Robert E. Lucey, archbishop of San Antonio, and Alonso S. Perales, a prominent Texas attorney, to advocate on his behalf directly to the FEPC chairman Rev. Msg. Francis J. Haas, a labor arbitrator and former member of the National Recovery Administration and National Labor Board, and FEPC Executive Secretary Lawrence W. Cramer, former governor of the U.S. Virgin Islands.[21]

New Mexico senator Dennis Chavez and John Haynes Holmes, chairman of the American Civil Liberties Union Board of Directors, also encouraged the FEPC chair and executive secretary to consider Castañeda for an appointment to the FEPC national board.[22] While his efforts may have fallen short of securing a seat with the FEPC, his campaign attests to his dedication to achieving the rights and privileges of first-class citizenship for Mexicans and his preferred strategy of interethnic solidarity to do so. Nonetheless, Monsignor Haas placed a phone call to Castañeda within weeks of receiving Senator Chavez's and Chairman Holmes's letters and thus began Castañeda's relationship with the FEPC.[23]

After Castañeda received Haas's initial phone inquiry in late June 1943, his appointment with the commission was simultaneously fast-tracked and slowed by the federal bureaucracy. Though Haas invited Castañeda to Washington, DC, in July for "an interview and a consultation," it appears that he never went through a formal interview process with an FEPC hiring committee.[24]

Instead Castañeda communicated with Haas in written correspondence that seemed to entail both an interview and a negotiation process. In mid-July Professor Castañeda wrote a letter to University of Texas at Austin president Homer P. Rainey in which he claimed, perhaps while still in the midst of negotiations with the FEPC and in haste to begin the process to secure a leave of absence from his academic appointment, that he had received a formal offer from the commission to serve as "Associate Director of the Regional Office" to be established in Dallas, Texas.[25] Although it is unclear whether Haas and Castañeda actually negotiated his official title and Civil Service rank, Castañeda apparently spent the latter part of July awaiting word from Washington regarding his federal appointment. By August 13 negotiations were over as Monsignor Haas dispatched a rather urgent telegram to Archbishop Robert E. Lucey of San Antonio seeking help in locating Castañeda "to supply us with proof of citizenship so his appointment can become effective without delay."[26] Ten days later Castañeda temporarily left his position as librarian and archivist of the University of Texas's Latin American Collection and part-time faculty member in the Department of History to assume his role with the FEPC's Region X.

As the sole staff member in the Dallas office, he diligently spent his first week on the job securing and setting up an office space and meeting with no fewer than six individuals, including the Mexican consul in Dallas and officials with the local office of the War Manpower Commission, regarding the FEPC's role on the home front and the status of "Latin Americans in the city."[27] On September 3, less than two weeks into Castañeda's tenure with the commission, Haas appointed him acting director of Region X. Before the year ended, Castañeda was promoted to special assistant to the chairman for Latin American problems.[28] Castañeda's original assignment with the FEPC was to specifically address discrimination complaints filed by "Latin Americans" in Region X, while his reassignment as the chairman's special assistant expanded his focus to include Mexican American workers in all FEPC jurisdictions. Castañeda subsequently spent his two and a half years with the FEPC traveling extensively to conduct personal interviews with and collect affidavits from workers, employers, union representatives, civil rights leaders, and government officials across the Southwest. He staged conferences with oil company officials, local labor organizers, and African American and Mexican American workers in Corpus Christi and El Paso, Texas, in order to carry out his mandate of ensuring that all workers in general, and Mexican American workers in particular, received equal pay for the same work and had equal access to promotions.[29] In February 1945 Castañeda received the assignment to serve as Region X's director, but unfortunately by June he learned that he had a mere $133 to run the office through July, the end of the fiscal year.[30] Political wrangling in Washington subsequently ensured the commission would not receive a reasonable budget to continue its work into the next fiscal year, and on December 15, 1945, Carlos E. Castañeda closed the doors to Region X's office for the last time.

Wartime Democracy and Carlos E. Castañeda's Challenge to the Black-White Racial Paradigm

Given the nature of the FEPC's creation as a direct response to African American civil rights demands and this country's rigid and deep-seated understanding of race as a black-white phenomenon, it is no surprise that in spite of the commission's nominal effort to address the wartime grievances of all ethnic and racial minority workers in the mobilization industry, the FEPC seemed to be preoccupied with prevailing notions of race.[31] At least seven official FEPC reports and studies produced during and immediately after the war focus primarily on the plight of African American workers and contain minimal references to workers of other ethnic and racial groups.[32] That is, FEPC discourse conflated race with African Americans and consequently federal policy and governmental resources privileged recourse for African American workers over workers with grievances based on creed, color (other than black), or national origin.

As noted above, the first FEPC primarily conducted hearings in cities such as Birmingham, Baltimore, and Detroit with large African American populations or in industries (railroads and shipyards) where African American workers predominated. Carlos E. Castañeda, whose academic work and longtime service centered on the Mexican American community in Texas, used his position with the commission not only to bring light to and reverse the deplorable working conditions of Mexican Americans but also to expand the country's racial perspective and alter the national discourse on racism.

On the FEPC's formation, the commission paid little attention to the struggles of Mexican American workers. For example, the cases of African American workers dominated their October 1941 hearings in Los Angeles, and only two Mexican Americans were among the fifty people who testified before FEPC staff.[33] Given this disparity, Castañeda wasted little time addressing concerns of Mexicana/o workers in Region X's mobilization industry. His commitment to securing equal employment opportunities on behalf of Mexican American workers is most evident in the drastic increase in cases docketed, or filed, in Region X during the first ten months of his term. These Mexican American workers filed complaints of discrimination with the FEPC based on unequal pay scales and unfair work assignments, among other problems.

Field Examiner Castañeda began his assignment with 26 cases pending; but by the year's end, he quadrupled that number, to 106 (see Table 5.1). He also seemed able to sustain his early pace of docketing more than 150 new cases every six months through at least June of the following year (see Tables 5.2 and 5.3). This productivity, moreover, was higher than seven of the twelve other FEPC regions in terms of the average number of monthly cases docketed between January and June 1944 (see Tables 5.4 and 5.5).[34]

Though not all of Region X's new cases docketed between August 1943 and June 1944 focused on Mexicana/o laborers, Castañeda's fastidious work in the field undoubtedly served to expand the FEPC's attention to the concerns of Mexican Americans. This became glaringly evident when in June 1944 he finally received the long-awaited approval from the Washington office to conduct a conference with American Smelting and Refining Company executives and local labor leaders in El Paso, Texas, to ascertain the

Table 5.1. Case Load Region X, July 1943–December 1943

Month	Docketed	Closed	Pending	Percent Closed
July	7	0	17	0
August	10	1	26	3.7
September	18	4	40	9.1
October	45	10	75	11.8
November	64	25	114	18.0
December	20	26	108	19.4

Source: Summary Table of Disposition of Case Load, July 1, 1943–December 31, 1943, Operational Statistics & Case Loads, Folder 1, Docketed Cases, 1944–1945, Operational Statistics, Division of Review & Analysis, Entry 35, RG 228, NACP.

Table 5.2. Disposition of Case Load Region X, July–December 1943

Total Complaints Docketed	Total Complaints Handled	Total Cases Closed	Percent Closed
164	174	66	38

Source: Summary Table of Disposition of Case Load, July 1, 1943–December 31, 1943, Operational Statistics & Case Loads, Folder 1, Docketed Cases, 1944–1945, Operational Statistics, Division of Review & Analysis, Entry 35, RG 228, NACP.

Table 5.3. Disposition of Case Load Region X, January–June 1944

Month	Docketed	Closed	Pending	Percent Closed
January	19	33	75	30.6
February	46	18	103	16.7
March	40	18	125	12.6
April	39	32	132	19.5
May	32	27	127	17.6
June	6	10	123	7.6

Source: Case Load Activity by Month, January 1, 1944–June 1944, Docketed Cases, 1944–1945, Entry 35, RG 228, NACP.

Table 5.4. Disposition of Case Load Region X, January–June 1944

Total Complaints Docketed	Total Complaints Handled	Total Cases Closed	Percent Closed
172	261	138	52.9

Sources: Case Load Activity by Month, January 1, 1944–June 1944, Docketed Cases, 1944–1945; and Comparative Summary of Office and Examiner Case Load Activity, January 1, 1944–June 30, 1944; Entry 35, RG 228, NACP.

Table 5.5. Summary of Case Load Activity in All FEPC Regions, January–June 1944

Region	Total Cases Handled	Monthly Average Docketed	Monthly Average Closed	Percent Closed
I	50	5.2	5.3	64.0
II	582	72.7	50.3	51.9
III	540	34.8	41.7	46.3
IV	292	16.2	26.8	55.1
V (Cleve)	291	19	24.8	51.2
V (Det)	268	11.5	27.3	61.2
VI	471	35.3	39	49.7
VII	377	39	12.2	19.4
VIII	33	1.6	3	54.5
IX	212	20	13.5	38.2
X	261	28.7	23	52.9
XI	40	3.7	1.3	20.0
XII (SF)	333	32.8	30.7	55.3
XII (LA)	293	31.3	24.3	49.8

Source: Case Load Activity by Month, January 1, 1944–June 1944, Docketed Cases, 1944–1945; and Comparative Summary of Office and Examiner Case Load Activity, January 1, 1944–June 30, 1944, Entry 35, RG 228, NACP.

status of Mexican American workers in their mines.[35] And if Castañeda's impressive caseload did not oblige the FEPC or the general public to pay heed to Mexican American struggles and to expand notions of race, then his public actions surely did.

Castañeda spent his early days on the job acutely aware of the constraints his civil service position put on his ability to speak freely about racial, social, and economic discrimination in the United States. After he attended a convention of the Texas Mid-Continent Oil and Gas Association in October 1943 he composed a letter to William Maslow, director of field operations and his immediate supervisor, stating, "I took no part in the discussion but I took full notes."[36] Maslow nonetheless felt compelled to remind Castañeda to "AVOID PUBLIC CONTROVERSY OR THREATS OF HEARINGS" in a concisely worded letter in mid-1944.[37] By early 1945 Castañeda's public actions came to exemplify his efforts to extend principles of wartime democracy and fair employment practices as a means to secure military victory abroad, specifically economic and social equality for Mexicans, beyond the realm of the mobilization industry and most certainly beyond the current hostilities. His actions were particularly striking perhaps because of the FEPC's inability to actually enforce fair and equitable employment practices and the slow pace by which the agency seemed to prefer to effect any positive social change. Castañeda thus brought Mexican American civil rights issues to national attention by publicly testifying before the Senate Committee on Labor and Education on March 13, 1945, a point I explore further below. Chairman Ross did not take issue with Castañeda's testimony before the Senate committee; instead, his distress stemmed from an opinion column, "Ley Antidiscriminatoria o Comisión de Buena Vecindad," Castañeda subsequently wrote for *La Prensa*, San Antonio's Spanish-language newspaper.[38] Ross firmly reminded Castañeda that "complete abandon of opinion, publicly expressed, is one of those things which public servants must do."[39] It appears Ross's concern was Castañeda's not so subtle critique of Texas's Good Neighbor Commission.[40] He offered Castañeda a stern admonishment:

> The only safe rule is not to make any public statements which criticize other agencies or which take sides on legislative matters. Does that mean that you cannot continue to explain to the public the work of the Committee? Certainly not. Do so by all means. Our purposes and how we operate offer a wide platform which you have usefully utilized on many occasions. Keep it up—but keep out of the political field![41]

Regional Director Castañeda's piece is indicative of his frustration with FEPC policy and his vested interest in and long-term efforts to dismantle systems of oppression used to subjugate Mexicans and Mexican Americans in the United States.[42] He understood, moreover, that to do so meant exposing to the nation the racial discrimination that Mexicana/os experienced. His goal was to illustrate that they were in fact treated as second-class citizens regardless of their citizenship.

"The Problem of the Mexican": Third-Space Subjectivity and the Fight for First-Class Citizenship

Castañeda's fight to achieve first-class citizenship for Mexican Americans in the United States reflects the same steadfast resolve he applied to his scholarly endeavors.[43] His research subsequently informed his understandings of the racialization of Mexicana/os in the United States, notions of citizenship, and the precariousness of Mexican American wartime subject positions in the body politic. In an unpublished essay, "The Problem of the Mexican," he not only outlines the way in which U.S. Mexicans occupy a "third" racial category, he also notes the general disregard for all Mexicans in the United States regardless of their citizenship status. He explains:

> Because of the predominance of the darker shades of brown in pigmentation, the tendency to class them as "non-white" has become general. They are not classed as "colored" or "black," but they are definitely not considered "white." With the general acceptance of this false assumption, the prejudice against the Negro, which characterizes the South, from which the larger part of the English speaking settlers of the Southwest came, [has] attached to the "Mexican," who is not only generally looked upon as non-white, but also as "non-American" or foreign, regardless of his nationality. In other words, it makes little to no difference in the Southwest whether a member of this group is or is not an American citizen. He is still a "Mexican."[44]

His wartime work ultimately served to illuminate the third-space subjectivity of Mexican Americans as "impossible subjects" even as he advocated for their access to equal rights as first-class citizens.[45] His efforts are especially evident in the arguments he carefully crafted in correspondence, meetings, speeches, and personal conversations and most significantly in his testimony before a U.S. Senate committee hearing.

Castañeda's monotonous bureaucratic duties and a federal mandate limited to wartime industries ultimately restricted the "official" measures he could take in his crusade for Mexican American civil rights. He made sure, nonetheless, to craft his written and verbal arguments in a manner that called attention to the unconstitutionality of discriminating against U.S. citizens regardless of their racial or ethnic background. Castañeda, moreover, frequently invoked language from the Declaration of Independence and the U.S. Constitution in written correspondence and in meetings with business owners, work supervisors, union officials, and military personnel to buttress his position. His letters reflected his moral authority over those who dared to exhibit unpatriotic behavior during a time of total war by denying the rights inherent to all citizen-workers. In a 1944 letter to the commanding general at Kelly Field in San Antonio, Castañeda argued that "in presenting the complaint this complainant has exercised the inalienable right of all citizens to voice a protest against what she conscientiously considers a violation of her rights."[46]

In another letter to the same commanding officer he reiterated how informal and formal practices used to discriminate against U.S. citizens of Mexican descent did not reflect "the basic principles of true Americanism."[47] His simple but profound argument that Mexican Americans, as U.S. citizens, deserved the same rights and treatment as white workers underscored what he saw as the untenable contradiction of expecting Mexican Americans to participate in the fight against fascism abroad while continuing to be subjugated at home. A year later Castañeda expanded his campaign to access the rights and privileges of first-class citizenship for all Mexican Americans by going directly to the floor of the U.S. Senate.

New Mexico senator Dennis Chavez proved early on to be a formidable ally not only of Carlos E. Castañeda but also of the FEPC. Chavez's commitment to the struggle for Mexican American civil rights is evidenced by his nomination of Castañeda to the FEPC, as mentioned above, but more important it was manifest in his Senate bill to create a permanent postwar FEPC. Senator Chavez and five colleagues introduced Senate Bill 2048 on June 28, 1944.[48] Chavez's introduction of the bill provided him with the occasion to call a hearing of the Senate Committee on Labor and Education in order to discuss the merits of equal opportunity employment and ultimately gave Castañeda the chance to make the case for Mexican American civil rights before a national committee of elected officials. Regional Director Castañeda's testimony, in his oral statement and the subsequent question-and-answer session with committee members, reflected his generation's chosen strategy of highlighting the unjust ways U.S. citizens of Mexican descent experienced discrimination in their economic, so-cial, and political lives prior to and during the war. Almost immediately on beginning his statement he emphatically articulated the citizenship sta-tus of Mexican Americans. He proclaimed, "Our Spanish-speaking pop-ulation in the Southwest, made up almost entirely of American citizens of Mexican extraction and Mexican nationals, are ill-dressed, ill-fed, ill-cared for medically, and ill-educated."[49] He subsequently provided the senators with a litany of examples where institutionalized discrimination in the mo-bilization industry not only hampered the war effort but also denied Mex-ican American workers the rights to which they were entitled. Castañeda spoke of dual-wage labor systems, glass ceilings, and moratoriums on hir-ing workers of Mexican descent in virtually every aspect of industry across the Southwest. Yet the most intriguing attempt to convince the committee and the national public of the evils of racism toward Mexicans in the United States came during the question-and-answer session.[50]

In that session, Regional Director Castañeda and Senator Chavez col-luded to advance the argument that Mexican Americans deserved to be treated as first-class citizens at their workplaces and in their everyday lives. In Castañeda's response to the senator's question regarding economic dis-crimination he deviated from the topic at hand and instead discussed Mexi-can experiences during the Great Depression:

> During the days of relief, the various agents who distributed relief allowed much less to Mexican families on relief than to Anglo-American families, anybody with a Spanish name, be he an American citizen or not, and they did it on the assumption that a Mexican does not have to eat so much, that he is not used to eating butter and bacon and other rich foods, and that if they gave it to them it might make them sick.[51]

Chavez added, "Well, we have heard that a similar argument was used by some of the State governments in the South. So it is not particularly new."[52] At first glance their exchange appears innocent or even dismissive but when understood in the context of Castañeda and his Mexican Amer-ican colleagues' shift in strategy, the dialogue gains significance. Chavez equated strategies to subordinate Mexicana/os with similar tactics used against African Americans in order to foreground the absurdity of discrim-inating against U.S. citizens. Unlike some scholars' assertion that Mexicans of Castañeda's generation primarily claimed racial privilege by using "the other white" strategy, Castañeda's comment reflects an effort to expand the black-white racial paradigm and put discrimination against Mexicana/os on par with the experience of African Americans.[53] Because it was more generally acknowledged that African Americans experienced systematic discrimination, linking the treatment of these two groups is invaluable for a long-term solution to systemic inequities because it broadens the scope and urgency of this enduring social problem. The success of this shift from a war of maneuver to a war of position, one fought not in the streets but through discourse, depended on successfully challenging normative ideological discourses regarding race and citizenship.[54]

Intra- and Interethnic Organizing: The Mexican American Generation and the Making of a Historical Bloc

Castañeda and his Mexicana/o contemporaries across the state, in particular LULACers (members of LULAC), worked in tandem to expand the social and civic services in Mexican American communities, improve the quality of education for Mexican American students, and, ultimately, challenge Texas's social and racial order.[55] Cynthia E. Orozco argues that for these men of Mexican descent, numerous factors necessitated the rise of a Mexican American political consciousness in early-twentieth-century South Texas. Those factors, Orozco asserts, included the Mexican consulate's inability to intervene on behalf of U.S. citizens and a nationwide preoccupation with "the Mexican problem."[56]

Castañeda and his colleagues' shift in strategy at once honored their lived reality as second-class citizens and undermined the racialization processes that indiscriminately classified them as nonwhite immigrants. Their new tactic, moreover, predicated their subject position on U.S. hegemony, thereby constituting themselves as what Gramsci refers to as a "historical bloc."[57] That is, Castañeda and his cohort's political project of privileging their American citizenship simultaneously located their subject position within, but insubordinate to, the state.[58]

Castañeda's tenure at the FEPC represents the Mexican American historical bloc's deliberate attempt to reconstitute hegemonic understandings of racial equality even while it relied on affirming the legitimacy of the state to expand a coalition to reform state practices. In other words, Castañeda's work with the FEPC allowed him to nurture old relationships with colleagues and allies in the fight for racial justice but also gave him the opportunity to establish new alliances with other ethnic and racial minorities, religious groups, and other institutions fighting for wartime and, more important, postwar advancements in equal rights.

The material conditions of total war provided the Mexican American historical bloc with the opportunity to further its war of position against the nation-state, and they used state rhetoric, wartime democracy and equal opportunity employment, and state institutions, the FEPC specifically, to do so. Castañeda's tenure with the commission, in particular, allowed him to appropriate the ideological underpinnings of wartime rhetoric to shore up each distinct element of the Mexican American historical bloc in Texas and in fact managed to expand the sphere of that bloc across state lines, or at least throughout Region X. Through his almost constant FEPC-related traveling he managed to cultivate new relationships with Mexican American civil rights leaders and rank-and-file union members in Texas, New Mexico, and Arizona. He spent his time—sometimes weeks on end—in field meetings, listening and talking, essentially gathering evidence, and organizing Mexican Americans of all socioeconomic backgrounds to use the rhetoric of wartime democracy to dismantle institutionalized racism in the mobilization industries. His time in the field in essence functioned as state-sanctioned organizing on behalf of an ever-expanding Mexican American historical bloc. Moreover, Castañeda's service with the president's commission also presented the Mexican American historical bloc with access to a nationwide cohort of like-minded individuals.

As Zamora claims, Carlos E. Castañeda's service with the FEPC subsequently served as a foundation for fostering new alliances with African American leaders and various civil rights organizations across the country and thus formed partnerships with seemingly separate historical blocs.[59] Senator Chavez's and ACLU Chair Holmes's nominations of Professor Castañeda to the FEPC were an early indication that Castañeda's appointment would bridge the Mexican American historical bloc with others also committed to an antiracist political agenda. Senior Examiner Castañeda's alliance-building activities became glaringly evident three months after his appointment to Region X when his supporters organized a drive to name him permanent director of the region. Chairman Ross received at least seven letters in support of Castañeda's promotion, not just from supporters in Region X, but from across the country. Castañeda garnered local support from the Texas Negro Chamber of Commerce, the Progressive Voters League, the Dallas NAACP, and the Dallas Council of Negro Organizations, among others, and national support from the secretary general of the Catholic University of America and New Mexico Congressman Antonio M. Fernández.[60] Castañeda's political strategy to cultivate interethnic and cross-class solidarity stands as a testament to his long-term goal of dismantling structures of oppression through the politics of negotiation. He, in other words, seems to have understood the importance of political strategies that transcended ethnic and racial lines and realized that a state in total war had to offer some concessions to the masses of mobilized citizens who had heretofore been treated as permanent outsiders.

Castañeda and Texas's Mexican American historical bloc's work to achieve social justice for people of Mexican descent in the United States preceded the country's entry into World War II and continued long after the war's conclusion. In anticipation of the commission's demise and subsequent postwar fight for racial and class equity, Castañeda and his Texas Mexican colleagues crafted a political platform designed to advance racial equality for all and not just Mexican Americans. Castaneda's longtime friend and colleague Alonso S. Perales, among other Mexican American activists, also testified before Chavez's Senate committee about the efficacy of a permanent FEPC. Castañeda and his Mexican American colleagues stood before the Senate as part of a diverse coalition that also included African American and Jewish leaders advocating not only for equal employment opportunities, but for federal action to alter the racial dynamics of a postwar United States.[61] Their fight to save the FEPC from ruin and to establish a permanent commission represents Castañeda's and his colleagues' participation in an increasingly growing and diverse historical bloc.

While the war certainly gave rise to this newly formed bloc, its collective goal of social and economic justice had far-reaching implications. Castañeda continued to work with his Texas Mexican American cohort and his new allies to create a viable resolution, albeit a state-sponsored resolution, to end formal and informal practices of discrimination following the war. In 1946 Senator Chavez called on Professor Castañeda to assist him in raising funds for his reelection campaign, and former FEPC officials Clarence Mitchell and Malcolm Ross both asked for his support in their respective postwar social justice work.[62] He continued his work with LULAC and played an instrumental role in the Mexican American civil rights organization the Committee of One Hundred of Bexar County, Texas, which advocated for "the progress and welfare of ALL the people of our community."[63] Dr. Carlos E. Castañeda, Alonso S. Perales, and the rest of Texas's Mexican American historical bloc and their wartime allies ultimately stand as agents of historic change whose social justice work paved the way for the civil rights movements of the 1960s and 1970s.

II

CULTURAL AGENCY

The *Mexican Voice* Goes to War: Identities, Issues, and Ideas in World War II–Era Mexican American Journalism and Youth Activism

FÉLIX F. GUTIÉRREZ

The weekend of December 6 and 7, 1941, was sure to be a big one for many youths of Mexican descent in Arizona. It was the weekend set for the Third Annual Conference of Los Conquistadores, a group founded in 1937 by students at Arizona State Teachers College at Tempe to bring more Mexican American youths to college and increase the Mexican American presence on campus. Los Conquistadores members traveled across the state talking about college opportunities, organized cultural programs on campus, raised funds for scholarships, and joined forces with other youth activists across the Southwest. By December 1941 the group had grown to forty-five members. Their annual conferences drew community leaders, educators, and students to discuss issues facing Mexican American youths and encourage them to improve their lives and their communities through education.

On Saturday morning, December 6, 150 high school and college students were welcomed by Arizona State's president, Grady Gammage, who had approved the establishment of Los Conquistadores four years earlier. They then moved through twelve sessions on topics such as jobs in industry, opportunities for teachers, California and Arizona events and organizing activities, and the importance of a college education. Presenters included the Mexican consul in Phoenix, the Arizona State Youth administrator, and college students or recent graduates, including representatives of the Mexican Youth Conference in California.[1] Some youths came from as far away as Flagstaff, 160 miles north, where students translated the name of the Flagstaff High School mascot Eagles to form the Aguilas after school administrators would not allow a club with the word *Mexican* in its name.[2]

After Saturday's program wrapped up with a social recess at 4:15 P.M., some Conquistadores and Mexican Youth Conference members went to dinner and then dancing at a venue open to Mexican Americans. Among them was Rebecca Muñoz, a founding member of Los Conquistadores who was teaching at the Webster School for Mexican American children in nearby Mesa and who had led a discussion on the topic "Why Go To College?" With her was her fiancé, Félix J. Gutiérrez, a UCLA student and editor of the Mexican Youth Conference's magazine, *The Mexican Voice*, who had spoken on "Progress in California."[3]

On Sunday, December 7, 1941, the conference began as scheduled. Although leaders learned of the attack on Pearl Harbor that morning they did not interrupt the conference.[4] However, by the time activities ended early in the afternoon attendees knew something big had happened. As they returned to their homes or campuses in Arizona and Southern California the young women and men knew their world would change. But they had no way of knowing how war would affect the challenges and opportunities facing people identified as "Mexicans" in the United States.

Some of these young activists found journalistic voices and successfully published their own perspectives, raising important points about discrimination, assimilation, and identity. In fact, journalism became a vehicle for Mexican American political and ideological mobility before, during, and immediately after World War II.

War on the Horizon and Mexican American Youth Journalism

Long before December 7, 1941, the awareness of imminent world war was on the minds of young people later to be called the nation's "Greatest Generation." The only question was when the United States would become involved. In April 1938 Gutiérrez, a freshman at Pasadena Junior College, published a cartoon in the school's *Pasadena Chronicle* showing Adolf Hitler teaching Italian Fascist leader Benito Mussolini how to march in goosestep while Mademoiselle France and England's John Bull "look on with interest amounting to alarm." The headline warned, "Democracy, Beware!!"[5]

In January 1940 the front page of *Juventud*, a newspaper begun in 1939 in Mesa by the Progressive Juvenile Division organization, featured a front-page photo under the three-column headline, "Members of the Mexican-American Section," illustrating the lead story, "Many Latins in National Guard Maneuvers Here."[6] In the picture seven Spanish-surnamed National Guardsmen smile for the camera as one digs a trench. More than 1,300 men, about two-thirds of the Arizona National Guard, participated in the maneuvers. "Of the troops, 261 were Spanish American," *Juventud* reported, adding that "companies from Douglas and Nogales were made up almost entirely of citizens of Mexican extraction; the percentage of Latins in the Casa Grande, Tucson and Yuma companies was also large."[7]

Participation in the January 1940 Arizona National Guard exercises was a source of dual pride in being both Mexican and American. Ethnic pride was expressed in the Progressive Juvenile Division's slogan, "Better Mexicans Make Better Americans," and its use of the term *Mexican-American*. Organized by Mesa civic leader Pedro W. Guerrero, owner of a successful sign company, the group and its newspaper sought to advance the "Cultural, Social, and Educational Betterment of Latin-American Youth."[8] *Juventud* urged readers to "FIGHT for economic security and social equity through cultural eminence."[9]

The duality extended to *Juventud* seeing both military training and educational advancement as keys to a better future. Daily activities at the Juvenile Division's ten-day 1940 and 1941 summer camps held at the Phoenix YMCA's Sky-Y Camp near Prescott began with a bugler summoning boys to stand in formation as the American flag was raised and they were reviewed by a young adult in military uniform.[10] To promote education, *Juventud* ran profiles of Mexican youths who had gone to college, promoted attendance at Los Conquistadores' programs at Arizona State, and sent delegations to youth conferences in California.[11]

The Southern California group's publication, *The Mexican Voice*, also reflected dual pride in being identified as "Mexican" while advocating equal rights as Americans. In addition to using the term *Mexican* in its name when it launched in 1938, early covers of the magazine featured distinctly Mexican images to attract attention and readers. These included the September–October 1939 issue featuring a Mexican eagle with a serpent in its beak, a 1940 cover of the eagle and serpent behind a young man and woman, and the Winter 1941 cover featuring a young man wearing a sombrero and serape and a young woman in traditional Mexican attire.[12]

As war drew closer, the covers and coverage of *The Mexican Voice* reflected what was on the minds of its readers. The Summer 1941 issue ran a red, white, and blue cover by Juan Acevedo featuring a rifle-carrying young soldier facing the same direction as an attacking American eagle in the background. Published several months before the attack on Pearl Harbor, the cover was headlined "We Do Our Share."

An article in the same issue by Cosme J. Peña listed the names and activities of twenty-three Mexican Americans who were in the military or working in defense plants, using the term *American-Mexican* to designate them. Reflecting on dual, and sometimes dueling, identities as Mexican and American, Peña wrote, "We don't believe in an over-dose and over-playing

Figure 6.1. *Mexican Voice*, summer 1941. This magazine was produced by boys and young men who took part in the YMCA's Mexican Youth Conference in 1938. The name of the publication, using *Mexican*, was considered a bold assertion of ethnic pride. Published months before the attack on Pearl Harbor, this issue listed the names of twenty-three Mexican Americans who were serving in the military or working in defense plants. The title on the cover: "We Do Our Share." Gutiérrez Family Collection.

of patriotism but we do like to present both sides of the question. In do-ing so we do not want any back-slapping or hurrahs but just an understand-ing that the American-Mexican is an American . . . and a true American."[13]

The dual identity of the younger generation was not widely recognized or accepted by many older Mexicans or whites at the time. There was little to gain by displaying a Mexican identity to whites as the young people sought to advance in a Eurocentric society. Yet both publications boldly advocated showing pride in being Mexican as a first step to becoming American while also reporting how their readers were denied equal rights by being identi-fied as Mexican.

A front-page article in *Juventud*'s first issue in December 1939 reported that "skating parties for the Mexican public" on Monday nights at the Ren-dezvous Skating Rink "have been discontinued indefinitely."[14] In the next issue an editorial noted the contributions of Mexican culture to the United States and urged readers to strengthen their Mexican identity in order to "be fully proud of being Mexicans and . . . become better Mexicans in order to become excellent Americans."[15]

The *Mexican Voice* used the word *Mexican* in its name to demonstrate pride in the heritage despite legal and social segregation its readers faced because of their Mexican identity. The Spring 1939 issue roundup of youth club activities across Southern California reported that one goal of the Monrovia club was to "again work for better cooperation in the municipal plunge."

Mexicans in Monrovia were allowed to swim only on days reserved for people of color, the magazine reported. In 1938 a club delegation had "vis-ited the City Council asking for equal rights as White Americans; but no action was taken." *The Mexican Voice* connected treatment of Mexicans in the United States to news from Europe: "Their [the Mexican American youths'] opinion is, 'We tch, tch over what Germany is doing to the Jews; but look at what Americans are doing to Americans in America.'"[16]

Equal access to the swimming pool was of special importance to editor Gutiérrez, whose cement contractor father, Francisco J. Gutiérrez, had laid the sidewalks and completed other cement work for the Monrovia plunge in 1925. Before it opened he learned his son would be able to swim only on a segregated basis. Modeling the complex strategies the next generation would use to expand their rights, the elder Gutiérrez had a plan of his own to temporarily subvert segregation. When construction was completed and the pool filled with water he used his contractor's key to open the gates so his son and friends could use the pool the evening before white patrons en-tered on opening day.[17]

With a drive to reinforce their Mexican identities as part of their efforts to gain rights promised (but not delivered) to all Americans, youths involved with both publications prepared for the future. They were both *a part of* the United States by virtue of their birth or residence and also *apart from* the United States because of their Mexican identity. Yet they did not see an inherent conflict in being loyal to both as they faced World War II.

Their United States was a nation that fell far short of delivering equal liberty, justice, and pursuit of happiness to all. Racial and ethnic disparities were part of their daily lives, as was the attachment of many parents to maintaining Mexican culture and values in a nation that did not know or appreciate Mexican Americans. Now they would be called to fight and possibly die abroad for others to have rights that their own country did not offer them at home. The multiple identities, issues, and ideas that had shaped their lives to this point provided a foundation on which they, and later generations, would develop complex understandings of themselves and American society. As they and their generation went to war, so did *The Mexican Voice*.

The Mexican Voice and Emergent Mexican American Activism

Pasadena Junior College student Félix J. Gutiérrez, editor of *The Mexican Voice*, began in journalism while attending Monrovia-Arcadia-Duarte High School, eighteen miles northeast of Los Angeles in the San Gabriel Valley. A talented artist and writer, he drew cartoons for the high school newspaper and yearbook and wrote a short story titled "Mi Tía" for the English department's literary magazine when he was a senior in 1937.[18] The descendant of ancestors who first arrived in the San Gabriel Valley in the 1770s, he later recalled being unable to speak English when he entered grammar school. He developed an "I'll show 'em" attitude as he made his way educationally at a time when few Mexican Americans attended or graduated from high school. The Great Depression cost his father first his cement contracting business and then his home. To continue in school, Gutiérrez worked in the high school print shop and picked oranges in nearby citrus groves when jobs were not taken by newcomers from Oklahoma and Arkansas. After high school he continued picking oranges, but fellow crew members would not ask him to pay his share of gas money to the orchards because Félix needed the money for college.[19]

A two-year letterman on the high school track team and basketball player, Gutiérrez became involved in sports and other activities at the local

YMCA. This led to camps and conferences organized by the YMCA across Southern California in the 1930s, including the YMCA's Older Boys Conference, which began in 1934. Characteristic of the YMCA in that era, the group work was open only to boys and often segregated by racial groups. In the summer, the YMCA held the Southern California Mexican Boys Camp, where boys from different YMCAs across the region met each other, shared activities and ambitions, and formed the Mexican Youth Conference to sponsor athletic contests, club events, and conferences during the rest of the year.

Reflecting issues on their minds, the Sixth Annual Mexican Youth Conference at the San Pedro YMCA in 1939 featured youths speaking on "The Emancipation of Mexican Youth," "Values of Education," and "You Haven't a Chance." The Oratorical Contest winner was a speech titled "Forging the Mexican American" by the *Mexican Voice*'s feature editor, Bert Corona, who was forging his long career as an equal rights activist.[20]

In addition to camping, sports, and conferences, the YMCA-sponsored group activities built friendships among Mexican youths attending or recently graduated from college and encouraged others to improve themselves through education. Most knew few *paisanos* on campus who shared their educational ambitions as they moved into high school and college. "I didn't know what to expect," recalled Stephen Reyes, who attended his first Mexican Youth Conference in 1936 after graduating from UCLA. He added:

> I felt like I was an oddball. There was no one around [my hometown of Orange] that had gone through high school and junior college and the university. When I hit this conference [I] met people like Tom Garcia, who had gone to college or was going to college. . . . That's why I looked forward to the Mexican Youth Conference meetings; to meet these other guys that were in the same boat and, if not already there, were on the way.[21]

Other prewar activities launched by the Mexican Youth Conference included leadership training institutes (1939), a Mexican college student fraternity named Quetzal (1939), the Mexican-American Girls' Conference (1940) and the Mexican-American Teachers' Association (1940). In 1939 members established links with Los Conquistadores at Arizona State Teachers College at Tempe and Mesa's Progressive Juvenile Division, publisher of *Juventud*. Mexican Youth Conference members also traveled to El Paso in 1941 "to carry out the work of the conference."

In 1938 the Mexican Youth Conference launched a magazine to report on its activities and other efforts to advance Mexican American youth achievement. Even before *The Mexican Voice* had a name it was clear that the publication hoped to be an agent of change for ambitious Mexican American youths working to improve their lives and their communities. In a pink mimeographed prospectus before the first issue, editor Gutiérrez encouraged readers to share their opinions and reactions for publication. "Opinions on what? Reactions on what? On you. The Mexican Americans of the United States, the fellows who live in Mexican Town, with its dirty shacks, its dirtier streets and its dirtiest children!" Gutiérrez wrote. He added, "That's the impression others get of us. And that's why we're publishing this paper (which is only a pamphlet now). We want to help you change as times are changing. We don't want people to always think of us as *dirty race*. That's what they think of us, and it's true. Let's change now!"[22]

Gutiérrez suggested nine topics for possible articles: cleanliness, personal cleanliness, citizenship, birth control, delinquency, education, vocations, religion, and social contacts. He also asked for Mexican American club news at local YMCAs and urged articles on "a Mexican who has accomplished something." The suggested names reflected a strong Mexican identity: *Mexican Forum* and *Mexican Bugle*. The bimonthly issues would sell for a penny and would be distributed by club leaders, YMCA leaders, and Mexican Youth Conference heads. The flyer concluded, "Help this paper help yourself—for we are forging a new destiny!"

Within a year *The Mexican Voice* had developed into a twenty- to thirty-page mimeographed news magazine with illustrated covers and typewritten stories under stenciled headlines. In addition to coverage of club activities and accomplishments, it carried articles on segregation and discrimination the Mexican Americans faced in the United States and criticized Mexican American youths who did not take advantage of available opportunities. It also covered sports and named "All Mexican" teams in basketball and football to showcase *paisanos* who were athletic standouts.

In 1939 *The Mexican Voice* added an Arizona correspondent, Arizona State Teachers College at Tempe senior Rebecca Muñoz, after publishing a letter she wrote describing Arizona activities. The Mexican-born daughter of Methodist Reverend Esau P. and Febronia Muñoz, a pastoral couple assigned to Spanish-speaking churches in Texas, Arizona, and California from 1918 to 1950, she and her six siblings were raised in the United States and went to college, five of them before World War II. She, her sisters Lucinda and Elizabeth, and her brother, Rosalio, were founding members of Arizona State College's Los Conquistadores in fall 1937. A younger sister, Josefina, joined after enrolling.

Figure 6.2. Los Conquistadores Breakfast, pre–World War II. The Conquistadores had been founded in 1937 by students at Arizona State Teachers College in Tempe to encourage more youths to attend the school and to raise the profile of Mexican Americans on campus. The Rebecca Muñoz Gutiérrez Photographs, Chicana/o Research Collection, Arizona State University Libraries.

"The first letter I wrote, he put in the *Voice*. And then after that he kept asking me to write more articles," she recalled.[23] Muñoz's submissions included reports of Arizona activities and commentaries, including some of the few articles *The Mexican Voice* ran in Spanish. A romance developed between editor and correspondent after the two met when she passed through Monrovia on a summer trip to visit relatives in Fresno. They were engaged in spring 1941 and married in 1942.

By fall 1939 *The Mexican Voice* was describing itself as an "Inspirational-Educational Magazine" and the "Voice of Modern Mexican Youth" and featured illustrated covers, some in color. The following year it had a staff of at least ten and was sent to three hundred persons, with 150 more copies distributed at YMCAs in the area. In winter 1941 the magazine moved from mimeograph to typeset issues of eight pages, listed thirty-eight persons in California, Arizona, and Texas authorized to collect subscriptions and donations, and shortened its name to *Mexican Voice*. During the war

Figure 6.3. Newly engaged *Mexican Voice* editor Félix J. Gutiérrez and Arizona correspondent Rebecca Muñoz arrive at Los Conquistadores Third Annual Conference, Arizona State Teachers College–Tempe, December 6, 1941. The Rebecca Muñoz Gutiérrez Photographs, Chicana/o Research Collection, Arizona State University Libraries.

leaders of the Mexican Youth Conference separated their activities from the YMCA to form an organization incorporated as the Mexican-American Movement (MAM).

World War II and the *Mexican Voice*: Fighting on Two Fronts

The *Mexican Voice* continued to publish as a typeset magazine on a reduced schedule during the war years, beginning in 1942. From the war's start it recognized its readers had to fight on two fronts: one against Axis forces overseas and one for equality in the United States. The spring 1942 cover, the first after war was declared, featured a young man wearing a Mexican sombrero and a young woman with traditional braids in front of a red, white, and blue shield with stars and stripes, symbolizing the blended identities of Mexican American youths. These dual images symbolized complex issues of identity, citizenship, and participation faced by Mexican-origin youths during an era of wartime nationalism and patriotism in the United States.

For instance, the magazine offered war coverage on the home front by quoting top government leaders as possible allies in efforts to improve the conditions of Mexicans in the United States. An article by Cosme J. Peña headlined, "DISCRIMINATION—AND US," began with quotes by President Franklin D. Roosevelt saying no law prohibited aliens from working in defense plants and U.S. Attorney General Francis Biddle stating a federal policy that there be "no discrimination in the employ of workers in defense industries because of race . . . creed . . . color . . . or even national origin." Peña asked, "How many of us know of people, of Mexican descent, who have been refused work on account of their national origin?"[24] He told readers how to file reports of discrimination in hiring or firing to the Minority Group Branch of the War Production Board and noted Mexican-American Movement leaders working to resolve issues of discrimination.

The same issue quoted a letter on hemispheric solidarity from Carey Mc-Williams, chief of the California State Division of Immigration and Housing, to Nelson Rockefeller, coordinator of Inter-American Affairs in Washington, DC. McWilliams urged that "the most obvious and most effective way to improve Latin-American relations is for the national government to take cognizance of the problems faced by this resident Mexican population . . . by taking immediately feasible steps to improve the social, economic and political status of this group and, of course, to publicize this fact widely through Latin America." McWilliams added, "In other words, Inter-American feeling could well begin at HOME."[25]

The issue featured the usual stories of youth activities across Arizona by Solomon Muñoz, sports news featuring Mexican American athletes, and news of regional conferences in Arizona and in California (Pasadena, Pomona, Watts-Willowbrook, Tulare, and Orange County). It added reports of Mexican youths serving in the military or working in defense plants. On the back page, the "*Nosotros*" column by Gutiérrez using the pen name Manuel de la Raza, described wartime conflicts faced by Mexican youths serving a country that had not treated them as equal to whites. After reporting that he was rated "highly opposed to war" on an attitude test, he noted he had responded affirmatively to the test statement, "War has some benefits."

"When we answered 'yes' on 'war has some benefits,' we were thinking of our Mexican American youth," Gutiérrez wrote. He noted that the military had taken young men from the "Mexican Town" and "Mexican school" and put them into "constant contact with all backgrounds." In addition, the military put everyone in the same uniforms, provided training, and had "given opportunities for advancement on merit and work." He reported that Mexican Americans reporting to his draft board were classified as "White" and that locally "a high rate of volunteers of Americans of Mexican descent" had entered the military without waiting to be drafted. "What this proves, we cannot venture to guess," he wrote.

> But it is heartening because they have less to fight for than the fellows "north of the railroad tracks." These fellows had never felt American. They had never been given a chance. At home, their parents derided "Americans." Any sign of gruffness, of coldness, of unpoliteness and of excessive noise was considered as "American" to them. In the schools, by attending "their own," they couldn't feel American. In the municipal plunge, a day was reserved for "Mexicans." In the theater the right side was for "them." Certain restaurants would not cater to "Mexicans." Yet . . . somehow, these fellows enlisted, joined the ranks and shouldered the responsibility *as theirs*.[26]

The staff of the *Mexican Voice* and Mexican-American Movement members joined the war effort. The magazine published one eight-page typeset issue per year during some of the war and identified current staff members in military service with asterisks. Six of the eleven names listed in the 1943 staff box had asterisks. An article listed the names and wartime whereabouts of twelve current and former staff members, including four working in defense plants. Rejected for military service because of poor eyesight, Gutiérrez continued studying art at UCLA and worked as a technical illustrator in the engineering department of the Douglas Aircraft Company during the war.

In 1943 he produced a *Mexican Voice* cover of a young woman next to a young man in uniform for an issue dedicated to three staff members serving in the army:

- Juan Acevedo, a UCLA graduate who had designed many magazine covers and was now with the camouflage corps;
- Cosme J. Peña, a Los Angeles City College graduate who had contributed as an editor or writer since 1939 and was serving as a clerk in the medical corps; and
- Manuel Ceja, a Chapman College graduate who was the first to join the magazine and wrote the sports columns, also a clerk in the medical corps.

The issue was sprinkled with articles recognizing Mexican participation in the war effort, including those awarded military decorations for wartime bravery. Among those mentioned was Margarite Sanchez, WAC in basic training in Massachusetts, the first female vice president of the Mexican Youth Conference. Another article reported that a short study of "Los Angeles County paisanos" in the military revealed that as of June 30, 1943, "38 have been wounded in action, 22 have given their lives and there are 44 prisoners of war."

Another article reported that "Mexican workers from Mexico" reached a peak of 1,300 weekly and that the previous May close to 23,000 workers had been sent with the cooperation of the Mexican government. A new feature was a "What Do You Say?" column featuring short quotes from prominent whites, including First Lady Eleanor Roosevelt, on the positive qualities of Mexican Americans and deploring the conditions they faced in the United States.

The Zoot Suit Riots, Yellow Journalism, and Alternative *Mexican Voice* Coverage

Along with noting that Mexicans from both sides of the border were contributing to the war effort, the 1943 *Mexican Voice* reported on the big news story involving Mexican American youths that year: the June 1943 Zoot Suit Riots in Los Angeles.[27] Three articles focused on the Mexican American youths called "pachucos" who had been attacked by servicemen, the causes of the riots and their aftermath. "The Pachuco Problem," by Paul Coronel, analyzed the second-generation adjustment problems of young Mexican Americans and traced the "undesirable channels of youthful activities" to "the failure of our institutions to assimilate the Mexican citizens into the channels of American citizenship."[28] Coronel placed responsibility on both sides, first criticizing Mexican parents for not encouraging education, Mexicans for hanging on to their cultural heritage, language, and food, and Mexican Americans for failing to intermingle with the rest of the American population.

On the other side, he noted "American" people did not regard Mexican Americans as their equal; that American institutions—schools and churches—saw Mexicans as a problem, not an asset, to white American society; and that American communities "have followed a policy of segregating the Mexican from the normal process of our American life." Coronel closed by calling for Mexican American professionals—particularly teachers, social workers, probation officers, and city officials—to be "encouraged and allowed to work within the Mexican-American communities" and urged both white Americans and Americans of Mexican descent to become educated to appreciate each other's contributions and background.

Another article reported the youth work of the Latin-American Coordinating Council of Los Angeles, which the magazine reported was formed two years earlier "when the first inklings of 'Pachuquismo' came to the public's attention."[29] The council, which included some members of the Mexican-American Movement, worked with police, educators, and juvenile delinquency workers to organize athletic leagues and clubs, helped develop the Latin American trade school in East Los Angeles, and had a speakers' bureau to "appear before all types of groups to discuss delinquency among Mexican youths." The group's goal was to "give our youth other goals and activities than just congregating on the streets and not being occupied with constructive things."

An editorial for readers in the military stationed abroad linked the riots to the need to fight for freedom both overseas and at home.[30] Headlined "A Challenge . . . " it began by quoting headlines over the sensational zoot suit news stories: "Zoot Suiters Attack Sailors," "Pachucos Invade Dance Hall, Kill One," and "Zoot Gangster Incites Riots." The editorial noted that such headlines "strike fear into your own people who go about their business of earning a living" and make it easier for others "to blame your group to segregate it, hate it, to feel superior to it."

It contrasted these negative images to the Mexican American military forces serving their country overseas as they "wallow in the jungles of the South Pacific, freeze in Attu, bake in India." In a message similar to the World War II Double V campaign of the *Pittsburgh Courier* and other black newspapers, the *Mexican Voice* called on military readers to fight for victory on two fronts:

> Fighter for freedom, when you return, you will return another person and you will return to a different world. You will say, "Ah, I am glad we got that job done over there." Yes, that job! But we have another job. One that will take a different sort of courage; not the courage of facing death, but the courage to face the future and to fight for your group, to fight for a better America, at home.

That two-front mission would drive the Mexican-American Movement's activities and its media through the end of the war and in postwar years.

The *Mexican Voice* Marches On:
Extending Wartime Homefront Victories

A picture of a helmeted Mexican American soldier produced by Cpl. Juan Acevedo was featured on the summer 1944 *Mexican Voice* cover, which continued its reports of Mexican-American Movement conferences and other activities from Santa Barbara to Orange County and as far east as San Bernardino. The issue listed six of eleven staff members in the armed forces, featured Mexican Americans serving in the military, sports news, references to the accomplishments of Mexican American youths, and quotes by whites on the contributions of Mexican Americans to the war effort.

Several stories reported on the widening influence of the Mexican-American Movement in promoting interracial cooperation in cities across the region. Paul Coronel wrote that the MAM had organized local councils "made up of Mexican-Americans and Non-Mexican Americans . . . interested in the problems faced by Mexican people residing in this country."[31]

In a *Nosotros* column on home front progress, Gutiérrez, writing as Manuel De La Raza, noted that several servicemen had written asking for the "'lowdown' on things 'Mexican' in Southern California" during the war.[32] He wrote that "discrimination and prejudice have slackened a little" and that "things are better than before the war":

> For example, we see things that we never saw much of before. Young fellows of Mexican descent with commissions in the Air Corps, Infantry Signal Corps, Navy—walking down First Street or Broadway in Los Angeles. We see Mexican girls walking down the street arm in arm, or in groups with others not of Mexican descent. Ditto for the boys. We see paisanos dating blondes from the westside. And yet, in the other extreme, we still see our gang groups dating their own chicks of their own social neighborhood groups.

He turned to other changes:

> The above-average American of Mexican descent is moving away from his "vecindad." The trend is to move into American neighborhoods. . . . We see intermarriage. . . . Even the newspapers who once capitalized on a few pachuco and servicemen incidents to make them large gang wars are now cooperating by giving gang juvenile delinquency very little news space. . . . Personnel of Mexican descent [are] moving into social work, especially in areas where we have a large concentration of our paisanos. . . . The Police

department has put on, through civil service, several officers of Mexican descent. . . . The Probation department is still seeking more qualified probation officers.

Although he assessed that "things Mexican" at home were better, Gutiérrez questioned whether wartime advances would continue in the postwar era. He called on those in uniform to continue to fight as veterans if they wanted home front advances to continue. The column concluded: "We as a group have made quite a few social gains, but whether we keep them . . . somehow depends on you . . . and us. We have been given a chance . . . because it was coming to us. But, what is going to happen after the war is something that very few of us venture to guess."

Some reasons for questioning whether wartime gains would continue in postwar America were shown in quotes that reflected the contrasting views on Mexican Americans held by Anglos who had worked with them during the war. Among the quotes in the summer 1944 "What Do You Say?"[33] column were the following:

Floyd L. Wohlwend, California Shipbuilding Corp:
"Given an opportunity to learn and practice, a Mexican moves ahead more rapidly than employees generally. . . . Mexican-Americans are not different from other employees in sobriety, tardiness, sickness and to discipline."

Leonard Gordon, Grocers Packing Co.:
"Our experience has shown that as a whole Mexican-Americans do not attain the standard of performance achieved by other groups we employed before the war. . . . We have found comparatively few Mexican-Americans with the ability and patience necessary to supervise others."

Sid Panush, Los Angeles County Civil Service Commission:
"Mexican-Americans have proven themselves to be as good as any other national group employed by the County. Man for man, on the same job, there can be no differentiation."

John F. Fisher, Los Angeles City Civil Service:
"There seems to be a slight tendency towards the viewpoint that the Mexican-American is less ambitious, less energetic than the American employee."

A. O. Anderson, Lockheed:

"There will be keen competition for jobs in the aircraft industry after the war. If Mexican-Americans wish to compete, they should take advantage of training opportunities."

Though some questioned the capabilities and ambition of Mexican Americans, there were no doubts that the Mexican-American Movement's organizing and advocacy for equal rights would continue when the war ended. Nor was there any doubt that the MAM's publications would spread the word.

Moving Forward on Postwar Issues

When Mexican American veterans and defense industry workers returned to more peaceful pursuits after the war, they also found changes in Mexican-American Movement publications. The MAM launched a newspaper, *Forward*, which was staffed by many of those who contributed to the *Mexican Voice*: Juan Acevedo, Roger Anton, Angelo Cano, Paul Coronel, Félix Gutiérrez, Dora Ibañez, Solomon Muñoz, Stephen Reyes, Gualberto Valadez, and others. In a front-page editorial in the first issue on October 28, 1945, the leaders told readers that the MAM had chosen the name *Forward* "because to us it symbolizes our attitudes, our philosophy, our Movement."[34] Although the newspaper said the MAM would continue publishing the *Mexican Voice* as a magazine, it appears that efforts that had gone into the magazine were transferred to the newspaper.

The newspaper continued under Gutiérrez's editorship and reported on the expanding activities of the MAM chapters throughout Southern California, commented on issues important to Mexican Americans, noted achievements, and invited comments from readers. Unlike the *Mexican Voice*, *Forward* ran advertising, mostly from local merchants in Southern California communities where the MAM had active chapters, such as Anaheim, Placentia, and Chaffey.

Major themes in *Forward* coverage and MAM activities in the late 1940s focused on the challenges facing Mexican Americans in the postwar period and the opportunities for leadership and change afforded MAM chapters and members. A standing feature in the newspaper was a column by Hilario T. Alvarado called "THE VETERAN of Mexican Descent." Alvarado opened a May 1946 column by noting Southern California's growth after the war and the potential for Mexican American veterans to play a positive role in the region's development.

"Los Angeles holds the distinction of being the second largest city with people of Mexican descent next to Mexico City," Alvarado wrote.[35] "This distinction can be a great asset to both a community or communities of people of that descent or to the city itself or it may be a bad reflection . . . In the city of Los Angeles, the veteran of Mexican descent has a contribution to make to himself and to the community." In order to play that role, he urged Mexican American veterans to take advantage of education benefits provided by the GI Bill of Rights:

> Today! Now! Not tomorrow, is the time when every veteran of Mexican ancestry should take advantage of the education and training opportunities offered by the G.I. Bill of Rights. . . . Veterans of Mexican descent, let us take advantage of the opportunities offered us in the fields of education and training. Let's better ourselves and our families. A challenge has been thrust upon us, let's take it and make the most of it for ourselves and our loved ones.

The next January, Alvarado observed that veterans of Mexican ancestry were making less use of the GI Bill's educational benefits than "veterans of different national antecedents."[36] He said he felt the reasons for the reported gap "'boil down' to two things."

> FIRST—Many young veterans of this ancestry still feel that they are not wanted here. . . . This attitude tends to create an inferiority complex, which keeps them from progressing. . . . They segregate themselves to a world of their own. After all they are Americans and are entitled to everything due an American. If they are not getting it they should fight for it.

Alvarado continued: "SECOND—many of them seem content with what little they have in wealth and/or knowledge. . . . They have to learn to wish and acquire nothing but the best within their own means."

Forward committed its coverage to creating a positive image of Mexican Americans in the minds of readers of all races by citing individual and group progress. It featured photos of MAM scholarship winners on the front page, covered regional and local conferences, and reported on efforts to advance integration on many fronts. It also noted continuing prejudice against people identified as Mexican and criticized those who changed their self-identification as they moved into a white-dominated society. *Forward* commented in a 1947 editorial headlined "INSECURITY":

> We think it is a shame that some people think they have to say that they are "Spanish" to get jobs. We know of a person who could not live in a privately sponsored housing development until he changed his "race classification" from Mexican to Spanish."[37]

The editorial continues:

> Why is it that time and time again you will see restaurants that read "Spanish food." When the owner himself will admit "it looks better to have a sign that says 'Spanish' than 'Mexican.' It is classier to the average American." . . . Why do people ask you if you are "Spanish" when you know that they later will call you "Mexican" when your back is turned? Yes, American society too often, in this case sets the standard: to be Spanish is superior. And we, too often, in self-defense and fear, cater to this erroneous thought.

On a related humorous note, a front-page article reported the wartime experience of Sgt. William Hornelas when he was based in Florida. Tired of a military diet of potatoes and Spam and homesick for tamales, chili con carne, and tortillas he came upon a restaurant with a big sign screaming, "Spanish Food."[38] He rushed in and without looking at the menu "ordered the old standbys," only to find they were not offered. "Puzzled he asked the proprietor, 'What's cooking? I thought you sold Spanish food. Your sign outside says, 'Spanish Food,'" *Forward* reported. "*Seguro paisano*, I have '*comida Española*,' but the stuff you want is Mexican food. Nobody eats that stuff around here."

Aside from commentaries and anecdotes, *Forward* focused most of its coverage on youth achievements, regional conferences, and the importance of organizing to gain rights promised to all Americans. The May 12, 1946, edition featured two award-winning essays on the U.S. Constitution by high school students Susie Madrid of Clifton, Arizona, and Consuelo Espinosa of Valencia High School in Placentia, California. On the same page was an article in Spanish titled "El Movimiento México-Americano" by Enrique M. Mestre.[39]

The activist roles of GI generation veterans were reported throughout the newspapers. An article headlined "Use of Pool" reported efforts of veterans in Tempe, Arizona, "protesting discrimination in the public swimming pool at Tempe Beach."[40] Arguing that allowing persons of Mexican ancestry to use the pool would "hurt business," swimming pool officials raised $1,500 to make a separate pool for "Spanish-speaking people use." But the veterans rejected the proposal "because they still consider this discriminatory." A group composed of members of "both cultural backgrounds" was established to appeal the action of the swimming pool committee.

Advocacy of equal rights and challenges to established practices also brought government scrutiny of the MAM and its activities. In 1946 MAM president Gualberto Valadez reported, "Several government agencies have investigated our organization looking for any possible subversive element. None has been found and the M.A.M. has been rated highly as an Americanizing influence."[41] Valadez went on to mention efforts of MAM members to work "in the advancement of Mexican Americans" with more established organizations: schools, the Boy Scouts, Girl Scouts, YMCAs, YWCAs, churches, service clubs, health departments, and other public agencies.

Developing strategies to advance racial and cultural integration in postwar America was the goal of the Tenth Annual Mexican American Youth Conference, sponsored by the MAM and YMCA and held at the Pacific Palisades conference grounds in May 1946. Among topics discussed by Mexican American and Anglo speakers at the conference, titled "Post War Problems and Opportunities for Mexican Americans," were "Post War America and Your Part in It," "Our Contributions to American Culture," "Merging of Cultures," and "Obstacles Facing the Mexican-American Youth."[42]

The two-day conference drew more than 130 youths from California and Arizona and recommended a seventeen-point program that recognized postwar Mexican Americans "face segregation and prejudice in American life." The program proposed two coordinated avenues of action. One avenue urged youths on ways to integrate into white society: "avoid self-segregation as much as possible," "encourage their parents to seek American citizenship and learn English," "overcome their inferiority complex when applying for jobs," and "be discriminate in the use of Spanish, especially in public places where it may create more barriers with those who do not speak the language." The other avenue urged equal rights and pride in being Mexican Americans: "segregated schools should be abolished," job applicants "should not deny their national background," and "persons of Mexican background should present themselves [as] Mexican-Americans or Americans of Mexican descent, use of terms such as 'Spanish-American,' 'Latin American' or 'Spanish' is not true to the group in general and should be discouraged."

Figure 6.4. Mexican Youth Conference, Pacific Palisades, Los Angeles, April 25 and 26, 1942. The conference separated from the YMCA during the war years, and participants created a new organization, incorporated as the Mexican-American Movement (MAM). Many of the activists were involved in the *Mexican Voice*. The Rebecca Muñoz Gutiérrez Photographs, Chicana/o Research Collection, Arizona State University Libraries.

The postwar Mexican-American Movement sent its message to a national audience. After the 1946 conference Gutiérrez published an article titled "U.S.-Mexican Youth Plan Set Up" for the Boston-based *Christian Science Monitor*, the only general circulation national newspaper, reporting the MAM's action plan to readers across the country. The message of reinforcing Mexican American pride while seeking equal rights in a white society that began on *The Mexican Voice*'s typewritten mimeographed sheets eight years earlier was now reaching readers across the country.[43]

The *Mexican Voice* and Mexican American Mobility

Whether published before, during, or after World War II, the pictures and articles in *The Mexican Voice*, its later iteration as *Mexican Voice*, and other

Mexican American youth publications tell stories of ambitious youths who saw no conflict in reinforcing a Mexican identity while advocating full participation in a "melting pot" society that denied equal rights to those who would not, or could not, melt into a white identity. Though facing discrimination by being identified as Mexican, they reinforced that identity as they moved into college and the military. They saw the war as an opportunity to prove their worth through service in the military or defense industries in support of a country that did not afford them equal opportunities. They fought on the battlefront against the nation's enemies and then on the home front for the nation's promise of equal rights for all.

When they reentered a peacetime society, they did not seek return to the normalcy they knew before the war. Instead, they worked to maintain and build on gains made during the war. In evolving from identifying as Mexicans to calling themselves Mexican Americans, they also built blended identities for themselves, their children, and their communities. This set the stage for future generations to seek advancement by reinforcing their Mexican heritage and Mexican American identity to themselves and to others as they worked for equality in American society.

"Capitán, ¿a qué huele la sangre?": Mexicana/o Vaudeville and Militarized Citizenship during World War II

PETER C. HANEY

Dios bendiga América

At midnight on the evening of December 3, 1941, four days before the Japanese strike on Pearl Harbor, San Antonio's Mexican *colonia*[1] gathered at the Teatro Nacional to celebrate the second anniversary of the theater's renovation.[2] Standing at the western edge of downtown, at the corner of Commerce and Santa Rosa Streets, the Nacional had been the city's premier venue for live Spanish-language theater since its opening in 1917. By the beginning of the 1940s, however, it had become more movie house than performance venue, and the renovation had expanded seating capacity and adapted the space to this new reality. Indeed, one of the evening's primary attractions was a screening of the comedy "Miente y serás feliz" (Lie and You'll Be Happy). Before the film, some thirty *artistas* (performers) shared the stage with Mexican consul Miguel Alvarez-Acosta, who served as master of ceremonies and featured speaker, and the consulate's consulting attorney, Manuel C. González.

Among the evening's highlights was the variety company of Ernestina Egdell de Rodríguez ("La Bella Netty") and her brother-in-law Carlos Rodríguez-Valero ("Don Suave") presenting an original *revista* (musical revue) by local actor Leonardo García Astol titled "Dios bendiga América" (God Bless America). We may never know whether the term *América* in that title refers to a country or a continent, and the ambiguity may have been intentional. Nevertheless, the obvious nod to Irving Berlin's patriotic anthem suggests an increasing engagement with U.S. citizenship on the part of performers and audience. Here "engagement" should not be mistaken for what has usually been understood as "assimilation." People of Mexican de-

Figure 7.1. Netty Egdell de Rodríguez and her husband, Jesús Rodríguez, performing at the Teatro Nacional in San Antonio, Texas, 1938. The Rodríguezes debuted a musical revue in 1939 that was titled *Votamos o nos botan* (Let's Vote or They'll Kick Us Out). San Antonio Light Collection, University of Texas at San Antonio, Libraries Special Collections.

scent in San Antonio did not simply abandon earlier loyalties or forget the abuses their community had suffered even before World War II. What is clear, however, is that the war that would begin for the United States in a few days made the demands of the U.S. state increasingly difficult to ignore. Although theater was very much a part of the Mexicana/o community's adaptation to that reality, it did not speak about the process with a single, unified voice.

This is true in part because the world of Mexicana/o theater in San Antonio was divided in ways that echoed and reinforced class divisions in its audience. Along with smaller, less prestigious theaters, *carpas* (tent shows) continued to present their eclectic, carnivalesque mix of acrobatics, comedy, song and dance, contortionists, and magicians to predominantly working-class audiences throughout the city during the years of the war. Furthermore, traveling *carpa* companies used San Antonio as a home base but continued to follow the migrant stream and visit small towns throughout South and West Texas. Many *artistas*, of course, worked both the tent shows and the theaters, but most performers identified themselves as either *artistas de teatro* or *artistas de carpa*. In general, the former group appears to have weathered the war better than the latter. While the theaters and the artists associated with them were at least able to continue performing throughout the war, those who worked on the more marginal side of San Antonio's Spanish-language entertainment industry often faced career-ending changes. Lack of documentation prevents a full assessment of the war's impact on the *carpas*, but what information is available from written and oral sources suggests that neither the tent shows' closeness to their audience nor the low cost of their productions would be enough to save them from the forces that challenged the live performance industry as a whole.

Among the most significant of these challenges was the large-scale repatriation of much of the theater's audience base during the depths of the Depression. It is impossible to know for sure how many Mexicana/os returned to their home country voluntarily or involuntarily from San Antonio after the stock market crash of 1929. This is true in part because the nationwide repatriation campaign that followed the crash unfolded as a decentralized collaboration between federal and local relief agencies, local repatriation boards, state militias, and the Mexican government.[3] Facing a hostile climate, many Mexican nationals surely returned to their communities of origin without being counted. Estimates for the country as a whole reach as high as two million between 1929 and 1939, and this number includes U.S. citizens.[4] In San Antonio and other large cities, the combined effects of the economic crisis and the forced removal of the audience contributed to the end of serious drama as a commercial enterprise in the most important Spanish-language theaters.[5] Although vaudeville held its own at the city's key *teatros* through the end of the 1930s, competition from film added to the economic and demographic challenges to live entertainment. For this reason, the industry was in decline when the war began. And though they limped along in one form or another through the early 1950s, the variety shows that had once dominated urban theaters and traveling tent shows never regained the stature they had enjoyed before the Depression. Shortages of gasoline and tires stymied touring plans, and the draft siphoned off performers and fans. Through it all, dedicated *artistas* continued to appear before Mexicana/o audiences in Texas throughout the years of the war. Indeed, the early 1940s saw an assertion of ethnic Mexican commercial control over an outsider-dominated local entertainment industry. In the area of content, themes of military triumphalism and U.S. patriotism gained ground in a field once defined by exile nationalism. Furthermore, participation in and support of the war effort became more and more important for Mexicana/o claims to belonging in the United States, a process that I call the militarization of citizenship.

But Mexicana/o vaudeville simply could not leave any authoritative ideology intact. Having long derived artistic energy from a tension between heavy moralism and saucy titillation, the *artistas* spoofed dominant rhetorics of heroic masculinity even as they reproduced them onstage. In these performances, their key resources were the comic potential of the human body and the bodily reality of war itself. By putting flesh, blood, and bowels on the skeleton of patriotic U.S. citizenship, performers highlighted aspects of the experience of combat that audiences on the home front could never fully grasp. By doing so, they implicitly challenged the abstract, reified loyalties and hatreds that made the horrors of World War II so disturbingly novel.[6] Nevertheless, both the content of theatrical entertainment and the actions of *artistas*, managers, and impresarios show a Mexicana/o public in San Antonio moving toward an increasingly militarized identification with the U.S. state. The elements of contestation and carnivalesque parody mentioned above make it clear that this movement was full of ambivalence and contradiction, but its reality is undeniable. Perhaps the clearest evidence of the change lies in the use of theater as a fund-raising tool. Where live performance had once served as a source of financial support for Mexicana/o community-based institutions, voluntary giving during World War II moved increasingly toward the U.S. war effort. At the same time, the stage shows pressed Mexico's official culture into military service. Inspired by the wartime alliance between the United States and Mexico, *artistas* came to use symbols formerly associated with exile nationalism and difference to mark a culturally distinctive version of U.S. citizenship.

Los teatros Go to War

In a way, the U.S. military was already present at the creation of San Antonio's commercial Spanish-language entertainment industry. In 1912 the Sicilian immigrant entrepreneur Sam Lucchese, who had become prosperous selling boots to the military and to the cattle industry in Texas during the late nineteenth century, constructed the Teatro Zaragoza at 805 West Commerce, at the corner of Commerce and Santa Rosa Streets, specifically to cater to the niche Spanish-language market.[7] This investment of money earned from what we now call "defense contracts" proved so lucrative that Lucchese was able to build the larger Teatro Nacional alongside the Zaragoza five years later. These spaces became the centerpieces of "an empire in San Antonio and Laredo that was unrivalled."[8] As Elizabeth Ramírez notes, Lucchese began his theatrical venture by hiring Carlos Villalongín, head and patriarch of the acting company that bore his name, as theater manager. By 1915, however, Lucchese took over the management of the theater, even traveling to Mexico himself to book the most prominent artists, among them the touring dramatic company of María del Carmen Martínez. With this move, he effectively turned formerly "independent artists" such as Carlos Villalongín and Juan Padilla into "employees" to be hired and fired at will based on their drawing power.[9] Whatever its relations with performers, the Lucchese family itself enjoyed close ties with the exiled Mexican elite, who saw the theater as a way of teaching morality and preserving cultural identity. This alliance may be seen as a flamboyant example of the cordial relationships that David Montejano has described between "Anglo" merchants and their Mexicana/o customers throughout southern Texas during the early twentieth century.[10] Although economic difficulties and stricter border controls made it more difficult for Mexican artists to travel to San Antonio during the 1930s,[11] performers associated with the Mexico City film industry's *época de oro* (Golden Age) gained renewed prominence on the city's stage during the war.

At the war's beginning, performance spaces owned by the Luccheses, including the Guadalupe Theater farther west, continued to dominate the landscape of San Antonio's Mexicana/o entertainment industry, offering variety acts, screenings of the latest Mexican and U.S. films, and music and dance, along with regular raffles and amateur talent shows. Although existing sources do not mention newsreels, it is possible that they were shown. To the extent that Lucchese's theaters continued to offer live performance, the racialized relations of production that had begun in the 1910s remained in force. I am suggesting, in other words, that management had come to occupy the "Anglo," or white, slot in the system of racial meanings that existed in early-twentieth-century Texas and exerted managerial authority over what was often referred to as "Mexican" talent even though performers came from a variety of Latin American backgrounds. By characterizing this situation as a case of racialized relations of production, I am arguing that identities related to beliefs about ancestry and phenotype were salient in the situation and that the elimination of ethnic Mexican middle management by the 1920s must be understood in racial as well as class terms. Here we see the precursor to the relations of production that characterized Spanish-language radio in the United States in the late 1970s and which Gutiérrez and Schement interpret as internal colonialism.[12]

In the big venues' shadow, traveling and neighborhood tent shows continued to operate, as did numerous smaller, less prestigious theaters. Prominent in this second tier of theaters were the Obrero at 416 W. Houston Street and the Progreso at 1306 Guadalupe, operated by Paul Garza and his uncle Juan Garza, respectively.[13] Although these spaces may once have housed live performances, they were dime movie houses specializing in second-run Hollywood action films by the end of the 1930s. Even after live performance in Spanish disappeared from many theaters, neighborhood church halls kept it alive. Throughout the Depression, the West Side churches had nurtured the serious full-length comic and dramatic productions that vaudeville and films had displaced from the commercial stage.[14] The hall at San Fernando Cathedral, the monumental centerpiece of Catholic life in downtown San Antonio and a visible sign of the city's connection to its Spanish/Mexican past, also hosted such performances. In the 1940s variety acts began to appear in the benefit functions and amateur productions of the churches. In the church halls, immigrant artists continued to create original comic theatrical pieces based on current events, providing the city's Mexicana/o public with opportunities for public reflection on their situation.

For much of the early twentieth century, a nostalgic exile nationalism had defined the Spanish-language stage. By the end of the 1930s, however, *artistas* who had made careers dramatizing their audiences' longing for the homeland and ridiculing Tejana/o code-switching were clearly not going back to Mexico. Onstage, new ways of thinking about citizenship and belonging were emerging. In 1939, for example, Netty and Jesús Rodríguez's variety company debuted a humorous *revista* (one-act musical revue) at the Nacional written by Astol and Carlos Rodríguez-Valero, the comic dandy Don Suave, titled *Votamos o nos botan*, "Let's Vote, or They'll Kick Us Out." According to *La Prensa*, the piece was "inspired by current events that are developing in Exterior Mexico with the desire that our *colonia* participate in the presidential elections."[15] This effort may seem unsurprising, but it is striking when placed in the context of the Rodríguez duo's earlier comedy. In a series of dialogues that the couple recorded for the Blue Bird and Vocalion labels between 1928 and 1937, partisan jokes about Mexican political figures occur frequently, but references to formal U.S. politics do not. Commentary on social conditions in the United States, however, became prominent in the couple's recorded work beginning in the mid-1930s. In these later dialogues, repatriation figures prominently. Several highlighted the suffering of deportees and their families and the abuses of immigration law enforcement. At the same time, they urged Mexicans to escape the consumerist anomie and topsy-turvy gender relations of the United States by returning home to *"la tierra de María Santísima"* (the land of the most Holy Virgin) where love and patriarchy still reigned.[16] For those who remained, hard work and good behavior, rather than collective action, were the answer. In this context the novelty of *Votamos o nos botan* becomes clear.[17]

In some ways, this program continued the *costumbrista* (folkloric) nationalism of the Rodríguezes' previous work.[18] Its musical score, according to the newspaper, centered on the popular song "Guadalajara." Furthermore, its comic scenes played themselves out before a backdrop painted by Jesús showing the sun setting between the volcanoes Popocatépetl and Ixtaccíhuatl as Aztec nobles bowed in worship. All of these details gave the *revista* what *La Prensa*'s correspondent called an *"intenso sabor mexicano"* (intense Mexican flavor). Clearly neither performers nor audience saw anything contradictory about the juxtaposition of these visual symbols of Mexican nationalism with calls to active citizenship in the United States. Although the 1939 *revista* may have represented a shift in political orientation, its title's darkly humorous reference to the repatriation campaigns of the preceding decade suggests that performers and audience knew that their shift from denizenship to citizenship was occurring under duress.

In the first full year of the war, San Antonio's Mexicana/o artists added benefit performances for causes linked to the war effort to their usual schedule of commercial appearances. While Jesús Rodríguez recovered from an illness in a private hospital, Netty and Don Suave alternated between tours outside of town and a regular gig as midnight entertainers at the Zaragoza, where they often partnered with visiting Mexican artists in providing warm-up entertainment for film screenings. Their performances appear to have been showcases of "typical" Mexican music and dance and broad comedy in the style that immigrant artists had maintained in the city for over twenty years but with greater emphasis on music. On January 17, 1942, the performers appeared with other San Antonio notables in a midnight benefit show at the Nacional for the singer Esperanza Espino.[19] Then, beginning in February, the duo shared the stage with the legendary Lydia Mendoza both at the Zaragoza and at an anniversary banquet for *La Prensa*.[20] After returning from a tour in March, the duo joined with Espino and the singing duo Lauro y Lola at the Zaragoza and at an April 15 benefit for the Red Cross at the Nacional.[21] Appearances with Lydia Mendoza and her family continued through June, when the magician "El Caballero Rosas" performed with Netty and Don Suave, first at the Zaragoza and then at a late June program for soldiers at the city's USO building.[22] Later, the duo shared the stage with a musical group known as the Trío Dragones who performed numerous stage shows and private parties to much critical acclaim before

Figure 7.2. José Abreu performs on the high wire, late 1930s, as a member of the Carpa Cubana, owned by his parents, Virgilio and Federica Abreu. (Virgilio Abreu was born in Cuba.) José Abreu was killed in action in Italy on July 8, 1944. Hertzberg Circus Collection of the Witte Museum, San Antonio, Texas.

returning to Mexico in July.[23] In July, after a few appearances at private parties and benefits, Jesús Rodríguez resurfaced at the Nacional in a lavish midnight performance that included an original *revista* of his own composition, along with the film *Mi General Pistolas*. The *revista*'s title was *Matrimonio, Estilo 1942*.[24]

Even though live performers were increasingly reduced to supplemental entertainment for film screenings at the Lucchese theaters, numerous local artists formed new touring variety companies in 1942. In June Lydia Mendoza and her brothers and sisters performed for several weeks at the Zaragoza before setting off on a tour of South and West Texas.[25] Five months later, the U.S.-born children of Micaela González, an immigrant performer who had arrived in San Antonio in the 1910s, formed the company "Las Perlitas y Ramirín." Featuring musical clown Ramiro ("Ramirín") González-González and with his brothers and sisters, the company debuted at the Nacional on November 2 before setting out on a tour of small towns in South and West Texas.[26] Ramirín would soon take his musical bottles and frying pans to the stage of the Teatro Hispano in New York with La Chata Noloesca's company, and he appeared frequently with her and with other noted San Antonio artists during the 1940s. "Discovered" by Hollywood after the war, he played supporting roles in numerous U.S. films and television shows during the next forty years under the name Pedro González-González, a name he adopted in part because English-speaking audiences found "Pedro" easier to remember than "Ramiro."[27] He is best remembered for his appearances as a comic "Mexican sidekick" in such John Wayne vehicles as *Rio Bravo*, and although many of his roles seem demeaning and stereotypical today, some Mexican American actors in Hollywood see him as a pioneer. Although San Antonio's commercial Spanish-language stage produced numerous notable and talented actors and musicians, no other performer enjoyed González's modest level of success in the U.S. film industry.

Finally, on November 2, 1942, a new company starring Esperanza Espino and Don Suave debuted at the Zaragoza.[28] In the remaining years of the war, we hear less of Netty and Jesús, although Don Suave's name appears continuously in announcements of daily variety acts. In these new variety companies, as with several that followed in 1943 and 1944, music seems to have become the show's central focus, while sketch comedy increasingly played a supporting role. Espino's group held down the stage at the Zaragoza until May 1943.[29] In July la Chata Noloesca's company returned, playing regularly through December.[30]

In 1944 military themes and wartime demands on U.S. residents gained prominence on the city's stages, as old favorites reorganized in new companies performed night after night at the Zaragoza. Even though many of the immigrant performers who dominated the Zaragoza and Nacional were past military age, the war touched their lives. This was particularly true of Jesús and Carlos Rodríguez-Valero, whose younger brother Enrique was naturalized at sea in 1943 after initially enlisting in the Army Corps of Engineers.[31] In April 1944, San Antonio's Mexicana/o theater community, long accustomed to holding benefit performances for charitable causes, organized the midnight debut of Lalo Astol's revista *Con sangre y con arena* (*With Blood and with Sand*) in support of a blood drive by the Red Cross.[32] Three months later, an even more ambitious benefit took place, this time aimed at encouraging San Antonio's *colonia mexicana*, or Mexican community, to buy war bonds. Instead of buying tickets for this midnight function at the Nacional, audience members were required to buy either an $18.75 bond for double admission or a $1.50 war stamp for single admission. This vast difference in contributions surely reflects the stark and long-standing economic stratification of the Nacional's audience. Beginning with a parade of soldiers and WACS, the eclectic program starred dancers Estrella Morales and Julio Cervantes and culminated in the screening of the film *El pecado de una madre* (*A Mother's Sin*). Music and dance ranged from a Liszt nocturne to an Afro-Cuban number titled "Bim, Bam, Bum." In what would seem a particularly jarring moment, a piano rendition of Wagner's "Ride of the Valkyries" preceded a dance number set to the popular samba "Tico Tico Tico." Surely the highlight of the evening was a comic sketch, apparently about the making of the night's film. Titled "En Hollywood," it featured local actors impersonating the transplanted Mexican film stars Dolores del Río and Arturo de Córdova.[33]

With this event, San Antonio's Mexicana/o stage clearly reached the moment described by Tomás Ybarra-Frausto "when the screen extolled the triumphs of the Escuadrón 201 . . . [and] the *tandas de variedad* [variety shows] included patriotic routines of khaki-clad performers singing '*Me voy de soldado razo*.'"[34] Interviews with performers echo Ybarra-Frausto's observation that "rousing finales always included the presentation of both the Mexican and the American flags." What is striking, however, is the variety of interpretations performers assign to that juxtaposition. For Carlos Monsiváis of the Carpa Monsiváis, for example, the flag display referred to the fact that "*somos Mexicanos.* . . . *Pero le daban respeto a* United States" (we're Mexicans. . . . But they gave respect to the United States).[35] Other performers have suggested that the juxtaposition meant allegiance to rather than respect for the United States, along with recognition of a Mexican heritage. The interpretations do not stop there, and they certainly do not stop with what performers are willing to say on tape. What is clear is that the openness of the variety show format allowed *artistas* to bring together disparate elements without imposing a common interpretive framework, allowing for multiple meanings. Furthermore, the presentation of the two flags suggests a community moving toward a "both-and" rather than an "either-or" understanding of its relationship to Mexico and the United States.

On the economic side, however, less flexibility was possible. After years of organizing benefit performances for individual artists, Mexicana/o-controlled private charitable causes, and home-country infrastructure, the Spanish-language theater now channeled the community's voluntary contributions directly to the U.S. war apparatus and Red Cross. Given this fact, it is interesting to note that there is no mention in the Spanish-language press of any special theatrical performances to mark the war's end in August 1945. Daily variety shows continued after the end of the war at the Zaragoza with a company headed by Lauro "El Gordo" Jiménez, while a large group headed by the actor Donato visited the Nacional from August 11 through 19.[36] The only real novelty after the war's end is the phasing out of daily variety acts at the Zaragoza. From July 29 of that year through August 25, its advertisements for films contain no announcements of live entertainment, and more such gaps would follow in the months and years to come. Whether this was a simple business decision on management's part or whether the content of the live shows themselves were in some way at issue we will never know.

Ideology and Mexicano Entrepreneurs
at the San Antonio Municipal Auditorium

The year 1944 also saw the emergence of a decidedly new dynamic of competition in San Antonio's Mexicana/o entertainment industry. On January 9 a large advertisement in *La Prensa* announced that a "rain of stars" would fall on the city's Municipal Auditorium, courtesy of entrepreneur Raoul A. Cortez and radio personality Ramiro "Dr. Nopal" Cortés. To celebrate the ninth anniversary of their program *La Hora Comercial Mexicano* (The Mexican Commercial Hour) on radio station KMAC, the duo would bring to San Antonio a cavalcade of Mexican film idols and recording artists on Tuesday, January 25, and Thursday, January 27, 1944. The lineup included the actor and composer Joaquín Pardavé, singer Esther Fernández, the *son jarocho* stylings of the Hermanas Huesca, the one-armed guitarist Victor Manuel, and many more.[37] For the city's *colonia mexicana*, the Municipal Auditorium had been a familiar gathering place since its dedication in 1926. An ornate Spanish Colonial Revival building seating 6,500, it housed numerous artistic programs organized to celebrate the Mexican independence day, *el diez y seis de septiembre*, and el Día de la Raza (what is observed as "Columbus Day" in the Anglophone United States) throughout the 1930s. Mutual aid societies, labor unions, and other organizations regularly used the auditorium for social events. In one famous 1939 incident, mob violence erupted after the city granted the Communist Party permission to use the facility. And if the quantity of advertising is any indication, wrestling and boxing matches there attracted a substantial Mexicana/o following. In some cases, prestigious theater troupes from Mexico such as the Virginia Fábregas company had performed at the auditorium in the past, and opera companies also used the facility. But allowing for hucksterism, Cortés and Cortez could justly claim that this celebration was *"sin precedente en San Antonio"* (without precedent in San Antonio).

Negotiations about the program may have lasted until practically the last minute, for it was not until January 16, nine days before the event, that *La Prensa* announced in a brief front-page story that Mario Moreno "Cantinflas" himself would appear at the auditorium.[38] On Sunday, January 23, 1944, a story in *La Prensa* added more artists to the program, including Edmundo Santos, a Mexican-born actor known for supplying the voices for the dubbed versions of Disney films distributed in the Spanish-speaking world.[39] The Lucchese enterprise responded quickly to this challenge. That Sunday, *La Prensa*'s readers also learned that singer and film idol Pedro Infante along with the Trío Janitzio would grace the stages of the Nacional and Guadalupe Theaters on Tuesday, January 25, and Friday, January 28.[40] The program at the Lucchese theaters included a screening of the Infante vehicle *Jesusita en Chihuahua*. Fans of Mexican cinema and music faced an enviable dilemma: whether to see Pedro Infante at the Nacional, the variety company of Polo Guerrero at the Zaragoza, or an enormous program featuring Cantinflas at the Municipal Auditorium.

The Luccheses, as mentioned earlier, had established their dominance in San Antonio's Mexicana/o theater industry by traveling directly to Mexico to recruit talent, bypassing their Mexican immigrant artist-managers. Suddenly in 1944, they found themselves in competition with the emerging Mexicana/o middle class. No doubt recognizing that they could not top the Lucchese theaters in daily entertainment, Cortés and Cortez continued to supplement the commercial success and public impact of their radio venture during and after the war by bringing occasional extravagant showcases of Mexican film and music stars to the Municipal Auditorium. Cortez applied for an FCC license for the Spanish-language radio station KCOR during the war, citing the station's value in raising support for the war effort in San Antonio's Mexican *colonia*. The Federal Communications Commission, however, did not grant the request until 1946.[41]

The shows in the Auditorium appear not to have followed a regular schedule. After their initial success with Cantinflas and company, Cortés and Cortez sponsored what appears to have been an equally successful appearance by the Ecuadorian-born ventriloquist Paco Miller, the singer "La Panchita," and an orchestra of eighty musicians in February.[42] In mid-May the film stars Pedro Armendáriz, Jorge Negrete, and Gloria Marín filled the Auditorium.[43] After touring Houston and the Coastal Bend, Miller and his group returned on May 22 and 23. After this rush of major programs, there followed a lull of several months, broken only by what appears to have been a less spectacular presentation in October.[44] Then, in 1945, Pedro Infante appeared at the Municipal Auditorium on January 14 and 15, headlining an extravagant program.[45] The duo's next big show did not come until September, when the famous Roberto Soto's "folkloric" company filled the Auditorium from the twenty-first through the twenty-third. An extravaganza featuring the actress Mapy Cortés, along with the Trío Calaveras, Amelia Wilhelmy, and many other notables followed in late November.[46] These irregular dates suggest a strategy that depended on filling a large performance space for occasional special events. Although the focus was always on the glitz and glamour of Mexico City stardom and the romantic nationalism of "typical" music and dance, the war and its aftermath were never far from the minds of performers and audience alike. In prepa-

Figure 7.3. Exterior of the Teatro Nacional, 1937, San Antonio, Texas. Standing on the western edge of downtown, at the corner of Commerce and Santa Rosa Streets, it had been the city's premier venue for live Spanish-language theater since 1917. In the 1940s it became more of a movie house than a performance venue. Zintgraff Studio Photograph Collection, University of Texas at San Antonio, Libraries Special Collections.

ration for his appearance at the Municipal Auditorium, for example, Cantinflas and his fellow *artistas* paraded through San Antonio's streets on military jeeps, encouraging the public to buy war bonds and receiving applause throughout the city.[47] This episode places both the increasing militarization of Mexicana/o claims to U.S. citizenship and the continued engagement of Mexican Americans with Mexico's official culture in stark relief.

In addition to being a venue for commercial extravaganzas and celebrations of the *fiestas patrias*, the Municipal Auditorium also hosted artistic and ceremonial expressions of the Mexicana/o community's commitment to the war effort. Notable among these was the swearing-in of the all-Latina Benito Juárez Air-WAC squadron that occurred on March 26, 1944. The campaign to recruit women in San Antonio and other parts of southern Texas for the squadron appears to have been vigorous. In addition to blanketing the Spanish-language press with advertisements, the army established a recruiting tent on Alamo Plaza and a booth in the Teatro Nacional specifically for the squadron.[48] This may well be the first case of a U.S. military recruiting presence in a theater catering to Mexicana/os in Texas. According to *La Prensa*, the first two San Antonio enlistees in this squadron, Francisca Fierros and Dora Salas, joined with the explicit goal of avenging the deaths of friends on the front.[49] Fierros already worked at Kelly Field when she was accepted as a WAC.[50] The artistic program for the swearing-in, which included Spanish dancers, a song performance by Lydia Mendoza, piano music by Luis Dorantes, and a dance number by the duo Johnnie and Evon, attracted such enthusiastic applause that several performers were obliged to repeat their numbers. Because of its artistic success and the distinguished retinue of guests from as far away as Monterrey, Nuevo León, *La Prensa*'s reporter characterized the ceremony as *"una verdadera comunión espiritual de las dos razas"* (a true spiritual communion of the two races).[51] Presumably, the two "races" in question were "white (Anglo)" and "Mexican." As the historian Leisa Meyer has noted, the army relied heavily on reports of this ceremony, and of others like it, for women of other colonized and minoritized communities, to project a public image of an all-inclusive Women's Army Corps.[52] Theatrical activity and civic ceremony in spaces like the Municipal Auditorium contributed to that effort, symbolically resolving the contradiction between capital's need for a diverse, racially stratified labor force and the state's need "to constitute a homogeneous nation with a unified culture."[53]

The Carpas: From *Los files* to *las filas*

Given the increasing involvement of San Antonio's commercial theater industry with the war effort during the 1940s, it is striking that there is little evidence for similar engagement by the *carpas*. Tent show performers interviewed for this project do not describe benefit shows pushing war bonds or presentations by military recruiters or consular officials. They do, however, describe experiences that were common to musicians, actors, and other working performers all over the country: a struggle to maintain their craft at a time of total social mobilization for war. This is not to say that no such collaboration ever occurred in the *carpas* but rather that other dynamics are more prominent in the memories of a small selection of tent show performers and in the written historical record that is available.

One example is the experience of the best known and most prestigious tent show company in San Antonio, the Carpa Cubana. This company faced severe losses of its own during the war. Owned by the Cuban-born Virgilio Abreu and his wife, Federica, the Cuban Show appears to have been most active during the 1920s. Business records that survive from the company are most complete for the years 1925 and 1926, with nothing later than 1938. From press coverage, it is known that the company toured the Rio Grande Valley in 1939 and performed in San Antonio in January 1941 after a tour through the Texas Hill Country, west of the city, but the extent to which performances continued after that year is difficult to determine.[54] It is known, however, that the Abreus lost their son José (Joe), a wire walker, to the war. After reaching the rank of sergeant in the 88th Division of the army's 6th Infantry Brigade, the younger Abreu died in action in Italy on July 8, 1944, leaving behind his parents and a son, Ramón.[55] Notices of requiem masses in his memory appear in *La Prensa* in 1945 and 1946.[56]

Unlike the Abreus, the five Mexican-born sons of Ysavel Monsiváis who formed the core of the Carpa Monsiváis lost no one to the war itself. But in a 1999 interview, comedian Carlos Monsiváis reported that his family was compelled to participate in military support industries at home:

> *El cuarenta y dos paramos completamente porque no había ya chance de mover el negocio tocante a la que el gobierno estaba exigiendo que fuéramos a cumplir con los trabajos que ellos nos iban a imponer. Nos iban a llevar a la fábrica donde estaban fabricando carpas pa'l gobierno. Pa' mandarlas para donde estaban peleando. Porque mi hermano hacía eso. Hacía carpas y nosotros le ayudábamos a hacer el trabajo. Y nos daban trabajo el gobierno con él haciendo ese trabajo. Eso fue . . . ya cuando empezó Alemania a pelearle a la guerra grande. Ya no pudimos . . . nos separaron.*

(In forty-two we stopped completely, because there was no chance to move the business because of what the government was demanding, that we go do the jobs that they were going to impose on us. They were going to take us to the factory where they were making tents for the government. To send them to where they were fighting. Because my brother did that. He made tents and we all helped to do the job. And the government gave us work with him, doing that job. That was . . . when Germany started to fight the big war. We just couldn't do it anymore. They separated us.)[57]

Although Monsiváis was unable to provide specific information about the tent manufacturer that employed him and his brothers, his story was not an uncommon one for actors and musicians. In October 1942, a so-called Work or Fight order from the Selective Service System directed local draft boards to review the deferments of men younger than thirty-eight who worked in jobs deemed unessential to the war effort. Such men faced the choice of enlisting or working in war industries on the home front.[58] Although this order provoked protest throughout the country and although unionized performers in some areas successfully resisted misapplications of it, a lone family of *carperos* and *carperas* in Texas would likely not have been in a position to defy a draft board consisting of men who were used to disposing of Mexicana/o labor.[59] Some members of the Monsiváis family settled in the small town of Kenedy, pouring foundations and building up walls around the Airstream trailers in which they had lived while touring. After the war, they bought projectors and used their tent to show films, sometimes performing locally in benefits for the American GI Forum, the organization that pioneered the militarization of Mexican American civil rights claims after the war. And during the war, Carlos Monsiváis took it upon himself to record on paper the sketches, dialogues, and songs that his family had performed all over Texas. The family business never recovered.

One of the few *carpa* companies that remained active during and after the war was the Carpa Hermanos García. Founded by Saltillo-born Manuel García and his wife, Teresa González de García, the *carpa* went through many names during the early decades of the twentieth century. By 1941, according to don Manuel's son Rodolfo, the couple's U.S.-born children were the mainstays of the show, and the family moved from San Antonio to Corpus Christi. In many ways the Carpa García's program resembled the *variedades* in more prestigious venues. During the war, García's little nephew Manuel Jr. ("Meme") charmed audiences by singing "Soldado razo" in a tiny military uniform. Such an early introduction to the stage was commonplace for members of *carpa* families, but García himself did not take to the stage until his early twenties. Born in 1917, García was of military age during the war, and though he reports receiving a draft notice, he was disqualified from military service for reasons he was never willing to discuss. Because his brother Manolo, father of "Meme," who had previously been the comedian for the show, was needed at the piano, García assumed the role of comedian. His character, don Fito, epitomized the urban *"pelado"* stereotype, drawing style and language from the young pachucos of Corpus Christi's Agnes Street.

After entering the stage *a resbalas* (slipping and falling) and trading jokes with the master of ceremonies, García usually ended his act with a song parody. Among his parodies was a version of the 1942 Pedro Flores composition "La despedida," which was popularized by the Puerto Rican singer Daniel Santos. Popular in South Texas, both on the stage and on the radio, the song presents a soldier's tender farewell to friends, his beloved, and his mother. One of Santos's greatest hits, the song remains an icon of the U.S. Latina/o experience in World War II to this day. Ironically, there are reports that the U.S. government censored it in Puerto Rico because it inspired nostalgia in troops of Latin American origin.[60] Although García's memory of his own parody was incomplete, those portions he could recall make its general thrust clear.

Vengo a decirle adios	(I come to say goodbye
A mi librada	To my live-in girlfriend.
Porque pronto me voy	Because soon I'm off
Para las pizcas.	To the cotton harvest.
Y aunque vaya a pizcar	And though I'm going to pick cotton
En otros pueblos	In other towns,
Da dan da da dan da da dam	Da dan da da dan da da dam
Da da da da da dam.	Da da da da da dam.
Yo ya me despedí	Now I have said goodbye
De mi librada	To my live-in girlfriend
Y le pedí por Dios	And I ask her by God
Que nunca llore	Not to cry,
Que recuerde por siempre	That she always remember
La pantera que yo le di a ella	The beating that I gave her)[61]

This reference to domestic violence is jarring to the contemporary reader, and it is not the only such reference in García's repertoire. In general, these parodies replace flowery love lyrics with gritty, grotesque scenes of love gone wrong, and there is a misogynist edge to many of them. In this particular parody, the speaker performs the full dance of bad qualities that native elites and foreign bigots have assigned to the lower-class Mexican man. Here, in other words, García's character was perhaps more the cruel, lazy, half-wild *"pelado"* than the sympathetic *"peladito"* popularized by Cantinflas. Where the speaker of Flores's original is an upstanding, duty-bound young soldier called to leave behind his mother and his lady love, the speaker of García's parody is an abusive brute leaving his illegitimate domestic partner behind for the cotton harvest. Here the militarized rhetoric that both the United States and Mexico used to dress up the Bracero Program, casting agricultural workers as "soldiers in the fields," finds itself reduced to absurdity. The irony would not have been lost on an audience caught between the Scylla of *"las filas"* (the ranks) and the Charybdis of *"los files"* (the fields).

When he performed the parody in the *carpa*, García often accompanied it with a joke that highlighted his audiences' understandings of militarized masculinity and used verbal taboos to highlight the incommunicable trauma of combat.

—Marchen. One two three Marchen. Uno dos tres cuatro.—'Ora sí ya estamos. En estos momentos vamos a entrar en combate. Y quiero que todos mis soldados estén listos para atacar el enemigo.
Y luego llega el sargento y dice
—Capitán capitán . . .
—Cállese la boca. ¿Que no ve que estoy tomando lista con mis soldados que vamos a entrar en acción?
—Pero es muy importante lo que yo quiero decirle mi capitán.
—A ver. ¿Qué quiere decirme?
—Los soldados como nunca han estado en combate. Quieren saber a qué huele la sangre.
Y luego voltea el capitán y dice
—¿Qué? ¿Qué dice?
—Los soldados quieren saber a qué huele la sangre porque nunca han estado en combate.
Y el capitán muy enojado le dice
—Huele a . . . cagada
Luego dice
—Ay capitán entonces ya estamos todos heridos.
'Taban heridos . . .

("March. One two three march. One two three four.
"Now we're here. In these moments we're going to be in combat. And I want all my soldiers to be ready to attack the enemy."
Then the sergeant comes and says
"Captain Captain . . ."
"Shut your mouth. Can't you see my soldiers that we're going to go into action?"
"But it's very important what I want to tell you, Captain."
"Let's see. What do you want to tell me?"
"The soldiers since they haven't been in combat. They want to know what blood smells like."
And then the Captain turns and says
"What? What did you say?"
"The soldiers want to know what blood smells like because they've never been in combat."

And the captain real angry says to him
"It smells like . . . shit."
Then he says
"Ay Captain why we're all wounded then all of us."
They were wounded . . .)[62]

Motivated by a fear that contrasts with the ideal of militarized masculinity, the soldiers here ask their captain a question that has no answer. No human language can convey the particularities of smell in detail, and lacking appropriate words, we must all rely on comparisons when trying to make unfamiliar scents intelligible. But the question of what blood smells like is more than a request for information. Here the smell stands for the experience of combat itself, which words and even memories similarly fail to capture.

Furthermore, when the soldiers misunderstand their captain's sarcastic retort and admit to having fouled their pants, they draw attention not only to their fear, but to the anus itself, a vulnerable point that male primary group talk in greater Mexico acknowledges only through double entendres and tortured silence. Just as the postwar South Texas *carnales* (buddies) famously described by Limón used anal humor to highlight the ways that more powerful social actors "screwed" them,[63] García's fictional soldiers draw attention to a vulnerability that is as stigmatized as it is unavoidable. The joke thus invites the audience both to mock the soldiers with laughter and to covertly identify with their failings. The captain's response is harsh, particularly because words related to the verb *cagar* bear a strong taboo in Spanish. In interviews, and in narratives he recorded on his own, García never uses the word without an apology or a guilty laugh. Furthermore, his performances of other parodies, jokes, and sketches across multiple interviews show some signs of self-censorship. In this joke, however, *"cagada"* occurs without comment across multiple tellings. Clearly the word matters.

Fidelity to the stereotype of the abusive army officer is one likely reason for this. More important, the use of *"cagada"* violates the implicit understanding of *respeto* (respect) between performer and audience that made it taboo. In a theatrical genre known for lightness and frivolity, the shock of such a breach would likely have communicated something about the trauma of combat that respectful words could not. The coward-soldiers of the joke are thus ambivalent figures. In time of war, the coward is to be ridiculed, of course, but by foregrounding cowardice and anal vulnerability, the joke highlights "the total human being" for which neither militarized consciousness nor abstract citizenship has room.[64] For an audience whose sons and daughters, both in the *filas* and in the *files*, became instruments of grand designs animated by appeals to abstract loyalties and hatreds, the joke and the parody exposed the seamy side of patriotism and military discipline, exploiting gaps in the disembodied ideal of militarized masculinity.

Conclusion: Incorporation and Ambivalence

Such moments of rupture are notable, and the fact that they occur in the Mexicana/o theater world's most marginalized sector is likely no accident. Together with the ambiguities surrounding appeals to U.S. citizenship in the wartime *revistas*, they show a population engaged in a multivocal process of negotiating its relationship to the U.S. state and capital during the 1940s. In this process the symbolic repertoire of exile nationalism found itself not replaced but repurposed and redirected. With Mexico an official ally in the war and suspicion of Mexicana/o collaboration with Germany muted, the signs of the former country's official culture were, like able-bodied men, available for service. Of course, nobody forgot about the inequalities staring them in the face. For the Westside women who joined the Benito Juárez squadron, however, the deaths of neighbors half a world away and the lure of jobs at Kelly Field must have overshadowed the daily humiliation of segregation and memories of Texas Ranger terror farther south.

As theaters where artists had once raised funds for the Mexican Blue Cross directed their efforts toward war bonds, they were following a public that was moving steadily into the orbit of the U.S. war machine. And given the threat that the Axis powers represented, it is easy to understand this move. The generation of Mexican Americans who came of age during and after World War II is often seen as assimilationist, eager to abandon its cultural identity in a quest for full U.S. citizenship. But an examination of Mexicana/o theater in San Antonio during the war suggests an alternate interpretation. San Antonio's wartime stage did not suppress the trappings of Mexican nationalism in the name of full membership in the polity. Instead, it converted them into appendages of the war effort and emblems of militarized U.S. citizenship. In this process, militarized spectacles of ethnic distinctiveness offered a symbolic resolution to the contradiction between capital's demand for Mexicana/o labor and the state's demand for cultural homogeneity. And if Cantinflas, the embodiment of the Mexican outsider, was to be found in a Jeep urging fans to contribute to the war effort, then was there really any "outside" left?

CHAPTER 8

"Con dolor de corazón":
Militarization and Transracial Recognition among Mexican Americans and Filipinos in the Bataan Death March

JORDAN BELTRÁN GONZALES

Memory, Spectacle, and Farce in Bataan Death March Commemorations

Since 1989 veterans of World War II in the Philippines, as well as their descendants and supporters, have gathered annually in southern New Mexico for the Bataan Memorial March. Part ceremony honoring soldiers who died in the Bataan Death March and as prisoners of war, part oral history recollection by military veterans, and also a test of physical endurance, this weekend of events takes place on the dusty desert trails of White Sands Missile Range, located northeast of Las Cruces and approximately fifty miles north of El Paso, Texas. On March 28, 2011, more than six thousand participants crossing the starting line at dawn were greeted by hundreds of cheering volunteers, families, and friends—including ten World War II veterans. But despite the festive atmosphere, the event casts a somber and elegiac tone of remembrance on the "Battling Bastards of Bataan," a popular reference to the 200th/515th Coast Artillery regiments of the New Mexico National Guard.[1] In these contemporary depictions of the legendary soldiers and their experiences, however, much of their emotional depth, vulnerability, and psychological suffering remain effaced. Through this symbolic memorial, emotional tributes, and kitschy bracelets and T-shirts, this event commodifies and reifies the Bataan Death March and thus places another layer of violence atop those who actually experienced it in the 1940s.

That is, the recognition of New Mexico's military contributions creates a spectacle that lacks attention to more complex histories and inadvertently approaches farce, or mockery, of the seriousness of the events. Indeed, it features a perverse romanticized reenactment of the April 1942 forced march of Filipino and U.S. soldiers: participants engage in a seven-hour run/walk across the arid desert of southern New Mexico that is supposed to somehow relate to the ordeal that the soldiers endured in the war-torn, tropical jungles of the Bataan peninsula on the island of Luzon.

The reenactment overlooks the compelling experiences of the young men who joined the U.S. military in the wake of the Great Depression, including the approximately 480 Hispano-Americanos, referred to herein as Mexican Americans, or Manitos,[2] who were sent from New Mexico to the Philippines in September 1941. Since the early 1900s, the term *Hispano-Americano* conveyed a growing "Spanish American" consciousness and relieved Nuevomexicanos of the "Mexican" label that white Americans had used to disparage them. Yet for this chapter, I employ the term *Mexican American* to acknowledge the significance of race as an organizing principle for economic and social conditions in New Mexico in the 1930s; the legacy of U.S. colonization of the Southwest affected how Mexican Americans experienced their race, class, and gender in ways that were distinct from Anglo-Americans, or whites, before, during, and after World War II.[3] The young men were sent from New Mexico to the Philippines in September 1941. In total, the New Mexico National Guard accounted for approximately one in nine U.S. soldiers—1,462 of an estimated 12,500 U.S. soldiers in the Philippines—and New Mexico was more highly represented than any other state.[4] Ultimately, 687 of these 1,462 New Mexicans—47 percent of the entire regiment—died during the fighting, on the death march, or as POWs.[5]

What has frequently been described as "loyal" or "heroic" military service in the war against Japan is only part of these complex stories. The other part, which has garnered far less attention, involves the personal and descriptive oral histories that offer a richer understanding of social and economic factors that affected how New Mexicans in general and Mexican Americans from New Mexico in particular experienced World War II. This essay draws on four videotaped interviews in the World War II collection of the Voces Oral History Project—Lorenzo Banegas, José Fuljencio Martinez, Ralph Rodriguez, and Agapito Silva—to argue that their participation as soldiers stemmed from the U.S. military's foothold in New Mexico and that their perspectives as Manitos influenced how they interacted with Filipinos during the war. Their stories uncover the U.S. military presence in the early lives of these New Mexicans, the economic hardship in the 1930s that made the monthly military stipend an attractive option, racial solidarity with Filipinos who were similarly conscripted into U.S. military service, and Banegas's emotional *corrido* of vulnerability and melancholy that he sang in POW camps in the Philippines and Japan.

These interviews illustrate how New Mexican military service during World War II, and especially during the Bataan Death March, illuminates the role of ideology, interpellation, and militarized citizenship among subaltern populations. Indeed, ideological constraints affected Mexican Americans and Filipinos, both of whom were racialized subjects thrust into a U.S. military project of defending the Philippines, which had become a U.S. territory after the Spanish-American War that ended in 1898. Through their actions and reflections, we begin to understand how these Mexican Americans acknowledged and created particular meanings in the expectations placed on them by their families, the state, the military, and even themselves. Louis Althusser has noted that subjects are formed, or interpellated, in relation to both ideological and repressive institutions, and these male soldiers complicate this process before and during the war. Mexican Americans, as well as other racial minority veterans, were tremendously influenced by ideologies of patriotism and military service, which also made them complicit with the U.S. military buildup in the Philippines.[6] This militarization involved the physical military structures and programs that facilitated the recruitment, training, and overall construction of the U.S. military's numerous projects within and beyond New Mexico, as well as the ideology of colonialism in which the U.S. military is actually rooted.[7] More important, these firsthand accounts push us to reconsider the ways in which these soldiers were not simply pawns in a militarized social system. Rather, they show their agency as they reflect on their own situation and survival, both physically and spiritually. That is, these soldiers forged new liminal identities as "Mexipinos" even as they retained their individual Mexican American and Filipino identities. Their postwar interviews reveal how their citizenship had been militarized even as they resiliently reclaimed it in a variety of empowering ways.

Mexipino Identities: Ethnicity and Overlapping Colonial Histories in the U.S. Territory of the Philippines

The Filipinos and the Hispanos had similar historical roots.[8] As a result of Spain's history in the U.S. Southwest, Mexico, and the Philippines, many New Mexicans and Filipinos spoke and understood Spanish.[9] Similarly, the Catholic Church and Catholicism played a central role in both cultures.[10] In essence, the untold story is how the presence of Mexican Americans in the Philippines is part of a complex layering of competing colonial empires, each of which profited from dark-skinned and indigenous peoples, sources of cheap labor and cannon fodder. The colonial relationship between the

United States and the Philippines and the militarization of Filipino identity, culture, and masculinity inform the experiences of Mexican Americans in the Philippines. Soldiers from both backgrounds inevitably were placed in similar circumstances, which led to a multiplicity of interactions and mutual identifications, all of which ultimately complicate Mexican American and Filipino soldiers' identities.

World War II in the Philippines represented multiple colonial histories. For nearly three and a half centuries, from 1561 to 1898, Spain laid claim to the land, resources, and then-autonomous indigenous ethnic groups who lived throughout the seven-thousand-island archipelago. In June 1898 Filipinos declared independence from Spain, but the United States refused to recognize the Philippine Republic as an independent nation. In December 1898, under the terms of the Treaty of Paris that followed the Spanish-American War, Spain ceded the Philippines to the United States in exchange for $20 million. The United States then promised a colonial project that would, in theory, transition the Philippines from an unincorporated territory into an independent nation.[11] Then, in February 1899, the United States invaded the Philippines and sparked the Philippine-American War, which decimated the Philippine population until fighting formally ended in 1902, although some scholars assert that guerrilla warfare continued until at least 1910.[12] For Filipinos, the spread of war in the 1940s to the Pacific fit into a pattern of European colonialism that had been established for centuries.

By December 1941 between 130,000 and 140,000 Filipinos already filled the growing ranks of the Philippine Army.[13] Throughout the war, moreover, between 200,000 and 300,000 Filipinos were inducted into the Philippine Army, many of whom enlisted seemingly in exchange for the promises of U.S. citizenship and veterans' recognition and benefits.[14] Due to the Philippines' status as a colony since 1902 and as a U.S. commonwealth after 1934, Filipinos had been U.S. "nationals," meaning that they were neither "aliens" nor "citizens." Following World War II, in January 1946, the Philippines gained formal independence through the Tydings-McDuffie Act, and Filipinos subsequently were categorized as "aliens."[15] To complicate matters for most Filipino *veteranos* after the war,[16] the attainment of U.S. citizenship and veterans' status became empty promises due to the 1946 Rescission Act. Passed by the U.S. Congress in February 1946, the act rescinded the promises of citizenship, veterans' status, and veterans' benefits for nearly all Filipinos. As a sleight-of-hand legal maneuver that eventually catalyzed decades of activism and campaigns on behalf of Filipino *veteranos*, the Rescission Act granted full veterans' status and the accompanying financial and medical benefits to only the surviving members of the Old Philippine Scouts,[17] who numbered fewer than twelve thousand, and to the few thousand Filipinos who had already extended their U.S. military service and pledged U.S. citizenship prior to December 1946.[18] The Rescission Act was finally lifted in 2009.

Militarized citizenship is a concept that describes how societal expectations of being patriotic and supporting the U.S. nation influenced citizens—or nationals, in the case of Filipinos—to serve in the military. Assessing the role of militarized citizenship for both Filipinos and Mexican Americans in the early 1940s requires us to understand how both groups related to the military. While Filipinos were explicitly deemed nationals and subjected to a persistent subordinate status through U.S. colonial policies and practices with the Philippines, Mexican Americans were effectively second-class citizens in the United States through a legacy of underdevelopment, unequal access to resources, and continued discrimination.[19] In the Philippines and in New Mexico, military service was a key example of how both Filipinos and Mexican Americans interpellated their perceived duties and responsibilities. Yet in the process of recognizing and acting on societal expectations to become soldiers, these groups claimed the role of subjects of empire and were complicit with the militarization of the Philippines. In an ironic twist, the similar subordinate status of Filipinos and Manitos was ultimately illuminated through the force of a competing empire—Japan—as it challenged the U.S. military's buildup in the Philippines.

Thus, as we return to the commemoration of the Bataan Death March survivors—who were captured after the Philippines fell from U.S. to Japanese control in March 1942—we need to attend to the complex racial and ethnic fusions, specifically, the ways Mexican American and Filipino soldiers identified with each other's background and circumstances. In one sense, this mutual identification of Mexican Americans as Asians also complicates convenient attempts to demonize Asian allies as absent, which the commemorations usually do in their effacement of Filipino allies and their portrayal of Asians as villains, such as the ever present representations of the Japanese atrocities committed by servicemen.[20]

"We had to just do with what we had": Chaos and U.S. Surrender in the Philippines

On December 8, 1941, only hours after Japan's air force bombed Pearl Harbor and two sites near Manila, its Imperial Army invaded Luzon.[21] Two weeks later, on December 22, regiments of Japan's Fourteenth Imperial Army landed in northwestern Luzon and began their trek toward southeastern Luzon and the Bataan peninsula. Japan's ground invasion prompted Filipino and U.S. soldiers on Luzon—estimated to be between 80,000 and 90,000 Filipinos[22] and roughly 12,500 U.S. soldiers—to begin mobilizing. Following orders from Gen. Douglas MacArthur, who commanded the Allied troops in the Pacific throughout World War II, Filipino and U.S. soldiers attempted to slow the Japanese forces until more reinforcements might arrive from the already depleted U.S. reserves and war chests.[23] Yet despite outnumbering the Japanese Army, the Filipino and U.S. soldiers were hamstrung by the loss of Allied planes in the Philippines, obsolete artillery equipment, limited supplies of ammunition, food, and medicine, and general confusion among officers and soldiers. Agapito Silva, who came from Gallup, New Mexico, and served in Battery "D" of the 200th Coast Artillery, summarized, "We had to just do with what we had."[24] In Battery D, there was familiarity and camaraderie; "about half and half" Mexican American and white. "That never kept us from speaking our language," Silva recalled. "We all looked after each other, especially during the Death March."[25]

Within two months, though, the greater numbers of Filipino and U.S. troops had still not deterred the advancing Japanese Army, which continued southward toward Manila and the Bataan peninsula. By mid-February 1942, the Battle of Bataan had escalated: U.S. and Filipino forces were backed onto the Bataan peninsula and faced the island of Corregidor in Manila Bay. For two months, from mid-February to April 9, 1942, Japan's regiments waged intense and prolonged fighting against several thousand soldiers from the U.S. Armed Forces of the Far East (USAFFE), several U.S. National Guard regiments, and tens of thousands more troops from the Philippine Scouts and the Philippine Army. The Philippines had represented a strategic location for U.S. foreign policy interests for the half century prior to World War II, but Pearl Harbor changed this role. After December 1941 the Philippines were a remote and inaccessible location for U.S. military support: the bombing of Pearl Harbor had decimated the naval fleet and resources had shifted to the war in Europe. Additional soldiers, ammunition, and resources never arrived at Bataan.[26] Without these resources, the Philippines were written off at this stage of the war.[27]

The ground invasion and the Battle of Bataan were a prelude to a major World War II trauma that began on April 9, 1942, an event subsequently known as the Bataan Death March. Finally, with his men out of munitions, food, and medication, U.S. Maj. Gen. Edward P. King surrendered. The

Japanese took as prisoners an estimated 67,000 to 78,000 Allied troops—between 55,000 and 66,000 Filipino soldiers[28] and 11,796 U.S. soldiers,[29] as well as thousands of Filipino civilian refugees.[30] Together, they faced constant threats of violence and the actuality of starvation, disease, and sheer exhaustion from Japanese soldiers. This infamous march went on for five days; the men struggled seventy-five miles, beginning at Mariveles, on the Bataan peninsula, and ending at Capas, near Camp O'Donnell and Camp Cabanatuan, two U.S. military supply bases. Less than one month later, on May 6, 1941, Filipino and U.S. soldiers, led by Gen. Jonathan M. Wainwright, capitulated on the nearby island of Corregidor, which represented the last U.S. military defense of the territorial capital and Manila Bay. Many of the prisoners of Bataan and Corregidor stayed at one of the two camps for the duration of the war; others were transferred to prison camps in China or Japan. Thousands of these soldiers died in April and May 1942 alone. At Camp O'Donnell and Camp Cabanatuan and, later, en route to and at other POW camps thousands more died.[31]

The demographics of ethnic representation in New Mexico's National Guard relate directly to militarized citizenship. The 200th Coast Artillery regiment was 33 percent Mexican American, 7 percent Native American, and 60 percent white.[32] At the beginning of the war, the average age among the four interviewees featured here was twenty-one; Matson, moreover, reports that the "majority of the men in the 200th were between twenty-three and twenty-seven at the time of the surrender."[33] Below I elaborate on some of the factors and institutions that led these Mexican Americans to join the 200th Coast Artillery.

The New Mexico Army National Guard and the Militarization of Mexican American Identity

The militarization of Manito citizenship included efforts to promote the military through education and leadership programs, publicity campaigns, and the draft. As they recounted their experiences, Silva, Rodriguez, and Martinez traced their decision to enter the military. Their respective paths arguably show as much about how they each entered the military as they reveal how the military entered their lives. Historical precedents for Mexican Americans in New Mexico's military, furthermore, trace back several wars and decades earlier. For example, New Mexico's National Guard was only the most recent iteration of militias and cavalries that preceded the territory's statehood in 1912. While the extent of the military's influence and pressure varied for each of these men, the theme of militarization in New Mexico is significant because the 200th Coast Artillery immediately began to train for the defense of the Philippines. In comparison to National Guard regiments from other states, the 200th Coast Artillery's extensive antiaircraft training set in motion its role against imminent Japanese air and ground forces.[34]

This chapter focuses on the perspectives of Mexican Americans by recovering previously unknown personal testimonies. Historical narratives of World War II and in particular the Bataan Death March are shaped by the concept of archival power, or the process by which archives are created and how they produce certain "facts" and narratives while obscuring other vantage points. Michel-Rolph Trouillot explains archival power as a phenomenon that leads to silences in historical narratives and, in turn, exposes the biases of historians, such as the dearth of attention to the experiences of Mexican American soldiers in World War II.[35] For this chapter, the Voces Oral History Project archive is vital in making these interviews available because most accounts of the Bataan Death March efface the racial minority presence. Among these profiles are similar attempts by the soldiers to reclaim and refashion their militarized citizenship in a context in which options were extremely limited both before and during the war.

Agapito Silva, for instance, who witnessed the bombardments of Corregidor firsthand before he was sent to Camp Cabanatuan and a POW camp in Omuta, Japan, reflected on the economic circumstances of his childhood during his videotaped interview. At ten years old, Agapito Silva and his parents and four siblings moved to Gallup, in northwestern New Mexico, after the Rio Grande again flooded their home in San Marcial, twenty miles south. Agapito's father, Mauricio, worked as a car inspector for the Santa Fe Railroad and his mother, Isabel Encinia Silva, took care of the household; young Agapito worked part-time taking and delivering orders at a grocery store to help with his family's income during the Great Depression. In 1939 Silva graduated from his local public high school. Military leadership training that Silva participated in as a high school student would influence his decision to join the military in 1941.

"I took military training back in 1937, when I was younger, at Fort Bliss [in El Paso, Texas]," Silva recalls. "I think I went for two years—1937 and 1938—and I guess that helped me when I joined the National Guard because they made me a corporal right away." This leadership training program took place during the summers before his junior and senior years in high school. Silva formally entered the army in late December 1939, then joined the 200th Coast Artillery when it was called to active duty in Jan-

Figure 8.1. Agapito Silva in August 1941, Fort Bliss, Texas, before departing for the Philippine Islands. Silva said that about half of his Battery D of the 200th Coast Artillery were Mexican American and the other half were white. And although the Mexican Americans spoke Spanish to one another, all the men "looked after each other, especially during the Death March." Voces Oral History Project, Nettie Lee Benson Latin American Collection, University of Texas at Austin.

Figure 8.2. Ralph Rodriguez was drafted and assigned to the 200th Coast Artillery Regiment (Anti-Aircraft) of the New Mexico Coast Guard in February 1941. He began translating the Articles of War to non-English-speaking Latinos so that they might understand the conflict they were entering. Eventually he was transferred to the medical corps and was later taken prisoner in the Bataan Peninsula, Philippines. Voces Oral History Project, Nettie Lee Benson Latin American Collection, University of Texas at Austin.

uary 1941. When asked why he initially enlisted, Silva replied, "Kids are kids. They set up the three-inch guns in front of the courthouse [in Gallup], and that enticed us." Silva's reflection "Kids are kids" symbolized how he admired and felt "enticed" by the power of the three-inch guns displayed in the center of his hometown—and closely associated with the McKinley County courthouse, a major government building and symbol of power and authority.[36]

One hundred fifty miles east, in Bernalillo near Albuquerque, Ralph Rodriguez, a graduate of the Sisters of Loretto Catholic high school, worked full-time at a local lumber company. Rodriguez took pride in his Spanish-to-English translation skills and entertained dreams of a career as a U.S. ambassador, possibly in Central America. In February 1941, when Rodriguez was drafted into the army, these aspirations were his priority. In his pursuit of educational attainment and a career in the civil service, Rodriguez faced a path that required military service. This is an example of militarized citizenship because societal expectations of being patriotic and supporting the U.S. nation, such as compliance with the draft, directly led to Rodriguez serving in the military. Rodriguez explained, "It didn't bother me too much. I know we had to serve, and it would just be a year. . . . I was working from 1937 to 1940, for three years before I was drafted. At that time, I was trying to work out a system where I could go to college. I wanted to be an ambassador—that was my prime ambition . . . Nicaragua, Guatemala, even Mexico. It was in all these thoughts and ideas that February 1941 came around and I was drafted."[37]

Furthermore, through his career aspirations in the foreign service, Rodriguez probed the topic of class strata among Mexican American soldiers. Based on his leadership roles as a medical translator in Bataan and his insights in his interview in 2001, it seems that Rodriguez might have pursued these career goals if he had had further schooling and job opportunities. While they represented a broad spectrum of backgrounds, Mexican Americans were charged with fighting alongside the U.S.-led Philippine Army and Philippine Scouts to defend the Philippines. Rodriguez was not alone as a draftee or as a resident of Bernalillo County; 272 New Mexicans in the 200th Coast Artillery came from this county, which includes Albuquerque, the state's most populous city.[38]

And in Las Vegas, New Mexico, 124 miles north of Albuquerque, José Fuljencio Martinez, originally from Mosquero, was a resourceful teenager during the Great Depression. His father, Felípe, earned only $1 a day with the Works Progress Administration. Martinez also worked at several neighbors' farms, doing "everything and anything they wanted me to do—bring in the cows—except milk the cows. . . . [I] plowed the fields, helped the women with their gardens."[39] He was paid in meat, eggs, and milk, which helped feed his family, as did the fruits and vegetables he picked and the coyotes, wild cats, and skunks that he trapped, skinned, and sold for money for school. Martinez's experience was a bit different from that of Silva and Rodriguez. Martinez came from very meager economic means; he sought financial stability for his family through military service, a motivation that has been echoed in other research.[40] When faced with military recruitment efforts prior to the war, Martinez chose what he assumed was the lesser of two evils, enlistment instead of conscription.

In March 1941 Martinez and a close friend enlisted in the army. He explained, "At that time, it was something you had to do. I figured that maybe we would get a chance to do what we wanted. . . . We figured that by joining, we would have a choice. Instead of riding on a stupid horse in the cavalry, we might be able to just fire the gun, which would be more fun." While Martinez interpellated his military service as a duty, or "something you had to do," he also attributed to the military his opportunity for adventure and autonomy that included his choice of military jobs. What seems most telling from this part of his interview, moreover, is Martinez's description of how far his expectations diverged from reality: "We're going to go over there to the Philippines, halfway around the world, and then come back. We figured for a year. We were just going to go as guards. Kids from the boondocks, we didn't know nothing."[41]

"Corrido de Bataan" and Transracial Recognition Scenes between Mexican American and Filipino Soldiers

The 200th Coast Artillery regiment was popular among New Mexican Hispanos because of a sense of camaraderie and shared ethnic backgrounds. Men like Miguel Enciñias, of Las Vegas, sought it out because they knew they would find other Spanish-speaking men. "The reason for the rush to join was that the battalions were predominantly Hispanic . . . from Las Vegas, Albuquerque and Socorro . . . almost 100 percent Hispanic," Enciñias said in 2001. Enciñias said he worried that he would be unable to understand officers in the units without large numbers of Latinos. This regiment would become home to Lorenzo Banegas, whose observations and expression through music illuminate connections between Mexican American and Filipino soldiers.

Before he even knew that the Philippines would be his destination, Lorenzo Banegas sought to join the army against difficult odds. In February 1941 Banegas was farming in Las Cruces, in southern New Mexico, but wanted to enlist. Despite being turned away by the army several times for medical reasons and because he provided for his family through his farmwork, Banegas persisted. He explained, "I wanted to go into the service, so I volunteered. Three times the doctor refused me—I was underweight, flat-footed, and—I don't know—there was always an excuse. But I told him I wanted to go, and the doctor said that he could fix the papers for me to enlist."[42] On February 22, 1941, Banegas was sworn into the army in Santa Fe and then promptly sent to the 200th Coast Artillery at Fort Bliss.

From Fort Bliss, Banegas was shipped to the Philippines, where he soon perceived connections between the native population and Mexican Americans. "I remember very distinctly, on September 16, 1941, when we arrived in Manila, the Filipino bands started playing 'South of the Border'—at that time it was a very popular song. They thought we were from Mexico. Even though we were from *New* Mexico, they thought we were from Mexico," Banegas recalled. Regarding the prevalence of the Spanish language in the Philippines, moreover, Banegas observed, "The old people speak Spanish, but the younger ones, they know very little. All the islands know Tagalog, but they have different dialects throughout the islands. But everyone understands Tagalog."[43]

The ways in which Banegas and his fellow Manitos were interpellated as Mexicans, rather than as New Mexicans, represents an instance of misrecognition as well as transracial recognition, in which ethnic and racial differences and similarities between and among Filipinos and Mexican Americans were more visible and acknowledged. To be sure, unity among soldiers is sometimes idealized, and these transracial recognition scenes were not exclusive to Mexican Americans and Filipinos. They extended to Native American and white soldiers allied with Mexican Americans and Filipino soldiers and civilians in many instances during the Battle of Bataan, the Bataan Death March, and throughout their years as POWs. However, the parallel colonial histories that led Manitos to the Philippines illuminate our understanding of how they were both subjects and agents of change as they grappled with their circumstances in World War II. Through their unique ties across two U.S. frontiers—New Mexico and the Philippines—it seems that Manitos served roles as colonial palimpsests, or subjects, of one previous U.S. colonial territory who had been transplanted and subjected to this more recent territory in the Pacific. In order to reclaim some agency—a sense of civic duty, manhood, adventure, and relative autonomy—Manitos joined the U.S. military that continued to govern and control the Philippines. For Filipinos who joined the Philippine Army, moreover, it seems that military service was also an interpellated, or perceived, duty, a means of economic subsistence, as well as a path toward citizenship. For each group, though, important trade-offs resulted from joining the military. In a perverse irony for both Manitos and Filipinos, a consequence of seeking this figurative and literal U.S. citizenship and financial stability was that these soldiers became subjects of empire and were complicit with U.S. imperial efforts in the Philippines.

As a reflection of his agency and voice, Banegas made sense of his geopolitical and transnational circumstances in a *corrido*, a Spanish-language ballad known for telling a significant story. Banegas emphasized the importance of how he and his friends cared for each other as POWs in Camp O'Donnell and then Camp Cabanatuan. Banegas stated his gratitude for Adolfo Rivera, a close friend from his National Guard unit who had saved his life when he was on the verge of exhaustion. Banegas credited Rivera for inspiring him to write the "Corrido de Bataan":

> When I composed that song, right on the bottom, I said, "My name is Lorenzo Banegas and I'll be seeing you soon," because I thought in about two or three months Americans would liberate us. But golly, it took a long, long time. And then I wanted to change the verse, *"Algún día, te veré"* (Some day, I will see you.)[44]

Despite scarce food, water, and medicine and afflicted with the crippling disease beriberi, associated with malnutrition, and the contagious disease diphtheria, Banegas channeled his hopes into his *corrido*. While tilling fields with minimal tools, walking barefoot, and avoiding punishment from prison guards, Banegas created his song:

Año de cuarenta y uno	(The year of 1941
Presente lo tengo yo.	Is clearly in my mind.
El día ocho de diciembre	On the 8th day of December
La guerra se declaró.	War was declared.
Como a las doce del día	About twelve o'clock noon
Cuando el caso sucedió	When the event took place
Se dejó venir Japón	The Japanese planes flew
Y a Clark Field nos bombardeó.	In and bombarded Clark Field.
Se fueron los aeroplanos	The warplanes departed
Y todo se asilenció	And everything went silent
Quedaron muertos y heridos	A great many were left
Un gran numeración.	dead and wounded
Había tantos heridos	There were so many wounded
Que era muy grande el total	The total was great
Los levantaron del campo	They were carried from the field
Derechito al hospital.	And taken straight to the hospital.

Pobrecitos los pilotos	Poor American pilots
Los siento de corazón	My heart breaks for them
Quedaron toditos muertos	They were all left dead
En un lado de su avión.	Beside their airplane.
Los pilotos americanos	The American pilots
Son muy buenos al volar	Are very good in flight
Les cayeron de sorpresa	They just couldn't take off
Fallaron al levantar.	When taken by surprise.
Cumplimos los cuatro meses	After four months of war
El día ocho de abril	On April 8th
No pudimos ya pelear	We could not continue to fight
Nos tuvimos que rendir.	We had to surrender.
El día que nos rendimos	The day of surrender
Quisiera no recordar	I would like to not recall
Nos pusieron en filas	We were placed in single file
Y nos forzaron a marchar.	And we were forced to march.
Marchamos de Mariveles hasta	We marched from Mariveles
Mero San Fernando	Clear to San Fernando
Nos hecharon en el tren	We were put on a train
Hasta mero Camp O'Donnell.	Clear to Camp O'Donnell.
Llegamos a Camp O'Donnell	We arrived at Camp O'Donnell
Ya tarde como a las dos	Late, at about two
Nos echaron en el cerco	We were placed in an enclosure
Con guardias alrededor.	With guards all around.
Ay! Japoneses ingratos	Oh! Cruel Japanese
Ya no tienen compasión	They show us no compassion
Aquí nos tienen sufriendo	They keep us suffering here
En campo de concentración.	In a concentration camp.
Nos trabajaban a pico y pala	They work us with pick and shovel
Todo el santo día de Dios	All of God's blessed day
No nos quieren dar comida	They don't want to feed us
Mas que un platito de arroz.	But a tiny plate of rice.

Ya con esta me despido	And with that I say goodbye
Con dolor de corazón	With an ache in my heart
Y nomás de estar pensando	And I only keep on thinking
En la muy triste prisión.	Of the very sad prison camp.
Si quieren saber quien soy	If you care to know who I am
Mi nombre les daré	I will tell you my name
Lorenzo Ybarra Banegas	Lorenzo Ybarra Banegas
Que muy pronto los veré.[45]	Who will see you very soon.)

In the seventh stanza, Banegas draws a connection to militarized citizenship when he explains that the Battle of Bataan lasted until April 8, 1942. When Banegas sings, *"No pudimos ya pelear / No tuvimos que rendir"* (We could not continue to fight / We had to surrender), his phrasing about continuing to fight and being forced to surrender is not uncommon among World War II veterans of the Philippines. Although circumstances were dire and their lives were threatened, Banegas implies that the decision to surrender was a choice made by their commanding officers, as opposed to the soldiers themselves. Banegas and his fellow soldiers—from the Philippines and the United States alike—were willing to die to fulfill their perceived soldierly duties, but the April 9, 1942, surrender interrupted those convictions. Despite his ability to recount the Death March, which he does in detail in the eighth and ninth stanzas—*"Marchamos de Mariveles hasta / Mero San Fernando / Nos hecharon en el tren / Hasta mero Camp O'Donnell"* (We marched from Mariveles / Clear to San Fernando / We were put on a train and/ to the Camp O'Donnell)—Banegas first acknowledges that he would prefer not to remember these experiences. As he prefaces his narrative of the dangers and exhaustion of the Bataan Death March with the lyrics, *"El día que rendimos / Quisiera no recordar"* (The day of surrender / I would like to not recall), Banegas shows us the toll imposed by his interpellated military duty and willingness to sacrifice for his country.

Banegas further recounts the life-and-death predicaments shared by tens of thousands of U.S. and Filipino soldiers, beginning with the first bombs dropped on Manila in December 1941 and continuing into the uncertainty of the prison camps. In terms of an identifiable subject throughout the *corrido*, Banegas refers either to himself or to a collective "we," as seen in *nosotros* (first-person plural). Though he depicts Japanese pilots and prison guards as cruel, Banegas does not distinguish among other ethnic or racial groups with whom he endured the war. He mentions only *"Los pilotos Ame-*

ricanos," which can be read as U.S. military pilots. Still, there is no reason to narrowly interpret his frequent use of *nosotros* to include only soldiers who were Mexican American, or even New Mexican or from the United States, because he portrays a broad array of experiences that included Filipino soldiers and civilians as well. During his interview, in fact, Banegas actually refers to "Americans" separately from "us" prisoners. As noted, the majority of the prisoners were Filipino. As historian Luís Alvarez has noted in his chapter in this volume, Latino soldiers "felt a kinship and solidarity with Filipinos based on shared culture, skin color, and recognition of one another's historical struggle with Spanish colonialism." Later, Banegas said he was expecting to be freed within a matter of months. "But by golly, it took a long, long time."[46] The ensuing time as a POW helped further consolidate a nascent Mexipino identity with other prisoners.

This *corrido* thus indirectly incorporates aspects of transracial recognition and solidarity among Mexican Americans and Filipinos. In particular, in addition to describing his heavy heart and his desire to reunite with family, his broader recollections suggest identifications not only with his family and the United States but also the Philippine nation that was caught in war.

The uniqueness of the Bataan experience—the unprecedented scale of U.S.-led soldiers who were surrendered and the timing of the Death March early in World War II—led to complex revisions of Mexican American and Filipino soldier identities and citizenship. The imperative, "Remember Bataan," was the subject of propaganda and campaigns to sell war bonds during World War II and has since been a subject of mainstream and documentary films, memoirs, and innumerable annual vigils. Though Manitos and Filipinos faced circumstances that were militarized by forces outside their control, they still reclaimed and remade their agency in new ways. This includes a nascent Mexipino political and multiracial identity as World War II veterans in the Philippines and Bataan Death March survivors that synthesized shared colonial histories and subordinate roles at the time of the war.

Personal Reflections on the Annual Bataan Memorial March

One of the most challenging aspects of learning about these World War II histories is navigating the stories by and about veterans and the ways in which their war experiences are represented in memorial events. Since 2006 this author and his mother—descendants of Ludovico Beltran, a Philippine Scout who survived the Bataan Death March—have participated in the Bataan Memorial March by running either the 15-mile or the 26.2-mile course. We participate in order to publicly remember my Lolo (Tagalog for "grandfather"), to reunite with a Filipino veteran, Menandro Parazo, who actually knew my Lolo in the Philippines and, years later, in Fort Bliss, as well as to represent Filipinos among the many descendants and participants at this event.

Although there are volunteers with water, snacks, and medical care along the route, the Bataan Memorial March feels very different from most marathons. Officially sponsored by the U.S. Army and Veterans of Foreign Wars of the United States, the weekend events champion the contributions and service of heroic New Mexicans, past and present. Many participants pay homage to veterans by carrying thirty-five-pound backpacks—full of weights, rice, or sand—and active members of the military run in full uniforms and boots. Descendants often carry photographs or wear T-shirts with silkscreened images of a father, grandfather, or uncle who was in the Bataan Death March. The distinct atmosphere of respect and reflection for these war veterans, as well as the prevalence of "teams" who run and attempt to finish together, make this feel like a macabre reenactment of some of the terrors of World War II.

During the weekend of presentations and events, we participants are taught that from the first moments of April 9, 1942, U.S. and Filipino soldiers' survival—hour by hour, footstep by footstep—was uncertain, nor were they free from torture by Japanese soldiers. The suffering and isolation of the 200th Coast Artillery is a badge of honor of sorts, captured in a short limerick, "Battling Bastards of Bataan," by war correspondent Frank Hewlett:

> We're the battling bastards of Bataan
> No mama, no papa, no Uncle Sam
> No aunts, no uncles, no nephews, no nieces
> No rifles, no planes, or artillery pieces
> And nobody gives a damn![47]

Here, "bastard" referred to soldiers who had been abandoned by General MacArthur and left without supplies in March 1942, during the Battle of Bataan. In their own reflections about the Battle of Bataan, though, none of these four interviewees spoke at length about General MacArthur. This limerick is ubiquitous at the Bataan Memorial March—it is printed on the complimentary T-shirts for participants and on sweatshirts, identification tags, and keychain souvenirs for purchase.

Despite the potential to critique the circumstances of the abandonment, however, the Bataan Memorial March elides any criticism of U.S. military or government actions that further endangered the lives of U.S. and Filipino soldiers and civilians. While the histories of the Bataan Death March and POW camps receive a certain focus throughout this weekend, the broader context surrounding war in the Philippines, as well as postwar campaigns for reparations for Filipino *veteranos* is beyond the scope of these memorial events. On a related note, moreover, a Congressional Gold Medal was proposed on December 15, 2011, in a bill by U.S. Sen. Tom Udall (D-NM) "in honor of the troops from the United States and the Philippines who defended Bataan and were subsequently prisoners of war."[48] Though this bill celebrates the legendary heroism and courage of Filipino and U.S. soldiers, particularly New Mexicans, it remains silent on postwar struggles for citizenship and veterans' benefits for the many thousands in the Philippine Army.

In essence, despite the intimate connections some of us have to these reenactment rituals and memorial events, they risk oversimplifying historical events.[49] Exploring these stories of Mexican Americans who survived World War II in the Philippines directs our attention to military experiences that began in New Mexico much earlier in the U.S colonization of half of Mexico after the U.S.-Mexico War. Portrayals of World War II veterans through redemptive narratives—ones that emphasize soldiers' contributions and themes of honor and loyalty to the United States—also overlook important themes of militarization and militarized citizenship that affected the circumstances of each soldier's participation. Transracial recognition scenes among Manitos and Filipinos complicate our understanding of the ways in which Mexican Americans recognized their own interpellated roles, as well as their agency to resist, in the colonial project of securing the Philippines from Japan.

CHAPTER 9

Tejanas on the Home Front: Women, Bombs, and the (Re)Gendering of War in Mexican American World War II Literature

PATRICIA PORTALES

Factory, Home, and Public Sphere

On December 29, 1940, during his Fireside Chat radio broadcast, President Franklin Delano Roosevelt called for America to become "the arsenal of democracy" against the Nazis and assist Britain with the production of military supplies.[1] When the United States prepared to enter World War II following the Japanese attack on Pearl Harbor one year later, American factories increased their production of weapons, ships, and aircraft. Consequently the surge in production coincided with thousands of male factory workers taking leave from work to enlist in the military. As a result, the increase in defense production necessitated an expanded workforce. Factory managers considered "the degree to which womanpower might take the place of manpower . . . on the factory floor."[2]

The demand for factory workers reached San Antonio, Texas, where the *San Antonio Light* reported that "one successful San Antonio bidder [made] vital secret parts for battleship turbines [while] another fabricat[ed] mushroom ventilators."[3] East of downtown San Antonio, a factory run by the Friedrich Refrigeration Company known for its quick-freezing processors and refrigerators, was "on contract to the Dallas Chemical Warfare Procurement District to produce . . . M10 and M69 cluster adapters, bomb boxes, nose cups, and parts bins."[4] Much of the company's workforce included local Mexican American women, who found themselves working higher-paying jobs, wearing nontraditional clothing, and learning a new way of life. In a 2008 interview, Juana Portales Esquivel, who was born and raised in San Antonio, recalled, "I was working during the war at Friedrich's air condition place on the Eastside. They were doing bombs, and we were welding the tops to the bombs. I worked for them during the war, 1942 to '45."[5] Be-

Figure 9.1. Mexican American women working at Friedrich Refrigeration, sanding cabinets, November 8, 1942. The factory, east of downtown San Antonio, procured a contract to produce "M10 and M69 cluster adapters, bomb boxes, nose cups, and parts bins." Mexican American women who took jobs there were soon welding the tops onto bombs. San Antonio Light Collection, University of Texas at San Antonio Libraries Special Collections.

fore the United States entered the war she had helped rear six siblings while employed as a domestic worker in San Antonio. When Friedrich's Refrigeration turned to defense production, the company bought ads in the *San Antonio Light*, and many local Mexican American women responded, including Esquivel, her cousin Clemencia Jasso, and their friend Rosie Vidal.

As Brenda Sendejo notes, the mobilization of women, especially Mexican American women, into the wartime workforce inevitably made them the "beneficiaries of wartime opportunities and relaxed gender roles, and they represented a transition from the experiences of the Great Depression to life in the postwar period."[6] Esquivel not only found transitional work in the new defense industry, she found new agency as a woman. She recalls, "We had to wear coveralls because [of] the sparks. We had to cover up. I still have spots [points to scars on her neck]. We wore shields and a cap and gloves and heavy shoes. Pants. I used to buy coveralls."[7] Beyond the

Figure 9.2. Juana Portales Esquivel, far right, Rosie Vidal, center, and Gloria Lopez, left, 1942. Esquivel holds the *San Antonio Light* classifieds publicizing welding positions at the Friedrich plant in San Antonio, Texas. Voces Oral History Project, Nettie Lee Benson Latin American Collection, University of Texas at Austin.

uniforms, scarred skin, and new skills that marked these women's transitions from domestic workers to factory workers, their new occupations undergirded significant shifts in their gendered societal roles.

Previous scholarship on Mexicans Americans in World War II includes the biographies and oral histories of military veterans, studies about ethnic tension between Mexican American zoot-suiters and white American sailors in Los Angeles and other cities, and documentation of the ensuing creation of Latina/o civil rights organizations such as the American GI Forum.[8] After decades of work historicizing Mexican American agency in the twentieth century, the male narrative remains foregrounded as representative of a collective experience. Recent feminist historiographies, however, illustrate the contributions of women of color, yet further scholarship on the image and contributions of Mexican American women to the war effort and home front remains necessary. The image of Rosie the Riveter, for example, embodied Mexican American female welders at Friedrich in San Antonio, even if the War Manpower Commission depicted her only as a white woman in propaganda posters.[9] Historian David M. Kennedy situates Rosie in the context of a Jim Crow society that could no longer continue its prejudices while it struggled to integrate its workforce:

> Rosie was a fictional symbol for a complex social reality that eluded tidy description. Rosie's denim-clad, tool-wielding, can-do figure was meant to personify . . . the women who worked during the war. In fact, she typified very few of them. . . . Rosie was a misleading symbol, though one whose heroically iconic stature powerfully molded memories of the war.[10]

In historical literature as well as creative literature, each of which I address in this chapter, Mexican American women's contributions challenge the World War II national imaginary as well as many Chicana/o Studies historiographies of the era. Recent scholarship has examined, for example, the 1940s Mexican American woman in the position of the *pachuca*, who alongside the zoot-suiters complicated the image of the home front civilian as both national patriot and cultural resister. In *The Woman in the Zoot Suit*, Catherine S. Ramirez reexamines the women linked to the 1943 Sleepy Lagoon Trial in Los Angeles and their representation as Mexican American "zooterinas" or *pachucas* in literature, film, and art. Ramirez reinserts this forgotten group into history but not merely as secondary to the zoot-suiters. Instead, she casts the *pachucas'* style—long "fingertip" coats, dark lipstick, and high bouffant or "ratted" hair—as symbols of newly attained mobility and agency for women during World War II. Ramirez's eleven interviewees express a respect for their own boldness intertwined with the *pachuca* attitude, which challenged gender norms and led to their exclusion from history because they did not fit the masculine profile. Though contradictory perceptions of female zoot-suiters emerged, Ramirez delineates their contributions to the war effort as defense workers, letter-writers, and patriots. Ramirez does not romanticize these women. Instead, she examines the overlooked collective identity of the female zoot-suiter, recognizing that the image communicated contradictory messages as a "symbol of independence" or as a "uniform of the impudent adolescent."[11] Similarly, Elizabeth Escobedo informs us of the power of the *pachucas'* aesthetic that challenged traditions during the war and still resulted in their enhanced agency within their communities.[12]

I want to add that Mexican American women on the home front challenged cultural norms not only through the aforementioned mappings of *pachuca* resistance, which in itself may be examined through multiple frames, but even within their complex patriotic roles as defense workers. For example, the *pachuca* served not only as the female counterpart to the pachuco, but she also resisted the role of passive girlfriend by appropriating the male zoot suit jacket. Similarly, women challenged the static and invariable Rosie the Riveter image not only through aesthetics but also through their labor, both in the factories and in their daily domestic routines. Moreover, I submit that their labor and production is the site at which their agency becomes potentially revolutionary.

As noted, Ramirez and Escobedo provide significant contributions to World War II Latinas as *pachuca* resisters who forged new spaces for a nuanced Mexican American identity. My analysis extends this work by examining Mexican American wartime laborers who also created counter-hegemonic feminist opportunities in the patriarchal and racist context of the World War II era. By placing oral historiographies alongside creative literature, a genre that fills in the gaps with imaginative interpretations, I situate the Latina laborer in a new paradigm for further mapping Latina agency. The images of the resister and the patriotic laborer were not, however, mutually exclusive; they were simultaneous. As historian Emma Pérez notes of the historiography of Mexican American women, "The contradictions women faced compelled them to accept existing structures and create their subjecthood within those structures."[13] The trope of World War II women's agency through the government-produced image of Rosie the Riveter provided the ultimate contradiction.

I thus examine Esquivel's oral history about her work as a welder in San Antonio and I analyze her agency alongside theatrical models of feminism represented by female characters in Severo and Judith Pérez's *Soldierboy* and Luis Valdez's *Zoot Suit*, plays that depict Mexican Americans during World War II.[14] *Soldierboy* is of particular value to this study because it is grounded in San Antonio's locales and historical processes: Santa Rosa Hospital, Zarzamora Street, Waverly Drive, Fort Sam Houston, the San Antonio River, Kelly Field, the Gunter Hotel, and the urbanization of Westside neighborhoods.

The historical depictions in *Soldierboy* firmly ground the events in the circumstances of 1940s San Antonio as it relies not only on locale but also on other significant sites where power was negotiated during the World War II era. Though the play is an imaginative rendering of historical events, it nonetheless informs our understanding of the era by seeking to fill in the blanks and silences in the historical record. As I illustrate further below, narrative has been theorized as a model of historiography by various scholars, and these plays illustrate the close relationships between narrative and historiography by incorporating facts alongside historical figures and composite characters to tell the story of Latina/os during this period. I submit that Esquivel's oral history and these two theatrical productions collectively illustrate and dramatize how women on the home front accepted their temporary patriotic duty in the defense industry while challenging both the patriarchal and nationalistic foundations.

Since the events in the plays are grounded in historical events and places, with select episodes set in a barrio household in which largely unseen gender conflicts and negotiations of power occur, I use the performance as a touchstone for remapping Mexican American women's emergent and imagined agency during World War II. In *Historia: The Literary Making of Chicana and Chicano History*, Louis G. Mendoza explains the possibilities of a symbiosis between literature and historiography:

> On the one hand, "fiction" writers reconstruct the past imaginatively. Historians, on the other, utilize their knowledge and evidence of "factual" events to tell us the truth about the past. These two seemingly very different tasks have a similar end, however—to create a narrative of the past in such a way as to offer a simultaneous representation and interpretation of some discrete dimension of time, space, and experience.[15]

In assessing the historical dimensions of literature and corresponding narrative elements of historiography, Mendoza asserts that "seeing literature as valid historical evidence enables a new way of conceptualizing the nature of power and its negotiation with more complexity and accuracy."[16] This interrelationship between history and literature enables a recovery of the real and complex people on which Dolores and Lupe in *Zoot Suit* and Esther and Petra in *Soldierboy* were based.

In this analysis of oral history and theater, I seek to trace what I call women's "liberatory layering," which maps women's multiple sites of struggle and simultaneous modes of agency while also examining the ways in which women's mobility affected cross-racial and cross-generational dimensions of a collective identity for Mexican Americans. Together these works illustrate how World War II–era Mexican American women negotiated their identities and viewed their multivalent roles *not* as contradictory but as simultaneous. Here I build on Emma Pérez's notion of "dialectical doubling"—where women "yielded a politics of contradiction to and with male centered policies"—to further problematize the nuanced roles women workers filled.[17] I see a similarity between Pérez's study of women's roles during the Mexican Revolution and my examination of Mexican American women during World War II. In both events, nationalism was high, women were asked to contribute to the effort, and women willingly agreed with the purpose of the effort. Here Pérez explains the circumstances:

> In essence, the male leaders idealized nationalism and in the name of revolution laid out duties for women. . . . A kind of "dialectics of doubling" was in play for women, who may have supported the "nationalist" cause of the revolution, but they intervened interstitially with their own rhetoric about their place and meaning in the revolution. . . . The women . . . mimicked men's ideas, in essence, agreeing with the greater cause of the revolution, but many female members performed activities in their own way, often expressing an interstitial feminism.[18]

I build on Emma Peréz's term *doubling* because it connotes both a reproduced and a binary state. Instead of doubling, however, the women of World War II were performing a "liberatory layering" of their roles. While working in factories as riveters, for example, they neither traded their citizenship nor shed their motherhood. Instead, these roles were simultaneously layered and cannot be studied merely as intersectionalities. Similarly, in her critique of feminism and Chicana Studies, Patricia Zavella points outs, "Chicana theorists implicitly were concerned with the *simultaneity* of experience: how race, class, and gender are experienced by Chicanas concurrently. We noted the impossibility of understanding the complexity of Chicanas' experiences with only the analytic category of gender."[19] This liberatory layering more appropriately encompasses each dimension of their identities.

In situating historical literature such as Esquivel's oral history and imaginative literature such as *Soldierboy* and *Zoot Suit*, I explore the complexities of the minority experience, specifically cross-racial and cross-gender collaborations. In order to extend the undertheorized position of Latina labor in World War II, I situate the war as the catalyst for recruiting women to factory defense work, which affected economic power, nontraditional roles, geographic mobility, patriotic duty, and subversive resistance. Thus Latina labor during World War II became a point of reference for meditating on the margins into which Latinas pushed their agency.

In several instances, women resisted the racist practices of their employers. Emma Pérez, in her analysis of the link between history and women's labor, notes, "Historical events . . . show that women's politics may have been subordinated under a nationalist paradigm, but women as agents have always constructed their own spaces interstitially."[20] During World War II, the War Manpower Commission created advertisements that encouraged women to work for the nationalist cause, which included returning to the domestic sphere once their factory work ended. A focus on these women and their nontraditional spaces reveals that past "studies marginalized women as the mothers or wives of men and denied them any contribution to a community."[21] Further examination reveals this layering created a unique form of Mexican American agency.

Negotiating Gender and Race through World War II Labor, San Antonio, 1942–1945

A November 1942 *San Antonio Light* article addressing the shifting workforce reads, "Five weeks ago, no woman had ever been employed in [the Friedrich] factory to use any machine besides the typewriter. Now 70 women work there and they are doing everything from turning lathes in the company's mill room to assembling the complete motor that makes the boxes run."[22] Like many of the wartime analogies between domestic work and factory work, the *San Antonio Light* aimed to portray women's aptitude for riveting: "Maybe knowing how to do things with their hands, even simple things like washing dishes, running the family sewing machine, cooking a meal, just naturally helps when they begin to turn the lathes, varnish and paint, connect up to the hundred and one parts of a motor."[23]

Though referencing only household chores as comparable to factory work, women had long mastered skills in other trades. In their analysis of labor and family, Louise Lamphere, Patricia Zavella, and Felipe Gonzales report that "fathers and their unmarried children were usually the wage earners in the United States until World War II with the very important exception of black mothers who (along with some Asian and Mexican workers) have always engaged in productive labor."[24] Much historiography initially claimed World War II as the watershed moment for women's entry in the workforce. However, this watershed included only middle-class white women who had not joined the labor force in sizable numbers. In *Claiming Rights and Righting Wrongs in Texas: Mexican Workers and Job Politics during World War II*, Emilio Zamora confirms that women's participation in the workforce preceded the United States' World War II campaign: "Women broke into the war industries earlier and with greater ease. It was not uncommon, even as early as 1941, to see women replace men who had taken up jobs vacated by other men who had entered the military."[25] For women of color, in this case Mexican American women, the notion of work outside the home already existed.

While employed in the defense industry, Mexican American women of the World War II generation addressed and performed their cultural citizenship pluralistically. Naomi Quiñonez illustrates that their agency affected "larger social incentives, shift[ing] women's sphere from the home to the workplace [while also] prov[ing] that Mexican American women were capable of taking advantage of changing social currents and were ready to move out of rigid cultural roles and traditions."[26] The broader implications of this production as a result of Mexican American women's participation included a shift not only in their work but in their identities as well. Women were then layering their roles as defense workers within their roles in the domestic sphere.

Esquivel's experiences as a welder convey the transformative agency of Latinas as laborers even in the face of a patriarchal and nationalistic cause. Esquivel's position as a welder afforded her movement outside the home, earning power that contributed not only to the family income but to her independence, and a shift in her self-representation. She recounts that she earned $3 per week cleaning homes in San Antonio's Woodlawn neighborhood, a largely working middle-class white community, before she applied for the defense job. She recalls her defense job with excitement:

> "I've got a picture . . . when we were downtown—the three of us. I think it is Rosie, Gloria, and me. We've got the [Friedrich employment] ad in our hands. We're walking right on Houston Street. There was this camera that used to take pictures of everybody."[27]

Once they were hired, she says, their family and the community did not object since many women were entering the workforce to aid defense manufacturing. The women were trained by their employer to weld the tops onto bombs. Their overnight shift, 7 P.M. to 7 A.M., meant they were away from their homes at night. The women also rewarded themselves modestly on payday when they ate breakfast at a restaurant called the Alamo. Esquivel also recalls that she and the other women had never worn coveralls and boots before.[28] Thus, Esquivel developed a consciousness that noted her newfound power not only in her work skills but also in her new uniform and pay. Patricia Zavella's research on labor offers a preliminary mapping of women's agency: "Working women develop a consciousness of their situation or recognition of their collective circumstances as workers by contrasting their work situations with their family situations."[29] In doing so, the women are situated not only as wives, mothers, or the appendages of men; they are contributors to society through their own autonomous labor.

Only a few months before obtaining the welding job, Juana met Homero Esquivel, the man she would marry at the end of the war. Shortly thereafter, he was drafted and served as a U.S. Navy Fireman aboard the USS *West Virginia* in the Pacific Theater. Juana Portales Esquivel's two brothers also served in the war. The eldest, Emilio Portales, fought with the Army's 17th Division of Combat Engineers on Utah Beach in Normandy, while her younger brother Raul Portales of the U.S. Navy served on the USS *Grumium* in the Pacific Theater. Esquivel then became the eldest sibling left at home to help her mother, Macedonia Portales, who also worked washing and ironing for families in the Woodlawn neighborhood. Esquivel then contributed to the family's income by working at the Friedrich plant.

The Hidden Transcript: Theatrical Recoveries of World War II Mexican American Women's Agency in *Soldierboy* and *Zoot Suit*

Imaginative literature reveals the influence of history and the models that, as historian David M. Kennedy argues, mold memories. With its roots as an educational tool and mechanism for political mobilization, Mexican American theater has instilled cultural pride while illustrating the complexities of myriad cultural negotiations. Fictional accounts of the home front during World War II, specifically the domestic sites in *Zoot Suit* and *Soldierboy*, enable me to build on the historical narrative of Esquivel's oral history. Norma Alarcón has critiqued the limiting and hegemonic function of history: "Insofar as it obeys ideological and metaphysical constraints, it does not truly recover human events and experience, nor is it capable of projecting change—thus, literature is allocated those functions."[30] Drawing on oral history as well as subjective literary texts such as theater, I situate my notion of liberatory layering in the context of the historical moment of World War II and the conditions—specifically labor, family, and economy—that affected women's agency.

My rereading of the plays as an imaginative expression of the power of women's work enables me to add to mappings of the subversive actions by women in World War II that have been documented by other means. The plays portray Mexican American women challenging their limited agency, which conclusively decenters the patriarchal paradigm and also introduces a permutation of the matriarchal paradigm. The plays reveal that women, even within the confines of a wartime nationalistic and patriarchal ideology, push against the limits placed on their prescribed agency, just as Esquivel did while welding at the Friedrich factory in San Antonio. These challenges are demonstrated by Judith Pérez and Severo Pérez, coauthors of *Soldierboy*, a play first produced in 1982 by El Teatro Campesino, under the direction of Luis Valdez in San Juan Bautista, California.[31] The play depicts the de la Cruz family and their post–World War II negotiations. Ostensibly about army veteran Frank de la Cruz's return from the European theater, the play illustrates the significant contributions to the family in the wake of his absence made by his wife, Esther, a uniform factory worker, and his mother, Petra, a pecan sheller during the Great Depression. Esther's and Petra's labor reflects the historical context of the war years that Brenda Sendejo observes:

> Mexican American women benefitting from wartime work represented a shift in a pattern of low-paying wage labor in sectors such as farmwork, canning, pecan shelling . . . during the early to mid-twentieth century, work that contributed to the racialization of women, that is, the social construction and oppression of the working class Mexican female. While wartime work was liberating for women, they still faced gender and racial discrimination.[32]

Similar to the experiences related in oral histories, the fictional characters in *Soldierboy* adjust to their post–World War II roles; Frank and Esther experience the same rites and negotiations as did the zoot-suiters and *pachucas*; they challenged their traditional roles while upholding their patriotic duty. Thus *Soldierboy* and *Zoot Suit* reveal parallel concepts of identity and gender negotiation between the military and the civilian, the Mexican American and the white American, and the traditional and the modern.

Though *Soldierboy* follows the life of Frank de la Cruz, it does not merely celebrate his return to society as a son, father, and war veteran; it problematizes the resulting negotiations his wife and mother face in their matriarchal home. His relationships with Esther and Petra are integral to showing the shift in agency for both men and women, and I examine the play's gendered spaces—masculinity, femininity, love, and work. I situate the notion of materialism in the context of the historical moment of World War II and the conditions—labor, family, and economic—that affected women's agency. The expression of the power of women's work thus enables the subversive actions of Esther and Petra to be foregrounded as integral to Frank's return to civilian life. The play signals that Mexican American women challenged their limited agency, finally shifting the patriarchal paradigm to a matriarchal paradigm, with elements of gynopoetics that feature women's culture and feminist alliances within the patriarchal spaces.

The Pérezes complicate *Soldierboy*'s plot by juxtaposing Esther's and Petra's newfound power within the family with Frank's position as a Mexican American whose earning power in the postwar economy is circumscribed by racism. In creating Frank, the Pérezes illustrate his readjustment to civilian life and reveal how his former roles are now ill-suited to his postwar attitudes and goals. What the Pérezes also illustrate is a mapping of the new positions the war created. Frank's shifting role, not only as a male, but also as a laborer, illustrates what Fredric Jameson calls the "traditional production [that] has disappeared and in which social classes of the classical type no longer exist."[33] However, on further examination, Esther reveals a similar shift. I situate her in Gloria Anzaldúa's notion of *nepantla*, an in-between state of "changing worlds, cultures, and . . . classes," where a reconfiguration of identity transpires.[34] Frank's return renders his military and now ill-fitting civilian clothing inappropriate, a phenomenon that Victor Turner identifies as the position of a liminal being:

> [A figure in the] middle ground [or] transitional period [yields] liminal beings . . . [who] have no status, property, insignia, secular clothing indicating rank or role, position in kinship system—in short, nothing that may distinguish them from their fellow neophytes or initiands.[35]

Frank certainly embodies this liminal being, especially since he is now lacking status or clothing indicating his rank. Esther, on the other hand, wholly appropriates Frank's clothing and reveals the liminality of his return. As a uniform maker, she recognizes the loss of Frank's military status within a civilian society, even though she knows it is just a role. Moreover, she is inversely linked to his new (lowered) status both on the material and political levels, since her employment is now an important source of family income.

In addition, Esther and Petra reveal that the power of their agency as workers is inflected in uniquely Mexican American terms, specifically, through language usage. Petra relates her past as a pecan sheller and the subversive singing she and her coworkers performed in reaction to the order her boss, who spoke only English, gave to stop singing. Though the Pérezes assign Petra the role of wife, mother, and moral conscience, it is her past as a 1930s laborer that informs her opinion of the present. The playwright's use of a pecan sheller is symbolically significant in San Antonio because of the resonance of the 1938 pecan shellers' strike by 12,000 mostly Mexican American women, who were aided by the Mexican American Communist and labor organizer Emma Tenayuca. Petra's contribution to her family helped when Beto's salary was insufficient, a fact he later affirms when he says to Frank, "All those years . . . even in the Depression, we never went hungry."[36] While Petra sings "Cuatro Milpas," Esther says she would like to learn the songs because singing as she works prevents her from "starting to think about something" too much, resulting in mistakes that make her fall behind. Petra recalls:

> Singing can help you keep from thinking. When we first came here from the Rio Grande, Beto could only get day work. It was never enough. And I had to go to work shelling pecans. I had never worked like that before, twelve, sometimes sixteen hours. I thought I'd go crazy with my thinking. What was I doing in this cold packing shed? *Mis dedos hinchados.* I felt even my mind didn't belong to me anymore. So I soon understood why the women sang. It was the only thing that gave the miserable work a little humanity. Some of the foremen would say in English, "Stop singing. You're having too much fun!" But when we stopped singing, we didn't clean as many pecans. So they let us sing.[37]

This scene reveals the contradiction inherent in Petra's otherwise subversive act. In singing, she and the other laborers resist and challenge the boss, both in terms of his authority and in terms of his proposed language restrictions. However, by resisting they increase production, and, in turn, contribute to his business profit. James C. Scott maintains that "every subordinate group creates, out of its ordeal, a 'hidden transcript' that represents a critique spoken behind the back of the dominant."[38] In *Soldierboy*, the songs and perhaps the use of Spanish are the hidden transcripts by which Petra and Esther create subversive empowering agency and alliances with their female coworkers, even as this agency is complex and still part of hegemony.

On several levels, Petra's experience as a laborer in the 1930s illustrates that she too moved outside of the domestic sphere when she negotiated her role as wife and mother with her role as financial contributor. She and Esther share the experience. However, Petra is a more multidimensional character who is seemingly contradictory when she advises Esther, "You don't have to work."[39] Since Petra recounts that her former foreman asked the women to stop singing, perhaps partly because they sang in Spanish, their continued cultural production became a subversive act of symbolic empowerment. Not only did they continue to sing, but they increased their production and subverted their employer's requests by showing the value in it; indeed, it was a marginal act that framed the center. While it aided the owner's profit, it also ensured their continued employment as exceptionally productive workers.

In fact, the use of Spanish among World War II–era factory workers was commonplace, whether or not employers permitted it. In her oral history, Esquivel also remembers vividly that while welding bombs for Friedrich Refrigeration, she, Vidal, and Jasso spoke Spanish. Though the women welders were warned not to discuss the war, an order she says they followed, they did speak about many other matters in Spanish. "The men bosses trained us. They were very nice to us. . . . They didn't mind [that we spoke Spanish]," recalls Esquivel.[40] As noted, Esquivel's empowerment in the form of wages and family decisions placed her in what Anzaldúa calls the *nepantla*, or in-between state, where a transitional equilibrium forms. Mexican American women negotiated their borderland positions and furthered their claim to ever more layers of empowerment. Petra, Esther, and Esquivel, because they brought Spanish into the workplace, temporarily erased racial duality, thus initiating what Anzaldúa has proposed as "a massive uprooting in dualistic thinking."[41] Their decision to communicate in Spanish became a cultural transition that marked their mobility in other social and economic spheres.

These transitions and new modes of women's empowerment also involved what some men viewed as "disruptions." In *Soldierboy*, for instance, Esther deals with the domestic disruption accompanying Frank's return from the war, a move that illustrates the difficulties involved in his negotiation of military and civilian life. Frank returns wearing his army sergeant's uniform and considers whether he can still fit into his old clothing hanging in the closet of his parents' home. In the stage directions, the Pérezes write that Frank "begins removing his uniform" and "takes [an old] suit out of the closet," while Esther "takes the [uniform] jacket and admires it at arms length."[42] Their conversation, however, further illustrates the new liminal space in which both Frank and Esther are positioned. In act 1, the Pérezes reveal Frank's liminality when he tries on his outgrown civilian clothes.

> ESTHER: You look good in uniform. But I'd rather see it in the closet. (*Frank takes a suit out of the closet and tries on the jacket.*) Sometimes I find myself still thinking that you are on the other side of the world. But here you are. Today's been . . . like a dream—the bands, the speeches, but I'm glad all that's over.
> FRANK: Let's see this. Do you think it's still in style? What do you think? Hum? It feels a little tight.
> ESTHER: It looks fine. Maybe if you leave it unbuttoned.
> FRANK: I'll have to wear it to my interview at Kelly Field. I'm supposed to see a fellow named, uh, Kroger.[43]

The Pérezes convey that while Frank's uniform is inappropriate for civilian life and his civilian clothes no longer fit, he occupies a new and uncomfortable middle ground. He loses his status as a World War II hero by having removed his uniform and is further emasculated by the ill-fitting civilian jacket, a symbol of his status at home. While Frank was overseas, his paternalistic dominance transferred to his brother Willie, a blow compounded by the fact that Esther earns her own living. (As I discuss further below, Frank's position parallels that of the disrobed World War II pachuco in Luis Valdez's play *Zoot Suit*, where a loss of clothing symbolizes his emasculation.)

Soldierboy illustrates the liminality of a war hero's traditional expectations in a changed society, and much more. In Frank's place, the Pérezes' choice to have Esther employed sewing uniforms not only enables her economic mobility; she is also creating the symbolic system—the uniform— by which her husband has been measured. A feminist critique of this paradigm shift reveals the extraordinary symbolic and actual power encoded in Chicana agency that is directly linked to Esther's war production. Vicki L. Ruiz situates the profound role that World War II labor had in transforming Mexican American women's agency:

> The World War II Era ushered in a set of new options for Mexican women wage earners. Not only did cannery workers negotiate higher wages and benefits, but many obtained more lucrative employment in defense plants.

As "Rosie the Riveters," they gained self-confidence and the requisite earning power to improve their standard of living.[44]

Although the Pérezes choose to set this provocative uniform scene in the privacy of the bedroom, Frank's ill-fitted suit is not simply a private matter. Frank also questions whether the suit will be appropriate for his interview at Kelly Field, where he is going to apply for a position as a radio repairman, a job he much prefers to selling produce for the family business with his father, Beto. Though Frank's civilian clothing illustrates his role has shifted, so too has Esther's. Despite the fact that Esther had never been to "the other side of the world," her role has nonetheless shifted from domestic to wartime production and represents a negotiation between the traditional Mexican and the mainstream. The Pérezes illustrate the shift in her agency, as she had "found work sewing in a uniform factory . . . working there to make extra money to help buy a house."[45] Esther's production, then, not only contributes to the war effort but also forges a new space outside the traditional home of her in-laws and makes her a contributor to the new home she and Frank plan to purchase.

Illustrating the patriarchal constraints on Mexican American women's newfound agency during the era, Frank has difficulty readjusting to this shift and shows his preference for her to return to the traditional. This tension is illustrated in the type of private bedroom exchanges that have been absent from documentary evidence but that theater is perfectly suited to imagining into new historiographies of the era.

> FRANK: (*Angrily.*) I got in [to Kelly Field]. What does that mean? Are you going to quit your job? Are you going to stay home now and take care of Junior, like a mother's supposed to?
> ESTHER: No, I'm not going to do that. I took the day off so we could have some time together.
> FRANK: There's no reason for you to work now . . . and you've always hated the job. You told me yourself. Your hair gets full of lint. Piecework, it's not for you . . .
> ESTHER: Frank, I don't know what you mean. Look, I make more money sewing than I would as a typist. And you know your mother. I couldn't be here all day.

The scene continues with a change in Frank's tone. He becomes more direct about the domestic role he expects Ester to follow, which would allow him to return to his role as patriarch.

FRANK: You don't have to work.

ESTHER: I know. But right now I want to work. Maybe I'll quit in a few
months . . . when everything's settled down.

FRANK: Junior needs you with him, Esther. A mother should be home.

ESTHER: Are you ordering me to stay home, Frank?

FRANK: No . . .

ESTHER: Frank. I think Junior's doing fine. If we're going to buy a house,
we could use the extra money. When we live in our own house, Frank
. . . then I'll want to stay home.[46]

Though Esther has been home in San Antonio while Frank was fighting abroad, she has not been "home" in the domestic sphere to care for her
young son, thus illustrating another negotiation between the military and
the civilian sphere. While Frank rejects Esther's factory work because it
represents something other than the domestic, she asserts that it is a position she will keep until they move—with the help of her financial contribution—to their own home. Her reaction is a revelation of her new identity
in what has been theorized as "a women-centered family life, a complicated
refuge and site of male authority and privilege where women negotiate autonomy and [contribute] support."[47]

Similarly, in her oral history, Juana Portales Esquivel and her husband,
Homero, built their financial security after the war by applying for the GI
Bill's business loan guaranty. "[He used the GI Bill] to start his job as a floor
finisher. They gave him a loan so he could buy all the machines he needed
and the equipment. [He was] self-employed," recalled Esquivel, who also
said they were able to buy a car in 1947 after their first child was born.
Though Esquivel stated that she enjoyed her welding position at Friedrich,
she did not mind when the job ended in 1945. In 1965, after her youngest
child began school, however, she contributed to the family income beyond
her domestic role by returning to work outside the home.[48] Like Esquivel's
oral history, *Soldierboy* illustrates the cultural negotiation present during
World War II when women worked for the war effort and—even in the
midst of a nationalist, patriarchal cause—created a new Latina paradigm.

Discursive Drapes on the Clothesline:
Performative Identity and Women's Agency in *Zoot Suit*

A feminist reexamination of Luis Valdez's *Zoot Suit* reveals that women,
even within the confines of a nationalistic and patriarchal ideology, pushed

the limits of their social location, just as Esquivel did while welding at the Friedrich factory in San Antonio and Esther did in *Soldierboy* while sewing uniforms in the factory. While the Sleepy Lagoon case involving the murder of a pachuco, and the broader "Zoot Suit riots" during the World War II era, have been the subject of numerous studies, this play proposes to fill in the blanks by imagining dialogues and debates that could not be reflected in the historical court records and other primary sources that have informed more standard historiographies of the era. While the play is not fact, it provides new perspectives for interpreting the facts beyond the Sleepy Lagoon case, its defendants, or the racism that undergirded the era.

In the play, Henry Reyna, the central character who is framed for the murder of another zoot-suiter, wears a zoot suit much to his parents' disapproval and shame. Various historiographies have proposed the zoot suit as a symbolic representation not only of youthful rebellion but also of the abject ways in which *pachucas* and pachucos have been viewed by the media and the judicial system.[49] In *Zoot Suit*, Dolores, Henry's mother, understands what the zoot suit represents and presides over its use. A feminist critique of Valdez's play reveals that Dolores maintains considerable agency not only for herself but also for her family. While Valdez has never been celebrated as a feminist, and has even been criticized for the masculinist dimensions in some of his plays, he nonetheless provocatively introduces Dolores standing next to a clothesline while asking Henry about his need to wear the suit. The scene opens:

> DOLORES: (*Sighs, resigns herself.*) *Mira, hijo*. I know you work hard for your clothes. And I know how much they mean to you. *Pero por Diosito santo*, I just don't know what you see in *ese cochinada de* "soot zuit."
> HENRY: Drapes, *amá*. We call them drapes.
> DOLORES: (*Scolding playfully.*) *Ay, sí*, drapes, *muy* funny, *verdad*? And what do the police call them, *eh*? They've put you in jail so many times. *Sabes que*? I'm going to send them all your clothes!
> HENRY: *A que mi amá*. Don't worry. By this time next week I'll be wearing my Navy blues. Okay?[50]

Much like Frank in *Soldierboy*, Henry Reyna in *Zoot Suit* uses "uniforms" to show his status, either in the form of a civilian in a zoot suit or the military uniform of World War II. Also similar to Esther's work as the maker of uniforms in *Soldierboy*, Dolores functions to supervise what Henry wears. That she is depicted at the clothesline, a trope for the maintenance of Henry's clothing and identity, marks her agency in the home beyond stereotypical depictions of this space as merely domestic.

Here, I part with the framing of *Zoot Suit* offered by Rosa Linda Fregoso, who argues that the play places female characters in dualistic categories: "the virgin or the whore, the long suffering mother or the 'cheap broad.'"[51] In her assessment, Ramirez repeats the refrain:

> Because it posits Mexican American women as either virgins or whores, *Zoot Suit* restricts and even bars their agency. . . . *Zoot Suit* fails to appreciate Chicanas' complex relationship to coolness and hipness and misrecognizes the ways in which they have expressed resistance via both language and silence.[52]

While I agree that these stereotypes exist in the play, I assert also that the female characters pressured their agency even while they were contained within a patriarchal framework. In her critique, Ramirez seeks for the women to equal the men in "coolness" and "hipness." I argue that women perform outside of these binaries. Dolores is more than a long-suffering mother; she has agency within the family as the sole proprietor of their clothing and, more significantly, their status.

This role as authority over her family's clothing is further exemplified in the play, thereby endowing it with even more symbolic significance. In the introduction to his survey of Chicano theater, for example, Jorge Huerta describes the overarching metaphor of the press:

> The use of newspapers for much of the set decoration, as well as the giant front page backdrop from which *El Pachuco* cuts his way at the top of the play is an effective metaphor for the all-pervading presence of the press. When Dolores Reyna hangs newspapers on the clothesline instead of actual laundry, the comment is complete.[53]

In several scenes, Dolores maintains her children's clothing, which in the play is intertwined with the metaphor of the press. When Rudy is set to go to war, "Dolores inspects his collar and gives him his hat."[54] Thus Dolores's clothesline becomes the axis for Henry's performative identity. The clothesline, though often associated with domesticity, also "signifies communities of women—namely working class women in urban settings . . . who gather around the clotheslines to share the news of the day."[55] Implicit on Dolores's clothesline is the zoot suit; however, Valdez's script depicts her explicitly hanging newspapers, not clothing. The metaphor of the clothesline then also serves as the narrative of Dolores's family, in addition to her role as narrator. Like the Brazilian literature *del cordel*, "literature on a string," the Reynas' story hangs on a clothesline.[56] Dolores, the only character who occupies this space, then enforces it.

Considering the racial injustices still pervasive during the 1940s, the treatment of the Mexican American youth in *Zoot Suit* depicts the racist nationalistic ideology of World War II. Thus the "Double V—Victory against racism at home and victory against fascism abroad" finally meant that the war would become the point of departure for civil rights. As early as 1941, President Roosevelt issued Executive Order 8802, banning discrimination in defense plants and government offices and services.[57] Though the severity of nationalistic ideology prompted the hysteria leading to race riots, it also forged cross-racial alliances among people of color. In *Zoot Suit*, it is Dolores who recognizes the community's cross-racial negotiations that led to the victory and release of Henry and the other Sleepy Lagoon defendants. She notes:

> Yes, but if it wasn't for the unselfish thoughtfulness of people like you and this beautiful lady—and all the people who helped out, Mexicanos, Negros, all Americanos—our boys wouldn't be home today.[58]

In her oral history, Esquivel also recalls that the war affected racial divisions in San Antonio, where she remembered that people of color were segregated from certain venues. "There was a lot of discrimination before the war with the colored people and with us, the Hispanics," recalls Esquivel of her school days at Pauline Nelson Elementary in San Antonio during the 1930s. "Colored people couldn't go to the Majestic [Theater]. There was a lot of discrimination. After the war, it started getting better."[59] In the years following 1945, after she and Homer Esquivel married, the integration of ethnicities became apparent. Esquivel recalls that when she and Homer went to San Pedro Park on Sundays, everyone—Mexicans, whites, and African Americans—went to watch people dance the jitterbug.

Esquivel's post–World War II experiences also reflect the new feminist agency in the domestic sphere. While Homero and his brother were serving in the war, his mother maintained the household, a responsibility she continued even on their return. Esquivel and her husband lived with his mother for a few years after the war and gave his mother approximately half of Homero's wages because, as Esquivel recalls, "she used to take care of everything."[60] Like Dolores in *Zoot Suit*, Esquivel's mother-in-law was more than "the long-suffering mother" confined to a domestic role. Her agency extended even over her veteran sons as she managed the family's income. Similarly, toward the end of the play *Zoot Suit*, it is again Dolores, the mother, who manages and deconstructs what the suit has done to her son:

> I know what you are feeling, *hijo*. I know inside you are afraid that nothing has changed. That the police will never leave you in peace. *Pero no le hace.* Everything is going to be fine now. Marry Della and fill this house with children. Just do one thing for me—forget the zoot suit clothes.[61]

That Dolores says "zoot suit clothes" instead of "zoot suit" signifies her understanding of them as mere clothes on the clothesline. This symbolic deconstruction contrasts with the symbolic identity Henry has worn and performed. In the same manner as *El Pachuco* and Rudy having been stripped of their zoot suits, Dolores figuratively strips Henry of his. Her assessment of her son outside of this signifier alters his subjectivity. He is, as she states in the closing scene, "our son,"[62] a person apart from the suit. I assert that Dolores, because she maintained her children's clothing at the clothesline, was the only true material challenger to the zoot suit. Her position at the line meant that even while contained within a patriarchal framework, her labor and domestic production—read hanging clothes—determined *when* and *if* Henry could wear it. His cultural performance could be carried out only because hers was the precursor.

The Subversive Demarcations of Labor: Mexican American Women and Cultural Performance

In mapping the complexity of Latina agency and labor in the home, at work, and in various public venues, Mexican American women progressed through their bilingual speech and labor acts even within the limits of patriarchal and nationalistic ideology. In the liberatory layering of their roles, Mexican American women on the homefront recuperated their borderlands *nepantlera* subjectivities. Mexican American women negotiated their roles as patriots, laborers, and resisters. They embody a model of third space consciousness, which enables them to move from the margin to the center and back again as they deem appropriate. As noted, the work of women of color, both as laborers and contributors to the national cause, intersects with white women's history while simultaneously being distinct from it. Women of color had a long tradition of working well before the United States entered the war in 1941. Nonetheless, the war did provide new opportunities and signal a shift in the type of work that had been available to women of color.

In *Becoming Mexican American*, George J. Sánchez examines the social construction of the border and gender roles; changes in labor outside the home "necessitat[ed] the flexibility of 'traditional roles' and norms for survival."[63] I seek to expand on those areas of women's roles that challenged what has been conceived as the "traditional." Thus their multivalent roles were couched in the nontraditional spaces through new skills and trades, especially in the defense industry. Through an examination of Mexican American women's agency of the World War II generation such as Juanita Esquivel's work as a munitions factory welder and corresponding oral history interviews, in addition to imaginative reconstructions of otherwise undocumented and effaced subversive proto-feminist agency, such as Severo Pérez and Judith Pérez's play *Soldierboy* and Luis Valdez's *Zoot Suit*, I situate these narratives in the complex negotiations between Mexican American women's agency, citizenship, and ideology. I ultimately argue that these remappings provide a fuller understanding of the realities and possibilities for Mexican American women to reclaim both private and public spaces as fully empowered women.

Interrogating the *Soldado Razo*: Masculinity, Soldiering, and Ideology in Mexican American World War II Memoir and Theater

B. V. OLGUÍN

The exclusion of Latina/o soldiers in Ken Burns's 2007 documentary, *The War*, touched a raw nerve in many Latina/o families who still gaze upon three-dimensional *retablos*, or photographic shrines, to uniformed grandfathers, brothers, uncles, and cousins who served in World War II. These family members recite the same prayers for uniformed sisters and brothers, daughters and sons, friends and neighbors in Afghanistan and Iraq. Burns and the Public Broadcasting Service, the film's underwriter, received thousands of emails, letters, and other expressions of outrage over this effacement of Latina/o service in World War II, as had Tom Brokaw for his equally blatant exclusion of Latina/os from his 1998 anthology on World War II veterans, *The Greatest Generation*.[1] The protests included a March 13, 2007, resolution by the American GI Forum that sought to block the airing of Burns's film, which was originally scheduled to premier on the symbolically significant Mexican Independence Day, el Dieciseis de Septiembre, that also is celebrated by Mexican Americans throughout the United States. The American GI Forum, which was founded by Mexican American World War II veterans in 1948, insisted that Ken Burns's taxpayer-funded project recognize—and, indeed, celebrate—Mexican American World War II soldiers.[2] The resolution proclaims that "Hispanic/Latino individuals during World War II were the most decorated minority group to receive this Country's highest award, 'The Congressional Medal of Honor.'" Ironically, and in many cases tragically, such claims are co-opted to support the eugenicist stereotype of a Latino "martial caste," which George Mariscal, a Vietnam War combat veteran, scholar, and activist, has critiqued as operative in military recruitment campaigns targeting Latino males.[3]

Even beyond the GI Forum's resolution, many of the oral histories, narratives, and historiographies by and about Latino soldiers feature masculinist spectacles of violence: their citizenship is articulated as racialized masculinity, masculinity as martial prowess, and soldiering as sexual virility. These militarized and problematically gendered models of male Latino citizenship are not confined to the battlefield. Tejano military veteran, author, and folklorist Américo Paredes reveals how the nineteenth- and early-twentieth-century acoustic Mexican American ballad form known as the epic heroic *corrido* features Mexican American social bandits firing their pistols as they hurl sexualized masculinist epithets at their white male Texan enemies, such as "come and meet your father" (e.g., "El Corrido de Jacinto Treviño").[4] Mexican American Medal of Honor recipient Roy Benavides also introduces his narrative of near-suicidal combat in Vietnam by recounting an episode when he pulled the testicles of a bull to prove his "bravery" and earn a quarter.[5] And in contrast to nostalgic attempts to recuperate Chicano masculinity and the Chicano male warrior hero by scholars such as Alfredo Mirandé and Miguel López, many more Latino-authored war narratives are replete with "male bonding" scenes involving sexual violence against women, such as Vietnam War veteran Charley Trujillo's account of a Chicano soldier biting the nipple off a Vietnamese woman during a group visit to a brothel in his semiautobiographical novel, *Dogs from Illusion.*[6]

These violent performances of soldiering as racialized, masculinist, and sexualized citizenship are not uniform. They involve myriad trajectories and slippages that are further nuanced by the historical and material specificities of each war. As I show in this chapter, the interplay between racialized gendered subjectivities and the performance of militarized citizenship by Mexican American male soldiers in World War II offers unique opportunities to complicate conventional historiographies of the Soldado Razo, or Mexican American buck private. Many Mexican American historiographies of World War II have posited male military service as a watershed moment in Mexican American claims to full citizenship that foregrounded a more or less oppositional model of Chicana/o identity in subsequent generations.[7] What remains unacknowledged, unaddressed, and undertheorized in historiographies of Mexican Americans in World War II is the degree to which Mexican American male performances of a militarized citizenship involved a wide array of political positions, cultural fusions, and ideological negotiations. George J. Sánchez locates a paradigm shift in Chicana/o historiography and cultural studies beginning in the late 1980s that recognized "the possibility of multiple identities and contradictory positions,"[8] which Chicana feminist theorists such as Norma Alarcón and Chela Sandoval more precisely have theorized as an interstitial third space agency that involves multiple, and sometimes simultaneous, migrations in and out of various subject positions.[9] Drawing on this liberation of the Mexican American subject from overdetermined binaries, I propose to interrogate the World War II Soldado Razo's racialized gendered citizenship, and the shifting relationships to hegemony, that is, the manner and degree to which they are interpellated in the dominant individualist, capitalist, and imperialist episteme. I argue that the World War II Soldado Razo is a central protagonist in the performance of a militarized Mexican American citizenship undergirded by various models of masculinist power that are as oppositional (even revolutionary) as they are hegemonic (and potentially fascist).

In her reading of the different, though similarly patriarchal, context of eighteenth- and nineteenth-century English literature, Eve Sedgwick has mapped the symbolic rehearsal of the patriarchal interdependence and solidarity among men—their homosocial bond—in their collective domination of women, especially through the figural and literal exchange of women in marriage as part of male-to-male property arrangements. She proposes the homosocial as

> social bonds between persons of the same sex; it is a neologism, obviously formed by analogy with "homosexual," and just as obviously meant to be distinguished from "homosexual." In fact, it is applied to such activities as "male bonding," which may, as in our society, be characterized by intense homophobia, fear and hatred of homosexuality.[10]

Scholars such as Michael J. Shapiro and Susan Faludi have extended Sedgwick to map the peculiarities of homosocial culture in U.S. military academies and male military culture in general.[11] I suggest that these mappings of male bonding as masculinist political subjectivity offer touchstones for rereading the masculinist World War II literature by Mexican American males beyond celebratory accounts of them as subaltern subjects claiming (or rejecting) U.S. citizenship with their pistols in their hands.

While George Mariscal, Lorena Oropeza, Stella Pope Duarte, and many more Chicana/o scholars, writers, and veterans have recuperated and presented alternative feminist and anti-imperialist discourses about Chicana/os and the Vietnam War—the war that continues to figure most prominently in virtually all accounts of Chicana/o social and political history—surprisingly little has been written about the complex performances of Mexican American masculinity in other wars, especially World War II.[12] As noted above, warfare has always involved—and in many cases is constituted by—sexualized violence. Yet no one has critiqued Mexican American soldiers for their use of sexual violence as the performance not just of soldiering but also of their Mexican American warrior hero subjectivities that undergird their U.S. citizenship, which is relatively empowering for them regardless of its antithetical dimensions due to lingering racism.[13] Even less has been written about the intersections of masculinity, homosocial bonding during war, and the complex racialized—and even transracial—aspects of Mexican American soldiering and supranational cultural citizenship in any war. This lacuna invites, and indeed demands, a reassessment of the ideology of Mexican American and Chicana/o spatial ontology. Pursuant to a more complex understanding of race and gender in the performance of Latino masculinities, specifically Mexican American soldiers in World War II, I seek to offer a preliminary mapping of the range of Mexican American racialized homosocial soldiering and citizenship. I submit that the Soldado Razo may be patriarchal, misogynist, and homophobic, even as his agency is located within a continuum of complexly racialized and gendered subjectivities that may also extend to a counterhegemonic politics.

By juxtaposing Mexican American masculinity in World War II Marine Corps veteran Guy Gabaldon's 1990 memoir as well as his related interview in the Voces Oral History Project to Judith Pérez and Severo Pérez's 1989 play, *Soldierboy*, which features a Mexican American World War II veteran from San Antonio, Texas, I seek to extend the range of possibilities for mapping the ideology of the Soldado Razo.[14] In both texts, I examine the utterances as well as the silences in order to identify the subtexts, or subliminal discourses, as well as the hidden transcripts, which the play, in particular, has sought to make more palpable and accessible. The use of a theatrical text is especially important to this project as few military veterans have been so willing or able to expose a less flattering, and self-critical, account of their experiences of soldiering, which is not surprising given the trauma involved in wartime military service. This is especially the case in regard to post-traumatic stress disorder, which is both difficult to discuss and in many cases even more difficult to recognize. That is, many soldiers have yet to come to terms with the psychological dimensions of their experiences in warfare. Judith Pérez and Severo Pérez's play thus becomes an important medium for imaginatively exploring the still-neglected psychosocial dimensions of warfare and masculinity. By reading the primary documentary evidence provided by Gabaldon in his self-published book and corresponding interview alongside theatrical renderings of composite soldiers in *Soldierboy*'s rendering of the Rapido River Crossing battle in Italy during World War II, new models of Mexican American masculinity emerge that challenge the more static binary of the oppositional subject versus the patriotic assimilationist.

Several questions emerge out of the eclectic pairing of a memoir cele-brating masculinity and an imaginative theatrical production that ex-plores the psychological and social complexities of it. How might the World War II narratives by and about Mexican American males inadvertently per-petuate the racist constructions of Mexican American males as a martial caste? How does the otherwise xenophobic practice of national soldiering paradoxically enable male-centered, cross-racial identifications with other men across battle lines? How far do these male-centered identifications go? What happens to U.S.-based theories of Latina/o identity when Mex-ican American soldiers reconstruct new identities in transnational battle-field contexts that also involve identifications with enemy combatants as fellow supranational subaltern grunts? In this chapter, I show that the inter-sections of masculinity, violence, and Mexican American citizenship ulti-mately pressure for a new paradigm in Mexican American, Chicana/o, and broader Latina/o Studies beyond progress narratives celebrating Mexican American heroism or equally celebratory Chicana/o resistance discourses proclaiming defiance to U.S. imperialism.

Motorcycles, the Marine Corps, and Capitalism in Guy Gabaldon's Transnational Masculinity

Since its inception, the field of Chicana/o Studies has been undergirded by theories of transnational spatial ontology, with Chicana/o subjects cel-ebrated for their complex transgressions and reappropriations of various lo-cal, national, and international sites of power and containment, particularly in the U.S.-Mexico borderlands.[15] The Latina/o spatial studies emphasis on the counterhegmonic potential of Latina/o claims to place also under-girds celebratory models of Latina/o cultural citizenship. William Flores and Rina Benmayor, for instance, propose that "cultural citizenship names a range of social practices which, taken together, claim and establish a dis-tinct social space for Latinos."[16] This expansive definition of Latina/o cul-tural citizenship allows for symbolic and material empowerment virtually anywhere Latina/os congregate, and intersects with various attempts to map Latina/o counterhegemonic agency across borders and globally. Male Mexican American soldiers, however, reveal some troubling aspects about Latino transnational cultural citizenship. One case in point is former ma-rine Guy Gabaldon. The recipient of the navy's Distinguished Service Cross and nominee for a Medal of Honor for his U.S. Marine Corps service in the Pacific theater during World War II, Gabaldon is symptomatic of the hegemonic dimensions of the Soldado Razo's identity and agency. Gabaldon has been the subject of a Hollywood film and numerous documentaries and books focusing on his unique bicultural, bilingual heritage as an East L.A. Chicano who grew up among Nisei, or second-generation Japanese Americans.[17] Ironically, Gabaldon gained fame for killing thirty-three Japanese soldiers and capturing over a thousand on the Pacific island of Saipan during World War II, which he often facilitated by speaking to his "enemy" in what he calls his East L.A. "backstreet Japanese." But Gabaldon's 1990 memoir, *Saipan: Suicide Island*, which bears the cover proclamation, "I killed 33 and captured 'over one thousand Japanese,'" reveals another dimension to his renowned bilingual and bicultural "heroism": a transnational fetish involving a transracial homosocial exchange of women. That is, he engages in male-bonding rituals with former enemies that are facilitated by the symbolic exchanges of Japanese and Mexican Japanese women. He also imbeds Mexican American class mobility in capitalism and U.S. imperialism in World War II and beyond. As such, Gabaldon exposes the underexamined subtext of celebratory readings of the World War II Soldado Razo warrior hero paradigm. A reinterrogation of his case—one of many—opens new possibilities for theorizing the intersections of Mexican American soldiering, citizenship, and U.S. hegemony following the war.

Gabaldon's memoir reveals that his main rationale for killing thirty-three Japanese soldiers was motivated by the same commodity fetish animating the World War II global contest between empires over who would emerge as one of the world's premiere superpowers. His book opens with an account of his materialist motivation to kill three Japanese soldiers he encountered during an early solo scouting expedition: a three-wheeled Harley Davidson motorcycle. "That bike is going to be mine," he recalls thinking to himself as he lurks nearby in a sugarcane field, adding, "All I've got to do is kill three 'Samurai' and I'll have a good ol' Harley."[18] Despite his celebrated acculturation into Nisei language and culture, Gabaldon reveals a racialized bias in his encounter with the Japanese "other" when he writes, "He should have had a Honda, not an American motorcycle."[19] Gabaldon subsequently kills these men for their American motorcycle, claiming the property for himself just as his service would enable the U.S. to claim Saipan as its own territory. That is, his desire for material goods, and the symbolic power that came with it, gains a metaphorical significance in relation to the U.S. desire to extend its might throughout the Pacific.

With the phallic Harley-Davidson engine roaring between his legs, Gabaldon rides back to the U.S. garrison victorious, thereby merging his previous barrio bad boy biker subjectivity with jungle warfare as a U.S. Marine.

SUICIDE ISLAND

BY
GUY GABALDON
"MAVERICK MARINE"

A TRUE STORY

NAVY CROSS

I killed 33 and captured "over one thousand Japanese"

Figure 10.1. *Saipan: Suicide Island.* In this account, Gabaldon details his childhood in Boyle Heights, living with a Japanese American family, and his exploits as a marine on the island of Saipan. Written, printed, and published by Guy Gabaldon, Saipan Island, U.S.A., March 1990.

He concludes that "fighting in the Pacific tropical jungles and living in the East Los Angeles ghettos had a lot in common—you had to be one step ahead of the enemy or adios Mother."[20] In the performance of his transnational persona—which involved local and global bilingual code-switching from English to Spanish to Japanese—Gabaldon ironically intersects with borderlands, interstitial, and, at least superficially, third space transnational subjectivities despite the hegemonic projection of his masculinist Mexican American soldiering. His soldiering tactics, after all, enable symbolic, social, and material class mobility. In addition, his claim to the status of a hero allows him the latitude to militate on behalf of additional subaltern subjects, such as fellow Mexican American soldiers, as well as his adopted Nisei family, which we learn in his memoir had been interned, though some of his childhood friends opted to join the army's all-Nisei 442nd Infantry Regiment instead.[21]

Gabaldon takes his interstitial agency a step further and ultimately undermines its potential counterhegemonic resonance. While performing a hybrid subjectivity in multiple transnational contexts—from East L.A. to the South Pacific to post–World War II counterinsurgency operations in Latin America—he instantiates a model of imperialist citizenship by celebrating Spanish conquistadors, who are anathema to the neo-indigenous basis of Mexican American Studies. He proclaims that "these pioneers were men of guts and stamina," adding, "I take pride in the valor of these men with big 'huevos' [balls]."[22] He then links colonialist conquest in sixteenth-century Mesoamerica to conquests in Saipan (which became a U.S. "territory" after World War II), the Bay of Pigs in Cuba (whose participants he helped recruit for additional counterrevolutionary ventures in Latin America), and the victorious anti-Sandinista Contra War in Nicaragua (in which he helped deliver supplies to anticommunist militias). While the American GI Forum insists on including soldiers such as Guy Gabaldon in the pantheon of the "Greatest Generation," Gabaldon's conflation of masculinity and the commodity fetish, which collapses transcultural citizenship with transnational imperialist conquest, is equally as pathological as it is patriotic. Indeed, in his own accounts, Gabaldon kills some Japanese soldiers for their gold teeth, watches, money, and souvenirs, including pistols, sabers, and other weapons. "I didn't know what the Geneva Convention had to say about War Booty," he reflects after complaining about having some of his goods confiscated by his officers. He responds, "I certainly didn't give a rat's ass what they say," then concludes:

> I'm not about to leave anything on their carcasses. That might sound ghoulish, but I know that the Marine behind me will strip the Nip I kill.[23]

Gabaldon is such a zealous killer of Japanese that he is threatened with a court-martial on several occasions for his unauthorized and expressly forbidden forays, which he frequently calls "hunts."

While it must be noted that Gabaldon's activities as a soldier were undertaken during warfare, in which killing is fundamental, though not always the main objective, in the execution of tactics and overall strategy, it is equally important to map the broader symbolic economy of his combat actions as well as his transracial and transnational identity. In many respects, Gabaldon is the quintessential subaltern subject who successfully navigates his marginality by transforming it into interstitial agency pursuant to his own enfranchisement. While Gabaldon shares uneasy similarities to other mestiza and mestizo icons who anchor Chicana/o Studies, he is not likely to ever be claimed as a paradigmatic subaltern Mexican American hybrid, or mestiza/o, subject by scholars in the field. And for good reason. Even as Gabaldon recuperates Japanese American citizenship through his celebration of the Japanese American soldiering exploits of some of his Nisei childhood friends who enabled his transculturation, he also freely uses exoticist and racist stereotypes that further place his transracial identity under erasure. Despite the hybrid performances of solidarity as a Mexican American and adopted Nisei subject, Gabaldon's bilingual flourishes in his memoir quickly degenerate into racist invective. He refers to Japanese soldiers, businessmen, and postwar politicians as "Nips" and "Japs." In a 1985 letter to Japanese Prime Minister Yasuhiro Nakasone, Gabaldon even mocks Japanese-accented English (e.g., "rots of ruck" for "lots of luck"). Prime Minister Nakasone apparently claimed that "Hispanics" "were a detriment to the advancement of the U.S.," to which Gabaldon offers the racist retort: "he stuck his hoof right between his buck-teeth."[24] Gabaldon does note, however, "I, too, cringe at the word 'Jap,'" adding, "after all, the person I love most, my wife, has her roots in Japan."[25] As a Mexican American/Nisei subject, Gabaldon alternately recognizes, rejects, and kills Japanese as the "other," then recognizes them anew as allies, enemies, family members, and even part of himself.[26] This is the complex yet clearly troubling dimension of Gabaldon's model of the *Soldado Razo* that undermines overly celebratory appraisals of his transnational and interstitial identity and agency.

Gabaldon's final "reunion" with the Japanese sniper who shot him during combat foregrounds how his soldiering-as-citizenship paradigm is informed by a transracial, transnational masculinity that is simultaneously part of hegemonic patriarchy and provocatively taboo. This reunion of macho men, which takes place on the same island forty years after they tried to pierce each other with bullets, climaxes in a symbolic exchange of women. As noted above, scholars have extended Sedgwick's exchange-of-women paradigm to a multiplicity of contexts, and I submit that a similar, though more figural, masculinist exchange of women may be occurring in a peculiar scene that Gabaldon recounts in his combat memoir. Amid photos of dead Japanese soldiers with captions such as "Jap burned to a crisp in a bunker," "Dead Japs by the Dozen," and "A Good Jap Soldier" that appear alongside the contorted bodies of U.S. Marines killed in combat, is a photo of Gabaldon hugging a former Japanese soldier, Saburo Arakaki, who also fought in the Saipan battle. Above them is a wrinkled rising sun flag of the Imperial Japanese Army that Japanese troops carried into battle and that subsequently adorned Gabaldon's postwar home in Saipan. Gabaldon notes that Arakaki was firm in his belief "that the Nisei were traitors to their race"[27] but also adds an ironic narrative about Arakaki's conversion to Christianity and his eventual lifelong friendship with Gabaldon and his Nisei Mexican American daughter.

The bond between two World War II soldiers from opposite sides of the battlefield climaxes in a chapter dedicated to the Japanese guerrillas who served under Arakaki's command and who ultimately wounded Gabaldon:

> We were both eighteen year old fighters for our respective countries and did our best to kill each other. If Arakaki had ever been in my rifle-sights I would have killed him as I did several of his friends. It was his friend, Corporal Horiguchi, who finally shot me. He got the drop on me and machine gunned me in the left arm and right ribs, grazing my right ear.
>
> Now when Arakaki comes to my home here on the Island where we fought each other, I feel honored by his presence. He prays with my family, and my ten year old daughter, Aiko, sings Japanese war-time songs to him, songs that I taught her when she was three years old. Arakaki's eyes get watery and I know spiritually, something I would never have thought possible—a former Japanese soldier who I had sought in the jungle, now influencing my religious philosophy. Incredible.[28]

As numerous soldier memoirs reveal, this sincere and highly personal episode has become a rite of postcombat soldiering that is undergirded by a transcendent bond among survivors of war horrors. This bond arises from a multiplicity of insights and emotions, including recognition of their exploitation and sacrifice by the elites who profit from war, as well as the sublime empathy sometimes shared by survivors of similar types of trauma. In some cases, it also involves the mutual recognition of each man's membership in a cult of masculinity. This homosocial soldiering appears as a martial cult that is embedded in a figural exchange of women in the form of Gabaldon's young daughter who is offered by her father to honor his guest with Japanese war songs. The implications of this transnational encounter are placed in greater relief when one considers the dissonance that would be created by a U.S. soldier encouraging a daughter to sing Nazi or Italian fascist war songs in honor of a former enemy soldier.

One of the enduring failures of postcolonial and subaltern studies—as well as Chicana/o Studies—is the persistent reluctance to account for the multiplicity of ways and degrees to which subaltern transnational hybrid subjects such as Gabaldon function within hegemony: in this case, capitalism and U.S. imperialism. Unlike the Chicana/o autobiographical writing, especially testimonial discourse, that has enabled the synthesis of an oppositional consciousness, Gabaldon remained a masculinist, misogynist, and homophobic promoter of empire throughout his life. He even based a failed congressional campaign on a xenophobic platform decrying "illegal immigrants" and "feminists,"[29] which he added to his memoir's pantheon of villains such as "faggots." As a symptomatic case, Gabaldon's memoir and subsequent interview in the University of Texas at Austin's Voces Oral History Project thus offer an aperture for nuancing simple celebratory accounts of Mexican American World War II "heroism" while simultaneously complicating the racialized gendered subjectivity and agency of the Mexican American World War II Soldado Razo.

Combat Trauma, (Anti)Masculinities, and Transgressive (Dis)Identifications in Judith Pérez and Severo Pérez's *Soldierboy*

Homosocial soldiering, as Gabaldon's hug with his former enemy illustrates, involves an intimate masculinity more powerful than nationalism. Their brotherhood, forged in the trauma of combat, transcends geopolitics even as Gabaldon synthesizes his transnational identifications into a fervent nationalist imperialist politics. *Soldierboy* offers an alternative synthesis of the political economy of the World War II Soldado Razo from a working-class perspective. Written during a residency with Teatro Campesino in San Juan Obispo, California, where it was produced in 1982 under the direction of Luis Valdez, this play presents a complex portrait of soldiering in which intimate combat masculinities overshadow—and overpower—heterosexual desire. Moreover, the play extends, and to some degree challenges, the resonance of Sedgwick's mapping of the continuum of male identifications by troping the racialized dimensions of the World War II Soldado Razo's homosocial soldiering toward a transracial underclass solidarity. Written by a Chicano and a white Jewish husband-and-wife team, the play features a provisionally taboo bonding between a Mexican American soldier and a white soldier from opposite sides of segregated tracks in World War II–era South Texas. As I show, this crossing of boundaries ultimately challenges the bourgeois desires of Mexican American cultural nationalist spectatorship.

Contemporary performance theorist José Esteban Muñoz proposes "disidentification" as an extension of various models of resistant spectatorship—or the act of rejecting offensive stereotypes and other denigrating images onscreen and onstage. He also explicates how multiethnic and gay performers deploy transgressive and relatively empowering reclamations and redeployments of stereotypes that enable actors and audience members to disidentify with them as they create new ones that are deployed toward new ends.[30] This practice of rejection, reclamation, and renovation ultimately liberates heretofore forbidden abjected subjectivities that, ideally, enable various types of enfranchisement beyond the models of empowerment proposed by Gabaldon. While none of the characters in *Soldierboy* are overtly gay, they deploy transgressive disidentification survival strategies to negotiate, and strategically disidentify with, in-group sexist and white racist stereotypes, as well as related expectations about their conduct from members of their own Mexican American community. Patricia Portales has mapped feminist agency in *Soldierboy* through a "liberatory layering," which involves disidentifications of sexist and racist expectations at the site of women's domestic and factory labor, which become consciousness-raising experiences.[31] I add that related gendered and racialized tensions in the play enable the playwrights to restage a transgressive homosocial soldiering through and beyond race. The related maneuvers and subversions of the characters also extend through and beyond heterosexual desire and ultimately enable a proletarian (though still ideologically inchoate) reconstruction of the World War II Soldado Razo.

The plot in *Soldierboy* revolves around the postwar life of Frank de la Cruz, a Mexican American World War II veteran who has returned to his home in San Antonio, Texas, after surviving one of the worst U.S. military disasters in the war: the Rapido River crossing in Italy that cost the lives of over two thousand soldiers from the U.S. Army's 36th Division, a unit that consisted primarily of poor Mexican Americans and whites from Texas and Oklahoma. Ostensibly a chronicle about the rise of the Mexican American middle class, the play focuses on Frank's efforts to leave his father's produce stand in favor of more lucrative employment as a radio repairman at Kelly

Field, a local air force base. Frank's wife, accustomed to her independence while her husband was at war, seeks to continue earning extra income and to preserve her growing autonomy by working in a garment factory, which her husband sees as an affront to his masculinity, his authority as a husband, and her duties as a mother. Frank's younger brother, an immature though de facto father figure to Frank's young son during his absence, is crippled after having been run over by an automobile in an act of drunken juvenile bravado. He now lives vicariously through newspaper and newsreel accounts of his older brother's "heroic" actions in the war.

Using these intersecting trajectories of warfare, gender, and labor, Judith Pérez and Severo Pérez synthesize a new discourse about the Soldado Razo that begins with the demystification of the Mexican American warrior hero mythos. The play opens with Frank's belated arrival home after the parade, brass bands, and speeches about heroism that he deliberately avoided because he rejects the male warrior hero paradigm such spectacles represent. For Frank, the war was less about bravery and manhood and more about subservience to military authority and primal attempts to survive by human beings who had been reduced to their barest animal essence. He remains traumatized by the death of a fellow soldier, Ernest Watts, who was killed saving Frank's life in the battle and now reappears in Frank's vivid dreams about the war. These ghostly visitations are juxtaposed to scenes illustrating Frank's strained relationship with his biological brother, Willie. They serve to foreground the explication of a different type of brotherhood that becomes less about masculinist models of soldiering and more about class war.

This linkage of soldiering with exploitation is underscored by Frank's and Watts's mutual roles in the deaths of powerless combatants and civilians alike, which extend the Soldado Razo's demystification to the level of a classical Greek tragedy that is preordained and continually gets worse. For instance, Frank de la Cruz, newly promoted to the rank of sergeant in charge of a platoon of reluctant soldiers, forces his men forward, knowing they will be slaughtered. He even goes so far as threatening to shoot a frightened draftee if he does not continue advancing toward the lethal German machine-gun nests. Frank's dreams revisit these leadership decisions and recall Watts's attempts to console him. Watts has an intimate knowledge of Frank's state of mind, since Watts previously had killed a group of Italian children with a grenade after mistaking them for German soldiers hiding in an abandoned house. This experience of survival—against desperate odds and by means of unspeakably horrible decisions that at the time seemed logical and reasonable even if they later appear to have been terribly

Figure 10.2. Actors performing a scene from the play *Soldierboy* at El Teatro Campesino in San Luis Obispo, California. This production of *Soldierboy* was directed by Luis Valdez and produced by Teatro Campesino. The play, by Severo Pérez and Judith Pérez, features a Mexican American soldier from San Antonio who is changed by his wartime experiences and returns home to a changed society. Courtesy of Teatro Campesino, Department of Special Collections, Davidson Library, University of California, Santa Barbara.

wrong—becomes the basis of their unique battlefield bond. They are mere pawns, and their collective agency has been co-opted to harm other pawns. And they know this.

The play presages this intimate bond between men in battle through an exchange of symbolically significant gifts that functions as a theatrically excessive device designed to foreground another level of synthesis in this restaging of the political economy of the Soldado Razo. During a lull in the battle, Frank gives Watts a medallion of St. Christopher, the 250 C.E. Christian martyr associated with dangerous river crossings who is believed to protect travelers, which initially was given to Frank by his fervently devout aunt. Watts returns the favor by offering a charred wooden case of toy soldiers he found on the battlefield for Frank's son, which ultimately gains a metonymic resonance in the play. These gifts are reminders of the model of manhood that neither of the men can escape. The play thereby offers an opportunity for the audience to entertain the option of disidentifying with the martial caste discourse surrounding Mexican American military service, and the male warrior hero mythos in general, but this is only part of the play's transgressive significance.

The corollary reconstruction of a potentially transracial materialist model of the Soldado Razo is presented through the unexpected, though quite common, battlefield bonding among soldiers of different racial backgrounds. This transracial bond is complicated by a postwar visit by Watts's mother, who had traveled with her husband to the de la Cruz home from their home in the rural white-majority enclave of Floresville, Texas. She seeks to know how her son died, especially since he remained listed by the army as Missing in Action. Frank, initially reluctant to tell her about the horrors they experienced as subjects and agents of warfare, eventually says that her son died instantly, ostensibly without pain. But he withholds the salient details of their wartime experiences. The conversation is punctuated by Mrs. Watts's matter-of-fact statement that her husband refuses to enter the de la Cruz home "because he wishes it was you that was missing, and Ernest [Watts] the one that came home." Frank retorts, "Look, I'm sorry about Ernest. But I'm not sorry about coming home," rejecting the bigoted view that Mexican Americans, and especially Mexican American soldiers, are surplus and expendable even as he commiserates with the Watts's grief.[32]

However, this scene involving Frank's refusal to identify with racist expectations does more than simply appeal to its targeted Mexican American audience, which had become accustomed to literary indictments of racism. By presenting such a powerful bond between a Mexican American and a white male, the play offers a revolutionary proposal for transracial sub-altern working-class solidarity, not as soldiers, but as victims of militarism. As such the play offers a potential indictment of Mexican American cultural nationalist claims to class mobility in the capitalist imperialist context of U.S. militarism during and after World War II, which the five military bases in San Antonio (dubbed by civic boosters "Military City, U.S.A.") continue to afford. Indeed, part of Frank's recipe for upward mobility was encouraging his father to seek a large produce supply contract with a military base that was reserved only for white suppliers. His own desire to work at the military base as a civilian contractor further illustrates the complicated material circumstances that undergird both his rejection of militarism and his recognition that military defense work offers the most lucrative options for him and his father.

The play's underlying critique of Mexican American middle-class desire for upward mobility reaches a crescendo in the penultimate scene, in which Watts saves Frank only to be killed in the process. Before his death, Watts shouts:

> You're crazy! You'll get yourself killed. We got to get you some help or you'll die here like the rest of them. Our company always went first. Why? The brass didn't think any better of us meskins and redneck farmboys. We didn't mean dirt to them. We always did what we was told. And you, Sarge, you were the best of what we had. We done enough. But no more. I'm saving our butts, de la Cruz. You're my ticket out of here. Goddamn it. We're not going to die here. Let's go.[33]

This dying soliloquy closes the drama and imbues the preceding act with a new troping of battlefield brotherhood as a tragic but significantly anti-masculinist cross-racial intimacy. (See Figure 10.2.) This homosocial bond no longer is defined by the exchange of women but by the figural and real exchange of blood. This new homosociality potentially forms the basis of the Soldado Razo's disarticulation from racialist and even simplistic anti-racist teleologies, so he can be relocated within a broader materialist critique of the political economy of warfare.

Yet the relationship between the two combat brothers is so powerful that it will extend beyond the grave and into Frank's home, casting a long, somber shadow over his postwar life that further complicates the Soldado Razo's homosocial soldiering. Indeed, the dead, and Frank's yearning for Watts's life, ultimately displace Frank's matrimonial intimacy. After his return from war, Frank never engages in sex, romantic touches, or any intimacy at all with his wife despite her entreaties, which includes a special dress bought for his exclusive gaze. In this play about post-traumatic stress disorder (which was diagnosed during World War II as "battle fatigue"), homosocial soldiering is forged in brutal annihilation and ultimately troped as a new model of the Soldado Razo that supersedes male warrior hero accolades and even heterosexual desire. In the end, the story is less about racism or marital estrangement than the potential for subaltern transracial class solidarity.

This is where the play itself disidentifies with the cultural nationalist politics of the venues such as the Farmworker Theater in San Juan Obispo where it was composed and staged or the Guadalupe Cultural Arts Center in San Antonio, which continues to host Chicana/o theater featuring archetypes of the "tragic" mestiza and mestizo or empowered Chicana/os opposing racism. The play instead presents the transracial aspects of homosocial soldiering beyond the archetype of the male warrior hero. It offers a vision of an egalitarian society no longer predicated on the domination and exploitation of patriarchy, or the annihilation resulting from nationalist imperialist wars. Watts, who vocalizes a class critique of the U.S. military's use of the poor as cannon fodder, is thus a necessary companion to Frank's immediate desire for upward mobility. The symbolic death of the male warrior hero, and the Soldado Razo warrior hero in particular, is less important than the synthesis of a new model of homosocial soldiering in which the Soldado Razo becomes a counterhegemonic transracial postsoldiering subaltern subject.

Conclusion: Mexican American Soldiering, Citizenship, and Chicana/o Studies

The World War II Soldado Razo, as these two literary texts illustrate, is an ideologically inchoate subject who engages in a multiplicity of migrations across geography—including geographies of race—within, and potentially beyond, hegemony. While *Soldierboy*, a play written by nonsoldiers, may seem anachronistic for its retrospective depiction of class critique during an era when Mexican Americans are not generally associated with radical working-class politics, World War II conscientious objector Carlos Cortez's poetry, art, and activism as a member of the Socialist Party and, later, Industrial Workers of the World suggests otherwise.[34] Additional World War II memoirs by Henry Cervantes and Frances X. Medina, as well as the World War II–era poetry by Américo Paredes, in addition to the nearly one thousand interviews in the Voces Oral History Project, reveal that the Soldado Razo resists easy classifications.[35]

The resultant slippage in the Soldado Razo's multiple negotiations of identity and ideology, it must be noted, was always a function of his subaltern social location, which earlier iterations such as military veteran and former zoot-suiter José Montoya's renowned poem, "El Louie," dramatically illustrated as early as 1969. While the poetic persona in Montoya's poem is a Korean War veteran who dies in obscurity as a drug addict, he nonetheless offered one of the earliest—and perhaps the first—attempts to offer a candid and self-critical yet compassionate assessment of Mexican American soldiering and truncated citizenship as subaltern yet ideologically complex. As such, "El Louie" implicitly is in dialogue with Raúl Morin's celebration of Mexican American soldiering in *Among the Valiant: Mexican Americans in WWII and Korea*, which bears an introduction by former President Lyndon B. Johnson, who would expand the U.S. war in Vietnam that, by some accounts, involved an over 25 percent casualty rate for Mexican American soldiers.[36] My preliminary reinterrogations of the World War II Soldado Razo reveal that Mexican American soldiering before, during, and after World War II involved myriad performances of homosociality. In other words, the de-mastery of knowledge that Sandra Soto advocates is always already at play in performances and rehearsals of the Soldado Razo.[37] Both Gabaldon and the Pérezes enable us to see the fissures in standard depictions of this Mexican American archetype.

With this recovery and de-mapping of the Soldado Razo's racialized gendered and (d)eroticized agency, important opportunities emerge to interrogate Mexican American citizenship and its varied relationships to hegemony. This interrogation must extend beyond simplistic proclamations and celebrations of the Soldado Razo, or condescending depictions of Mexican American soldiers as mystified agents of empire, tragic mestizo (anti) heroes, or proto-revolutionary protagonists of history. These authors reveal that the Soldado Razo has agency, but it is not always counterhegemonic; nor is it merely a performance of mystification by colonized subjects. The field of Chicana/o Studies has excelled, especially in the past two decades, in mappings of Chicana and Chicano subversive and proposed counterhegemonic negotiations of ideology, but it has yet to account for the highly problematic specter of the relatively empowered capitalist imperialist Mexican American subject illustrated by Guy Gabaldon and further exposed by Judith Pérez and Severo Pérez.

This masculinist, capitalist, and imperialist militarism has extended even more dramatically into the late-twentieth/early-twenty-first-century "war on terror" as Mexican American and Latina/o soldiers took leadership roles in the U.S. wars in Iraq and Afghanistan. One Mexican American soldier, Gen. Ricardo Sánchez, was the commanding officer in charge of troops in the Abu Ghraib prisoner abuse scandal, of which he attempts to absolve himself in his memoir, *Wiser in Battle: A Soldier's Story*.[38] Another Latino, Puerto Rican José A. Rodriguez Jr., is a CIA officer and the author of a book that recounts his role in designing and implementing the waterboarding torture of prisoners, *Hard Measures: How Aggressive CIA Actions after 9/11 Saved American Lives*.[39] The ideological pendulum of the Soldado Razo had swung this far right as early as World War II, as is illustrated in Robert Huddleston's biography, *Edmundo: From Chiapas, Mexico, to Park Avenue*.[40] Based on original correspondence to and from Edmundo Lassalle, this profile bears the cover tagline, "The true story of a Mexican-American who became a World War II spy and married a German Princess." This account of the Soldado Razo-as-spy features the imperialist philandering Mexican American agent of the World War II Office of Strategic Services, the precursor to the CIA (where Lassalle is rumored to also have served).

As the fields of Chicana/o and Latina/o Studies continue to recover and map the ever more complex nature of Latina/o racialized gendered identities and various claims to local, national, and transnational citizenship— as well as supranational and internationalist paradigms—scholars need to continue accounting for the material and cultural contexts undergirding (and still overdetermining) Latina and Latino enlistment in the U.S. military. The field also inevitably will need to account for the growing Latina/o middle classes, the increasing number of elected officials—most of whom are die-hard capitalists and wholeheartedly support U.S. imperialism—and even the growing number of Mexican American and Latina/o millionaires. Latina/o Studies can no longer continue to ignore the specter of its own imperialists—from Marine Corps privates to army generals to CIA officers— any more than it can ignore the complex, empowering, and potentially revolutionary aspects of the Soldado Razo.

Seeking "America": A Cuban Journey through the United States and Beyond during the World War II Era

GERALD E. POYO

On July 25, 1941, eighteen-year-old Sergio Poyo, accompanied to the Havana docks by his parents, José Poyo y Skillin and Sergia Alvarez y Rodríguez, boarded a ferry for the United States to attend professional school. Cuban American relatives in Miami whom he had never met until this visit put him on a bus to Atlanta the next day.[1] He spent a month with his brother, José (known as Bebo), who studied engineering at the Georgia Institute of Technology and, in early September, continued his bus trip to Flint, Michigan, where he enrolled in the General Motors Institute (GMI) for a three-year program in automotive dealership management. Sergio's engagement with Flint in fall 1941 was both daunting and exciting as he immersed himself in an American environment. Everything was alien about this U.S. working-class industrial city dotted with automobile and parts factories, and when winter arrived his excitement at seeing snowfall for the first time gave way to the chilling reality of freezing temperatures. At first he was comforted by the knowledge that this was a temporary residence preparing him for his future in Cuba, but the unexpected death of his father soon transformed him from visiting student to immigrant.

Sergio's entry directly into the Anglo-American mainstream rather than a Cuban American community required him to adjust quickly. Facilitated by his white racial background, good education, English-language proficiency, and familiarity with U.S. culture, Sergio took advantage of opportunities and mostly avoided the difficult barriers and often harsh treatment Latino immigrants faced during the 1940s, but not entirely. This chapter explores the adjustment experience of a Cuban immigrant, U.S. Army veteran, and businessman who embraced Americanization while simultaneously embarking on an unexpected transnational journey that created for him and his family a broader hemispheric understanding of what it meant to be "American."[2]

Neocolonial Lives and Transnational Legacies

Sergio Poyo's decision to attend the General Motors Institute stemmed from an interest in his father's profession. For almost twenty years José Francisco Poyo had worked at the Lawrence B. Ross Corporation, the General Motors distributorship in Cuba, which sold cars retail but also enjoyed the exclusive right of importing automobile stock for agencies across the island. José found a job with the Ross Corporation in 1914 as a clerk fresh out of Havana's San Agustín High School where he studied "*comercio*" (business). During the next decade he rose to become vice president of the company and managed day-to-day operations. In 1939 Ross sold the distributorship, and two years later General Motors offered José the managing directorship of a struggling automobile agency in Santiago de Cuba, promising to provide credit to purchase the dealership outright.

José was among the first generation in Cuba of an exile revolutionary and intransigently nationalist family that returned home with high expectations after the independence war against Spain. His grandfather, José Dolores Poyo, had lived in a thoroughly Cuban community in Key West since 1869 where he challenged Spanish rule as a nationalist newspaper editor, cigar factory reader, and revolutionary conspirator. In the early 1890s José Dolores collaborated with José Martí in helping launch the insurrection that led to Cuba's independence.[3] José's father, Francisco Andrés Poyo, worked as a cigar maker in Key West's famous Eduardo H. Gato factory and played baseball to raise funds for the revolutionary effort.[4] Born in Key West in 1896, José moved to Havana with his entire family—parents, grandparents, aunts, uncles, and cousins—three years later. They endured thirty years of exile and returned home to make their nationalist dream a reality.

Although fully Cuban in identity and culture, they faced the challenge of reintegrating into a devastated society, which inevitably did not live up to their idealistic nationalist expectations. Growing up in Havana, José experienced his father's and grandfather's disappointment with the Cuban republic's efforts to mature under the watchful eye of the United States. In addition to suffering the humiliation of the U.S.-imposed Platt Amendment to the Cuban constitution of 1902 that significantly compromised Cuba's sovereignty, they resented bitterly the corruption of Cuba's new political class, which did not act much differently than the Spaniards before them. As Francisco Andrés said, "We carry their blood in our veins," which accentuated the feelings of betrayal.[5] When the United States occupied Cuba in 1898 after defeating the Spanish army, the military government opened the island to Americans—some honest and many not—with capital, ambition, and the protection of the occupation authorities. U.S. citizens not only transformed Cuba's economy, but influenced its culture and values in many ways. Few Cubans had resources to compete with the flood of Americans who soon took charge of the country's economy. Those Cubans with land often had extensive acreage but little capital, so they sold to Americans and became their employees. Those few with capital and entrepreneurial ambitions did what they could to survive in a very competitive situation but often also ended up working for Americans and internalizing American economic, social, and cultural ways.[6] As noted historian of Cuba Louis A. Pérez Jr. wrote:

> Many Cubans were integrated into North American structures by virtue of their employment with U.S. companies, from large sugar corporations and mining operations to banks, department stores, and small shops and farms. . . . The employment of so many Cubans by North American enterprises affected behaviors and bearings, values and perspectives, appearances and attitudes.[7]

Cuba had gone from Spanish colonialism to a new economic colonialism that placed a premium on working with U.S. businesses and investors.

As a graduate of Colegio Nuestra Señora de Belén, a prestigious Jesuit high school in Havana, Sergio certainly could have attended any number of universities in the United States, but at the suggestion of his father José's bosses in New York, he decided to attend GMI's unique specialized Dealer Cooperative Program. According to GMI's yearbook, this program provided students with "training that enabled dealerships to obtain men qualified in automotive operation, construction, and repair." "Men thus trained," the yearbook assured readers, were prepared for "responsible jobs in sales promotion and automotive servicing." And for Sergio, this meant work in the family dealership.[8]

Besides his academic preparation, Sergio arrived in the United States ready culturally and linguistically to study at GMI. During the 1920s and 1930s, English-language skills in Cuba were increasingly indispensable for aspiring businessmen as the island's economy became thoroughly dependent on the United States. Sergio's mother made sure her children learned English. A shrewd woman from the small town of Caimito del Guayabal, thirty kilometers west of Havana, Sergia Alvarez always referred to herself as a *guajira* (a country woman lacking big-city sophistication), but she sized up the situation in Havana quickly and made sure to enroll her children in an English-language school. "Learn English," one school advertised, "the language of Progress. Increase your prestige and popularity—and earn more money. Never before have there been as many opportunities for men and women with knowledge of the English language."[9] Though Sergia did not speak English and knew little about the United States, she nevertheless could see the advantages of an "American" education. She enrolled her four sons in Havana's Phillips School, located on Avenida Central in the prestigious Kohly neighborhood, not far from the Poyo home.[10] The school offered classes from nursery school to seventh grade and provided "complete Spanish and English preparation for entrance to American and Cuban high schools."[11] One of many English-language private schools in Cuba modeled on North American curricula, the four children learned fluent English, even avoiding the inflections of a Spanish-language accent.[12] Sergio enrolled at Belén in eighth grade and completed his education in a Spanish-language Cuban curriculum but remembered being more proficient in English than Spanish vocabulary and composition. Sergio and his brothers also acquired English-language fluency in their Almendares neighborhood, which throughout the 1930s filled with children of families connected to foreign companies such as Coca-Cola, Swift Company, Trust Company, First National City Bank, and the Royal Bank of Canada.

Sergio completed his first semester in Flint, Michigan, uneventfully, except for the shocking attack on Pearl Harbor by Japan on December 7. Shortly after the outbreak of the war, he and his brother received letters from their father telling them he would be registering the family at the U.S. consulate in Havana. Born in Key West, José retained the right to U.S. citizenship, a right his bosses in New York encouraged him to claim as a way to facilitate wartime business travel between the United States and Cuba. José told his sons that they, too, were eligible to claim U.S. citizenship and apply for passports but cautioned that they would be subject to the draft and should consider their decision carefully. Both remained at school during the Christmas holiday to work, and Sergio spent Christmas with friends who invited him to their home.

But Sergio and Bebo quickly pushed aside concerns about the war when a Western Union cable from their mother informed them their father had fallen gravely ill. In Havana José and Sergia had spent a pleasant Noche Buena together with their two youngest sons, Jorge and Ernesto, and with the Poyo grandparents, no doubt discussing the war, business, school, and Bebo and Sergio in the United States. In the late evening José complained of feeling ill; he developed a fever, and in the following days the family physician diagnosed a particularly virulent and dangerous form of malaria. As soon as they received the cables from their mother, Sergio and Bebo set out on their journeys home. Unable to fly because of bad weather, Bebo spent a restless night at the Greyhound station in Atlanta waiting for his bus, which was delayed. In Miami he boarded a Pan American flight to Havana, where he arrived on Sunday afternoon, January 4, while Sergio arrived the next day.[13] They were too late. Their father had died on Saturday morning, and according to custom and law, the burial took place within twenty-four hours. Neither son had the chance to see their father's body or grieve his death at a funeral. This they had to do alone in the privacy of their thoughts, in their own ways.

The family's destiny changed in an instant. José Poyo's untimely death on January 3, 1942, underscored the family's economic fragility, not uncommon for that sector of Cuba's bourgeoisie highly dependent on salaried jobs with foreign companies. Family income disappeared, except for a small General Motors insurance policy on José. While they lived a comfortable life, the family had few resources beyond their home and José's salary, which they had little possibility of replacing. José's difficult and long trajectory to a comfortable standard of living did not include guarantees, and his sons now had to fend for themselves. Sergia recognized the need for her sons to complete their educations in the United States—only possible if they did not have to worry about the welfare of the family. Most middle-class women in Cuba did not work, and few jobs existed even if they wanted one, so she thought her chances would be better in the United States. The family soon immigrated to the United States and settled in Atlanta.

Sergio departed first on February 18 to resume studies in Flint using his Cuban passport and seven-month student visa.[14] Three weeks later, on March 9, the U.S. Department of State confirmed the family's registration as U.S. citizens, making them eligible for passports and facilitating their move.[15] In the meantime, Sergia and Bebo traveled to Santiago to close the dealership, and within weeks the family departed for Atlanta. Sergia leased the family's Havana home, and José's parents oversaw it. In Atlanta, Sergia rented an apartment not far from Georgia Tech, where Bebo returned to school. Younger brothers Jorge and Ernesto enrolled in school, Jorge in his second year of high school at Boys High and Ernesto in a nearby elementary school. Though she spoke no English, Sergia found a job at Woolworth's department store placing price tags on merchandise heading for the sales floor. She also supplemented the family income by regularly renting one of her apartment's three bedrooms to two Latin American students while her sons occupied the other. Up to this point, Sergia had been the wife of a successful businessman and lived a comfortable life in Cuba, but her origins in the small town of Caimito gave her a practical and down-to-earth perspective that facilitated this transition from a solid middle-class Cuban life to working for meager wages in a department store in downtown Atlanta.

In the month and a half in Havana after his father's funeral, Sergio not only helped his mother and brother decide the family's future but also pondered how one's destiny could change so unexpectedly and dramatically. Sergio's plan to join his father in running the car dealership in Santiago disappeared, and he returned to the United States with a different frame of mind: he needed to rethink his strategies about the future. He continued his already designed path but also recognized that his future would probably be in the United States rather than Cuba. With this in mind he focused on assimilating as best he could. If Sergio's formative years at Phillips School prepared him well for his experiences in the United States, so did the legacy of the family's exile during the final thirty years of the nineteenth century and their engagement with the world of American business on the island. Ironically, Cuba's neocolonial relationship with the United States inevitably drew the Poyo family into an economic, social, and cultural world that prepared and paved the way for moving north at some future time. The family shifted their focus from Cuba to forging a new life in the United States, and Sergio requested his American passport.

Work, Wartime Military Service, and Americanization

For millions of migrants all over the world, the act of leaving their homeland represents a strategy to improve life conditions for themselves and their families. Whatever the particularities, moving to new environments requires adjustments and the development of new identities, sometimes chosen, often not, and is informed by the political, socioeconomic, cultural, and even psychological background of migrants, the migration experience itself, and the demands of host countries. In the 1940s, when Sergio arrived, the United States generally insisted that immigrants "Americanize," that is, shed their culture and traditions and assimilate even if no intention existed of providing equitable access to socioeconomic and political opportunities.[16] During the late nineteenth and early twentieth century, the influx of millions of immigrants frightened many who believed foreigners threatened the foundations and traditions of American society. Anti-immigrant forces rallied and in 1924 succeeded in enacting the country's first comprehensive immigration reform known as the National Origins Act. This legislation closed borders, banned Asian and African immigration altogether, and favored the immigration of northern Europeans over southern and eastern Europeans whom the nation generally viewed as difficult to assimilate. The United States as "melting pot" became a well-accepted metaphor, which framed national attitudes about difference. Popularized in the early twentieth century, this idea envisioned the diverse peoples in the United States "melting" into a unified whole. Synonymous with Americanization, it encouraged assimilation and conformity as the surest path to good employment and mobility for those whose racial and ethnic characteristics permitted.[17]

In an era of war and nationalist fervor, those unable or unwilling to "melt" faced the certainty of intolerance and suspicion, most dramatically seen in the forced internment of California's Japanese for the duration of World War II. Certainly understanding this reality, Sergio did not resist Americanization, which yielded opportunities but also exposed deeply entrenched negative attitudes that affected even those who complied with societal requirements and expectations.[18] In the 1960s, intolerance for difference softened, and the Immigration Act of 1965 changed the composition of immigration streams to the United States. "Cultural pluralism" replaced the "melting pot," creating an entirely new environment of relative openness—but one that Sergio did not experience.[19]

Sergio was one of thousands of mostly Mexican, Puerto Rican, and Cuban migrants arriving and adjusting during the start of a new era of Latin American immigration to the United States after the Great Depression. The U.S. economic collapse in the 1930s had reduced migration from all three regions and spurred massive and systematic deportations of Mexican workers, which reversed with the outbreak of World War II.[20] Suddenly agribusiness and railroads in the Southwest again needed Mexican workers; a government sponsored guest-worker program known as the Bracero Program provided work to hundreds of thousands of laborers.[21] In Puerto Rico, rising unemployment during the first half of the twentieth century related to the island's economic transformation under U.S. tutelage forced thousands of Puerto Ricans, who enjoyed U.S. citizenship, to seek work in New York and other urban centers in the United States.[22] After the U.S. occupation of Cuba in 1898, which closely integrated the two economies, existing Cuban communities (established since the 1870s) in Florida and New York attracted more immigrants.[23] Migration north also gained strength after the Depression, and between 1946 and 1956 approximately fifty thousand Cubans received permanent resident visas.

Cubans of all classes regularly traveled north during this era for vacations, education, and work, especially to New York and Miami.[24] Professionals, workers, writers, baseball players, musicians, artists, and actors found the United States alluring, as did students. Since the nineteenth century, middle- and upper-class Cuban families sent their children to the United States for secondary and university education. They attended not only elite schools like Harvard and Yale, but any educational institution they believed provided an advantage in U.S.-dominated Cuba. Between 1923 and 1946 annual enrollments of Cubans in American colleges and university increased to 585 from 139.[25]

After the family's immigration to the United States, Sergio did his best to embrace an attitude of conformity and integration, for him an obvious response to the country's expectation of assimilation. Handsome, five feet eight inches, with black curly hair and an athletic build, Sergio was reserved and congenial, which helped him create a network of friends and gain acceptance at GMI. He was one of four "Hispanics" (probably all from Latin America) in the Dealer Program's 1941 entering class of fifty-nine students, and the only one in the Alpha Delta fraternity, which he joined in 1942. Besides the bonding activities inherent in fraternity life, Sergio developed friendships by joining the fraternity softball team.

Baseball had been an important part of his life in Cuba, and he had frequently accompanied his grandfather, Francisco Andrés, to watch their favorite Almendares baseball club. He starred on the Belén baseball team playing shortstop and second base and even played a bit of semi-pro ball before leaving for the United States. Now he shared this pastime with his fraternity brothers; the 1942 GMI yearbook, *The Reflector*, included two action photos of Sergio blasting a hit and sliding into home base.[26]

He also dated, and in early 1943 he met a young woman from Flint, Geraldine "Gerry" Darnell, at a fraternity party, and despite their differences, the two quickly became regular companions.[27] Communication with his girlfriend in Havana, whom he had last seen around the time of his father's funeral, lessened as it became clear he would not return to Cuba anytime soon. He appreciated Gerry's company and support during this difficult period in his life. They were an unlikely couple: he from a middle-class Cuban family and she from a working-class midwestern family. Sergio's privileged and stable childhood in Havana contrasted with Gerry's difficult early years.

She was born in Painton, in southeastern Missouri, on February 17, 1923, the same year as Sergio. Gerry's parents, Earl Vanoy Darnell and Edna Patterson, had a troubled marriage. Though Gerry mostly refused to discuss that painful aspect of her life, she did say that their family's difficult economic situation contributed to her parents' divorce. An unskilled worker, Darnell struggled to get along as the Great Depression enveloped the country. Sometime in 1933, Edna left Morehouse, Missouri, to join her parents in Flint, Michigan. Her parents had moved from Cape Girardeau, Missouri, in the early 1920s to work in the automobile factories.[28] Edna took her two children, Gerry and Robert, as well as her stepson, Elton, and joined the dramatic migration from the increasingly impoverished rural areas of the South and Midwest to the industrial North where she found a job at the AC Spark Plug plant.[29] During this era of great labor tensions, Edna Darnell joined the union and earned a living for her children. Gerry remembered fondly her years at Flint Central High School where she studied the Commercial I curriculum that taught business and secretarial skills, including bookkeeping and typing, which she put to use beginning in February 1940 during her final semester in high school.[30] She went to work as a secretary at H. W. Schaffer's retail store at 134 W. First Street in Flint, where she continued working after graduation and so avoided the more grueling work in the automobile and parts plants.

Sergio adapted to Gerry's world of friends and family, and their relationship strengthened. The extent of their attachment became especially evident during summer 1943 when Sergio moved to Indianapolis for training with the Allison Division of General Motors as part of the cooperative "hands-on" aspects of his education.[31] Wartime adjustments forced GMI to temporarily discontinue the dealership program and instead prepared students in aircraft engine repair and maintenance. Sergio pursued training as an airplane mechanic but knew that it was just a matter of time before he was drafted; that certainly inspired two important decisions.[32]

Feeling alone and anxious about what the war might bring, Sergio missed Gerry very much, and on one of her visits he proposed marriage and she accepted. Without funds and their families geographically scattered, they opted for a simple ceremony performed by the justice of the peace in Indianapolis on August 7, 1943.[33] In a letter to her mother several days later, written on Indianapolis Hotel Lincoln letterhead, where they spent their honeymoon, Gerry said, "I'm so happy, and I love my husband very, very much. He is so sweet."[34] She also gave her mother the address of the apartment they were moving to later that day: Mrs. Sergio Poyo, 1327 Park Ave., Indianapolis. "Sounds peculiar doesn't it?" she noted, referring to her new name.[35] They had known each other for about eight months, but they were not the only ones during this era that responded to the reality of war by accelerating relationships and marrying. Neither ever spoke of strains specifically associated with their differing ethnic backgrounds or of negative

Figure 11.1. Geraldine Darnell, left, her mother, Edna Darnell, center, and her brother, Robert Darnell, Flint, Michigan, ca. 1940. © Gerald E. Poyo. Courtesy of Gerald E. Poyo.

Figure 11.2. Sergio Poyo and Geraldine Darnell, wedding photograph, August 1943. Geraldine, a working-class midwestern Anglo woman, and Sergio, a middle-class Cuban man, married after knowing one another for only eight months. Geraldine learned to cook Cuban and Latin dishes from her mother-in-law. © Gerald E. Poyo. Courtesy Gerald E. Poyo.

Figure 11.3. Second Lt. Sergio Poyo, 1945. Poyo later attributed his penchant for order and routine to boot camp. © Gerald E. Poyo. Courtesy Gerald E. Poyo.

reactions from family or friends, but they understood theirs was an unconventional marriage. In later years, Sergio often pointed to Gerry's independent and adventurous streak that freed her to explore a world much different from her own.

Sergio's second big decision was to join the military. On September 11, 1943, less than a month after their marriage, Sergio enlisted in the Reserve Corps of the Army of the United States as an aviation cadet.[36] Earlier in the year, Bebo had done the same, and in 1945, after completing high school, Jorge joined the navy, leaving only fourteen-year-old Ernesto with their mother in Atlanta. In less than two years, Sergio's status changed dramatically from a Cuban student training abroad to a newly wed U.S. citizen preparing to go to war. Military training introduced Gerry and Sergio to the full flavor of U.S. culture and geography, from the Midwest to the South to the West. After induction in Indianapolis, he proceeded to Jefferson Barracks, Missouri, for boot camp with the 35th Training Group while Gerry returned to Flint.[37] Throughout his life afterward, he often commented that his penchant for order and routine stemmed from his military training, beginning with boot camp. Sergio afterward cut his hair biweekly, hung his clothes carefully to ensure that his pant creases were perfectly aligned, kept his shoes shined, and recounted how quickly he could make a bed "military-style." In December 1943 Sergio began Army Air Corps cadet training at Middle Georgia College in Cochran.

Gerry joined him in Cochran in the middle of January and rented a room in the house of the A. A. Holcombe family. Sergio lived in the college dormitories that now served as military barracks. While he trained, Gerry kept busy doing a variety of things, including making friends with wives of cadet trainees, planning dinners for Sergio on his days off, and even helping Mrs. Holcombe with her dress shop. She also kept up a regular correspondence with her family and friends, especially her mother who had recently remarried.

Describing what she and Sergio were doing, her letters also inquired about how her brother, Bob, and half brother, Elton, were doing in the military and why she did not get more letters. She also struggled to convince her mother, who had relied on her a great deal, that despite all the changes in their lives, they would be fine.[38] Gerry soon became pregnant and told her mother in the middle of March that she and one of the other wives took walks "out by the college." "I have to do something," she added, "as I'm getting so fat I can't walk." "Sergio," she complained, "said he would have to send me home in a cattle car."[39] They exaggerated since she was probably only about two months along, but she returned to Flint sometime before October 20 to give birth to a son, Sergio Jr.

Commissioned as a second lieutenant, Sergio left Cochran for Maxwell Field, in Montgomery, Alabama, before beginning navigator training in San Marcos, Texas, on November 16. He remembered the first time he navigated an aircraft back to San Marcos on a night training flight. It was a particularly cloudy and turbulent night, and the exercise tested his abilities and provoked considerable anxiety, but he managed well. Gerry and Sergio Jr. joined him, and they all remained in San Marcos until he received his navigation degree on April 7, 1945, and entered active duty.[40] Sergio then went to Fort Bragg, North Carolina, to undergo advanced navigational training at Pope Field before spending time at Shaw Field, Sumter, South Carolina. During this time, Gerry lived in Flint. Finally, he was assigned to George Field in Lawrenceville, Illinois, with the 805th AAF Base Unit where he prepared for service with the I Troop Carrier Unit, which was headed for the Pacific theater.[41]

As Sergio's unit prepared for overseas deployment, he suddenly suffered appendicitis, which left him ill for weeks. While still recovering, on August 6, the day before their second wedding anniversary, Sergio and the country learned of the atomic bomb that destroyed Hiroshima. Three days later another bomb devastated Nagasaki and the Japanese government surrendered unconditionally, abruptly ending the war. Sergio nevertheless expected to be deployed overseas, perhaps to Japan, when he returned to duty on September 21. "His days of leisure are over," Gerry commented to her mother in a letter. "I guess," she continued, "Sergio will be overseas by x-mas, but I still keep hoping for a miracle."[42] A miracle indeed; it came in the form of demobilization. At San Marcos Sergio had been commissioned a "temporary" second lieutenant in the U.S. Army who would serve "at the pleasure of the President of the United States for the time being, and for the duration of the war and six months thereafter unless sooner terminated." Much to Gerry's delight, his separation from the Army Air Corps came earlier than expected, on November 9, 1945.[43]

Sergio's first steps in becoming American involved navigating social relations and learning the ways of this new society, which overall proved a positive experience. School, fraternity, and marriage introduced him to the U.S. social and cultural environment, while his military experience tied him emotionally to his new country. He never faced combat or even went overseas, but military experience solidified his sense of citizenship and patriotism. As with other Latinos, the military experience and willingness to give his life for the United States influenced his identity transition. He proudly adopted nationalist World War II narratives and fiercely identified with the values of that American generation. "If it wasn't for the atomic bomb you probably wouldn't be here," Sergio declared years later in a conversation with his son Gerald who questioned the morality of using atomic weaponry to end the war against Japan. They were discussing a national controversy generated by an exhibition at the Smithsonian Institution's Air and Space Museum in 1994. The exhibit was built around the *Enola Gay*, the aircraft that delivered the bomb over Hiroshima. Veterans' groups around the country, with whom Sergio agreed, took the museum to task for including viewpoints of those who considered the bombs unnecessary. The controversy eventually caused the Smithsonian to cancel the exhibition. Sergio felt strongly about his time in the military and the rationale for using the bomb. Without the bomb he would certainly have participated in the inevitable assault on Japan and perhaps lost his life, which gave him little sympathy for those, including his son, who second-guessed the decision. Identification with this kind of narrative and argument linked him to U.S. national identity.[44]

Latinidad and the Racial Limits of the "American Dream"

After demobilization, Sergio, along with his family, returned to Indianapolis where he completed the cooperative aspects of the now reinstated GMI automotive dealer program. At the end of summer 1946 he received his GMI degree with a specialty in automobile engineering and dealership service and maintenance.[45] Sergio immediately put to use his father's superb reputation among General Motors Overseas Operations' (GMOO) executive leadership in New York and contacted Morris Clark, general manager of the Foreign Distributorship Division. It was Clark who five years earlier had encouraged his father to take charge of the General Motors dealership in Santiago and suggested Sergio attend GMI, and it was Clark who now offered Sergio his first professional job. The young Poyo family moved to Fair Lawn, New Jersey, from where he commuted to work to the Foreign Distributorship Division offices across the Hudson River in Manhattan on the second floor of the Argonout building on the corner of Broadway and 57th Street, opposite the General Motors Building. The job paid $250 per month and involved providing automotive technical training and support for the service departments of foreign distributors in Latin America, which put his GMI training to good use and required extensive travel throughout the region.[46]

During his first five years in the United States, Sergio set a path toward integration and expected to find a stable job working in the automobile industry consistent with his training and ambitions. The death of his father in Cuba in January 1942, which suddenly left him, his mother, and his brothers without resources, framed Sergio's outlook on life and firmly defined economic security as among his top priorities. He settled into work with the FDD but with a view to securing a dealership job in the New York–New Jersey region. In reality, he hoped eventually to achieve his father's dream of owning an automobile dealership. Working as an automobile service trainer with the FDD provided the opportunity for interesting and exciting travel throughout Latin America, but being away from home for months at a time quickly became burdensome. In summer 1950, for example, Sergio set out on a lengthy trip to Colombia, Ecuador, Bolivia, Peru, and Chile, leaving six-months'-pregnant Gerry alone to care for five-year-old Sergio Jr. Even though his brothers and friends helped Gerry, he felt uncomfortable leaving his wife during her pregnancy. Sergio returned in time for the birth of their second son, Gerald, in September and kept his eyes open for other work opportunities.

As he searched for work he kept in mind the importance of deemphasizing his Cubanness, a lesson he learned during his short stay with his brother in Atlanta in July 1941 before starting the GMI program. Working in a warehouse for a month, he partnered with an African American man in the stockroom. Young Sergio immediately saw the dynamics of the work environment for his adult counterpart, recognizing the limitations a black man faced in the United States. He learned that some Americans possessed characteristics that made full acceptance and mobility difficult if not impossible, signaling to him the need to integrate as best he could. Sergio also learned about the attitudes and barriers that condemned Latinos in the United States to second-class citizenship. During 1942 and 1943, violence against Mexican American zoot-suiters erupted in Los Angeles and made national headlines; and Sergio later saw, firsthand, the fierce anti–Puerto Rican attitudes in New York and other cities in the Northeast.[47] But he also recognized that, unlike most Latina/os in the United States, he enjoyed assimilative options they did not. His light skin, fluent English, and lack of an accent allowed him, when convenient, to avoid being identified as "Hispanic" and "pass" as an American.[48]

One day in the late 1940s, as they rode the bus into Manhattan, Sergio made clear to his brother, Bebo, his ideas for coping with anti-Latino discrimination. Though they usually conversed in Spanish, Bebo realized that when he spoke to his brother in Spanish on the bus Sergio always replied in English. Challenging him, Bebo asked if he was ashamed of being Cuban and speaking Spanish. Sergio asserted that he was not ashamed of his heritage or language but that American society certainly held it against him. He told his brother that he did not want to be mistaken for Puerto Rican, not because he had anything against Puerto Ricans, but because of the way they were treated in New York. Sergio even extended his assimilation strategy to the naming of his children. In military training and not present when his eldest son was born, Gerry named him Sergio Jr., which he only learned of during their first conversation after the birth. Later he acknowledged that he would have preferred to give his son an "American" name, and the next three children received clearly "American" names: Gerald, Cynthia, and Jeffrey. Sergio rarely spoke to his children in Spanish, and it was also during this time that he began to introduce himself as "Serge." Gerry apparently had no concerns about her husband's name and probably began to call him "Serge" at his insistence.[49]

An immigrant trying to carve out a life for himself and his family as a businessman in New York City, Sergio spent little time pondering life's inequities, except how to avoid them. If he could avoid discrimination, he would. Moreover, he had a wife and child to worry about, and he did not want unnecessary, and for him, he thought, avoidable handicaps. Certainly, the practical methods for achieving this goal outweighed any thought of challenging societal attitudes he did not think he could change. Seeing the harsh economic and social realities Latina/os faced, Sergio did not cultivate Hispanic friends. He spent most of his time with his brothers, Bebo and Jorge, who lived with them for a time in Fair Lawn, a suburb with few Latina/os. Gerry naturally developed relationships with Anglo-Americans who constituted their social network.[50]

Decisions about assimilating, however, were also tied to his attitudes about Cuba. Sergio had pleasant memories of Cuba, remembering fondly his family life, especially the time spent with his father at the car dealership and with his grandfather Francisco who encouraged his interest in baseball. He reminisced about his years at Belén Jesuit School, where he played baseball and basketball and developed a close relationship with friends in a study group. But Sergio's memories were definitely mixed and deeply influenced by his family's disillusionment with Cuba's experience as an independent republic. Sergio remembered the political instability and limited economic possibilities in Cuba that eventually disrupted his family life. When Bebo became involved in student politics at the University of Havana, their father immediately sent him to study at Georgia Tech and Sergio happily went to GMI. Though he always had a keen interest in politics and after retirement expressed strong conservative political viewpoints, he carried a suspicion and distaste for politicians wherever he lived. Sergio often told the story of how during the early 1930s his father had spent the night at the distributorship with a gun to protect it from insurgents intent on stealing cars. "Nobody should have to do that," he explained. When his father died and the family left Havana, Sergio concluded that Cuba offered little for him and his family. He rarely spoke of his homeland, at least not until his son Gerald, as an adult, began inquiring about the family's history.

Despite his best efforts, however, Sergio could not fend off others' deeply embedded discriminatory sentiments. Sergio's hopes of finding work in a dealership did not materialize even though he had been trained in exactly that line of work and had demonstrated his willingness to adapt to American ways. Frustrated and disappointed, he finally concluded that his Hispanic surname and background, which he did not hide or deny, trumped his willing attitude to conform to American ways. Although he never specified exactly how he thought this discrimination operated, daily contacts with the society around him made clear that Latina/os of all classes struggled to receive equal opportunities. He even detected anti-Latina/o attitudes among Gerry's friends and often heard their derogatory use of "spic" when speaking of Puerto Ricans. As friends, they did not consider him in that category, but they certainly reflected broader societal norms. Sergio's Americanization efforts remained insufficient for society's gatekeepers, so he sought an alternative path.

From America to América: Toward a Transnational Latinidad

This disappointing experience and Sergio's determination to work for a dealership inspired him to consider returning to Cuba when his boss Morris Clark in 1949 alerted him of an opportunity at a new automobile agency in Havana owned by an Italian national, Amadeo Barletta. The flamboyant Italian had briefly owned the distributorship where José Poyo had worked and remembered Sergio, who often accompanied his father to the office. With Clark's full endorsement, Sergio interviewed in Havana and toured the new, state-of-the-art Ambar Motors facility, an elegant two-story building with large glass windows around an ample showroom.[51] Barletta also flew Gerry to Havana so she could see the city for herself and meet the extended Poyo family, especially Sergio's grandparents whom he had not seen since he left Cuba in 1942.

Gerry immediately liked what she saw, and after a few days Sergio accepted the job on the condition of a higher salary. The Italian told Sergio not to worry about the salary; he would be taken care of. When Sergio insisted, Barletta became impatient and suggested he return to New York to think further about the offer. Years later, Sergio reflected on this critical juncture that determined the direction of his career. Despite his readiness to return to Havana and work in a thoroughly modern distributorship, Sergio felt uncomfortable with Barletta, who he thought represented a traditional Latin American (or perhaps Mediterranean) business model based on a *patrón* relationship. The *patrón* model required a strong and dependent personal tie between the employee and his employer. An employer's personal commitment to care for his employee and family, including awarding end-of-year bonuses, celebrating birthdays, and enjoying holidays with the "company family," defined the relationship, not salary. In return, the employer expected from his employees absolute loyalty and commitment to his interests. Having an independent streak and trained in U.S. business practices, Sergio rejected this "old school" business environment in Havana in favor of "modern" corporate values. Sergio never again entertained the idea of working for Barletta in Havana and was satisfied to seek his fortunes elsewhere.

Sergio then learned of another possibility, again through Morris Clark, who told him that William A. McCarthy, a longtime Foreign Distributorship Division sales representative who had worked in Mexico and Colombia, had recently purchased a Chevrolet, Buick, and GM truck distributorship in Bogotá called Compañía General Automotríz.[52] McCarthy lived in New York and thought Sergio and Bebo the perfect candidates to lead the service and sales departments, respectively. Satisfied with the terms of employment, the family departed for Colombia, and after a harrowing and what seemed endless flight on a twin-engine DC-4 propeller aircraft from New York via Miami and Panama finally arrived in Bogotá, on April 6, 1951. Ironically, the Latino traits that hampered chances in the United States now became an advantage in finding the employment he wanted. After eight years in Colombia he worked as a General Motors executive in Venezuela, Argentina, and Uruguay. Sergio interacted naturally with Latin Americans but also possessed the values and style of an American businessman on whom U.S. executives counted when interacting with Latin American cultures. This was his niche, one that he used to build a successful corporate career as one of only a few Latino executives in General Motors overseas operations.

Sergio's very intentional strategy of assimilating into North American society was driven by economic goals and not by a deep-seated need or desire to reject his cultural heritage wholesale. He retained many aspects of Latin culture, which Gerry also embraced, ensuring that Latino sensibilities remained within the family even while living in the United States. From early on, Gerry showed interest in learning the Spanish language. In two letters to Sergio soon after their marriage, in December 1943, she jotted *"mi amor"* and *"mi todo"* at the bottom left of the envelopes.[53] She also took to Cuban and Latin music and dance, which Sergio especially enjoyed. They enjoyed the Big Band sounds and dances of the World War II era, but Sergio also took Gerry to a club in Flint owned by a Colombian national where he taught her to dance Latino rhythms, including the cha-cha-cha, mambo, and merengue, which they enjoyed throughout their lives. Latin music from their extensive record collection—Tito Rodríguez, Tito Puente, Pérez Prado, Ernesto Lecuona, Trio Los Panchos, Jorge Negrete, and many other Latino artists—permeated the household and always played at their cocktail and dance parties wherever they lived. As a result, their children never perceived Sergio's "strategic" distancing from his Cuban background as somehow hostile to Latin American ways.

Gerry also learned about Cuban culture through her mother-in-law, Sergia, with whom she developed an enduring relationship. She first met Sergia in early 1944 after moving to Cochran, Georgia, to be with Sergio during Air Corps training. In early March Sergia visited from Atlanta with her youngest son, Ernesto. "She brought me a pair of earrings for my birthday. They are really nice ones too," Gerry wrote to her mother.[54] During Easter, Sergio and Gerry reciprocated and traveled to Atlanta.[55] The next year, Gerry again mentioned a visit to Sergia in Atlanta but this time from San Marcos.[56] These early visits established the foundation for a strong bond between the two women, which Sergia used to transmit her Cuban culture to her grandchildren.

But it was the move to South America that embedded the family's place between two cultural traditions and cemented their sense of Latinidad. Had they remained in the United States, their connection to Latin culture would have certainly weakened, and effective use of Spanish would have been lost since English remained the predominant household language. Few societal incentives existed during that era that would have bolstered the family's Latino identity and culture, especially living in the suburbs rather than in a U.S. Latino community. In Latin America, on the other hand, while attending bilingual international schools with U.S. curricula, the children grew up speaking Spanish, hearing Latin music, eating Cuban and South American dishes of many kinds, and internalizing pan-Hispanic sensibilities. Wherever Sergio and Gerry lived, which after 1950 was mostly in

South America, Sergia visited and taught Gerry how to prepare Cuban and Latin dishes, including *picadillo cubano* and *arroz con pollo*, and much about Hispanic culture generally. Since Sergia never learned much English the household switched to Spanish when she visited, and Gerry learned to communicate with her mother-in-law in Spanish. Thoroughly bilingual and bicultural, the family lived a transnational reality.

Conclusion: Memories and Legacies of a Cuban Americano

Sergio Poyo arrived in the United States on the eve of its entrance into World War II. The declaration of war against Japan on December 8, 1941, unleashed a nationalist fervor that demanded a deepening desire for social conformity and political unity. Although he initially planned to return home on completing his training, his father's death closed that option. Sergio remained in the United States and set out on an intentional path of assimilation, facilitated by his family's historical familiarity with U.S. culture and the English language, as well as his own personal characteristics as a white, middle-class, and educated Cuban. His studies at General Motors Institute, marriage to Gerry Darnell, and service in the Army Air Corps introduced Sergio to American life. This, combined with his late father's excellent reputation at General Motors, secured him a job in New York, which he considered a first step toward his ultimate goal of working in an automobile dealership. He integrated effectively, always demonstrating his willingness to fit in, but was surprised to learn that his efforts were insufficient. His name still signaled a Latino background, which he never denied. Dismayed at this reality, he took a very different career path rather than settle for the limited options he encountered trying to live in New York and New Jersey. In the completely different setting of American business enterprise in Latin America, Sergio used his ethnic traits, business education, and technical automotive skills to build a successful corporate career and the family retained and strengthened its Hispanic ethnic identity.

Sergio Poyo's story speaks to many issues Latina/os faced during the World War II era, especially the role of class, color, and ethnicity in negotiating integration into American society in the face of deep-seated animosity to the Hispanic presence. Although he was among a small minority of Latinos in the United States who had some possibility of "passing" as an American, even this path did not fully deflect negative societal attitudes about his ethnicity, which remained evident. In the United States, Sergio faced barriers that limited his ability to compete on an equal footing, but ultimately he found the opportunities he desired working outside the United States, where his Cuban background, hybrid manner, and U.S. training offered a useful combination in Latin American settings. In South America, Sergio served as an intermediary between the American business he worked for and local cultures. This experience did not divert the family's firm sense of U.S. nationality but added an enriching twist. They experienced a hemispheric reality containing many cultures and traditions that influenced Sergio, Gerry, and the children in multiple ways in Latin America and later in the United States. Sergio's efforts to assimilate and his subsequent automotive career in South America provided the opportunity for the family to blend U.S., Cuban, Colombian, Venezuelan, Argentine, and Uruguayan cultures and identities into a deeply complicated and enriched transnational understanding of what it meant to be an "American," in the broadest sense of the term, or rather a Cuban Americano.

Notes

Preface

1. The Botello brothers' discharge papers and photographs are part of the U.S. Latino & Latina World War II (Voces) Oral History Project. Their records were compiled by their younger brother, Thomas Botello.

2. Jane L. Delgado and Leo Estrada, "Improving Data Collection Strategies," *Public Health Reports* 108, no. 5 (Sept.–Oct. 1993). Delgado and Estrada outline the direct link between the failure to capture accurate enumeration and public policy: "An immediate effect of the lack of Hispanic mortality, morbidity, and health services utilization data has been the lack of Hispanic-specific objectives under the Healthy People 2000 initiative. Healthy People 2000 is a DHHS effort to detail and set the nation's disease prevention and health promotion goals. Because of a lack of baseline data to assess risk, only 25 of 300 Healthy People 2000 objectives contain specific components focusing on the Hispanic community. As a result, there are no Hispanic component objectives in the areas of alcohol and other drugs, mental health and mental disorders, unintentional injury, occupational safety and health, environmental health, food and drug safety, and sexually transmitted diseases. There are currently no plans to supplement the number of Hispanic component objectives under Healthy People 2000. In addition to collection of adequate data on Hispanic subpopulations, timely data analysis is necessary to ensure that the information becomes available to practitioners through the public health literature and is quickly put to use in the planning and delivery of health care services to Hispanic communities" (541–542).

3. Maria Eva Flores, "What a Difference a War Makes!" in *Mexican Americans and World War II*, ed. Maggie Rivas-Rodriguez (Austin: University of Texas Press, 2005), 182. Aniceto Nuñez was interviewed by Flores in Fort Stockton, TX, on 10 March 2000. Here, "White" appears to refer to social position, not only to racial categorization. Nuñez's statement appears to signify that "Mexicans" or "Mexican Americans" had gained social acceptance by the mainstream Anglo society.

4. Joe William Trotter Jr., "From a Raw Deal to a New Deal? 1929 to 1945," in *Make Our World Anew: A History of African Americans Since 1880*, vol. 2, ed.

Robin Kelley, D. G. Lewis, and Earl Lewis (New York: Oxford University Press, 2005), 161.

5. See chapters 2 and 4 of this volume, which include stories about Afro-Cubans who served in "colored units."

6. Alison R. Bernstein, *American Indians and World War II: Toward a New Era in Indian Affairs* (Norman: University of Oklahoma Press, 1991), 40.

7. Bill Yenne, *Rising Sons: The Japanese American GIs Who Fought for the United States in World War II* (New York: Macmillan, 2007), 247. Yenne's information derives from a War Department memo dated 1 August 1945.

8. Kevin Scott Wong, *Americans First: Chinese Americans and the Second World War* (Cambridge, MA: Harvard University Press, 2005), 1. See also James C. Mc-Naughton, "Chinese-Americans in World War II" (United States Army, 3 August 2009), www.history.army.html/topics/opam/chinese-americans.html. Scott estimates that the number represented nearly 20 percent of the adult Chinese male population.

9. Silvia Álvarez Curbelo, "The Color of War: Puerto Rican Soldiers and Discrimination during World War II," in *Beyond the Latino World War II Hero: The Social and Political Legacy of a Generation*, ed. Maggie Rivas-Rodriguez and Emilio Zamora (Austin: University of Texas Press, 2009), 115. Álvarez Curbelo writes that as racial segregation in the U.S. military became the topic of intense debate during World War II, the issue of how Puerto Ricans regard race entered into the discussion. William H. Hastie, the country's first African American federal judge served as a civil adjutant to the secretary of war, specifically to handle Negro affairs. Hastie raised his concern with Governor Tugwell: it appeared that Selective Service boards and military authorities were segregating the Puerto Rican troops racially. Tugwell explained the situation by saying that authorities were "merely observing an established local custom." Still, the Tugwell administration commissioned a study by Julio Enrique Monagas in which he found that the "color line . . . was part of the American culture and largely alien to the island" (117). "To divide the Puerto Rican soldiers in white and colored, to start here a division of races that [has] never existed, to bring to Puerto Rico the racial prejudices existing in the Continent, would constitute a dangerous menace to the stability of the Puerto Rican people" (118). Military authorities argued that there was not as much racial mixing as Monagas insinuated. In the end, Puerto Rico governor Rexford G. Tugwell would side with the military and defer to an interpretation of "local custom" that allowed segregation.

10. One area of scholarship is the "whiteness" of Latinos, in which some scholars conclude that some Latino civil rights leaders often argued that Mexican Americans should be legally considered "white," as a way to integrate public facilities and institutions, since state laws often mandated racial segregation. Using that logic, it is possible that some Mexican Americans, in particular, might have self-identified as "white."

11. The U.S. Latino & Latina World War II Oral History Project, asked to quantify military service of Latina/os, repeatedly gave as general an answer as possible: "up to 750,000."

12. Amado M. Padilla, "A Set of Categories for Combining Psychological and Historical Studies of Cultures, in *Contemporary Mexico Papers of the Fourth International Congress of Mexican History* (UCLA Latin American Studies), ed. James W.

Wilkie, Michael C. Meyer, and Edna Monzón de Wilkie (Los Angeles: UCLA Latin American Center, 1973), 585–586.

13. See Minnesota Population Center and Minnesota Population Center, "Integrated Public Use Microdata Set," Census Enumeration Forms, http://usa.ipums .org/usa/voliii/tEnumForm.shtml.

14. United States Office of the Assistant Secretary for Policy and Planning, "Veteran Population Model, VetPop2007," Department of Veterans' Affairs, Washington, DC, January 2008.

15. Frank D. Bean and Marta Tienda, *The Hispanic Population of the United States* (New York: Russell Sage Foundation, 1987); and Minnesota Population Center, "Integrated Public Use Microdata Set," Census Enumeration Forms, http:// usa.ipums.org/usa/voliii/tEnumForm.shtml.

16. Ibid.

17. Ibid.

18. Elizabeth Arias, Lester R. Curtin, Rong Wei, and Robert Anderson, "United States Decennial Life Tables for 1999–2001," *National Vital Statistics Report* 57, no. 1 (5 Aug. 2008), archived at www.cdc.gov/nchs/data/nvsr/nvsr57/nvsr57 _01.pdf.

19. See Glen Elder Jr., Elizabeth C. Clipp, James Scott Brown, Leslie R. Martin, and Howard W. Friedman, "The Life-Long Mortality Risks of World War II Experiences," *Research on Aging* 31, no. 4 (2009): 391–412; Kelly Bedard and Olivier Deschênes, "The Long-term Impact of Military Service on Health: Evidence from World War II and Korean War Veterans," *American Economic Review* 96, no. 1 (2006): 176–194; Xian Liu, Charles Engel, Han Kang, and David Cowan, "The Effect of Veteran Status on Mortality among Older Americans and Its Pathways," *Population Research and Policy Review* 24, no. 6 (2005): 573–592.

20. Elizabeth Arias, "United States Life Tables by Hispanic Origin," *Vital and Health Statistics* 2, no. 152 (2010): 1–41; Kyriakos S. Markides and Jeannine Coreil, "The Health of Hispanics in the Southwestern United States: An Epidemiological Paradox," *Public Health Reports* 101 (1986): 253–265; Ira Rosenwaike and Benjamin S. Bradshaw, "Mortality of the Spanish Surname Population of the Southwest," *Social Science Quarterly* 70, no. 3 (1989): 631–641; and Robert Schoen and Verne E. Nelson, "Mortality by Cause among Spanish Surnamed Californias, 1969–71," *Social Science Quarterly* 62 (1981): 259–274.

21. Anne Leland and Mari-Jana Oborocenau, *American War and Military Operations Casualties: Lists and Statistics* (Washington, DC: Congressional Research Service, 2010).

22. Bean and Tienda, *The Hispanic Population of the United States.*

23. Deborah Fenstermaker and Dawn Haines, *Summary of Estimated Net Coverage*, A.C.E. Revision II, 31 December 2002. Unpublished pdf accessed at www .census.gov/dmd/www/pdf/pp-54r.pdf.

24. Clara Rodriguez, *Changing Race: Latinos, the Census, and the History of Ethnicity in the United States* (New York: New York University Press, 2000). The cited discussion is in Appendix A, "Data Limitations and the Undercount."

25. Richard Alba and Tariqul Islam, "The Case of the Disappearing Mexican Americans: An Ethnic-Identity Mystery," *Population Research and Policy Review* 28 (2009): 109–121.

Introduction

1. Maggie Rivas-Rodriguez and Emilio Zamora, eds., *Beyond the Latino World War II Hero: The Social and Political Legacy of a Generation* (Austin: University of Texas Press, 2009).
2. Maggie Rivas-Rodriguez, ed., *Mexican Americans and World War II* (Austin: University of Texas Press, 2005).
3. Textbook publisher Pearson has used our photos. Several excerpts and photos were included in Vicki L. Ruiz and Virginia Sánchez Korrol, eds., *Latinas in the United States: A Historical Encyclopedia*, 3 vols. (Bloomington: Indiana University Press, 2006); and material from our interviews is included in Rodolfo Acuña's *Occupied America: A History of Chicanos*, 7th ed. (New York: Pearson Longman, 2007). Our photos have appeared in documentaries, including John Valadez's *The Longoria Affair*, as well as hundreds of newspaper and magazine stories.
4. Maria Eva Flores, "What a Difference a War Makes!" in Rivas-Rodriguez, *Mexican Americans and World War II*, 182.

Chapter One

1. The literature on Cubans in Key West is voluminous. See Gerald Eugene Poyo, *"With All and for the Good of All": The Emergence of Popular Nationalism in Cuban Communities of the United States: 1848–1898* (Durham: Duke University Press, 1989); L. Glenn Westfall, "Don Vicente Martínez Ybor: The Man and His Empire" (Ph.D. diss., University of Florida, 1977); Consuelo E. Stebbins, *City of Intrigue, Nest of Revolution: A Documentary History of Key West in the Nineteenth Century* (Gainesville: University Press of Florida, 2007).
2. Gary R. Mormino and George E. Pozzetta, *The Immigrant World of Ybor City: Italians and Their Latin Neighbors in Tampa, Florida, 1885–1985* (Urbana: University of Illinois Press, 1987), 1–92.
3. I have chosen to use the term *Hispanic* instead of *Latin* or the more current *Latino/a*. All three terms are inaccurate, imprecise, and unsatisfying, but "Hispanic" works best in this chapter simply because it encompasses Spaniards, who generally are not included in standard usages of "Latina/o."
4. Mormino and Pozzetta, *Immigrant World*, 55, 97–141; quote from the *Tampa Morning Tribune*, July 30, 1896.
5. Mormino and Pozzetta, *Immigrant World*, 67–68; Armando Méndez, *Ciudad de Cigars: West Tampa* (Cocoa: Florida Historical Society Press, 1994), 1–150.
6. The literacy figures are found in *Reports of the Immigration Commission, Immigrants in Industries*, 14, Tables 172–174, 192 (Washington, DC: U.S. Government Printing Office, 1911); Mormino and Pozzetta, *Immigrant World*, 286–291.
7. Mormino and Pozzetta, *Immigrant World*, 97, 98, 102–103, 175–209; Gary Mormino and George E. Pozzetta, "'The Reader Lights the Candle': Cuban and Florida Cigar Workers' Oral Tradition," *Labor's Heritage* 5 (Spring 1993): 4–27; Gary R. Mormino and George E. Pozzetta, "Spanish Anarchism in Tampa, Florida, 1886–1931," in *Struggle a Hard Battle: Essays on Working-Class Immigrants*, ed. Dirk Hoerder (DeKalb: Northern Illinois University Press, 1986), 170–198.

8. Yglesias did not accent his name.

9. Jose Yglesias, "The Radical Latino Island in the Deep South," *Nuestro: The Magazine for Latinos* 1 (August 1977).

10. Ferdie Pacheco, *Ybor City Chronicles* (Gainesville: University Press of Florida, 1994), 7.

11. Whites were often referred to as Anglos, and though both terms are imprecise, "white" is used throughout this chapter.

12. Mormino and Pozzetta, *Immigrant World*, 225–227, 251–252, 280–292; Ferdie Pacheco, interview by the author, audio recording, Tampa, FL, 12 June 1984, Special Collections, University of Florida Library.

13. Mormino and Pozzetta, *Immigrant World*, 142–163; Pacheco, *Ybor City Chronicles*, 134–142.

14. Braulio Alonso, conversation with the author, 24 May 2001; Mormino and Pozzetta, *Immigrant World*, 210–233; Frank Trebín Lastra, *Ybor City: The Making of a Landmark Town* (Tampa: University of Tampa Press, 2006), 167–168; Ana M. Varela-Lago, "*¡No Pasarán!*" The Spanish Civil War's Impact on Tampa's Latin Community, 1936–1939," *Tampa Bay History* 19 (Fall–Winter 1997): 5–34; Yglesias quoted in Studs Terkel, *Hard Times: An Oral History of the Great Depression* (New York: Pantheon Books, 1970), 109. The term and song "No pasarán" became a rallying cry during the Spanish Civil War. During the siege of Madrid, Communist leader Dolores Ibárruri Gómez used the phrase, vowing the National forces would be denied the city. When Franco's armies breached Madrid's walls, he responded, "Hemos pasado" (We have passed).

15. Maria Pasetti Leto, interview by the author, Tampa, FL, August 1, 2001; Pasetti, "Pearl Harbor," essay in author's possession.

16. Braulio Alonso, conversation with the author, Tampa, FL, 24 May 2001; also, Braulio Alonso file, Special Collections, University of South Florida. The file contains a series of essays Alonso wrote at the request of the author.

17. Josephine Acosta Pizzo, conversation with the author, Tampa, FL, 6 January 2000; Gary R. Mormino, *Hillsborough County Goes to War: The Home Front, 1940–1950* (Tampa, FL: Tampa Bay History Center, 2001), 42.

18. Mormino, *Hillsborough County Goes to War*, 41.

19. Ibid.

20. Ibid., 42–43; Willie García, conversation with the author, Tampa, FL, 7 May 2001.

21. Pacheco, *Ybor City Chronicles*, 251.

22. Mormino, *Hillsborough County Goes to War*, 46; René González, interview by the author, audio recording, Tampa, FL, 10 March 2001.

23. "En Guerra—Protección y Precaución," *La Gaceta*, 12 December 1941.

24. Roland Manteiga, conversations with the author, 1977–1998. Manteiga succeeded his father as editor and publisher of the Spanish-, Italian-, and English-language newspaper, *La Gaceta*.

25. "Por El Centro Asturiano," *La Gaceta*, 9 December 1941; Susan D. Greenbaum, *More than Black: Afro-Cubans in Tampa* (Gainesville: University Press of Florida, 2002), 257; "Centro Español Provides Benefits for 6000 Members," *Tampa Daily Times*, 21 January 1942; "Español Club Gives Pledge to President," *Tampa Daily Times*, 10 December 1941.

26. Bob Martínez, conversations with the author, 7 December 2008 and 31 March 2009.

27. Mormino, *Hillsborough County Goes to War*, 67–79, 83; "Mother Of Dead Flier Buys Bonds," *Tampa Morning Tribune*, 20 January 1944; *Tobacco Leaf*, 3 January 1942.

28. Mormino, *Hillsborough County Goes to War*, 74.

29. Ibid., 51–63; Pacheco, *Ybor City Chronicles*, 252.

30. Pacheco, *Ybor City Chronicles*, 252.

31. Mormino, *Hillsborough County Goes to War*, 78; Willie García, conversation with the author, Tampa, FL, 7 May 2001.

32. Mormino, *Hillsborough County Goes to War*, 79, 113; Frank Lastra, conversation with the author, 12 April 2000; Lastra, *Ybor City*, 143–144, 173–174; Alonso, conversation; "Mother Breaks in Tears at Gifts from Son in Pacific," *Tampa Morning Tribune*, 3 September 1944; "Tampa Soldier in Italy to Get Home Cooked Food," *Tampa Daily Times*, 2 March 1944.

33. "City's First Lady Butcher," *Tampa Daily News*, 19 November 1942; "War Is Putting Women Back on Old Jobs of Turning out Bread," *Tampa Morning Tribune*, 12 December 1942; Mormino, *Hillsborough County Goes to War*, 53–58, 71–77.

34. Andy Huse, *The Columbia Restaurant: Celebrating a Century of History, Culture, and Cuisine* (Gainesville: University Press of Florida, 2009), 14–35; Pacheco, *Ybor City Chronicles*, 93.

35. Mormino and Pozzetta, *Immigrant World*, 111–124, 239–247; Manuel Alfonso, interview by the author, audio recording, Tampa, FL, 21 July 1984.

36. "Sirviendo la Nación," *La Gaceta*, 16 July 1942; Gutiérrez profile, "With Our Boys on All Fronts," *Tampa Daily Times*, 28 January 1945; Alvarez and Meza profiles, "With Our Boys on All Fronts," *Tampa Daily Times*, 20 November 1942.

37. "Jose Yglesias, Novelist of Revolutions, Dies at 75," *New York Times*, 8 November 1995; Jose Yglesias, *One German Dead* (Leeds: Eremite Press, 1988), 6 (Yglesias became Tampa's greatest native-born author).

38. Lastra, *Ybor City*, 173; "Cousins Hurt in Germany within Day," *Tampa Sunday Tribune*, 5 November 1944; "Tampa Marine in Jap Prison Camp," *Tampa Morning Tribune*, 26 February 1945.

39. Huse, *The Columbia Restaurant*, 32–34; Pacheco, *Ybor City Chronicles*, 71–76.

40. "Veteran of Last War with Four Sons in This One," *Tampa Morning Tribune*, 26 February 1945.

41. Arsenio Sánchez, interview by the author, audio recording, Tampa, FL, 5 July 1999, University of South Florida; "Sánchez Diary," copy in author's possession and University of South Florida Special Collections; "Gilbert Salas Killed on Iwo Jima," *Tampa Morning Tribune*, 25 April 1945.

42. Alonso, interview; Alonso essay, "Entry into Rome," in author's possession and USF Special Collections.

43. Alonso, interview; Alonso essay, "German Surrender in the Dolomite Alps," in author's possession and USF Special Collections.

44. Denver Blanco, conversation with the author, Tampa, FL, 11 April 1995, notes from conversation in possession of author.

45. Benito profile, "With Our Boys," *Tampa Daily Times*, 31 May 1945; Pacheco, *Ybor City Chronicles*, 261–625.

46. "Tampan Lands on Sicily," *Tampa Morning Tribune*, 19 August 1943; "Oscar Ramos Killed in Italy Fight," *Tampa Morning Tribune*, 19 May 1945.

47. Emiliano Salcines Jr., interviews by the author, audio recordings, 1980–2010, Tampa, Fl; "Tampa Boy, Tank Gunner, Dies in France," *Tampa Morning Tribune*, 30 September 1944; Alvarez and Hernández files in "Hillsborough County, Florida Reference Materials. Selected Veterans and War Casualty Research and Reference Project. World War II, 1941–1945, U.S. Army and Army Air Corps. I. Alphabetical Casualty List."

48. "Hillsborough County, Florida Reference Materials . . . Alphabetical Casualty List"; Fernández and Parra files, in Florida National Guard World War II Roster, Hillsborough County.

49. Rodríguez profile in Florida National Guard, Hillsborough County; "Tampan Wins Bronze Star for Heroism on Franklin," *Tampa Morning Tribune*, 22 May 1945; "Tampan Killed in Action in Pacific Area," *Tampa Daily Times*, 24 July 1943.

50. "Survivor of 'Death March' Forced to Work in Jap Mines," *Tampa Morning Tribune*, 10 October 1945; "Tommy Gomez Says, 'I'm Full of Holes but out Of Danger,'" undated *Tampa Morning Tribune* clipping; "Tommy Gomez Quits Boxing Ring," *St. Petersburg Times*, 5 November 1946; Frank Adamo, interview by the author, 11 October 1980, University of Florida.

51. Lastra, *Ybor City*, 175, 189–190; Pacheco, *Ybor City Chronicles*, 260–275.

52. "Band of Brothers," *St. Petersburg Times*, 3 July 2005; "Band of Brothers Loses One," *St. Petersburg Times*, 10 January 2008.

53. Mormino, *Hillsborough County Goes to War*, 175–176; "Marine Hero's Parents Receive His Medal of Honor," *New York Times*, 31 August 1951; *The United States Naval Academy Alumni Association, Inc., Register of Alumni, Graduates and Former Naval Cadets and Midshipmen* (Annapolis, MD: Association Publishers, 1990); letter quoted in "Long-Desired Service Career Ends for Tampan at Inchon," *Tampa Daily Times*, 30 September 1950.

54. Mormino, *Hillsborough County Goes to War*, 123–130; Francisco González Jr., interview by the author, audio recording, Tampa, FL, 18 June 1983, University of Florida; "War's End Brings 'A Hot Time in the Old Town' to Tampans," *Tampa Daily Times*, 15 August 1945; "Tampa Gives Peace Wild Happy Welcome," *Tampa Morning Tribune*, 15 August 1945.

55. "Joy and Sorrow at Tampa's Union Station," *Tampa Morning Tribune*, 19 August 1945.

56. Grillo, quoted in Greenbaum, *More than Black*, 260.

57. "An Analysis of American Public Opinion Regarding the War," Presidential Personal Files (PPF) 4721, Franklin D. Roosevelt Library, Hyde Park, NY.

58. James M. McPherson, *Battle Cry of Freedom: The Civil War Era* (New York: Oxford University Press, 1988), 485–486.

59. Alonso, memoir; Lastra, *Ybor City*, 172; Jose Yglesias, *"Buscando un Sueño,"* 60.

60. Yglesias, *"Buscando un Sueño,"* 60.

61. *Turner v. Keefe, Chairman of Board of Public Instruction, et. al.*, Supp. 647 (1943).

62. Francisco Rodríguez Jr., interview by the author, audio recording, Tampa, FL, 1 August 1985, University of Florida, and conversation with the author, 18 June 1983; Mormino, *Hillsborough County Goes to War*, 58–60; Greenbaum, *More*

than Black, 258, 266, 281–282, 284, 286; "Tampa Student Hits Train for Poor Service," *Florida Sentinel*, 24 January 1948.

63. Alonso, memoir; Mormino and Pozzetta, *Immigrant World*, 298–300, 302–304; Lastra, *Ybor City*, 176–177; "Latin Pupils Who Speak Own Language Won't Be Whipped," *Tampa Morning Tribune*, 27 September 1944; "West Tampans Have No Worries about Zoot-Suit Hoodlums," *Tampa Daily Times*, 18 June 1943; Mormino, *Hillsborough County Goes to War*, 136–138.

64. Lastra, *Ybor City*, 176; Mormino, *Hillsborough County Goes to War*, 131–132.

65. "Veterans Lead in Enrollment at Tampa U," *Tampa Morning Tribune*, 5 September 1947; "Vets Predominate on Tampa 'U,'" *Tampa Daily Times*, 9 September 1947; Mormino, *Hillsborough County Goes to War*, 131–132; James W. Covington, *Under the Minarets* (Tampa, FL: University of Tampa Press, 1981), 35, 37.

66. Jose Yglesias, "Coming Down from the Mountain" (review of Martin Duberman, *Black Mountain College*), *University Review* (December 1972): 79–80; Yglesias, "Un Buen Obrero," *New Masses* 61 (November 26, 1946): 17–19.

67. Mormino and Pozzetta, *Immigrant World*, 300–301; Passiglia, quoted in Mormino and Pozzetta, *Immigrant World*, 300; Lastra, *Ybor City*, 176–177.

68. Manteiga, quoted in "Ybor Citians Would Preserve 'Latin Culture,'" *Tampa Daily Times*, 29 July 1955; Lastra, *Ybor City*, 214–220; Mormino and Pozzetta, *Immigrant World*, 304–307; "Ybor City Begins to Look Spanish Again," *Tampa Sunday Tribune*, 3 May 1953.

69. Lastra, *Ybor City*, 27–28; Gary R. Mormino, "Tampa, Cuba before Fidel," *Tampa Tribune*, 5 February 2006; Gary R. Mormino, "Rallying for the Revolution," *Tampa Tribune*, 15 February 2006; Greenbaum, *More than Black*, 270–273; Phil LoCicero, "My Meeting with Fidel Castro," *La Gaceta*, 28 May 1993; "Anti-Batista Revolutionist to Talk Here," *Tampa Daily Times*, 26 November 1955; "Cubans Here Give Funds to Aid Revolt against Batista," *Tampa Tribune*, 1 December 1955; "Cuban Government to Print Tampa Scene on Stamp Honoring Revolutionary Leader," *Tampa Morning Tribune*, 1 June 1953; "Tampa Cigar Industry in Revolution," *Tampa Tribune*, 1 June 1962; "Cuban Tobacco Embargo Begins to Hurt Tampa," *St. Petersburg Times*, 6 March 1962.

70. Interview with Rodríguez; Lastra, *Ybor City*, 216–225; Mormino and Pozzetta, *Immigrant World*, 303–309; "Cigar Factory Landmark Toppled by Expressway," *Tampa Tribune*, 3 February 1963; "Blacks Gain, Lose in Ybor," *Tampa Tribune*, 16 May 1979; "Only One Ybor Club Continues to Thrive," *Tampa Tribune*, 15 May 1979.

Chapter Two

1. The scholarly literature on Afro-Latina/os has grown steadily in recent years. A useful starting point is *The Afro-Latin@ Reader: History and Culture in the United States*, ed. Miriam Jiménez Román and Juan Flores (Durham: Duke University Press, 2010). My usage of "Afro-Latina/o" as a category is limited to those Latina/os of African descent who were born in the United States or have lived significant parts of their lives in the United States to highlight the particularities of the U.S. experience of Afro-Latina/os instead of the more expansive hemispheric understanding, which is evident in the Jiménez Román and Flores volume.

2. Norberto González, videotaped interview by Erika Martínez, 14 September 2002, Miami, FL. Evelio Grillo, videotaped interview by Mario Barrera, Las Vegas, NV, 7 April 2003. Both interviews and corresponding documentation in the Voces Oral History Project Collection, Benson Latin American Library, Rare Books, University of Texas at Austin.

3. Throughout U.S. history, Latinos who were not identified as "black" have often identified or self-identified as "white," "Castilian," "Spanish," and "Hispanic." See Suzanne Oboler, *Ethnic Labels, Latino Lives: Identity and the Politics of (Re)presentation in the United States* (Minneapolis: University of Minnesota Press, 1995).

4. On the experiences of Latino baseball players during the era of legalized segregation, see Adrian Burgos Jr., *Playing America's Game: Baseball, Latinos, and the Color Line* (Berkeley: University of California Press, 2007).

5. Evelio Grillo, *Black Cuban, Black American* (Houston: Arte Público Press, 2000).

6. My notion of transculturation is inspired by Fernando Ortiz's well-known formulation published in his classic study, *Cuban Counterpoint: Tobacco and Sugar* (Durham: Duke University Press, 1995).

7. The classic work on Ybor City remains Gary R. Mormino and George E. Pozzetta, *The Immigrant World of Ybor City: Italians and Their Latin Neighbors in Tampa, 1885–1985*, 2nd ed. (Gainesville: University Press of Florida, 1998). On the Afro-Cuban experience in Tampa, see Susan D. Greenbaum, *More than Black: Afro-Cubans in Tampa* (Gainesville: University Press of Florida, 2002).

8. On Cuban migration to Tampa and Key West, see Gerald Poyo, *"With All and for the Good of All": The Emergence of Popular Nationalism in the Cuban Communities of the United States* (Durham: Duke University Press, 1989).

9. Grillo, *Black Cuban, Black American*, 17–18. On Washington's recruitment of Cuban students to Tuskegee from Florida and Cuba, see Frank André Guridy, *Forging Diaspora: Afro-Cubans and African-Americans in a World of Empire and Jim Crow* (Chapel Hill: University of North Carolina Press, 2010).

10. Evelio Grillo, interview by Mario Barrera, videotape recording, Oakland, CA, 26 January 2003, Voces Oral History Project, Nettie Lee Benson Latin American Library, University of Texas at Austin.

11. Grillo, interview.

12. Grillo, *Black Cuban, Black American*, 61. Grillo lived with his older brother, Sergio ("Henry"), who had a close relationship with Mary McLeod Bethune, the prominent African American educator and Civil Rights activist. For more on the experience of the Grillos in Washington, DC, see Guridy, *Forging Diaspora*, chap. 4.

13. Grillo, *Black Cuban, Black American*, 129.

14. On the Black Panthers' deep roots in Oakland's African American community, see Donna Murch, *Living for the City: Migration, Education, and the Rise of the Black Panther Party in Oakland, California* (Chapel Hill: University of North Carolina Press, 2010).

15. Grillo, interview.

16. Hawley was a Republican congressman from Galveston from 1897 to 1901. He became president of Cubanaco in 1900. See Gillian McGillivray, *Blazing Cane: Sugar Communities, Class, and State Formation in Cuba, 1868–1959* (Durham: Duke University Press, 2009).

17. On the domination of Cubanaco's sugar mills in the region, see McGillivray, *Blazing Cane*, 86–117.

18. Norberto González, interview by Erika Martínez, videotape recording, Miami, 14 September 2002, Voces Oral History Project, Nettie Lee Benson Latin American Library, University of Texas at Austin.

19. The literature on sugar and slavery in Cuba is voluminous. See, for example, Manuel Moreno Fraginals, *El Ingenio: Complejo economico-social cubano del azúcar* (Havana: Editorial Ciencias Sociales, 1978); Franklin W. Knight, *Slave Society in Cuba during the Nineteenth Century* (Madison: University of Wisconsin Press, 1970); and, more recently, Matt Childs, *The 1812 Aponte Rebellion in Cuba and the Struggle against Atlantic Slavery* (Chapel Hill: University of North Carolina Press, 2006).

20. On Cuba during this period, see Luis E. Aguilar, *Cuba 1933: Prologue to Revolution* (Ithaca: Cornell University Press, 1972), 40–115; Jules Benjamin, "The Machadato and Cuban Nationalism, 1928-1932," *Hispanic American Historical Review* 55 (1975): 66–91; Louis A. Pérez Jr., *Cuba under the Platt Amendment* (Pittsburgh: University of Pittsburgh Press, 1986), 182–300; Instituto de Historia de Cuba, *Historia de Cuba: Organización y crisis desde 1899 hasta 1940* (Havana: Editora Política, 1998), 240–281; Robert Whitney, *State and Revolution in Cuba: Mass Mobilization and Political Change, 1920–1940* (Chapel Hill: University of North Carolina Press, 2001), 17–81. See also Lionel Soto, *La Revolución del 33*, 3 vols. (Havana: Editorial de Ciencias Sociales, 1979); and José Tabares del Real, *La Revolución del 30: Sus dos últimos años* (Havana: Editorial de Ciencias Sociales, 1975).

21. On the pervasiveness of U.S. cultural forms in Cuba during the pre-Castro era, see Louis A. Pérez, *On Becoming Cuban: Identity, Nationality, and Culture* (Chapel Hill: University of North Carolina Press, 1999).

22. Puerto Ricans constituted more than half of the total Latino population in New York, reaching 61,946 by 1940 and exploding to 831,000 in 1970. See Agustín Laó-Montes and Arlene Dávila, eds., *Mambo Montage: The Latinization of New York* (New York: Columbia University Press, 2001). On the Puerto Rican community in New York during this period, see Virginia Sánchez-Korrol, *From Colonia to Community: The History of Puerto Ricans in New York City* (Berkeley: University of California Press, 1994). On the presence of Cubans in the thriving Latin music scene in New York, see Ruth Glasser, *My Music Is My Flag: Puerto Rican Musicians and Their New York Communities, 1917–1940* (Berkeley: University of California Press, 1995).

23. González, interview.

24. Ibid.

25. Grillo, interview. His emphasis.

Chapter Three

1. In *re Rodriguez*, 81 Fed. 337 (W.D. Texas, 1897).

2. *Plessy v. Ferguson*, 163 U.S. 537, 539 (1896).

3. Arnoldo De León, *They Called Them Greasers: Anglo Attitudes toward Mexicans in Texas, 1821–1900* (Austin: University of Texas Press, 1983).

4. Gilbert G. Gonzalez, *Chicano Education in the Era of Segregation* (Philadelphia: Balch Institute Press, 1990).

5. Patricia Gándara and Gary Orfield, "Introduction: Creating a 21st Century Vision of Access and Equity in Higher Education," in *Expanding Opportunity in Higher Education: Leveraging Promise*, ed. Patricia Gándara, Gary Orfield, and Catherine L. Horn (Albany: State University of New York Press, 2006), 1–16.

6. Ibid.; United States Department of Veterans Affairs, "G.I. Bill History," www.gibill.va.gov/benefits/history_timeline/index.htm (last modified 9 February 2012).

7. United States Department of Veterans Affairs, "G.I. Bill History," www.gibill.va.gov/benefits/history_timeline/index.htm (last modified 9 February 2012).

8. David D. Henry, *Challenges Past, Challenges Present: An Analysis of American Higher Education since 1930* (San Francisco: Jossey-Bass, 1975); Gándara and Orfield, "Introduction: Creating a 21st Century Vision"; John Bound and Sarah Turner, "Going to War and Going to College: Did World War II and the G.I. Bill Increase Educational Attainment for Returning Veterans?" *Journal of Labor Economics* 20 (2002): 784–815.

9. Ronald Roach, "From Combat to Campus," *Black Issues in Higher Education* 14 (1997): 26.

10. Bound and Turner, "Going to War and Going to College."

11. Reginald Wilson, "G.I. Bill Expands Access for African Americans," *Educational Record* 75 (1994): 32–39; Roach, "From Combat to Campus," 26.

12. Suzanne Mettler, "'The Only Good Thing Was the G.I. Bill': Effects of the Education and Training Provisions on African-American Veterans' Political Participation," *Studies in American Political Development* 19 (2005): 31–52.

13. Ramón M. Rivas, interview by Maggie Rivas-Rodriguez, videotape recording, San Antonio, TX, 12 June 1999, Voces Oral History Project, Nettie Lee Benson Latin American Collection, University of Texas at Austin.

14. Nicanór Aguilar, interview by Maggie Rivas-Rodriguez, videotape recording, El Paso, TX, 29 December 2001, Voces Oral History Project.

15. Raymon A. Elizondo, interview by Israel Saenz, videotape recording, Salt Lake City, UT, 6 December 2013, Voces Oral History Project.

16. Julian L. Gonzalez, interview by Raquel C. Garza and Veronica Franco, videotape recording, San Antonio, TX, 13 October 2001, Voces Oral History Project.

17. Adam Gastelum, interview by René Zambrano, videotape recording, San Diego, CA, 8 September 2000, Voces Oral History Project.

18. Paul Gil, interview with Andrea Valdez, videotape recording, Austin, TX, 20 October 1999, Voces Oral History Project.

19. Lorenzo Terrones Lujano, interview by Patricia Aguirre, videotape recording, Newton, KS, 1 August 2003, Voces Oral History Project.

20. Virgilio Roel, interview by Angélica A. Rodríguez, telephone recording, 15 March 2011, Voces Oral History Project.

21. Virgilio Roel, interview by Oscar Torres, videotape recording, Austin, TX, 9 September 2002, Voces Oral History Project.

22. Ibid.

23. Ibid.

24. Ibid.

25. Three Rivers, TX, is known for the "Felix Longoria Affair," in which the family of a Mexican American World War II soldier who had been killed in battle

in the Philippines in the closing days of the war was denied use of the funeral chapel. The funeral home's explanation: "the Whites would not like it." The incident gained national notoriety through the widespread media attention. Tejanos rallied against the injustice under the newly created American GI Forum, an organization that gained prominence due to this incident. Then-Senator Lyndon B. Johnson secured a place for Private Longoria's remains to be interred at Arlington National Cemetery. For more information, see Patrick J. Carroll, *Felix Longoria's Wake: Bereavement, Racism, and the Rise of Mexican American Activism* (Austin: University of Texas Press, 2003).

26. Roel, interview with Rodriguez, 15 March 2011.

27. Tex. Att'y Gen. Op. No. V-128 (1947).

28. Leonard A. Valverde, "Equal Educational Opportunities since *Brown*: Four Major Developments," *Education and Urban Society* 36 (2004): 368–378; 64 F.Supp. 544 (C.D. Cal. 1946), *aff'd*, 161 F.2d 774, 9th Cir. 1947 (en banc).

29. Tex. Att'y Gen. Op. No. V-128 (1947).

30. Roel, interview with Rodriguez, 15 March 2011.

31. For a deeper discussion on American Samoa and colonialism, see Dan Taulapapa McMullin, "The Passive Resistance of Samoans to U.S. and Other Colonialisms," in *Sovereignty Matters: Locations of Contestation and Possibility in Indigenous Struggles for Self-Determination*, ed. Joanne Barker (Lincoln: University of Nebraska Press, 2005), 109–121.

32. Roel, interview with Rodriguez, 15 March 2011.

33. Ibid.

34. Ibid.

35. Ibid.

36. Ibid.

37. Mettler, "'The Only Good Thing Was the G.I. Bill,'" 31–52.

38. See Angela Valenzuela, *Subtractive Schooling: U.S.-Mexican Youth and the Politics of Caring* (Albany: State University of New York Press, 1999), for a detailed discussion about bilingualism and multilingualism.

39. A. D. Azios, interview by Angélica A. Rodríguez, telephone recording, 14 March 2011, Voces Oral History Project.

40. Ibid.

41. Ibid.

42. Ibid.

43. Ibid.

44. Ibid.

45. Ana Maria Merico-Stephens, "Latinos in Law Professions," in *Encyclopedia Latina: History, Culture, and Society in the United States*, ed. Ilan Stavans (Danbury, CT: Grolier, 2005), 425–427.

46. Diana Evans, Ana Franco, Robert D. Wrinkle, and James Wenzel, "Who's on the Bench? The Impact of Latino Descriptive Representation on Supreme Court Approval," paper presented at the annual meeting of the American Political Science Association, Seattle, WA, 1–4 September 2011.

47. Janet Moore, "Minority Overrepresentation in Criminal Justice Systems: Causes, Consequences, and Cures," *Freedom Center Journal* 3, no. 1 (2011): 35–38.

48. Azios, 2011 interview.

49. Julian L. Gonzalez, interview by Angélica A. Rodríguez, audio telephone recording, 14 March 2011, Voces Oral History Project.

50. National Survey of Student Engagement, *Student Engagement: Pathways to Collegiate Success* (Bloomington: Indiana University Center for Postsecondary Research, 2004); National Survey of Student Engagement, *Engaged Learning: Fostering Success for All Students* (Bloomington: Indiana University Center for Postsecondary Research, 2006). Part-time students' experiences can become invisible. They are on campus much less than their full-time peers, their responsibilities off-campus (e.g., child care, working) can consume their spare time, and they are more likely to be older than full-time students. They also take longer to graduate and are less likely to be successful. This marginalization may create a sense that their experience in higher education is less valuable, which Julian Gonzalez mentioned when he was asked to share his story.

51. National Center for Education Statistics, *Total Fall Enrollment in Degree-Granting Institutions, by Attendance Status, Sex of Student, and Control of Institution: Selected Years, 1947 through 2009*, http://nces.ed.gov/programs/digest/d10/tables /dt10_197.asp?referrer=list (accessed 20 April 2011).

52. Gonzalez, interview by Rodriguez, 14 March 2011.

53. Alamo Colleges, 2011, www.alamo.edu/.

54. Gonzalez, interview by Rodriguez, 14 March 2011.

55. Ibid.

56. Ibid.

57. Roach, "From Combat to Campus," 26.

58. The authors acknowledge Laurel Dietz and Michael Voloninno for their help with the research that underlies the introduction to the chapter.

Chapter Four

1. Rudy Acosta, interview by Louis Sahagun, videotape recording, Upton, CA, 14 November 2000, Voces Oral History Project, Nettie Lee Benson Latin American Collection, University of Texas at Austin.

2. Inderpal Grewal, *Transnational America: Feminisms, Diasporas, Neoliberalisms* (Durham: Duke University Press, 2005), 2–3. In a much different and more recent context, Grewal forcefully argues that "America cannot be studied only within the territories of the United States" and that "America produced subjects outside its territorial boundaries."

3. Ana Ramos Zayas, "Delinquent Citizenship, National Performances: Racialization, Surveillance, and the Politics of 'Worthiness' in Puerto Rican Chicago," *Latino Studies* 2 (2004): 26–44.

4. Neil Foley, *Quest for Equality: The Failed Promise of Black-Brown Solidarity* (Cambridge, MA: Harvard University Press, 2010), 17–18.

5. This essay draws from ten oral histories in the Voces Oral History Project.

6. Mary Louis Pratt, *Imperial Eyes: Travel Writing and Transculturation* (London: Routledge, 1992), 7. Pratt explains contact zones as "the spatial and temporal copresence of subjects previously separated by geographical and historical disjunctures, whose trajectories now intersect."

7. Acosta, interview.

8. Allison Varzally, *Making a Non-White America: Californians Coloring Outside Ethnic Lines, 1925–1955* (Berkeley: University of California Press, 2008), 160.

9. Raul Morin, *Among the Valiant: Mexican-Americans in WWII and Korea* (Alhambra, CA: Borden Publishing Company, 1966), 88.

10. Richard Dominguez, interview by Steven Rosales, videotape recording, Whittier, CA, 26 March 2003, Voces Oral History Project.

11. Acosta, interview.

12. Guy Gabaldon, interview by Maggie Rivas-Rodriguez, videotape recording, Washington, DC, 7 June 2000, Voces Oral History Project.

13. Edward Prado, interview by Ruben Ali Flores, videotape recording, San Antonio, TX, 26 February 2000, Voces Oral History Project.

14. Claire Jean Kim, *Bitter Fruit: The Politics of Black-Korean Conflict in New York City* (New Haven: Yale University Press, 2000), 10. Kim notes that "racial power operates not only by reproducing racial categories and meanings, per se, but by reproducing them in the form of a distinct racial order" and that the idea of "racial order emphasizes that each group gets racialized or positioned relative to other groups."

15. On the multiracial character of life in Los Angeles for ethnic Mexicans during World War II see, for example, Luis Alvarez, *The Power of the Zoot: Youth Culture and Resistance during World War II* (Berkeley: University of California Press, 2008); Anthony Macias, *Mexican American Mojo: Popular Music, Dance, and Urban Culture in Los Angeles, 1935–1968* (Durham: Duke University Press, 2008).

16. On the multiracial history of Boyle Heights, see George J. Sanchez, "What's Good for Boyle Heights Is Good for the Jews: Creating Multiracialism on the Eastside during the 1950s," *American Quarterly* 56, no. 3 (September 2004): 135–163.

17. Guy Gabaldon, *Saipan: Suicide Island* (Saipan Island: privately printed, 1990).

18. Acosta, interview; Dominguez, interview; Gabaldon, interview.

19. As Miriam Jimenez Roman and Juan Flores remind us, "Afro-Latino" is not just a referent for people of African descent in Latin America or the Caribbean but also the long history of African-descended Latina/os in the United States who share group history, transnational discourse, often navigate the U.S. color line as both African American and Latina/o, and share the lived experience of being Afro-Latino. Miriam Jiménez Román and Juan Flores, eds., *The Afro-Latin@ Reader: History and Culture in the United States* (Durham: Duke University Press, 2010), 3.

20. Evelio Grillo, *Black Cuban, Black American: A Memoir* (Houston: Arte Público Press, 2000), 6; Evelio Grillo, interview by Mario Barrera, videotape recording, Oakland, CA, 26 January 2003, Voces Oral History Project.

21. Grillo, interview.

22. Grillo, interview. Norberto Gonzalez, interview by Erika Martinez, videotape recording, Miami, FL, 14 September 2002, Voces Oral History Project.

23. Morin, *Among the Valiant*, 87, 139–140.

24. Ibid., 118–119.

25. Fred Gomez story, in Maggie Rivas-Rodriguez et al., eds., *A Legacy Greater than Words: Stories of U.S. Latinos & Latinas of the World War II Generation* (Austin: U.S. Latino & Latina World War II Oral History Project, 2006), 17.

26. Rudolfo "Rudy" Acosta story, in Rivas-Rodriguez, *A Legacy Greater than Words*, 25.

27. Rodolfo Tovar story, in Rivas-Rodriguez, *A Legacy Greater than Words*, 148.

28. Grewal, *Transnational America*, 23. Grewal notes the complex and multiple characters of transnational "connectivities" (as opposed to outright "connections") where there are a "variety of connections that exist," "weak and strong connectivities," "some unevenly connected, others strongly connected," "some get translated and transcoded," and "still others incommensurable and untranslatable."

29. Alicia Camacho Schmidt, *Migrant Imaginaries: Latino Cultural Politics in the U.S.-Mexico Borderlands* (New York: New York University Press, 2008), 5.

30. Fred Gomez, interview by William Luna, videotape recording, Chicago, IL, 17 September 2002, Voces Oral History Project.

31. Dominguez, interview.

32. Morin, *Among the Valiant*, 113–114.

33. Ibid., 203.

34. Ibid., 232–233.

35. Gabaldon, interview; Gabaldon, *Saipan: Suicide Island; Hell to Eternity: The Guts! Glory! Gallantry of America's Hell-Bent for Victory Marines!* (1960).

36. On Mexican American claims to whiteness during World War II, see Neil Foley, "Becoming Hispanic: Mexican Americans and the Faustian Pact with Whiteness," in *Reflexiones 1997: New Directions in Mexican American Studies*, ed. Neil Foley (Austin: University of Texas Press, 1997), 53–70.

37. Gomez, interview.

38. Gonzalez, interview; Norberto Gonzalez story, in Rivas-Rodriguez, *A Legacy Greater than Words*, 145.

39. Rudolph Tovar, interviewed by Henry Mendoza, videotape recording, Los Angeles, CA, 26 September 2003, Voces Oral History Project.

40. Gonzalez, interview; Rivas-Rodriguez, *A Legacy Greater than Words*, 144.

41. Gonzalez, interview.

42. Leo Moreno, interview by Paul R. Zepeda, videotape recording, Houston, TX, 8 August 2003, Voces Oral History Project.

43. Prado, interview.

44. Juan Flores, "Reclaiming Left Baggage: Some Early Sources for Minority Studies," *Cultural Critique* 59 (Winter 2005): 187–206.

Chapter Five

1. In 1943 the FEPC's Region X included Texas, Louisiana, New Mexico, and Arizona.

2. Félix D. Almaráz Jr., *Knight without Armor: Carlos Eduardo Castañeda, 1896–1958* (College Station: Texas A&M Press, 1999), 4–19 (quotation in this chapter's title from p. 68); Richard R. Flores, *Remembering the Alamo: Memory, Modernity, and the Master Symbol* (Austin: University of Texas Press, 2002).

3. Benjamin Johnson, *Revolution in Texas: How a Forgotten Rebellion and Its Bloody Suppression Turned Mexicans into Americans* (New Haven: Yale University Press, 2005).

4. The founding of the League of United Latin American Citizens (LULAC) on 17 February 1929 in Corpus Christi, Texas, is the most obvious manifestation of this *new* Mexican American political consciousness. Cynthia E. Orozco, *No Mexicans, Women, or Dogs Allowed: The Rise of the Mexican American Civil Rights Movement* (Austin: University of Texas Press, 2009), 65–91.

5. Mario T. García, *Mexican Americans: Leadership, Ideology, and Identity, 1930–1960* (New Haven: Yale University Press, 1989), 231–251.

6. Ibid., 233.

7. Ibid., 232; Almaráz, *Knight without Armor*, 68.

8. Emilio Zamora, *Claiming Rights and Righting Wrongs in Texas: Mexican Workers and Job Politics during World War II* (College Station: Texas A&M University Press, 2009), 8.

9. García, *Mexican Americans*; Zamora, *Claiming Rights and Righting Wrongs in Texas*. Richard Griswold del Castillo also argues for a more nuanced understanding of the Mexican American generation's civil rights endeavors in general and of their wartime efforts in particular. Richard Griswold del Castillo, ed., *World War II and Mexican American Civil Rights* (Austin: University of Texas Press, 2008).

10. First in a letter and then in a meeting, Eleanor Roosevelt, a strong supporter of equal rights for African Americans, requested that A. Philip Randolph cancel the March on Washington. Mrs. Roosevelt not only feared for the safety of African American demonstrators in the southern town of Washington, DC, but also worried the March on Washington would "set back the progress which is being made, in the Army at least, towards better opportunities and less segregation." Louis Ruchames, *Race, Jobs, and Politics: The Story of FEPC* (New York: Columbia University Press, 1953), 17–18; Herbert Garfinkel, *When Negroes March: The March on Washington Movement in the Organizational Politics for FEPC* (Glencoe: Free Press, 1959), 42.

11. Executive Order 8802, June 25, 1941; General Records of the United States Government, 1778–2006, Record Group 11, National Archives Building, Washington, DC (hereafter NAB).

12. "The President's Committee on Fair Employment Practice: Its Beginning and Growth and How it Operates," a report of the Division of Review and Analysis (FEPC), Washington, D.C., March 1944; Histories of the FEPC, Folder 14; Reference Files, July 1941–April 1946; Headquarters Records, Division of Review & Analysis; Records of the Committee on Fair Employment Practice, 1904–1946, Record Group 228 (hereafter RG 228), National Archives at College Park, MD (hereafter NACP).

13. Andrew E. Kersten, *Race, Jobs, and the War: The FEPC in the Midwest, 1941–1946* (Chicago: University of Illinois Press, 2000), 38.

14. Kersten, *Race, Jobs, and the War*; Ruchames, *Race, Jobs, and Politics*; C. Kesselman, *The Social Politics of FEPC: A Study in Reform Pressure Movements* (Chapel Hill: University of North Carolina Press, 1948).

15. Ibid.

16. White employees used work stoppages, also known as hate strikes, as a means to protest "the hiring or upgrading of blacks or other minority workers or because these industrial newcomers challenged racial discrimination in defense factories." Kersten, *Race, Jobs, and the War*, 52. For a comprehensive list of hate strikes in the Midwest, see Appendix B in Kersten, *Race, Jobs, and the War*. According to Ru-

chames, between July 1943 and December 1944 the FEPC settled eighteen strikes initiated by white workers protesting equal employment opportunities for African American workers. Ruchames, *Race, Jobs, and Politics*, 187.

17. Ruchames, *Race, Jobs, and Politics*, 188–193.

18. Ibid., 54–55.

19. Executive Order 9346; Executive Orders 8802 and 9346, Folder 14, Office Files of Cornelius Golightly, 1943–1945, Headquarters Records, Division of Review & Analysis, RG 228, NACP.

20. Ibid. During the FEPC's first year of existence it operated with a budget of $80,000. At the close of the FEPC's first year committee members and allies, and on approval of President Roosevelt, anticipated a budget of over $100,000 for fiscal year 1943. Unfortunately, Roosevelt's unexpected transfer of the FEPC to the War Manpower Commission prevented this increase. Nonetheless, on Roosevelt's issuance of EO 9346 the FEPC's budget increased, and Roosevelt subsequently requested that the House appropriate $585,000 for the FEPC for the fiscal year beginning July 1, 1944. While the House Committee on Appropriations approved an appropriation of $500,000, it did so with much opposition from southern politicians. On March 21, 1945, less than a month before Roosevelt's death (on April 12), he requested a $599,000 appropriation for the FEPC's upcoming fiscal year. This time the House Appropriations Committee granted the FEPC a mere $250,000 budget. While allies of the FEPC, such as Senators Dennis Chavez and Vito Marcantonio, attempted to secure the FEPC a larger budget, their lobbying proved unsuccessful. Because of the insufficient funds the FEPC reduced its staff and closed all but three field offices. Ruchames, *Race, Jobs, and Politics*, 27, 46, 88, 122, 132.

21. Carlos E. Castañeda, Archivist and Professor, to Alonso S. Perales, Attorney at Law, 29 May 1943, Alonso Perales, 1937–1957, Correspondences, 1920–1958, Personal and Biographical Material, 1911–1960, Carlos E. Castañeda Papers (hereafter CEC Papers), Benson Latin American Collection, University of Texas at Austin (hereafter BLAC).

22. Francis J. Haas, FEPC Chairman, to Dennis Chavez, U.S. Senator, New Mexico, 21 June 1943, C, Folder 3; Carbon Copies of Letters Sent, February 1943–May 1945, Office Files of the Chairman (hereafter OFC); Office of the Committee, Entry 6 (hereafter E 6), RG 228, NACP; and Lawrence W, Cramer, FEPC Executive Secretary, to John Haynes Holmes, Chairman, American Civil Liberties Union Board of Directors, 5 June 1943, H, Folder 8, OFC, E 6, RG 228, NACP.

23. Almaráz, *Knight without Armor*, 217.

24. Ibid.

25. Ibid.

26. Francis J. Haas, FEPC Chairman, to Robert E. Lucey, Archbishop, San Antonio, Texas, 13 August 1943, Folder 9, OFC, E 6, RG 228, NACP.

27. Carlos E. Castañeda, Senior Examiner, to Francis J. Haas, FEPC Chairman, 27 August 1943 and 2 September 1943, Mexicans (Miscellaneous), Folder 5; Aliens in Defense, U.S. Government, Central Files, 1941–1946, Administrative Division, Entry 25 (hereafter E 25), RG 228, NACP.

28. William Maslow, Director of Field Operations, to Carlos E. Castañeda, Special Assistant to the Chairman, 17 December 1943; H, Folder 8, OFC, E 7, RG 228, NACP; Almaráz, *Knight without Armor*, 220.

29. William Maslow, Director of Field Operations, to Carlos E. Castañeda,

Special Assistant to the Chairman, 23 June 1944, Folder 3, OFC, E 6, RG 228, NACP. In Castañeda's efforts to secure fair and equitable employment opportunities for African American and Mexican workers in Corpus Christi he met with officers and members of the Zinc Workers' Federal Labor Union (Local 23245, American Federation of Labor) and the Alkali Workers' Industrial Union (an affiliate of United Gas, Coke, Chemical and Allied Workers, Local 153, Congress of Industrial Organization [CIO]). In West Texas, New Mexico, and Arizona Castañeda conferred with leaders and rank-and-file members of affiliates of the CIO, the American Federation of Labor, the Brotherhood of Railway Trainmen, and the International Union of Mine, Mill and Smelter Workers. Almaráz, *Knight without Armor*, 226, 235–249; Griswold del Castillo, *World War II and Mexican American Civil Rights*, 75–78. Also see Zamora, *Claiming Rights and Righting Wrongs in Texas*; and Daniel, *Chicano Workers and the Politics of Fairness*, for a more detailed look at Castañeda's work with the FEPC.

30. Almaráz, *Knight without Armor*, 265.

31. Francis J. Haas, FEPC Chairman, to Robert W. Kinney, Attorney General, Los Angeles, CA, 13 August 1943, H, Folder 8, OFC, RG 228, NACP.

32. "The Wartime Enforcement of the Non-Discrimination Policy in the Federal Government," Folder 5; "The Fair Employment Practice Committee and Race Tensions in Industry," Folder 12; "The President's Committee on Fair Employment Practice: Its Beginning and Growth and How it Operates," Folder 14; "Justification for Continuation of Functions and the Appropriation during Period of Reconversion," Folder 14; ibid; "Outline for Study of Nonwhite Unemployment During Reconversion," Folder 18; "Impact of Reconversion on Minority Workers: A Report to the President," Folder 19; "Minorities in Defense," Folder 1. All citations are found in Studies & Reports Issued by FEPC, Reference Files, July 1941–April 1946, Division of Review & Analysis, Headquarters Records, Entry 33 (hereinafter E 33), RG 22, NACP.

33. Public Hearing in the Matter of Complaints of Discrimination in Employment in Defense Industries because of Race, Creed, Color or National Origin, 20–21 October 1941, Los Angeles, CA, Employment in Defense Industries, Folder 1, Cook Country Plumbers Union–Employment in Defense Industries (Public Complaints), Hearings, 1941–1946, Legal Division, Entry 19, RG 228, NACP. Griswold del Castillo, *World War II and Mexican American Civil Rights*, 22.

34. Region X's average of docketing 28.7 new cases a month did not measure up to Region II's average of 72.7, but it certainly outdid Region VIII and XI's monthly average of 1.6 and 3.7, respectively.

35. William Maslow, Director of Field Operations, to Dr. Carlos E. Castañeda, Special Assistant to the Chairman for Latin American Problems, 23 June 1944 (hereafter Maslow to Castañeda, June), C, Folder 3, OFC, RG 228, NACP.

36. Almaráz, *Knight without Armor*, 222–224.

37. Maslow to Castañeda, 23 June 1944, Folder 3, OFC, RG 228, NACP.

38. "Ley Antidiscriminatoria o Comisión de Buena Vecinidad," *La Prensa*, 24 March 1945, 5.

39. Malcolm Ross, FEPC Chairman, to Dr. Carlos E. Castañeda, Regional Director, 15 May 1945, Folder 3, OFC, RG 228, NACP.

40. For a detailed discussion of the Good Neighbor Policy's and Texas's Good

Neighbor Commission's implication for Mexican American civil rights endeavors, see Zamora, *Claiming Rights and Righting Wrongs*; and Griswold del Castillo, *World War II and Mexican American Civil Rights*, 23–33.

41. Malcolm Ross, FEPC Chairman, to Dr. Carlos E. Castañeda, Regional Director, 15 May 1945, Folder 3, OFC, RG 228, NACP.

42. Griswold del Castillo, *World War II and Mexican American Civil Rights*, 77.

43. For a detailed study of the pan-American identity Castañeda outlined in his work with the FEPC, see Zamora, *Claiming Rights and Righting Wrongs in Texas*.

44. The Problem of the Mexican, Manuscripts, 1923–1957 File, Literary Productions, 1924–1958, Personal and Biographical Material, 1911–1960, CEC Papers, BLAC. Quotation in the subhead above from this source.

45. Mae M. Ngai, *Impossible Subjects: Illegal Aliens and the Making of Modern America* (Princeton: Princeton University Press, 2004).

46. Carlos E. Castañeda, Special Assistant to the Chairman, to Commanding General, Kelly Field, Texas, 16 March 1944, 10–GN-246, Kelly Field, Folder 33, Closed Cases, Entry 70 (hereafter E 70), RG 228, National Archives and Record Administration Southwest Region, Fort Worth, TX (hereafter NARA FW).

47. Carlos E. Castañeda, Special Assistant to the Chairman, to General Vanaman, Commanding General, Kelly Field, Texas, 14 July 1944, 10–GN-283, Kelly Field, Folder 36, E 70, RG 228, NARA FW.

48. S. 2048, A Bill, 78th Cong., 2nd sess., Chavez Bill, Folder 17, C–D, Office Files of Marjorie M. Lawson, 1942–1945, Division of Review & Analysis, Entry 27, RG 228, NACP.

49. Statement of Dr. Carlos E. Castañeda, Special Assistant to the FEPC Chairman, before Senator Chavez's Subcommittee of the Senate Education and Labor Committee, 12–14 March 1945; Miscellaneous, Folder 1, Unarranged, Office Files of Evelyn H. Cooper, 1943–1945, Legal Division, Entry 18, RG 228, NACP.

50. Ibid.

51. Carlos E. Castañeda, "Statement of Dr. Carlos E. Castañeda, Regional Director, Fair Employment Practice Committee, Region 10, San Antonio, Texas," in *Are We Good Neighbors*, comp. Alonso S. Perales (New York: Arno Press, 1974), 102.

52. Ibid.

53. Ian F. Haney Lopez, "White Latinos," *Harvard Law Review* 6 (2003): 1–7.

54. David Forgacs, ed., *The Antonio Gramsci Reader: Selected Writings, 1916–1935* (New York: New York University Press, 2000), 225–229.

55. Griswold del Castillo, *World War II and Mexican American Civil Rights*, 26–31, 81–86.

56. Orozco, *No Mexicans, Women, or Dogs Allowed*, 59–91.

57. Forgacs, *The Antonio Gramsci Reader*, 193–194.

58. I would like to thank Luis Alvarez for encouraging me to pursue Gramsci's notion of historical bloc as my theoretical apparatus. His comments on an early draft of this chapter proved invaluable.

59. Zamora, *Claiming Rights and Righting Wrongs*, 136–137.

60. Malcolm Ross, FEPC Chairman, to A. Maceo Smith, President, Texas Negro Chamber of Commerce, 30 November 1943, Untitled, Folder 7, Carbon Copies of Letters Sent (February 43–May 45), J–Z; Ross to M. H. Jackson, President, Progressive Voters' League, 30 November 1943, Untitled, Folder 11, Carbon Copies

of Letters Sent (February 43–May 45), J-Z, OFC, Entry 6, RG 228, NACP; Ross to Ernest C. Estell, 14 December 43, Untitled, Folder 5, OFC, Entry 6, RG 228, NACP; Ross to B. W. Goodwin Jr., Dallas NAACP, 30 November 43, G, Folder 7, OFC, Entry 6, RG 228, NACP; Ross to Roy J. Deferrari, 29 November 43, D, Folder 4, OFC, Entry 6, RG 228, NACP; Almaráz, *Knight without Armor*, 228.

61. Perales, *Are We Good Neighbors*, 86–133.

62. Carlos E. Castañeda, Professor, to Clarence Mitchell, FEPC Director of Field Operations, 15 March 1946, Folder 6, Correspondence, 1920–1958; and Malcolm Ross, FEPC Chair, to Carlos E. Castañeda, Professor, 13 March 1946, Folder 3, Activities and Organizations, 1428–1958, Personal and Biographical Material, 1911–1960, CEC Papers, BLAC.

63. Newsletter, Committee of One Hundred, 1946; Minorities Affected, Folder 8, Office of the Committee, Entry 8, RG 228, NACP.

Chapter Six

1. Third Annual Conference Program, Los Conquistadores, Arizona State Teachers College at Tempe, 1941. For an overview and analysis of organizations formed by Mexican-origin college students prior to the Chicano Movement of the 1960s, with a chapter focused on California and Arizona in the 1930s and 1940s, see Christopher Tudico, "Before We Were Chicana/os: The Mexican American Experience in California Higher Education, 1848–1945" (Ph.D. dissertation, University of Pennsylvania, 2010).

2. Solomon Muñoz, conversation with author, 1 June 2001, Fresno, CA. In this chapter the terms *Mexican, Mexican-origin, Mexican American* and *American Mexican* are used to describe persons of Mexican descent living in the United States unless otherwise designated. The terms are used in a manner consistent with the interviews or publications cited.

3. Rebecca Muñoz and Félix J. Gutiérrez are the parents of the author of this chapter.

4. Muñoz, conversation with author, 1 June 2001.

5. "Democracy, Beware!!" *Pasadena Chronicle*, 22 April 1938, 2.

6. "Members Of The Mexican-American Section" and "Many Latins In National Guard Maneuvers Here," *Juventud* 1, no. 2 (12 January 1940): 1. Copies of *Juventud* were provided to the author by the Guerrero family.

7. "Many Latins in National Guard Maneuvers Here."

8. Masthead, *Juventud* 1, no. 1 (1 December 1939): 2. For more information on the organization and role of Mesa's Progressive Juvenile Division and *Juventud*, see Dean Smith, *La Gloria Escondida* (Phoenix: Sims Publishing Company, 1967), chap. 15, 147–159.

9. Front Page Ears, *Juventud* 1, no. 1 (1 December 1939). "Ears" refers in journalism to boxed text featured alongside a newspaper's nameplate on the front page.

10. Pedro W. Guerrero, *Division Juvenil Encampments, Picnics-Partys*, 16 mm film, Guerrero Family Archives, Mesa, AZ.

11. "California Sends Delegates to First Interstate Mexican Youth Parley Ever Held in Arizona," *Juventud*, 1 December 1939, 1.

12. For examples, see *Mexican Voice* covers for September, October 1939, 1940, and winter 1941.

13. See cover of issue cited and article by Cosme J. Peña, "We Do Our Share," *Mexican Voice*, summer 1941, 3, Gutiérrez Family Archives.

14. "Skatings Discontinued," *Juventud* 1, no. 1 (December 15, 1939): 1.

15. "Mexican Culture Has Influenced the American Social Pattern," *Juventud* 1, no. 2 (January 12, 1940): 2.

16. "Club News—Monrovia," *Mexican Voice*, spring 1939, 16.

17. Félix J. Gutiérrez, conversation with author, early 1950s.

18. "Mi Tía" (Monrovia-Arcadia-Duarte High School), *Anthology*, 1937, 20–21.

19. Isador Guardado, conversation with author, spring 1994, Duarte, CA. Guardado and Gutiérrez were members of a family picking crew. For profiles of Gutiérrez written while he was editor of the *Mexican Voice*, see Rodney L. Brink, "Youth Works to Eliminate Racial Hyphen," *Christian Science Monitor*, 25 July 1945, 9; and "Felix Gutierrez," *Juventud* 1, no. 1 (15 December 1939): 2.

20. Stephen Reyes, "The Mexican Youth Conference," *Mexican Voice*, Spring 1939, 2, 4. For additional information on the *Mexican Voice*, see references to the *Mexican Voice* and to the Mexican American movement in Carlos Muñoz Jr., *Youth, Identity, Power: The Chicano Movement*, rev. ed. (New York: Verso, 2007); F. Arturo Rosales, *Chicano! The History of the Mexican American Civil Rights Movement* (Houston: Arte Público Press, 1996); George J. Sánchez, *Becoming Mexican American: Ethnicity, Culture and Identity in Chicano Los Angeles, 1900–1945* (London: Oxford University Press, 1993); and David G. Gutiérrez, *Walls and Mirrors: Mexican Americans, Mexican Immigrants, and the Politics of Ethnicity* (Berkeley: University of California Press, 1995). Some information in this section is drawn from Félix F. Gutiérrez, "Mexican-American Youth and Their Media: *The Mexican Voice*, 1938–1945," Paper presented to the panel "The Formation of a Mexican American Consciousness and the Media in Los Angeles," Organization of American Historians, Los Angeles, CA, 1984.

21. Stephen Reyes, interview, Pasadena, CA, 27 March 1984.

22. Quote from Félix F. Gutiérrez, "Mexican-American Youth and Their Media," 7.

23. Rebecca Muñoz Gutiérrez, interview, South Pasadena, CA, 27 March 1984; and "Letters to the Editor," *Mexican Voice*, spring 1939, 17.

24. Cosme J. Peña, "DISCRMINATION—AND US," *Mexican Voice*, spring 1942, 3.

25. "BEGIN AT HOME . . . ," *Mexican Voice*, spring 1942, 2.

26. Manuel De La Raza (Félix J. Gutiérrez), "Nosotros," *Mexican Voice*, spring 1942, 8.

27. For information on the Zoot Suit Riots, see Mauricio Mazon, *The Zoot-Suit Riots: The Psychology of Symbolic Annihilation* (Austin: University of Texas Press, 1984).

28. Paul Coronel, "The Pachuco Problem," *Mexican Voice*, 1943, 3.

29. "The Latin-American Coordinating Council," *Mexican Voice*, 1943, 6.

30. "A Challenge . . . ," *Mexican Voice*, 1943, 2.

31. Paul Coronel, "As We Move . . . ," *Mexican Voice*, summer 1944, 2.

32. Manuel De La Raza (Félix J. Gutiérrez), "Nosotros," *Mexican Voice*, summer 1944, 8.

33. "What Do You Say?" *Mexican Voice*, summer 1944, 6.

34. Cited in Félix F. Gutiérrez, "Mexican-American Youth and Their Media," 19. A predecessor to *Forward* was *Youth Forward*, of which Gutiérrez was founding editor in October 1943. The newspaper was published by the Los Angeles Youth Advisory Council and incorporated many of the same editorial elements of the *Mexican Voice*. During the war he also worked with the mimeographed *Eastside Youth Council News*. Both publications apparently were part of efforts following the Zoot Suit Riots to expand youth services and activities and involved members of the Mexican Youth Council and the Mexican-American Movement.

35. H. T. Alvarado, "THE VETERAN of Mexican Descent," *Forward*, 12 May 1946, 2.

36. H. T. Alvarado, "THE VETERAN of Mexican Descent," *Forward*, 15 January 1947, 2.

37. "INSECURITY," *Forward*, 15 January 1947, 2.

38. M.D.R. (Félix J. Gutiérrez), "Spanish Food?" *Forward*, 15 January 1947, 1.

39. "Editorials-Opinions-Articles-Criticisms," *Forward*, 12 May 1946, 3.

40. "Use of Pool," *Forward*, 12 May 1946, 7.

41. Gualberto Valadez, "The President Speaks . . . ," *Forward*, 12 May 1946, 1.

42. "Youth Conference May 18–19," *Forward*, 12 May 1946, 1.

43. Félix Gutiérrez, "U.S.–Mexican Youth Plan Set Up," *Christian Science Monitor*, 19 June 1946, 1, 2. For other *Christian Science Monitor* coverage of the MAM, see "Mexican-American Movement Tells of Cultural Gains," 12 November 1945, 9; and Brink, "Youth Works to Eliminate Racial Hyphen."

Chapter Seven

I thank Maggie Rivas-Rodríguez, Ben Olguín, and the Voces Oral History Project for supporting my work and for including me in a symposium in 2006 and a seminar in 2009 that led to the writing of this chapter. Special thanks are also due to the families of the late Rodolfo García and the late Carlos Monsiváis, without whose memories I would not have a project. I am also grateful to Pancho and Evelyn García, who hosted me during a 2009 research trip to San Antonio. I also thank the participants in the 2009 seminar, along with Laura Padilla and Richard Flores, for their comments. Finally, thanks are due to the Guadalupe Cultural Arts Center, the Rockefeller Foundation, the Recovering the U.S. Hispanic Literary Heritage Project, the Wenner-Gren Foundation for Anthropological Research, and Grinnell College's Rosenfield Program in Public Affairs, International Relations, and Human Rights for financial support of my research.

1. The Spanish word *colonia* can be translated as "neighborhood" or "colony" and was the term that San Antonio's Spanish-language press used in the early twentieth century to refer to the ethnic Mexican presence in the city. I follow this usage, recognizing that *colonia mexicana* represents a way of understanding that presence from an expatriate's perspective. In this chapter, I use *ethnic Mexican* and *Mexicana/o* as roughly equivalent terms referring to people identified with the dominant Hispano-

phone culture of what is now Mexico. The term is intentionally ambiguous regarding nationality. "Mexican American" in this article refers specifically to people of Mexican descent born or naturalized in the United States. "Mexican" refers to citizens and nationals of the United Mexican States.

2. Anonymous author, "Hoy celebra el 2o. aniversario de su inauguración el nuevo Teatro Nacional," *La Prensa* (San Antonio), 3 December 1941, 4.

3. Francisco E. Balderrama and Raymond Rodríguez, *Decade of Betrayal: Mexican Repatriation in the 1930s* (Albuquerque: University of New Mexico Press, 2006), 149.

4. Rodolfo Acuña, *Occupied America: A History of Chicanos*, 7th ed. (Boston: Pearson Higher Ed., 2011), 208.

5. Nicolás Kanellos, *A History of Hispanic Theatre in the United States: Origins to 1940* (Austin: University of Texas Press, 1990), 199.

6. J. Glenn Gray, *The Warriors: Reflections on Men in Battle* (New York: Harper & Row, 1959), 147.

7. Sam Lucchese, with Tad Mizwa, *A Lifetime with Boots* (Houston: Cordovan Corp., 1980), 3.

8. Kanellos, *A History of Hispanic Theatre in the United States*, 77.

9. Elizabeth C. Ramírez, *Footlights across the Border: A History of Spanish-Language Professional Theatre on the Texas Stage* (New York: P. Lang, 1990), 70–71.

10. David Montejano, *Anglos and Mexicans in the Making of Texas, 1836–1986* (Austin: University of Texas Press, 1987), 240.

11. Ramírez, *Footlights across the Border*, 88.

12. Félix Gutiérrez and Jorge Reina Schement, *Spanish-Language Radio in the Southwestern United States* (Austin: Center for Mexican American Studies, 1979), 100.

13. "Rock Bottom Price Admits to S.A. Show," *San Antonio Light*, 13 November 1938, 1.

14. Kanellos, *A History of Hispanic Theatre in the United States*, 77.

15. "Estreno de la jososa revista 'Votamos o nos botan,'" *La Prensa* (San Antonio), 11 June 1939, 3. Author's translation.

16. "Una Mula De Tantas," phonograph recording featuring Netty and Jesús Rodríguez, Cat #B-2308, Matrix #BVE 87809–1 (Blue Bird, San Antonio, 1935), Collection of the Arhoolie Foundation.

17. For an extended discussion of the Rodríguez duo's depression-era recordings, see Peter Haney, "Bilingual Humor, Verbal Hygiene, and the Gendered Contradictions of Cultural Citizenship in Early Mexican American Comedy," *Journal of Linguistic Anthropology* 13, no. 2 (2003).

18. The term *costumbrismo* refers to an artistic and literary movement in the Spanish-speaking world that centers on the quasi-ethnographic depiction of local customs and mannerisms, especially those of peasants and indigenous people.

19. "Función a beneficio de la cantante Esperanza Espino," *La Prensa* (San Antonio), 17 January 1942, 4.

20. "Cantó en el aniversario de 'La Prensa,'" *La Prensa* (San Antonio), 22 February 1942, 5.

21. "Función para recaudar fondos para la Cruz Roja," *La Prensa* (San Antonio), 9 April 1942, 4.

22. "El 'Caballero Rosas' se presenta con éxito en el Zaragoza," *La Prensa* (San Antonio), 2; "Actos artisticos para los soldados," *La Prensa* (San Antonio), 27 June 1942, 4.

23. "Agasajo de despedida al Trio Dragones," *La Prensa* (San Antonio), 28 July 1942, 4.

24. "Reaparición del artista Jesús Rodríguez Valero," *La Prensa* (San Antonio), 25 July 1942, 4.

25. "El Trio Mendoza en jira artistica," *La Prensa* (San Antonio), 7 June 1942, 2.

26. "Naciona," *La Prensa* (San Antonio), 1 November 1942, sec. 2, 3.

27. "Pedro González González, 80, Film and TV Character Actor, Dies," *New York Times*, www.nytimes.com/2006/02/17/arts/television/17gonzalez.htm,l, 17 February 2006, accessed 29 January 2012.

28. "Zaragoza," *La Prensa* (San Antonio), 1 November 1942, 3.

29. Advertisement for the Teatro Zaragoza, *La Prensa* (San Antonio), 16 May 1943, sec. 2, 3.

30. "Zaragoza," *La Prensa* (San Antonio), 4 July 1943, 3.

31. "Combate contra el eje en el extranjero," *La Prensa* (San Antonio), 20 June 1943, 5.

32. "Función en el Teatro Nacional para recabar fondos para la Cruz Roja," *La Prensa* (San Antonio), 13 April 1944, 8.

33. "La función de esta noche en el Teatro Nacional," *La Prensa* (San Antonio), 8 July 1944, 4.

34. Tomás Ybarra-Frausto, "La Chata Noloesca: Figura del donaire," in *Mexican American Theatre: Then and Now*, ed. Nicolas Kanellos (Houston: Arte Público Press, 1983), 49.

35. Carlos and Amada Monsiváis, interview by Pete Haney, audio recording, Universal City, TX, 31 July 1990, University of Texas Institute of Texan Cultures at San Antonio. "They" in the second sentence refers to an unnamed group of artists who, according to Monsiváis, gave his family a tent.

36. "Zaragoza (Advertisement)," *La Prensa*, 26 August 1945, 4; "Función de despedida," *La Prensa*, 19 August 1945, 4.

37. Untitled advertisement, *La Prensa* (San Antonio), 9 January 1944, 12.

38. "Actuará Cantinflas en el Auditorio Municipal," *La Prensa* (San Antonio), 16 January 1944, 1.

39. "Destacados artistas mexicanos en San Antonio," *La Prensa* (San Antonio), 23 January 1944, 4.

40. "Un conocido galán del cine en los Teatros Nacional y Guadalupe," *La Prensa* (San Antonio), 23 January 1944, 4.

41. Gutiérrez and Schement, *Spanish-Language Radio in the Southwestern United States*, 9.

42. Untitled advertisement, *La Prensa* (San Antonio), 6 February 1944, 4.

43. Untitled advertisement, *La Prensa* (San Antonio), 30 April 1944, 4.

44. "Las Estrellas más destacadas del cine desfilarán por el escenario del Auditorio," *La Prensa* (San Antonio), 24 September 1944, 4.

45. Untitled advertisement, *La Prensa* (San Antonio), 14 January 1944, 6.

46. Untitled advertisement, *La Prensa* (San Antonio), 16 September 1945, 4; Untitled advertisement, *La Prensa* (San Antonio), 11 November 1945, 4.

47. "Hoy debieron haber partido los artistas mexicanos," *La Prensa* (San Antonio), 28 January 1944, 8.

48. U.S. Women's Army Advertisement, *La Prensa* (San Antonio), 27 February 1944, 6.

49. The story did not specify which friends had been killed.

50. "Las primeras del escuadrón 'Benito Juárez,'" *La Prensa* (San Antonio), 14 March 1944, 5.

51. "El festival en honor de las WAC," *La Prensa* (San Antonio), 28 March 1944, 5.

52. Leisa D. Meyer, *Creating GI Jane: Sexuality and Power in the Women's Army Corps during World War II* (New York: Columbia University Press, 1996), 49.

53. Lisa Lowe, "The International within the National: American Studies and Asian American Critique," *Cultural Critique*, no. 40 (Autumn 1998): 31.

54. "Esperan un circo en la Cd. de McAllen," *Herlado de Brownsville*, 4 May 1939, 1; Frank W. Brady, "The Bexar Facts," *San Antonio Light*, 31 January 1941, 14A.

55. "El Sargento Joe M. Abreu, muerto en acción de guerra," *La Prensa* (San Antonio), 6 August 1944, 3.

56. "Misa en el aniversario de su muerte en acción," *La Prensa* (San Antonio), 8 July 1945, 6; "Misa cantada en la Iglesia de San Felipe," *La Prensa* (San Antonio), 7 July 1946, sec. 2, 4.

57. Carlos Monsiváis, interview.

58. Albert A. Blum, "Work or Fight: The Use of the Draft as a Manpower Sanction during the Second World War," *Industrial and Labor Relations Review Journal* 16 (1963): 367.

59. In an article titled "Musical 3As not forced to war work or fight; No legality to local ruling," *Billboard* magazine noted the success of New York's American Federation of Musicians Local #802 in contesting orders from a draft board that would have forced married musicians with children to enlist; *Billboard*, 13 July 1943, 23.

60. Daniel Terán-Solano, "La historia del bolero latinoamericano," www.ana litica.com/va/hispanica/9288877.asp (accessed 11 March 2006).

61. Rodolfo G. García, tape recording, San Antonio, TX, 17 July 1990, University of Texas Institute of Texan Cultures at San Antonio.

62. Rodolfo García, interview by Peter C. Haney, audio recording, San Antonio, TX, 4 February 1999, author's collection.

63. José Limón, *Dancing with the Devil: Society and Cultural Poetics in Mexican-American South Texas* (Madison: University of Wisconsin Press, 1994), 31.

64. J. Glenn Gray, *The Warriors: Reflections on Men in Battle* (New York: Harper & Row, 1970), 148.

Chapter Eight

1. The 200th Coast Artillery regiment of the New Mexico National Guard was called to active duty status on January 6, 1941. During the Battle of Bataan, in late December 1941, several hundred soldiers from the regiment were reorganized into

the 515th Coast Artillery for a defensive mission. Marcus Griffin, *Heroes of Bataan, Corregidor, and Northern Luzon,* 2nd ed. (Carlsbad, NM: M. Griffin, 1989), 1–15.

2. "Manitos" signified *hermanito,* or younger brother, to evoke a connection with people of Spanish origins.

3. John M. Nieto-Phillips, *The Language of Blood: The Making of Spanish-American Identity in New Mexico, 1880s-1930s* (Albuquerque: University of New Mexico Press, 2004), 81–82.

4. Eva Matson, *It Tolled for New Mexico: New Mexicans Captured by the Japanese, 1941–1945* (Las Cruces, NM: Yucca Tree Press, 1994), 4.

5. Ibid., 12.

6. Louis Althusser, in *Lenin and Philosophy and Other Essays* (New York: Monthly Review Press, 1972), 174.

7. Setsu Shigematsu and Keith L. Camacho, eds., "Introduction: Militarized Currents, Decolonizing Futures," in *Militarized Currents: Toward a Decolonized Future in Asia and the Pacific* (Minneapolis: University of Minnesota Press, 2010), xv.

8. Rudy P. Guevarra Jr., *Becoming Mexipino: Multiethnic Identities and Communities in San Diego* (New Brunswick, NJ: Rutgers University Press, 2012), 8–10; "Filipinos in Nueva Espana: Filipino-Mexican Relations, Mestizaje, and Identity in Colonial and Contemporary Mexico," *Journal of Asian American Studies* 14 (2011): 392.

9. Tagalog, regarded as the Philippines' national language, incorporates some Spanish and English words into its vocabulary, as well as Malay and Chinese words. Languages such as Ilocano, spoken mainly in Luzon and the northern islands, and Cebuano, spoken in the southern islands, predate Spanish colonization. For languages in the Philippines, see Austin Craig, *Philippine Progress Prior to 1898* (Metro Manila: Cacho Hermanos, 1985), 106.

10. Neferti Tadiar, *Things Fall Away: Philippine Historical Experience and the Makings of Globalization* (Durham: Duke University Press, 2009), 31.

11. Craig, *Philippine Progress Prior to 1898,* 77–78; Susan K. Harris, *God's Arbiters: Americans and the Philippines, 1898–1902* (New York: Oxford University Press, 2011), 11–14, 182.

12. Oscar V. Campomanes, "Casualty Figures of the American Soldier and the Other: Post-1898 Allegories of Imperial Nation-Building as 'Love and War,'" in *Vestiges of War: The Philippine-American War and the Aftermath of an Imperial Dream, 1899–1999,* ed. Angel Velasco Shaw and Luis H. Francia (New York: New York University Press, 2002), 136; E. San Juan, *Racial Formations, Critical Transformations: Articulations of Power in Ethnic and Racial Studies in the United States* (Atlantic Highlands, NJ: Humanities Press, 1992), 117; Abe Ignacio et al., *The Forbidden Book: The Philippine-American War in Political Cartoons* (San Francisco: T'Boli, 2004).

13. Ricardo Trota Jose, *The Philippine Army, 1935–1942* (Manila: Ateneo de Manila University Press, 1992), 193.

14. Ibid., 139; Antonio Raimundo, "The Filipino Veterans Equity Movement: A Case Study in Reparations Theory," *California Law Review* 98, no. 2 (2010): 593; Rick Rocamora, *Filipino World War II Soldiers: America's Second-Class Veterans* (San Francisco: Veterans Equity Center, 2008), 12.

15. Mae M. Ngai, *Impossible Subjects: Illegal Aliens and the Making of Modern America* (Princeton, NJ: Princeton University Press, 2004), 100.

16. "The term '*veteranos*' refers to Filipinos who fought on behalf of the U.S. military in the Philippines during World War II. Due to the Rescission Act of 1946, Filipino soldiers in the Philippine Army are not officially recognized as American veterans, but we use the term to respectfully acknowledge their participation alongside soldiers from other Allied nations." Tracy Lachica Buenavista and Jordan Beltrán Gonzales, "DREAMs Deferred: Filipino Experiences and an Anti-Militarization Critique of the Development, Relief, and Education for Alien Minors Act," *Harvard Journal of Asian American Policy Review* 20 (2011): 37; Rocamora, *Filipino World War II Soldiers*, 22.

17. Raimundo, "The Filipino Veterans Equity Movement," 594–596.

18. "While in 2009 the American Recovery and Reinvestment Act provided lump sum settlements to surviving Filipino *veteranos*, the attempt was vastly symbolic because a majority of *veteranos* had died before this recognition and survivors had only one year to apply and access their money." Buenavista and Gonzales, "DREAMs Deferred," 35. For photographs and narratives of San Francisco's Filipino *veteranos*, see Rocamora, *Filipino World War II Soldiers*.

19. Mario Barrera, *Race and Class in the Southwest: A Theory of Racial Inequality* (Notre Dame: University of Notre Dame Press, 1989), 40.

20. John W. Dower, *War without Mercy: Race and Power in the Pacific War*, 7th ed. (New York: Pantheon Books, 1993), 79.

21. Everett M. Rogers and Nancy R. Bartlit, *Silent Voices of World War II: When Sons of the Land of Enchantment Met Sons of the Land of the Rising Sun* (Santa Fe, NM: Sunstone Press, 2005), 40.

22. Jose, *The Philippine Army*, 194–195.

23. Rogers and Bartlit, *Silent Voices of World War II*, 43.

24. Agapito E. Silva, interview by Brian Lucero, videotape recording, Albuquerque, NM, 30 November 2001, Voces Oral History Project, Nettie Lee Benson Latin American Collection, University of Texas at Austin.

25. Ibid.

26. Jose, *The Philippine Army*, 209–210.

27. Teodoro Agoncillo, *The Fateful Years* (Quezon City, Philippines: Garcia, 1965), 898.

28. Chris Schaefer, *Bataan Diary: An American Family in World War II, 1941–1945* (Houston, TX: Riverview Publishing, 2004), 60; Dower, *War without Mercy*, 328.

29. Rocamora, *Filipino World War II Soldiers*, 81.

30. Jonathan Wainwright, *General Wainwright's Story: The Account of Four Years of Humiliating Defeat, Surrender, and Captivity* (Garden City, NY: Doubleday, 1946), 81.

31. Felipe Fernandez, *Memoirs of a Philippine Scout Cavalryman* (self-published, 2007), 54–59; Hampton Sides, *Ghost Soldiers: The Forgotten Epic Story of World War II's Most Dramatic Mission* (New York: Doubleday, 2001); Griffin, *Heroes of Bataan*, iv.

32. Matson arrives at these figures by calculating the percentages of soldiers

who were "liberated" and who died according to army enrollment personnel and payroll rosters. "As with any statistics concerning people, there are always exceptions. Several men had one Anglo and one Hispanic parent. An arbitrary decision was made to place them on the basis of their surname. If the surname was Hispanic, they were classified as Hispanic/Anglo and put into the Hispanic group. Conversely, if the surname was Anglo, their classification was Anglo/Hispanic and they were included in the Anglo group." Matson, *It Tolled for New Mexico*, 127.

33. Ibid., 15.

34. Griffin, *Heroes of Bataan*, 38–43; Banegas, interview.

35. Michel-Rolph Trouillot, *Silencing the Past: Power and the Production of History* (Boston, MA: Beacon Press, 1995), xix.

36. Silva, interview.

37. Ralph Rodriguez, interview by Brian Lucero, videotape recording, Albuquerque, NM, 23 and 31 January 2002, Voces Oral History Project, Nettie Lee Benson Latin American Collection, University of Texas at Austin.

38. Matson, *It Tolled for New Mexico*, 75.

39. Silva, interview.

40. Matson, *It Tolled for New Mexico*, 7.

41. José Fuljencio Martinez, written memoir, Fort Garland, CO, 1 September 2002, Voces Oral History Project, Nettie Lee Benson Latin American Collection, University of Texas at Austin.

42. Lorenzo Banegas, interview by Robert C. Moore, audio recording, Las Cruces, NM, 27 April 1992, Voces Oral History Project, Nettie Lee Benson Latin American Collection, University of Texas at Austin.

43. Ibid.

44. Ibid.

45. Ibid. Lorenzo Banegas may be heard singing the "Corrido de Bataan" at http://reta.nmsu.edu/bataan/corrido/index.html (accessed 4 November 2011).

46. Banegas, interview.

47. Manuel De Veyra, *Doctor in Bataan, 1941–1942* (Quezon City: New Day, 1991), 34.

48. A bill to grant the Congressional Gold Medal to the troops who defended Bataan during World War II, S. 2004, 112th Cong., 1st sess.

49. Trouillot, *Silencing the Past*, 29.

Chapter Nine

1. David M. Kennedy, *Freedom from Fear: The American People in Depression and War, 1929–1945* (Oxford: Oxford University Press, 2001), 465.

2. Ibid., 632.

3. "S.A. Delivers War Goods," *San Antonio Light*, 9 January 1942, 12A.

4. U.S. Department of the Interior, National Park Service, *Historic Preservation Certification Application for the Friedrich Building* (San Antonio, TX: National Park Service, 1999), 3. http://thefriedrich.com/Friedrich%20Part%201.pdf.

5. Juana Portales Esquivel, interview by Patricia Portales, audio recording, San

Antonio, TX, 23 February 2008, Voces Oral History Project, Nettie Lee Benson Latin American Collection, University of Texas at Austin.

6. Brenda Sendejo, "Mother's Legacy: Cultivating Chicana Consciousness during the War Years," in *Beyond the Latino World War II Hero: The Social and Political Legacy of a Generation*, ed. Maggie Rivas-Rodriguez and Emilio Zamora (Austin: University of Texas Press, 2009), 156.

7. Esquivel, interview.

8. See Raul Morin, *Among the Valiant: Mexican Americans in World War II and Korea* (Los Angeles: Valiant Press, 1963); Mauricio Mazon, *Zoot Suit Riots: The Psychology of Symbolic Annihilation* (Austin: University of Texas Press, 1988); and Henry A. J. Ramos, *The American GI Forum: In Pursuit of the Dream, 1948–1983* (Houston, TX: Arte Público Press, 1998).

9. "Women in War Jobs: Rosie the Riveter (1942–1945)," Ad Council, Historic Campaigns, www.adcouncil.org/default.aspx?id=128.

10. Kennedy, *Freedom from Fear*, 776.

11. Catherine S. Ramirez, *The Woman in the Zoot Suit: Gender, Nationalism, and the Cultural Politics of Memory* (Durham, NC: Duke University Press, 2008), 4.

12. Elizabeth Escobedo, "The *Pachuca* Panic: Sexual and Cultural Battlegrounds in World War II Los Angeles," *Western Historical Quarterly* 38 (2007): 133–156.

13. Emma Pérez, *The Decolonial Imaginary: Writing Chicanas into History* (Bloomington: Indiana University Press, 1999), 81.

14. Severo Pérez and Judith Pérez, *Soldierboy*, in *Necessary Theater: Six Plays about the Chicano Experience* (Houston, TX: Arte Público Press, 1989); Luis Valdez, *Zoot Suit and Other Plays* (Houston, TX: Arte Público Press, 1992).

15. Louis Gerard Mendoza, *Historia: The Literary Making of Chicana and Chicano History* (College Station: Texas A&M University Press, 2001), 21.

16. Ibid., 19.

17. Pérez, *The Decolonial Imaginary*, 32.

18. Ibid., 59.

19. Patricia Zavella, "The Problematic Relationship of Feminism and Chicana Studies," *Women's Studies* 17 (1989): 28.

20. Pérez, *The Decolonial Imaginary*, 33.

21. Ibid., 12.

22. "Women Handle Man-Size Jobs in S.A. Factory: Perform Highly Complicated Tasks," *San Antonio Light*, 8 November 1942, 3:4.

23. Ibid.

24. Louise Lamphere, Patricia Zavella, and Felipe Gonzales, *Sunbelt Working Mothers: Reconciling Family and Factory* (New York: Cornell University Press, 1993), 15.

25. Emilio Zamora, *Claiming Rights and Righting Wrongs in Texas: Mexican Workers and Job Politics during World War II* (Austin: University of Texas Press, 2009), 52.

26. Naomi Quiñonez, "Rosita the Riveter: Welding Wartime Tradition with Wartime Transformations," in *Mexican Americans and World War II*, ed. Maggie Rivas-Rodriguez (Austin: University of Texas Press, 2005), 266.

27. Esquivel, interview.

28. Ibid.

29. Patricia Zavella, "Abnormal Intimacy: The Varying Work Networks of Chicana Cannery Workers," *Feminist Studies* 11 (1985): 542.

30. Norma Alarcón, "Traddutora, Traditora: A Paradigmatic Figure of Chicana Feminism," *Cultural Critique: The Construction of Gender and Modes of Social Division* 13 (1989): 66.

31. Jorge Huerta, Introduction to *Necessary Theater: Six Plays about the Chicano Experience* (Houston: Arte Público Press, 1989), 13.

32. Sendejo, "Mother's Legacy," 175.

33. Fredric Jameson, *Postmodernism, or The Cultural Logic of Late Capitalism* (Durham, NC: Duke University Press, 1990), 53.

34. Gloria Anzaldúa, *Borderlands: La Frontera* (San Francisco: Aunt Lute Press, 2007), 226.

35. Victor Turner, quoted in Mauricio Mazon, *Zoot Suit Riots: The Psychology of Symbolic Annihilation* (Austin: University of Texas Press, 1988), 91.

36. Pérez and Pérez, *Soldierboy*, 41.

37. Ibid., 61.

38. James C. Scott, *Domination and the Arts of Resistance: Hidden Transcripts* (New Haven, CT: Yale University Press, 1992), xii.

39. Pérez and Pérez, *Soldierboy*, 61.

40. Esquivel, interview.

41. Anzaldúa, *Borderlands*, 102.

42. Pérez and Pérez, *Soldierboy*, 43.

43. Ibid., 43–44.

44. Vicki L. Ruiz, *From Out of the Shadows: Mexican Women in Twentieth-Century America* (New York: Oxford University Press, 1998), 82.

45. Pérez and Pérez, *Soldierboy*, 21.

46. Ibid., 48–49.

47. Latina Feminist Group, *Telling to Live: Latina Feminist Testimonios* (Durham, NC: Duke University Press, 2001), 5.

48. Esquivel, interview.

49. Ramirez, *The Woman in the Zoot Suit*, xiv.

50. Valdez, *Zoot Suit and Other Plays*, 34.

51. Rosa-Linda Fregoso, quoted in Ramirez, *The Woman in the Zoot Suit*, 104.

52. Ibid., 106.

53. Jorge Huerta, Introduction to *Zoot Suit and Other Plays*, 15.

54. Valdez, *Zoot Suit and Other Plays*, 86.

55. Wendy S. Hesford, *Framing Identities: Autobiography and the Politics of Pedagogy* (Minneapolis: University of Minnesota Press, 1999), 129.

56. "Curran's Cordel Connection," Arizona State University, 8 December 2010, www.public.asu.edu/~atmjc/introduction.html.

57. Kennedy, *Freedom from Fear*, 768.

58. Valdez, *Zoot Suit and Other Plays*, 87.

59. Esquivel, interview.

60. Ibid.

61. Valdez, *Zoot Suit and Other Plays*, 91.

62. Ibid., 94.

63. George J. Sánchez, *Becoming Mexican American: Ethnicity, Culture, and Identity in Chicano Los Angeles* (New York: Oxford University Press, 1993), 132.

Chapter Ten

This chapter is written in honor of my cousin Victor Montez Ledesma, who died on June 14, 1944, from wounds received in the invasion of Normandy on the same date; my uncle Adán Valdez, who fought in the North Africa campaign; *y mi 'buelito* Silva, who served in the Philippines during World War II.

1. Tom Brokaw, *The Greatest Generation* (New York: Random House, 1998); Ken Burns and Lynn Novick (dir.), *The War* (Public Broadcasting Service, 2007).

2. For a discussion of the American GI Forum, see Henry Ramos, *The American GI Forum: In Pursuit of the Dream, 1948–1983* (Houston: Arte Público Press, 1998).

3. George Mariscal, *Aztlán and Vietnam: Chicano and Chicana Experiences of the War* (Berkeley: University of California Press, 1999); "Yo Soy El Army: US Military Targets Latinos with Extensive Recruitment Campaign," Roundtable Discussion hosted by Amy Goodman, *Democracy Now*, National Public Radio, 18 May 2010.

4. Américo Paredes, *A Texas-Mexican Cancionero: Folksongs of the Lower Border* (Austin: University of Texas Press, 1995); *With His Pistol in His Hand: A Border Ballad and Its Hero* (Austin: University of Texas Press, 1958).

5. Roy P. Benavides and John R. Craig, *Medal of Honor: One Man's Journey from Poverty and Prejudice* (Washington, DC: Brassey's, 1999), 9.

6. Alfredo Mirandé, *Hombres y Machos: Masculinity and Latino Culture* (Boulder, CO: Westview Press, 1997); Miguel R. López, *Chicano Timespace: The Poetry and Politics of Ricardo Sánchez* (College Station: Texas A&M Press, 2000); Mario T. García, *Memories of Chicano History: The Life and Narrative of Bert Corona* (Berkeley: University of California Press, 1995); Charley Trujillo, *Dogs from Illusion* (San Jose: Chusma House, 1994), 133.

7. For more complex historiographies of pachucos and zoot-suiters, see Luis Alvarez, *The Power of the Zoot: Youth Culture and Resistance in World War II* (Berkeley: University of California Press, 2008); and Catherine Sue Ramírez, *The Woman in the Zoot Suit: Gender, Nationalism, and the Cultural Politics of Memory* (Durham, NC: Duke University Press, 2008). For alternative materialist feminist explications of *Zoot Suit*, see Patricia Portales, "Women, Bombs, and War: (Re)Gendering the Liberatory Layering of Mexican American Women on Homefront in World War II Literature, Theater, and Film" (Ph.D diss., University of Texas at San Antonio, 2012).

8. George J. Sánchez, *Becoming Mexican American: Ethnicity, Culture and Identity in Chicano Los Angeles, 1900–1945* (Oxford: Oxford University Press, 1995), 8.

9. Norma Alarcón, "Conjugating Subjects: The Heteroglossia of Essence and Resistance," in *An Other Tongue: National and Ethnicity in the Linguistic Borderlands*, ed. Alfred Arteaga (Durham, NC: Duke University Press, 1994): 125–139; Chela Sandoval, *Methodology of the Oppressed* (Minneapolis: University of Minnesota Press, 2000).

10. Eve Kosofsky Sedgwick, *Between Men: English Literature and Male Homosocial Desire* (New York: Columbia University Press, 1985), 1.

11. Michael J. Shapiro, *Violent Cartographies: Mapping Cultures of War* (Minneapolis: University of Minnesota Press, 1997); Susan Faludi, "A Reporter at Large: The Naked Citadel," *New Yorker* (5 September 1994): 62–65.

12. George Mariscal, *Brown Eyed Children of the Sun: Lessons from the Chicano Movement, 1965–1975* (Albuquerque: University of New Mexico Press, 2005); Lorena Oropeza, *¡Raza Sí! ¡Guerra No! Chicano Protest and Patriotism during the Viet Nam War Era* (Berkeley: University of California Press, 2005); Stella Pope Duarte, *Let Their Spirits Dance* (New York: Harper Perennial, 2002).

13. Lisa Lowe, *Immigrant Acts: On Asian American Cultural Politics* (Durham, NC: Duke University Press, 1996), proposes the concept of "antithetical" citizenship in her discussion of the racist legislation directed at Asian immigrants and Asian Americans and thus offers an important touchstone for mapping the circumscribed nature of Mexican American citizenship during World War II, in which increased class mobility also coincided with formal segregation.

14. Guy Gabaldon, interview with Maggie Rivas-Rodriguez, videotape recording, Washington, DC, 7 June 2000, Voces Oral History Project, Nettie Lee Benson Latin American Collection, University of Texas at Austin. Guy Gabaldon, *Saipan: Suicide Island* (Saipan: Privately printed, 1990); Judith Pérez and Severo Pérez, *Soldierboy, Necessary Theater: Six Plays about the Chicano Experience*, ed. Jorge Huerta (Houston, TX: Arte Público Press, 1989), 20–75.

15. See Gloria Anzaldúa, *Borderlands/La Frontera: The New Mestiza* (San Francisco: Aunt Lute Press, 1999); and Raúl Homero Villa, *Barrio-Logos: Space and Place in Urban Chicano Literature and Culture* (Austin: University of Texas Press, 2000).

16. William Flores and Rina Benmayor, eds., "Introduction: Constructing Cultural Citizenship," in *Latino Cultural Citizenship: Claiming Identity, Space, and Rights* (Boston: Beacon, 1998), 1.

17. See Phil Karlson, *Hell to Eternity* (Warner Brothers, 1960); and Steven Jay Rubin, dir., *East L.A. Marine: The Untold True Story of Guy Gabaldon* (Fast Carrier Productions, 2006).

18. Gabaldon, *Suicide Island*, 16.

19. Ibid., 18.

20. Ibid., 19.

21. It must duly be noted that Chela Sandoval distinguishes between the use of various subaltern tactics—in which various subject positions are deployed, as hegemonic circumstances warrant, toward an egalitarian emancipatory end—and strategy. Hegemonic agents and mystified subaltern subjects can involve hybrid performances as tautological that do not involve any substantive challenges to power. See Sandoval, *Methodology of the Oppressed* (Minneapolis: University of Minnesota Press, 2000), 59. Sandra Soto's concerns about the potential limits of intersectionality models are apt in gauging Gabaldon's slippery agency. She notes that the intersections of various subjects alone do not necessarily constitute solidarity or counter power. See Sandra Soto, *Reading Chican@ Like a Queer: The De-Mastery of Desire* (Austin: University of Texas Press, 2010), 3–5.

22. Gabaldon, *Suicide Island*, 25.

23. Ibid., 19.

24. Ibid., 228.

25. Ibid., 10. Gabaldon's second wife was of Japanese and Mexican heritage and born and raised in Mexico.

26. For a discussion of the transnational fetish that accompanies Mexican American encounters with Japanese during World War II, see discussion of Américo Paredes's poetics by B. V. Olguín, "Reassessing Pocho Poetics: Américo Paredes and the (Trans)National Question," *Aztlán: A Journal of Chicano Studies* 30, no. 1 (Spring 2005): 87–121; Ramón Saldívar, *The Borderlands of Culture: Américo Paredes and the Transnational Imaginary* (Durham, NC: Duke University Press, 2006); and Américo Paredes, B. V. Olguín and Omar Vasquez Barbosa, translators, *Cantos de Adolescencia/Songs of Youth (1932–1937)* (Houston: Arte Público Press, 2007).

27. Gabaldon, *Suicide Island*, 205.

28. Ibid., 206.

29. Guy Gabaldon, interview; Gabaldon, *Suicide Island*, 206–207.

30. José Esteban Muñoz, *Disidentifications: Queers of Color and the Performance of Politics* (Minneapolis: University of Minnesota Press, 1999).

31. Patricia Portales, "Women, Bombs, and War" (Ph.D. diss., University of Texas at San Antonio, 2012).

32. Pérez and Pérez, *Soldierboy*, 58.

33. Ibid., 74.

34. Carlos Cortez, *De Kansas a Califas and Back to Chicago* (Chicago: March/Abrazo Press, 1992); Carlos Cortez, *Crystal-Gazing the Amber Fluid and Other Wobbly Poems* (Chicago: Charles H. Kerr, 1990); Carlos Cortez, *Where Are the Voices? and Other Wobbly Poems* (Chicago: Charles H. Kerr, 1997). For discussions of Cortez's poetry, art, and activism, see Scott H. Bennet, "Workers/Draftees Of the World Unite! Carlos A. Cortez Redcloud Koyokuikatl: Soapbox Rebel, WWII CO, & WWI Artist/Bard," in *Carlos Cortez Koyokuikatl: Soapbox Artist and Poet* (exh. cat.), ed. Víctor Alejandro Sorell (Chicago: Mexican Fine Arts Center Museum, 2001), 12–56.

35. Henry Cervantes, *Piloto: Migrant Worker to Jet Pilot* (Central Point, OR: Hellgate Press, 2002); Frank X. Medina and Dorothy B. Marra, *Ciao, Francesco* (Kansas City: Medina Marra Publications, 1995); Américo Paredes, *Between Two Worlds* (Houston, TX: Arte Público Press, 1990).

36. Raul Morin, *Among the Valiant: Mexican Americans in WWII and Korea* (Vista, CA: Borden Publishing, 1963). For discussions of casualty rates by Mexican American soldiers in Vietnam, see Carlos Vélez-Ibañez, *Border Visions: Mexican Cultures of the Southwest* (Tucson: University of Arizona Press, 1996).

37. Soto, *Reading Chican@ Like a Queer*, 2010.

38. Ricardo Sánchez and Donald T. Phillips, *Wiser in Battle: A Soldier's Story* (New York: Harper, 2008).

39. José A. Rodriguez, *Hard Measures: How Aggressive CIA Actions after 9/11 Saved American Lives* (New York: Threshold Editions, 2012).

40. Robert Huddleston, *Edmundo: From Chiapas, Mexico, to Park Avenue* (College Station, TX: VirtualBookWork, 2007).

Chapter Eleven

1. República de Cuba, Pasaporte #1885, expedido junio 28, 1941, Sergio Poyo Alvarez, Poyo Family Archives.

2. The essential narrative of this story is derived from conversations and interviews with Sergio and Geraldine Poyo (some formal, others less so) from the mid-1980s until their deaths in 2005 and 1997, respectively. Unless otherwise noted, they are the sources for the stories and events in this chapter.

3. Gerald E. Poyo, *"With All, and for the Good of All": The Emergence of Popular Nationalism in the Cuban Communities of the United States, 1848–1898* (Durham, NC: Duke University Press, 1989).

4. Gerald E. Poyo, "Baseball in Key West and Havana, 1885–1910: The Career of Francisco A. Poyo," *Florida Historical Quarterly* 87, no. 4 (Spring 2009): 540–564.

5. Family story related to the author by his father, Sergio Poyo, and uncles, José and Jorge.

6. Louis A. Pérez Jr., *On Becoming Cuban: Identity, Nationality, and Culture* (Chapel Hill: University of North Carolina Press, 1999).

7. Pérez, *On Becoming Cuban*, 394.

8. *The Reflector, 1942* (GMI Yearbook), 50–51.

9. Pérez, *On Becoming Cuban*, 402.

10. "English Teaching in Cuban Schools," *Cuba Review* 7, no. 2 (January 1909): 17.

11. *Anglo American Directory of Cuba, 1951* (Marianao, Cuba: Almendares), 213.

12. See Pérez, *On Becoming Cuban*, 402, for an interesting discussion of how these schools operated and tried to form Cuban youth in the image of the United States.

13. "The American Poyo Family," 9–10, brief family history by José Francisco Poyo (1997).

14. República de Cuba, Pasaporte #1885, expedido junio 28, 1941, Sergio Poyo Alvarez, Poyo Family Archives.

15. See Letter, Harold S. Tewell to Mr. Sergio Poyo, Havana, Cuba, 24 March 1942, American Consulate General, Department of State and Speedletter, Department of State to Mr. Sergio Poyo, 24 April 1963, Washington, DC, Poyo Family Archives.

16. On "Americanization" programs directed at Mexican immigrants, see George J. Sánchez, *Becoming Mexican American: Ethnicity, Culture and Identity in Chicano Los Angeles, 1900–1945* (New York: Oxford University Press, 1993), 87–107.

17. Suzanne Oboler, *Ethic Labels, Latino Lives: Identity and the Politics of (Re) Presentation in the United States* (Minneapolis: University of Minnesota Press, 1995), 27–31.

18. On attitudes about non-European immigrants during World War II and before, see David M. Reimers, *Still the Golden Door: The Third World Comes to America* (New York: Columbia University Press, 1992), 11–38.

19. On the Immigration Act of 1965, see Reimers, *Still the Golden Door*, 63–90. For a good overview of identity debates in the United States, see Ronald Takaki, ed., *Debating Diversity: Clashing Perspectives on Race and Ethnicity in America*, 3rd ed. (New York: Oxford University Press, 2002).

20. Marisa Alicea, "The Latino Immigration Experience: The Case of Mexicanos, Puertorriqueños, and Cubanos," in *Handbook of Hispanic Cultures in the United States: Sociology*, ed. Félix Padilla (Houston: Arte Público Press, 1994), 35–56. On repatriation of Mexican workers in the 1930s, see Sánchez, *Becoming Mexican American*, 209–226.

21. On the Bracero Program, see Reimers, *Still the Golden Door*, 39–62.

22. Virginia E. Sánchez-Korrol, *From Colonia to Community: The History of Puerto Ricans in New York City, 1917–1948* (Westport, CT: Greenwood Press, 1983), 11–50.

23. Gary Mormino and George Pozzetta, *The Immigrant World of Ybor City: Italians and Their Latin Neighbors in Tampa, 1888–1985* (Urbana: University of Illinois Press, 1990).

24. Pérez, *On Becoming Cuban*, 412.

25. Ibid., 408.

26. *The Reflector, 1942* (GMI Yearbook), 54–55, 75, 100–101; and family photographs, Poyo Family Archive.

27. The earliest photo of Sergio in Gerry Darnell's photograph album is March 1943, Poyo Family Archive. Sergio told his eldest son, Sergio Jr., about meeting Gerry at a fraternity party.

28. Certainly, other difficulties plagued Edna and Earl's relationship, but this is a subject about which Gerry refused to speak. She must have had affection for her father, however, because she attended his funeral in St. Louis in 1947.

29. Geraldine Darnell's report cards reveal a change in school in 1933. Morehouse Public Schools, Six Week and Annual Report, 1932–1933, and Public Schools–Flint, Michigan, Report of Pupil's Grade, 1933–1934, Poyo Family Archive.

30. Geraldine S. Darnell's Flint Central High School diploma, Poyo Family Archive.

31. *The Reflector, 1942* (GMI Yearbook), 54–55.

32. "Army of the United States, Certificate of Service, Sergio Poyo, November 9, 1945." See also "Identification Card—Enlisted Reserve Corps, Sergio Poyo, September 11, 1943," which identifies his occupation as "Air Mechanic Instructor."

33. Marion County Court House, Indiana, Marriage License of Sergio Poyo and S. Geraldine Darnell, 7 August 1943, Poyo Family Archive.

34. Geraldine Poyo to Edna Darnell (Mom), 10 August 1943, Poyo Family Archive.

35. Ibid.

36. See "Headquarters, 153rd Service Unit, Armed Forces Induction Station, Indianapolis, Indiana, Special Orders, 11 September 1943"; and "Identification Card—Enlisted Reserve Corps, Sergio Poyo, Aviation Cadet, Indianapolis, Indiana," Poyo Family Archives.

37. Dated envelope, Mrs. Sergio Poyo to Sergio Poyo, 2 December 1943, and photographs of Sergio Poyo at Jefferson Barracks, Poyo Family Archive.

38. See Letters, Gerry Poyo to Edna Darnell, 1943–1945, Poyo Family Archive.

39. Gerry Poyo to Edna Root, Robert Darnell, and Russell Root, 14 March 1944, Poyo Family Archive.

40. Mrs. Sergio S. Poyo to A/C S. Poyo, 6 September 1944, Maxwell Field, Al-

abama, Army Air Forces Training Command, Aircraft Observer (Aerial Navigator) Diploma, Presented at Army Air Forces Navigation School, San Marcos, Texas, to 2nd Lt. Sergio Poyo, 7 April 1945; Gerry Poyo to Edna Root and Russell Root, 27 February 1945, postmarked in San Marcos, Texas, 28 February 1945, Poyo Family Archive.

41. See "Army of the United States, Certificate of Service, Sergio Poyo, November 9, 1945," and photographs of Sergio at Shaw Field, Sumter, SC, Poyo Family Archive.

42. Gerry Poyo to Edna Root and Russell Root, 20 September 1945, Poyo Family Archive.

43. See "Army of the United States, Certificate of Service, Sergio Poyo, November 9, 1945"; and "Headquarters, Army Air Forces Central Flying Training Command, Office of the Commanding General, Randolph Field, Texas, From D. F. Herbst, Lt. Col., AGD, to Aviation Cadet Sergio Poyo, Subject: Temporary Appointment, April 7, 1945."

44. Sergio Poyo, personal communication, 1994.

45. *The Reflector, 1946* (GMI Yearbook), 52.

46. Telephone conversation with José Poyo, 30 December 2006.

47. For a discussion of the process of Latino exclusion from full citizenship in the United States, see Oboler, *Ethnic Labels, Latino Lives*, 32–40. On Puerto Ricans in New York, see Jesús Colón, Edna Acosta-Belén, and Virginia Sánchez Korrol, eds., *The Way It Was and Other Writings* (Houston, TX: Arte Público Press, 1993).

48. For a contrasting Cuban experience in the United States, see Evelio Grillo, *Black Cuban, Black American: A Memoir* (Houston, TX: Arte Público Press, 2000).

49. In photos of Sergio Poyo from Gerry Poyo's photograph album from the early 1940s, he is identified as "Sergio." Poyo Family Archive.

50. For a discussion of how class and race historically influenced Latino integration into United States society, see Oboler, *Ethnic Labels, Latino Lives*, 23–26. See also Oscar Hijuelos, *Our House in the Last World* (New York: Persea Books, 1983), for an account of a Cuban family's immigration and adjustment in New York during this same period.

51. "Ambar Motors Corporation Inaugurates Building," *Havana Post*, 20 January 1949.

52. "W. A. McCarthy," *General Motors World* 7, no. 3 (March 1928): 10.

53. See envelopes, Mrs. Sergio Poyo to Sergio Poyo, 2 December 1943; and Mrs. Sergio Poyo to Sergio Poyo, 26 December 1943, Poyo Family Archive.

54. Gerry Poyo to Edna Root, Robert Darnell, and Russell Root, 14 March 1944, Poyo Family Archive.

55. Gerry Poyo to Edna Root, Robert Darnell, and Russell Root, 26 March 1944, Poyo Family Archive.

56. Gerry Poyo to Edna Root and Russell Root, 27 February 1945, Poyo Family Archive.

Selected Bibliography

Books and Journal Articles

Acuña, Rodolfo. *Occupied America: A History of Chicanos*. 7th ed. Boston: Pearson Higher Ed., 2011.

Agoncillo, Teodoro. *The Fateful Years*. Quezon City, Philippines: Garcia, 1965.

Alarcón, Norma. "Conjugating Subjects: The Heteroglossia of Essence and Resistance." In *An Other Tongue: Nation and Ethnicity in the Linguistic Borderlands*, edited by Alfred Arteaga. Durham, NC: Duke University Press, 1994.

Alba, Richard, and Tariqul Islam. "The Case of the Disappearing Mexican Americans: An Ethnic Identity Mystery." *Population Research and Policy Review* 28 (2009): 109–121.

Aldrich, Mark. "The Gender Gap in Earnings during World War II: New Evidence." *Industrial and Labor Relations Review* 42, no. 3 (1989): 415–429.

Alicea, Marisa. "The Latino Immigration Experience: The Case of Mexicanos, Puertorriqueños, and Cubanos." In *Handbook of Hispanic Cultures in the United States: Sociology*, edited by Felix Padilla. Houston, TX: Arte Público Press, 1994.

Almaráz, Félix D., Jr. *Knight without Armor: Carlos Eduardo Castañeda, 1896–1958*. College Station: Texas A&M Press, 1999.

Althusser, Louis. *Lenin and Philosophy and Other Essays*. New York: Monthly Review Press, 1972.

Alvarez, Luis. *The Power of the Zoot: Youth Culture and Resistance during World War II*. Berkeley: University of California Press, 2008.

Anderson, Karen Tucker. "Last Hired, First Fired: Black Women Workers during World War II." *Journal of American History* 69, no. 1 (1982): 82–97.

Anzaldúa, Gloria. *Borderlands/La Frontera*. San Francisco: Aunt Lute Press, 1977.

Balderrama, Francisco E., and Raymond Rodríguez. *Decade of Betrayal: Mexican Repatriation in the 1930s*. Albuquerque: University of New Mexico Press, 2006.

Barrera, Mario. *Race and Class in the Southwest: A Theory of Racial Inequality*. Notre Dame, IN: University of Notre Dame Press, 1989.

Bean, Frank D., and Marta Tienda. *The Hispanic Population of the United States*. New York: Russell Sage Foundation, 1987.

Bedard, Kelly, and Olivier Deschênes. "The Long-Term Impact of Military Service on Health: Evidence from World War II and Korean War Veterans." *American Economic Review* 96, no. 1 (2006): 176–194.

Benavides, Roy P., and John R. Craig. *Medal of Honor: One Man's Journey from Poverty and Prejudice.* Washington, DC: Brassey's, 1999.

Benjamin, Jules. "The Machadato and Cuban Nationalism, 1928–1932." *Hispanic American Historical Review* 55 (1975): 66–91.

Bennet, Scott H. "Workers/Draftees Of the World Unite! Carlos A. Cortez Redcloud Koyokuikatl: Soapbox Rebel, WWII CO, & WW I Artist/Bard." In *Carlos Cortez Koyokuikatl: Soapbox Artist and Poet,* exh. cat., ed. Víctor Alejandro Sorell. Chicago: Mexican Fine Arts Center Museum, 2001.

Bernstein, Alison R. *American Indians and World War II: Toward a New Era in Indian Affairs.* Norman: University of Oklahoma Press, 1991.

Blanton, Carlos. *The Strange Career of Bilingual Education in Texas, 1836–1981.* College Station: Texas A&M University Press, 2004.

Blum, Albert A. "Work or Fight: The Use of the Draft as a Manpower Sanction during the Second World War." *Industrial and Labor Relations Review* 16, no. 3 (1963): 366–380.

Boris, Eileen. "'You Wouldn't Want One of 'Em Dancing with Your Wife': Racialized Bodies on the Job in World War II." *American Quarterly* 50, no. 1 (1998): 77–108.

Bound, John, and Sarah Turner. "Going to War and Going to College: Did World War II and the G.I. Bill Increase Educational Attainment for Returning Veterans?" *Journal of Labor Economics* 20 (2002): 784–815.

Brokaw, Tom. *The Greatest Generation.* New York: Random House, 1998.

Buenavista, Tracy Lachica, and Jordan Beltrán Gonzales. "DREAMs Deterred: Filipino Experiences and an Anti-Militarization Critique of the Development, Relief, and Education for Alien Minors Act." *Harvard Journal of Asian American Policy Review* 20 (2011): 29–39.

Burgos, Adrián, Jr. *Playing America's Game: Baseball, Latinos, and the Color Line.* Berkeley: University of California Press, 2007.

Campomanes, Oscar V. "Casualty Figures of the American Soldier and the Other: Post-1898 Allegories of Imperial Nation-Building as 'Love and War.'" In *Vestiges of War: The Philippine-American War and the Aftermath of an Imperial Dream, 1899–1999,* edited by Angel Velasco Shaw and Luis H. Francia, 134–162. New York: New York University Press, 2002.

Carroll, Patrick J. *Felix Longoria's Wake: Bereavement, Racism, and the Rise of Mexican American Activism.* Austin: University of Texas Press, 2003.

Castañeda, Carlos E. "Statement of Dr. Carlos E. Castañeda, Regional Director, Fair Employment Practice Committee, Region 10, San Antonio, Texas." In *Are We Good Neighbors?* compiled by Alonso S. Perales, 59–63. New York: Arno Press, 1974.

Cervantes, Henry. *Piloto: Migrant Worker to Jet Pilot.* Central Point, OR: Hellgate Press, 2002.

Childs, Matt. *The Aponte Rebellion in Cuba and the Struggle against Atlantic Slavery.* Chapel Hill: University of North Carolina Press.

Colón Jesús, Edna Acosta-Belen, and Virginia Sanchez Korrol. *The Way It Was and Other Writings.* Houston, TX: Arte Público Press, 1993.

Cortez, Carlos. *De Kansas a Califas and Back to Chicago*. Chicago: March/Abrazo Press, 1992.

———. *Crystal-Gazing the Amber Fluid and Other Wobbly Poems*. Chicago: Charles H. Kerr, 1990.

———. *Where Are the Voices? and Other Wobbly Poems*. Chicago: Charles H. Kerr, 1997.

Covington, James W. *Under the Minarets: The University of Tampa, 1931–1981*. Tampa: University of Tampa Press, 1981.

Craig, Austin, and Conrado Benitez. *Philippine Progress Prior to 1898*. Metro Manila: Cacho Hermanos, 1985.

Curbelo, Silvia Álvarez. "The Color of War: Puerto Rican Soldiers and Discrimination during World War II." In *Beyond the Latino World War II Hero: The Social and Political Legacy of a Generation*, edited by Maggie Rivas-Rodriguez and Emilio Zamora, 110–124. Austin: University of Texas Press, 2009.

Daniel, Clete. *Chicano Workers and the Politics of Fairness: The FEPC in the Southwest, 1941–1945*. Austin: University of Texas Press, 1991.

De Leon, Arnoldo. *They Called Them Greasers: Anglo Attitudes toward Mexicans in Texas, 1821–1900*. Austin: University of Texas Press, 1983.

De Veyra, Manuel. *Doctor in Bataan, 1941–1942*. Quezon City: New Day, 1991.

Delgado, Jane I., and Leo Estrada. "Improving Data Collection Strategies." *Public Health Reports* 18, no. 5 (September–October 1993): 540–545.

Dower, John W. *War without Mercy: Race and Power in the Pacific War*. 7th ed. New York: Pantheon Books, 1993.

Duarte, Estela Pope. *Let Their Spirits Dance*. New York: Harper Perennial, 2002.

Elder, Glen, Jr., Elizabeth C. Clipp, James Scott Brown, Leslie R. Martin, and Howard W. Friedman. "The Life Long Mortality Risks of World War II Experiences." *Research on Aging* 31, no. 4 (2009): 391–412.

Escobedo, Elizabeth. "The *Pachuca* Panic: Sexual and Cultural Battlegrounds in WWII Los Angeles." *Western Historical Quarterly* 38 (2007): 133–156.

Fernandez, Felipe. *Memoirs of a Philippine Scout Cavalryman*. Self-published, 2007.

Flores, Juan. "Reclaiming Left Baggage: Some Early Sources for Minority Studies." *Cultural Critique* 59 (Winter 2005): 187–206.

Flores, Maria Eva. "What a Difference a War Makes!" In *Mexican Americans and World War II*, edited by Maggie Rivas-Rodriguez, 177–200. Austin: University of Texas Press.

Flores, Richard R. *Remembering the Alamo: Memory, Modernity, and the Master Symbol*. Austin: University of Texas Press, 2002.

Flores, William, and Rina Benmayor, eds. *Latino Cultural Citizenship: Claiming Identity, Space, and Rights*. Boston: Beacon, 1998.

Foley, Neil. "Becoming Hispanic: Mexican Americans and the Faustian Pact with Whiteness." In *Reflexiones 1997: New Directions in Mexican American Studies*, 53–70. Austin: Center for Mexican American Studies, 1997.

Forgacs, David, ed. *The Antonio Gramsci Reader: Selected Writings, 1916–1935*. New York: New York University Press, 2000.

Gabaldon, Guy. *Saipan: Suicide Island*. Saipan Island: Privately published, 1990.

Gamboa, Erasmo. *Mexican Labor and World War II: Braceros in the Pacific Northwest, 1942–1947*. Seattle: University of Washington Press, 2000.

Gándara, Patricia, and Gary Orfield. "Introduction: Creating a 21st-Century Vision of Access and Equity in Higher Education." In *Expanding Opportunity in Higher Education: Leveraging Promise*, edited by Patricia Gándara, Gary Orfield, and Catherine L. Horn, 1–16. Albany: State University of New York Press, 2006.

García, Maria. "Agents of Americanization: Rusk Settlement and the Houston Mexicano Community, 1907–1950." In *Mexican Americans in Texas History: Selected Essays*, edited by Emilio Zamora, Cynthia Orozco, and Rodolfo Rocha, 121–137. Austin: Texas State Historical Association, 2000.

García, Mario T. *Memories of Chicano History: The Life and Narrative of Bert Corona*. Berkeley: University of California Press, 1995.

———. *Mexican Americans: Leadership, Ideology, and Identity, 1930–1960*. New Haven: Yale University Press, 1989.

Garfinkel, Herbert. *When Negroes March: The March on Washington Movement in the Organizational Politics for FEPC*. Glencoe, IL: Free Press, 1959.

Glasser, Ruth. *My Music Is My Flag: Puerto Rican Musicians and Their New York Communities, 1917–1940*. Berkeley: University of California Press, 1995.

Gluck, Sherna Berger. *Rosie the Riveter Revisited: Women, the War, and Social Change*. New York: New American Library, 1987.

Gonzalez, Gilbert G. *Chicano Education in the Era of Segregation*. Philadelphia: Balch Institute Press, 1990.

Gray, J. Glenn. *The Warriors: Reflections on Men in Battle*. New York: Harper & Row, 1970.

Greenbaum, Susan. *More than Black: Afro-Cubans in Tampa*. Gainesville: University Press of Florida, 2002.

Grewal, Inderpal. *Transnational America: Feminisms, Diasporas, Neoliberalisms*. Durham, NC: Duke University Press, 2005.

Griffin, Marcus. *Heroes of Bataan, Corregidor, and Northern Luzon*. 2nd ed. Carlsbad, NM: M. Griffin, 1989.

Grillo, Evelio. *Black Cuban, Black American: A Memoir*. Houston, TX: Arte Público, 2000.

Griswold del Castillo, Richard, ed. *World War II and Mexican American Civil Rights*. Austin: University of Texas Press, 2008.

Guevarra, Rudy P., Jr. *Becoming Mexipino: Multiethnic Identities and Communities in San Diego*. New Brunswick, NJ: Rutgers University Press, 2012.

———. "Filipinos in Nueva España: Filipino-Mexican Relations, Mestizaje, and Identity in Colonial and Contemporary Mexico." *Journal of Asian American Studies* 14, no. 3 (2011): 389–416.

Guridy, Frank André. *Forging Diaspora: Afro-Cubans and African-Americans in a World of Empire and Jim Crow*. Chapel Hill: University of North Carolina Press, 2010.

Gutiérrez, David. *Walls and Mirrors: Mexican Americans, Mexican Immigrants, and the Politics of Ethnicity*. Berkeley: University of California Press, 1995.

Gutiérrez, Félix, and Jorge Reina Schement. *Spanish-Language Radio in the Southwestern United States*. Austin: Center for Mexican American Studies, 1979.

Haney, Peter. "Bilingual Humor, Verbal Hygiene, and the Gendered Contradictions of Cultural Citizenship in Early Mexican American Comedy." *Journal of Linguistic Anthropology* 13, no. 2 (2003): 163–188.

Harris, Susan K. *God's Arbiters: Americans and the Philippines, 1898–1902*. New York: Oxford University Press, 2011.

Henderson, Alexa B. "FEPC and the Southern Railway Case: An Investigation into Discriminatory Practices during WW II." *Journal of Negro History* 61, no. 2 (1976): 173–187.

Henry, David D. *Challenges Past, Challenges Present: An Analysis of American Higher Education since 1930*. San Francisco: Jossey-Bass, 1975.

Hesford, Wendy S. *Framing Identities: Autobiography and the Politics of Pedagogy*. Minneapolis: University of Minnesota Press, 1999.

Hijuelos, Oscar. *Our House in the Last World*. New York: Persea Books, 1983.

Honey, Maureen. *Bitter Fruit: African American Women in World War II*. Columbia: University of Missouri Press, 1999.

———. *Creating Rosie the Riveter: Class, Gender, and Propaganda during World War II*. Amherst: University of Massachusetts Press, 1984.

———. "Maternal Welders: Women's Sexuality and Propaganda on the Home Front during World War II." *Prospects* 22 (1997): 479–519.

Huddleston, Robert. *Edmundo: From Chiapas, Mexico, to Park Avenue*. College Station, TX: VirtualBookWork, 2007.

Huerta, Jorge, ed. *Necessary Theater: Six Plays about the Chicano Experience*. Houston, TX: Arte Público Press, 1989.

Huse, Andy. *The Columbia Restaurant: Celebrating a Century of History, Culture, and Cuisine*. Gainesville: University Press of Florida, 2009.

Ignacio, Abe, Enrique de la Cruz, Jorge Emmanuel, and Helen Toribio. *The Forbidden Book: The Philippine-American War in Political Cartoons*. San Francisco: T'Boli, 2004.

Instituto de Historia de Cuba. *Historia de Cuba: Organización y crisis desde 1899 hasta 1940*. Havana: Editora Política, 1998.

Jameson, Fredric. *Postmodernism, or The Cultural Logic of Late Capitalism*. Durham, NC: Duke University Press, 1990.

Johnson, Benjamin. *Revolution in Texas: How a Forgotten Rebellion and Its Bloody Suppression Turned Mexicans into Americans*. New Haven, CT: Yale University Press, 2005.

Jose, Ricardo Trota. *The Philippine Army, 1935–1942*. Manila: Ateneo de Manila University Press, 1992.

Kanellos, Nicolás. *A History of Hispanic Theatre in the United States: Origins to 1940*. Austin: University of Texas Press, 1990.

Kanellos, Nicolás, and Helvetia Martell. *Hispanic Periodicals in the United States, Origins to 1960: A Brief History and Comprehensive Bibliography*. Houston, TX: Arte Público Press, 2000.

Kennedy, David M. *Freedom from Fear: The American People in Depression and War, 1929–1945*. Oxford University Press, 2001.

Kesselman, Louis C. *The Social Politics of FEPC: A Study in Reform Pressure Movements*. Chapel Hill: University of North Carolina Press, 1948.

Kessler-Harris, Alice. "'Rosie the Riveter': Who Was She?" *Labor History* 24, no. 2 (1983): 249–253.

Kersten, Andrew E. *Race, Jobs, and the War: The FEPC in the Midwest, 1941–1946*. Chicago: University of Illinois Press, 2000.

Kim, Claire Jean. *Bitter Fruit: The Politics of Black-Korean Conflict in New York City.* New Haven, CT: Yale University Press, 2000.

Knight, Franklin W. *Slave Society in Cuba during the Nineteenth Century.* Madison: University of Wisconsin Press, 1970.

Kossoudji, Sherrie A., and Laura J. Dressler. "Working-Class Rosies: Women Industrial Workers during WW 2." *Journal of Economic History* 52, no. 2 (1992): 431–446.

Lamphere, Louise, Patricia Zavella, and Felipe Gonzales. *Sunbelt Working Mothers: Reconciling Family and Factory.* New York: Cornell University Press, 1993.

Laó-Montes, Agustín, and Arlene Dávila, eds. *Mambo Montage: The Latinization of New York.* New York: Columbia University Press, 2001.

Lastra, Frank Trebín. *Ybor City: The Making of a Landmark Town.* Tampa: University of Tampa Press, 2006.

Latina Feminist Group. *Telling to Live: Latina Feminist Testimonios.* Durham, NC: Duke University Press, 2001.

Limón, José Eduardo. *Dancing with the Devil: Society and Cultural Poetics in Mexican-American South Texas.* Madison: University of Wisconsin Press, 1994.

Liu, Xian, Charles Engel, Han Kang, and David Cowan. "The Effect of Veteran Status on Mortality among Older Americans and Its Pathways." *Population Research and Policy Review* 24, no. 6 (2005): 573–592.

López, Ian F. Haney. "White Latinos." *Harvard Law Review* 6 (2003): 1–7.

López, Miguel R. *Chicano Timespace: The Poetry and Politics of Ricardo Sánchez.* College Station: Texas A&M Press, 2000.

Lowe, Lisa. "The International within the National: American Studies and Asian American Critique." *Cultural Critique*, no. 40 (Autumn 1998): 29–47.

Lucchese, Sam, with Tad Mizwa. *A Lifetime with Boots.* Houston, TX: Cordovan Corp., 1980.

Macias, Anthony. *Mexican American Mojo: Popular Music, Dance, and Urban Culture in Los Angeles, 1935–1968.* Durham, NC: Duke University Press, 2008.

Marín, Christine. "Mexican Americans on the Home Front: Community Organizations in Arizona during World War II." *Perspectives in Mexican American Studies* 4 (1993): 75–92.

Mariscal, George. *Aztlán and Vietnam: Chicano and Chicana Experiences of the War.* Berkeley: University of California Press, 1999.

———. *Brown-Eyed Children of the Sun: Lessons from the Chicano Movement, 1965–1975.* Albuquerque: University of New Mexico Press, 2005.

Markides, Kyriakos S., and Jeannine Coreil. "The Health of Hispanics in the Southwestern United States: An Epidemiological Paradox." *Public Health Reports* 101 (1986): 253–265.

Matson, Eva. *It Tolled for New Mexico: New Mexicans Captured by the Japanese, 1941–1945.* Las Cruces, NM: Yucca Tree Press, 1994.

Mazon, Mauricio. *The Zoot Suit Riots: The Psychology of Symbolic Annihilation.* Austin: University of Texas Press, 1984.

McGillivray, Gillian. *Blazing Cane: Sugar Communities, Class, and State Formation in Cuba, 1868–1959.* Durham, NC: Duke University Press, 2009.

McMullin, Dan Taulapapa. "The Passive Resistance of Samoans to U.S. and other

Colonialism." In *Sovereignty Matters: Locations of Contestation and Possibility in Indigenous Struggles for Self-Determination*, edited by Joanne Barker, 109–121. Lincoln: University of Nebraska Press, 2005.

Medina, Frank X., and Dorothy B. Marra. *Ciao, Francesco*. Kansas City: Medina Marra Publications, 1995.

Méndez, Armando. *Ciudad de Cigars: West Tampa*. Cocoa Beach: Florida Historical Society Press, 1994.

Mendoza, Louis Gerard. *Historia: The Literary Making of Chicana and Chicano History*. College Station: Texas A&M University Press, 2001.

Merico-Stephens, Ana Maria. "Latinos in Law Professions." In *Encyclopedia Latina: History, Culture, and Society in the United States*, vol. 4, edited by Ilan Stavans, 425–427. Danbury, CT: Grolier, 2005.

Mettler, Suzanne. "'The Only Good Thing Was the G.I. Bill': Effects of the Education and Training Provisions on African-American Veterans' Political Participation." *Studies in American Political Development* 19 (2005): 31–52.

Meyer, Leisa D. *Creating GI Jane: Sexuality and Power in the Women's Army Corps during World War II*. New York: Columbia University Press, 1996.

Milkman, Ruth. *Gender at Work: The Dynamics of Job Segregation by Sex during World War II*. Urbana: University of Illinois Press, 1987.

———. "Redefining 'Women's Work': The Sexual Division of Labor in the Auto Industry during World War II." *Feminist Studies* 8, no. 2 (1982): 337–372.

Mirandé, Alfredo. *Hombres y Machos: Masculinity and Latino Culture*. Boulder, CO: Westview Press, 1997.

Montejano, David. *Anglos and Mexicans in the Making of Texas, 1836–1986*. Austin: University of Texas Press, 1987.

Moore, Janet. "Causes, Consequences, and Cures of Racial and Ethnic Disproportionality in Conviction and Incarceration Rates: An Introduction." *Freedom Center Journal* 3, no. 1 (2011): 35–38.

Moreno Fraginals, Manuel. *El Ingenio: Complejo economico-social cubano del azúcar*. Havana: Editorial Ciencias Sociales, 1978.

Morin, Raul. *Among the Valiant: Mexican-Americans in WWII and Korea*. Alhambra, CA: Borden Publishing Company, 1966.

Mormino, Gary R. *Hillsborough County Goes to War: The Home Front, 1940–1950*. Tampa, FL: Tampa Bay History Center, 2001.

Mormino, Gary R., and George E. Pozzetta. *The Immigrant World of Ybor City: Italians and Their Latin Neighbors in Tampa, Florida, 1885–1985*. Urbana: University of Illinois Press, 1987.

———. "'The Reader Lights the Candle': Cuban and Florida Cigar Workers' Oral Tradition." *Labor's Heritage* 5 (Spring 1993): 4–27.

———. "Spanish Anarchism in Tampa, Florida, 1886–1931." In *Struggle a Hard Battle: Essays on Working-Class Immigrants*, edited by Dirk Hoerder, 170–198. DeKalb: Northern Illinois University Press, 1986.

Muñoz, Carlos. *Youth, Identity, Power: The Chicano Movement*. New York: Verso Books, 2007.

Muñoz, José Esteban. *Disidentifications: Queers of Color and the Performance of Politics*. Minneapolis: University of Minnesota Press, 1999.

Murch, Donna. *Living for the City: Migration, Education, and the Rise of the Black Panther Party in Oakland, California.* Chapel Hill: University of North Carolina Press, 2010.

Nelson Laird, Thomas F., and Ty M. Cruce. "Individual and Environmental Effects of Part-Time Enrollment Stats on Student-Faculty Interaction and Self-Reported Gains." *Journal of Higher Education* 80 (2009): 290–314.

Ngai, Mae M. *Impossible Subjects: Illegal Aliens and the Making of Modern America.* Princeton, NJ: Princeton University Press, 2004.

Nieto-Phillips, John M. *The Language of Blood: The Making of Spanish-American Identity in New Mexico, 1880s–1930s.* Albuquerque: University of New Mexico Press, 2004.

Oboler, Suzanne. *Ethic Labels, Latino Lives. Identity and the Politics of (Re)presentation in the United States.* Minneapolis: University of Minnesota Press, 1995.

Olguín, B. V. "Reassessing Pocho Poetics: Américo Paredes and the (Trans)-National Question." *Aztlán: A Journal of Chicano Studies* 30, no. 1 (Spring 2005): 87–121.

Olson, Keith, W. "The G.I. Bill and Higher Education: Success and Surprise." *American Quarterly* 25 (1973): 596–610.

Oropeza, Lorena. *¡Raza Sí! ¡Guerra No!: Chicano Protest and Patriotism during the Viet Nam War Era.* Berkeley: University of California Press, 2005.

Orozco, Cynthia E. *No Mexicans, Women, or Dogs Allowed: The Rise of the Mexican American Civil Rights Movement.* Austin: University of Texas Press, 2009.

Ortiz, Fernando. *Cuban Counterpoint: Tobacco and Sugar.* Durham, NC: Duke University Press, 1995.

Pacheco, Ferdie. *Ybor City Chronicles.* Gainesville: University Press of Florida, 1994.

Padilla, Amado M. "A Set of Categories for Combining Psychological and Historical Studies of Culture." In *Contemporary Mexico of the Fourth International Congress of Mexican History.* Edited by James W. Wilkie, Michael C. Meyer, and Edna Monzón de Wilkie. Los Angeles: UCLA Latin American Center, 1973.

Paredes, Américo. *Between Two Worlds.* Houston, TX: Arte Público Press, 1990.

———. *A Texas-Mexican Cancionero: Folksongs of the Lower Border.* Austin: University of Texas Press, 1995.

———. *Cantos de Adolescencia/Songs of Youth (1932–1937).* B. V. Olguín and Omar Vasquez Barbosa, translators. Houston, TX: Arte Público Press, 2007.

———. *With His Pistol in His Hand: A Border Ballad and Its Hero.* Austin: University of Texas Press, 1958.

Pascarella, Ernest. "How College Affects Students: Ten Directions for Future Research." *Journal of College Student Development* 47 (2006): 508–520.

Pérez, Emma. *The Decolonial Imaginary: Writing Chicanas into History.* Bloomington: Indiana University Press, 1999.

Pérez, Louis A., Jr. *Cuba under the Platt Amendment.* Pittsburgh: University of Pittsburgh Press, 1986.

———. *On Becoming Cuban: Identity, Nationality, and Culture.* Chapel Hill: University of North Carolina Press, 1999.

Pérez, Severo, and Judith Pérez. *Soldierboy.* In *Necessary Theater: Six Plays about the Chicano Experience,* edited by Jorge Huerta, 13–75. Houston, TX: Arte Público Press, 1989.

Poyo, Gerald E. "Baseball in Key West and Havana, 1885–1910: The Career of Francisco A. Poyo." *Florida Historical Quarterly* 87, no. 4 (Spring 2009): 540–564.

———. *"With All, and for the Good of All": The Emergence of Popular Nationalism in the Cuban Communities of the United States: 1848–1898.* Durham, NC: Duke University Press, 1989.

Pratt, Mary Louis. *Imperial Eyes: Travel Writing and Transculturation.* London: Routledge, 1992.

Quiñonez, Naomi. "Rosita the Riveter: Welding Wartime Tradition with Wartime Transformations." In *Mexican Americans and World War II*, edited by Maggie Rivas-Rodriguez, 245–268. Austin: University of Texas Press, 2005.

Raimundo, Antonio. "The Filipino Veterans Equity Movement: A Case Study in Reparations Theory." *California Law Review* 98, no. 2 (2010): 575–624.

Ramirez, Catherine S. *The Woman in the Zoot Suit: Gender, Nationalism, and the Cultural Politics of Memory.* Durham, NC: Duke University Press, 2008.

Ramírez, Elizabeth C. *Footlights across the Border: A History of Spanish-Language Professional Theatre on the Texas Stage.* New York: P. Lang, 1990.

Ramos, Henry A. J. *The American GI Forum: In Pursuit of the Dream, 1948–83.* Houston, TX: Arte Público Press, 1998.

Reed, Merl E. *Seedtime for the Modern Civil Rights Movement: The President's Committee on Fair Employment Practice, 1941–1946.* Baton Rouge: Louisiana State University Press, 1991.

Reimers, David M. *Still the Golden Door: The Third World Comes to America.* New York: Columbia University Press, 1992.

Rivas-Rodriguez, Maggie, ed. *Mexican Americans and World War II.* Austin: University of Texas Press, 2005.

Rivas-Rodriguez, Maggie, Julianna Torres, Missy DiPiero-D'Sa, and Lindsay Fitzpatrick, eds. *A Legacy Greater than Words: Stories of U.S. Latinos & Latinas of the World War II Generation.* Austin, TX: U.S. Latino & Latina World War II Oral History Project, 2006.

Rivas-Rodriguez, Maggie, and Emilio Zamora, eds. *Beyond the Latino World War II Hero: The Social and Political Legacy of a Generation.* Austin: University of Texas Press, 2009.

Roach, Ronald. "From Combat to Campus." *Black Issues in Higher Education* 14, no. 2 (1997): 26–29.

Rocamora, Rick. *Filipino World War II Soldiers: America's Second-Class Veterans.* San Francisco: Veterans Equity Center, 2008.

Rodriguez, Clara. *Changing Race: Latinos, the Census, and the History of Ethnicity in the United States.* New York: New York University Press, 2000.

Rodriguez, José A. *Hard Measures: How Aggressive CIA Actions after 9/11 Saved American Lives.* New York: Threshold Editions, 2012.

Rogers, Everett M., and Nancy R. Bartlit. *Silent Voices of World War II: When Sons of the Land of Enchantment Met Sons of the Land of the Rising Sun.* Santa Fe, NM: Sunstone Press, 2005.

Román, Miriam Jiménez, and Juan Flores, eds. *The Afro-Latin@ Reader: History and Culture in the United States.* Durham, NC: Duke University Press, 2010.

Rosales, F. Arturo. *Chicano! The History of the Mexican American Civil Rights Movement.* Houston, TX: Arte Público Press, 1996.

Rosenwaike, Ira, and Benjamin S. Bradshaw. "Mortality of the Spanish Surname Population of the Southwest." *Social Science Quarterly* 70, no. 3 (1989): 631–641.

Ruchames, Louis. *Race, Jobs, and Politics: The Story of FEPC*. New York: Columbia University Press, 1953.

Ruiz, Vicki L. *From Out of the Shadows: Mexican Women in Twentieth-Century America*. New York: Oxford University Press, 1998.

———. "South by Southwest: Mexican Americans and Segregated Schooling, 1900–1950." *Organization of American Historians* 15, no. 2 (Winter 2001): 20–22.

Saldívar, Ramón. *The Borderlands of Culture: Américo Paredes and the Transnational Imaginary*. Durham, NC: Duke University Press, 2006.

San Juan, E. *Racial Formations/Critical Transformations: Articulations of Power in Ethnic and Racial Studies in the United States*. Atlantic Highlands, NJ: Humanities Press, 1992.

San Miguel, Guadalupe, Jr. "Status of Historical Research on Chicano Education Report." *Review of Educational Research* 57, no. 4 (Winter 1987): 467–480.

Sánchez, George J. *Becoming Mexican American: Ethnicity, Culture, and Identity in Chicano Los Angeles*. New York: Oxford University Press, 1993.

———. "What's Good for Boyle Heights Is Good for the Jews: Creating Multiracialism on the Eastside during the 1950s." *American Quarterly* 56, no. 3 (September 2004): 135–163.

Sánchez, Ricardo, and Donald T. Phillips. *Wiser in Battle: A Soldier's Story*. New York: Harper, 2008.

Sanchez-Korrol, Virginia E. *From Colonia to Community: The History of Puerto Ricans in New York City, 1917–1948*. Westport, CT: Greenwood Press, 1983.

Sandoval, Chela. *Methodology of the Oppressed*. Minneapolis: University of Minnesota Press, 2000.

———. *Reading Chican@ Like a Queer: The De-Mastery of Desire*. Austin: University of Texas Press, 2010.

Santillán, Richard. "Rosita the Riveter: Midwest Mexican American Women during World War II, 1941–1945." *Perspectives in Mexican American Studies* 2 (1989): 115–147.

Schaefer, Chris. *Bataan Diary: An American Family in World War II, 1941–1945*. Houston, TX: Riverview Publishing, 2004.

Schmidt, Alicia Camacho. *Migrant Imaginaries: Latino Cultural Politics in the U.S.– Mexico Borderlands*. New York: New York University Press, 2008.

Schoen, Robert, and Verne E. Nelson. "Mortality by Cause among Spanish Surnamed Californians, 1969–71." *Social Science Quarterly* 62 (1981): 259–274.

Scott, James C. *Domination and the Arts of Resistance: Hidden Transcripts*. New Haven, CT: Yale University Press, 1992.

Sedgwick, Eve Kosofsky. *Between Men: English Literature and Male Homosocial Desire*. New York: Columbia University Press, 1985.

Sendejo, Brenda. "Mother's Legacy: Cultivating Chicana Consciousness during the War Years." In *Beyond the Latino World War II Hero: The Social and Political Legacy of a Generation*, edited by Maggie Rivas-Rodriguez and Emilio Zamora, 156–177. Austin: University of Texas Press, 2009.

Shapiro, Michael J. *Violent Cartographies: Mapping Cultures of War*. Minneapolis: University of Minnesota Press, 1997.

Shigematsu, Setsu, and Keith L. Camacho, eds. *Militarized Currents: Toward a De-*

colonized Future in Asia and the Pacific. Minneapolis: University of Minnesota Press, 2010.

Sides, Hampton. *Ghost Soldiers: The Forgotten Epic Story of World War II's Most Dramatic Mission.* New York: Doubleday, 2001.

Smith, Dean. *La Gloria Escondida.* Phoenix, AZ: Sims, 1967.

Soto, Lionel. *La Revolución del 33.* 3 vols. Havana: Editorial de Ciencias Sociales, 1975.

Stebbins, Consuelo E. *City of Intrigue, Nest of Revolution: A Documentary History of Key West in the Nineteenth Century.* Gainesville: University Press of Florida, 2007.

Tabares de Real, José. *La Revolución del 30: Sus dos últimos años.* Havana: Editorial de Ciencias Sociales, 1975.

Tadiar, Neferti. *Things Fall Away: Philippine Historical Experience and the Makings of Globalization.* Durham, NC: Duke University Press, 2009.

Takaki, Ronald. *Debating Diversity: Clashing Perspectives on Race and Ethnicity in America.* 3rd ed. New York: Oxford University Press, 2002.

———. *Double Victory: A Multicultural History of America in World War II.* Boston: Little, Brown, 2000.

Terán-Solano, Daniel. "La historia del bolero latinoamericano." Analitica.com (2000). www.analitica.com/va/hispanica/9288877.asp (accessed 11 March 2006).

Trotter, Joe William, Jr. "From a Raw Deal to a New Deal: 1929 to 1945." In *Make Your World Anew: A History of African Americans since 1880,* vol. 2, edited by Robin Kelley, D. G. Lewis, and Earl Lewis, 131-381. New York: Oxford University Press, 2005.

Trouillot, Michel-Rolph. *Silencing the Past: Power and the Production of History.* Boston: Beacon Press, 1995.

Trujillo, Charlie. *Dogs from Illusion.* San Jose, CA: Chusma House, 1994.

Tucker, Barbara. "Agricultural Workers in World War II: The Reserve Army of Children, Black Americans, and Jamaicans." *Agricultural History* 68, no. 1 (1994): 54–73.

United States Naval Academy Alumni Association. *Register of Alumni, Graduates and Former Naval Cadets and Midshipmen.* Annapolis, MD: Association Publishers, 1990.

Valdez, Luis. *Zoot Suit and Other Plays.* Houston, TX: Arte Público Press, 1992.

Valencia, Richard R. *Chicano Students and the Courts: The Mexican American Legal Struggle for Educational Equality.* New York: New York University Press, 2008.

Valenzuela, Angela. *Subtractive Schooling: US–Mexican Youth and the Politics of Caring.* Albany: State University of New York Press, 1999.

Valverde, Leonard A. "Equal Educational Opportunities since Brown: Four Major Developments." *Education and Urban Society* 36 (2004): 368–378.

Varela-Largo, Ana. "'¡No Pasarán!': The Spanish Civil War's Impact on Tampa's Latin Community, 1936–1939." *Tampa Bay History* 19 (Fall–Winter 1997): 5–35.

Varzally, Allison. *Making a Non-White America: Californians Coloring Outside Ethnic Lines, 1925–1955.* Berkeley: University of California Press, 2008.

Wainwright, Jonathan. *General Wainwright's Story: The Account of Four Years of Humiliating Defeat, Surrender, and Captivity.* Garden City, NY: Doubleday, 1946.

Washburn, Patrick S. *A Question of Sedition: The Federal Government's Investigation of the Black Press during World War II.* New York: Oxford University Press, 1986.

Wilson, Reginald. "G.I. Bill Expands Access for African Americans." *Educational Record* 75 (1994): 32–39.

Wilson, Steven. "Brown over 'Other White': Mexican Americans' Legal Arguments and Litigation Strategy in School Desegregation Lawsuits." *Law and History Review* 21, no. 1 (2003): 145–194.

Wong, Kevin Scott. *Americans First: Chinese Americans and the Second World War.* Cambridge, MA: Harvard University Press, 2005.

Ybarra-Frausto, Tomás. "La Chata Noloesca: Figura del donaire." In *Mexican American Theatre: Then and Now,* edited by Nicolás Kanellos, 41–51. Houston, TX: Arte Público Press, 1983.

Yenne, Bill. *Rising Sons: The Japanese American GIs Who Fought for the United States in World War II.* New York: Macmillan, 2007.

Yglesias, Jose. "Black Mountain College." *University Review* 19 (December 1972): 17–19.

———. *One German Dead.* Leeds, MA: Eremite Press, 1988.

Zamora, Emilio. *Claiming Rights and Righting Wrongs in Texas: Mexican Workers and Job Politics during World War II.* College Station: Texas A&M University Press, 2009.

———. "The Failed Promise of Wartime Opportunity for Mexicans in the Texas Oil Industry." *Southwestern Historical Quarterly* 95, no. 3 (1992): 23–50.

———. "Mexico's Wartime Intervention on Behalf of Mexicans in the United States: A Turning of Tables." In *Mexican Americans and World War II,* edited by Maggie Rivas-Rodríguez, 221–243. Austin: University of Texas Press, 2005.

Zavella, Patricia. "Abnormal Intimacy: The Varying Work Networks of Chicana Cannery Workers." *Feminist Studies* 11 (1985): 541–557.

———. "The Problematic Relationship of Feminism and Chicana Studies." *Women's Studies* 17, no. 1 (1989): 25–36.

Zayas, Ana Ramos. "Delinquent Citizenship, National Performances: Racialization, Surveillance, and the Politics of 'Worthiness' in Puerto Rican Chicago." *Latino Studies* 2 (2004): 26–44.

Unpublished Works

Portales, Patricia. "Women, Bombs, and War: Remapping Mexican American Women's Home Front Agency in World War II Literature, Theater, and Film." Ph.D. diss., University of Texas at San Antonio, 2012.

Westfall, L. Glenn. "Don Vicente Martínez Ybor: The Man and His Empire." Ph.D. diss., University of Florida, 1977.

Speeches

Lopez, Joe. "Acknowledgement of the Little Special One." Lecture at the Annual Meeting of the Philippine Scouts Heritage Society, Long Beach, CA, 21 May 2011.

Reyna, Tony. "My Experiences in the Bataan Death March." Lecture at the Bataan Memorial March, White Sands, NM, 26 March 2011.

Magazine Articles

Faludi, Susan. "A Reporter at Large: The Naked Citadel." *New Yorker*, 5 September 1994, 62–65.

Yglesias, Jose. "The Radical Latino Island in the Deep South." *Nuestro: The Magazine for Latinos* 1 (August 1977): 5–6.

———. "Un Buen Obrero." *New Masses*, 26 November 1946: 17–19.

Collections/Archives/Files

Arhoolie Foundation

Netty and Jesús Rodríguez, "Una Mula De Tantas." Phonograph Recording, Cat. #B-2308, Matrix #BVE 87809–1. San Antonio: Blue Bird, 1935.

Nettie Lee Benson Latin American Collection, University of Texas at Austin

Carlos E. Castañeda Papers. Personal and Biographical Material, 1911–1960.

U.S. Latino & Latina World War II Oral History Project/Voces Oral History Project, Nettie Lee Benson Latin American Collection, University of Texas at Austin

Acosta, Rudy. Interview by Louis Sahagun. Videotape recording. Upton, CA. 14 November 2000.

Aguilar, Nicanór. Interview by Maggie Rivas-Rodriguez. Videotape recording. El Paso, TX. 29 December 2001.

Azios, A.D. Interview by Paul Zepeda and Ernest Eguia. Videotape recording. Houston. 13 December 2002.

———. Interview by Angélica A. Rodríguez. Telephone recording. 14 March 2011.

Banegas, Lorenzo. Interview by Robert C. Moore. Audio recording. Las Cruces, NM. 27 April 1992.

Dominguez, Richard. Interview by Steven Rosales. Videotape recording. Whittier, CA. 26 March 2003.

Elizondo, Raymon A. Interview by Israel Saenz. Videotape recording. Salt Lake City, UT. 6 December 2003.

Esquivel, Juana Portales. Interview by Patricia Portales. Audio recording. San Antonio, TX. 23 February 2008.

Gabaldon, Guy. Interview by Maggie Rivas-Rodriguez. Videotape recording. Washington, DC. 7 June 2000.

Gastelum, Adam. Interview by René Zambrano. Videotape recording. San Diego, CA. 8 September 2000.

Gil, Paul. Interview with Andrea Valdez. Videotape recording. Austin, TX. 20 October 1999.

Gomez, Fred. Interview by William Luna. Videotape recording. Chicago, IL. 17 September 2002.

Gonzalez, Julian L. Interview by Raquel C. Garza and Veronica Franco. Videotape recording. San Antonio, TX. 13 October 2001.

———. Interview by Angélica A. Rodríguez. Telephone recording. 14 March 2011.

Gonzalez, Norberto. Interview by Erika Martinez. Videotape recording. Miami, FL. 14 September 2002.

Grillo, Evelio. Interview by Mario Barrera. Videotape recording. Oakland, CA. 26 January 2003.

Lujano, Lorenzo Terrones. Interview by Patricia Aguirre. Videotape recording. Newton, KS. 1 August 2003.

Martinez, José Fuljencio. Interview by Rea Ann Trotter. Audio recording. Fort Garland, CO. 1 September 2002.

Moreno, Leo. Interview by Paul R. Zepeda. Videotape recording. Houston, TX. 8 August 2003.

Prado, Edward. Interview by Ruben Ali Flores. Videotape recording. San Antonio, TX. 26 February 2000.

Rivas, Ramón M. Interview by Maggie Rivas-Rodriguez. Videotape interview. San Antonio, TX. 12 June 1999.

Rodriguez, Ralph. Interview by Brian Lucero. Videotape recording. Albuquerque, NM. 23 January 2002.

Roel, Virgilio. Interview by Oscar Torres. Videotape recording. 9 September 2002.

———. Interview by Angélica A. Rodríguez. Telephone recording. 15 March 2011.

Silva, Agapito E. Interview by Brian Lucero. Videotape recording. Albuquerque, NM. 30 November 2001.

Tovar, Rudolph. Interview by Henry Mendoza. Videotape recording. Los Angeles, CA. 26 September 2003.

University of Texas at Arlington, Tejano Voices Collection

Peña, Albert, Jr. "Oral History Interview with Albert Peña, Jr., 1996." Interview by Jose A. Gutierrez. Tejano Voices. 2 July 1996. Accessed 1 November 2010. http://library.uta.edu/tejanovoices/TV.jsp?x=015.

University of Florida Library, Oral History Project

Adamo, Dr. Frank. Interview by Gary Mormino. Tape recording. Tampa, FL. 20 April 1980.

University of South Florida Library, Special Collections

Alfonso, Manuel. Interview by Gary Mormino. Tape recording. Tampa, FL. 21 July 1984.

Gary Mormino Personal Archives

Rene, Gonzalez. Interview by Gary Mormino. Tape recording. Tampa, FL. 2001.

Pacheco, Ferdie. Interview by Gary Mormino. Tape recording. Tampa, FL. 12 June 1984.

Salcines, Emiliano José. Interviews with Gary Mormino, Tampa, FL. 1980–2000.

Sánchez, Arsenio. Interview by Gary Mormino. Tampa, FL. 5 July 1999.

Franklin D. Roosevelt Library, Hyde Park, New York

"An Analysis of American Public Opinion Regarding the War." Presidential Personal Files (PPF) 4721.

University of Texas Institute of Texan Cultures at San Antonio

Monsiváis, Carlos, and Amada Monsiváis. Interview by Pete Haney. Audio recording. Universal City, TX. 31 July 1990.

National Archives and Records Administration, College Park, MD

Records of the Committee on Fair Employment Practice, 1904–1946. Record Group 228. Headquarter Records. Division of Review and Analysis. Office of the Committee. Office Files of the Chairman. Administrative Division. Central Files 1941–1946. Legal Division. Hearings, 1941–1946.

National Archives and Records Administration, Southwest Region, Fort Worth, TX

Records of the Committee on Fair Employment Practice, 1904–1946. Record Group 228. Closed Cases, August 1941–March 1946.

National Archives and Records Administration, Washington, DC

General Records of the United States Government, 1778–2006. Record Group 11. Records of the Select Committees of the House of Representatives, Chapter 22. www.archives.gov/legislative/guide/house/chapter-22–select-guaranty-programs .html.

Private Collections

García, Rodolfo. Interviewed by Peter C. Haney. Audio recording. San Antonio, TX. 4 February 1999.

Court Cases, Legal Opinions, Treaties

Delgado v. Bastrop ISD. 2 Race Rel.L.R. 329 (S.D. Tex. 1957).
Mendez v. Westminster. 64 F. Supp. 544 (C.D. Cal. 1946), aff'd, 161 F.2d 774 (9th Cir. 1947) (en banc).
Op. Tex. Att'y Gen. No. V-128 (1947).
Plessy v. Ferguson, 163 U.S. 537 (1896).
Treaty of Peace, Friendship, Limits, and Settlement with the Republic of Mexico, Art. IX, Feb. 2, 1848, U.S.-Mex., 9 Stat. 922.

Reports

Arias, Elizabeth. "United States Life Tables by Hispanic Origin." *Vital and Health Statistics*, ser. 2, no. 152 (2010): 1–41.

Arias, Elizabeth, Lester R. Curtin, Rong Wei, and Robert Anderson. "United States Decennial Life Tables for 1999–2001." *National Vital Statistics Report* 57, no. 1 (5 August 2008).

Fenstermaker, Deborah, and Dawn Haines. Summary of estimated net coverage. A.C.E. Revision II, 31 December 2002. www.census.gov/dmd/www/pdf/pp -54r.pdf.

Immigration Commission. *Reports of the Immigration Commission, Immigrants in Industries*. 14. Washington, DC: U.S. Government Printing Office, 1911.

Leland, Anne, and Mari-Jana Oborocenau. "American War and Military Operations Casualties: Lists and Statistics." Washington, DC: Congressional Research Service. 26 February 2010. Available at www.fas.org/sgp/crs/natsec /RL32492.pdf.

Minnesota Population Center. "Integrated Public Use Microdata Set." Census Enumeration Forms. http://usa.ipums.org/usa/voliii/tEnumForm.shtml.

National Center for Education Statistics. "Total Fall Enrollment in Degree-Granting Institutions, by Attendance Status, Sex of Student, and Control of Institution: Selected Years, 1947 through 2009." Accessed 20 April 2011, retrieved from http://nces.ed.gov/programs/digest/d10/tables/dt10_197.asp?referrer=list.

National Survey of Student Engagement. *Student Engagement: Pathways to Collegiate Success*. Bloomington: Indiana University Center for Postsecondary Research, 2004.

Snyder, Thomas D., Alexandra G. Tan, and Charlene M. Hoffman. *Digest of Education Statistics 2005* (NCES 2006–030). U.S. Department of Education, National Center for Education Statistics. Washington, DC: U.S. Government Printing Office, 2006.

United States Bureau of the Census. "Net Undercount and Undercount Rate for U.S. and States (1990)." www.census.gov/dmd/www/pdf/understate.pdf. n.d.

United States Department of Health, Education, and Welfare. "Life Tables for 1949–1951." *Vital Statistics Special Reports*, 41 (1–5).

———. Public Health Service. "United States Life Tables, 1959–1961." Washington, DC, 1964.

———. "United States Life Tables, 1969–1971." Rockville, MD, May 1975.

United States Department of Health and Human Services, Public Health Service. National Center for Health Statistics. "United States Decennial Life Tables for 1979–1981," 1, no. 1. DHHS Pub. No. (PHS) 85–1150–1. Washington, DC: Government Printing Office, August 1985.

United States Department of Health and Human Services, National Center for Health Statistics. "United States Decennial Life Tables for 1989–1991," 1, no. 1. Hyattsville, MD, 1997.

United States Department of the Interior, National Park Service. Historic Preservation Certification Application for the Friedrich Building. San Antonio, TX, 1999.

United States Department of Veterans' Affairs. "G.I. Bill History." Last modified 6 November 2009. www.gibill.va.gov/GI_Bill_Info/history.htm.

———. Office of the Assistant Secretary for Policy and Planning. "Veteran Population Model." VetPop2007. Washington, DC: Released January 2008.

Author Biographies

LUIS ALVAREZ is associate professor of history at the University of California, San Diego. He is the author of *The Power of the Zoot: Youth Culture and Resistance during World War II* (University of California Press, 2008) and coeditor of *Another University Is Possible* (University Readers Press, 2010). He has won numerous awards for his research and teaching, including fellowships from the Warren Center for Studies in American History at Harvard University, the Ford Foundation, the University of California's Office of the President, and the Institute for Humanities Research at Arizona State University, and the Teaching Excellence Award from the University of Houston.

JORDAN BELTRÁN GONZALES is coauthor, with Tracy Lachica Buenavista, of "DREAMs Deferred: Filipino Experiences and an Anti-Militarization Critique of the Development, Relief, and Education for Alien Minors Act," *Harvard Journal of Asian American Policy Review* (2011). He graduated with a bachelor's degree in history from Yale University and is currently a Ph.D. candidate in the Department of Ethnic Studies at the University of California, Berkeley. His dissertation topic is the Philippines and the Bataan Death March in World War II, postwar social movements for Filipinos' citizenship and veterans benefits, and various memorial projects in the present day.

MARIANNE M. BUENO received her M.A. and Ph.D. degrees in history from the University of California, Santa Cruz. Her research interests include Chicana and Chicano history, women's and gender studies, and military studies. She has taught at the University of Minnesota and the

University of North Texas. She is currently working on a book manuscript based on her dissertation research, which examines the experiences of Mexican Americans on the World War II home front and front lines.

KARL ESCHBACH is a professor in the Departments of Internal and Preventive Medicine and Community Health, Division of Geriatric Medicine, and director of Population Research, Sealy Center on Aging, at the University of Texas Medical Branch.

FRANK ANDRÉ GURIDY is an associate professor of history and African and African diaspora studies at the University of Texas at Austin. He is the author of *Forging Diaspora: Afro-Cubans and African Americans in a World of Empire and Jim Crow* (University of North Carolina Press, 2010), which won the Elsa Goveia Book Prize from the Association of Caribbean Historians and the Wesley-Logan Book Prize, conferred by the American Historical Association. He is also the coeditor of *Beyond el Barrio: Everyday Life in Latino/a America* (New York University Press, 2010).

FÉLIX F. GUTIÉRREZ is professor of journalism and communication in the Annenberg School for Communication and Journalism and professor of American Studies and Ethnicity in the Dana and David Dornsife College of Letters, Arts, and Sciences at the University of Southern California. He curated the exhibit *Voices for Justice: 200 Years of Latino Newspapers in the United States* (2010), received the Association for Education in Journalism and Mass Communication Lionel C. Barrow Jr. Award for Distinguished Achievement in Diversity Research and Education (2011), and coauthored *Racism, Sexism, and the Media: Multicultural Issues into the New Communications Age* (Sage, 2013).

PETER C. HANEY is assistant director at the Center for Latin American and Caribbean Studies at the University of Kansas. His work on Mexican American performance has appeared in the *Journal of Linguistic Anthropology*, the *Journal of American Folklore*, *Pragmatics*, and *Language and Communication*. He served as a consultant for the museum exhibition *Las Carpas: Mexican American Tent Shows*, which opened in 1998 at San Antonio's Herzberg Circus Museum and remained until the museum's closure in 2001. He also served as a consultant for the Galán Productions documentary *Visiones: Latino Arts and Culture*, which aired on most PBS stations in 2004.

GARY R. MORMINO is the Frank E. Duckwall Professor Emeritus in Florida history at the University of South Florida, St. Petersburg. A co-author of *The Immigrant World of Ybor City* (1987), his most recent book is *Land of Sunshine, State of Dreams: A Social History of Modern Florida* (2005). He is currently working on a history of Florida and World War II.

JULIAN VASQUEZ HEILIG is an award-winning researcher and teacher. He is currently an associate professor of Educational Policy and Planning and African and African Diaspora Studies (by courtesy) at the University of Texas at Austin. He is also a faculty affiliate of the Center for Mexican American Studies and the Warfield Center for African and African American Studies. His current research includes an examination of how educational policies affect urban minority students. His research interests also include issues of access, diversity, and equity in higher education. He was inspired to contribute to this volume by the stories his grandfather William B. Heilig told him about service in World War II.

B. V. OLGUÍN is the author of *La Pinta: Chicana/o Prisoner Literature, Culture, and Politics* (University of Texas Press, 2010); co-translator, with Omar Vásquez Barbosa, of *Cantos de Adolescencia/Songs of Youth (1932–1937)* by Américo Paredes Manzano (Arte Público Press, 2007); and author of the forthcoming *Violentologies: Warfare and Ontology in Latina/o Literature, Film, and Popular Culture*. He is a published poet, community journalist, prison educator, and volunteer Emergency Medical Technician. Olguín currently is an associate professor in the Department of English and assistant director of the Honors College at the University of Texas at San Antonio.

PATRICIA PORTALES is currently an associate professor of English at San Antonio College. She received her Ph.D. in U.S. Latina/o literature from the University of Texas at San Antonio. She earned a B.A. in English with a minor in history and an M.A. in English from St. Mary's University. Her research interests include Mexican American oral history, literature, and semiotics of World War II. For over a decade she has also been a freelance journalist and fiction writer.

GERALD E. POYO is professor of history at St. Mary's University in San Antonio. He is the author of *"With All, and for the Good of All": The Emergence of Popular Nationalism in the Cuban Communities of the United States*

(Duke Univiversity Press, 1989), *Cuban Catholics in the United States: Exile and Integration* (University of Notre Dame Press, 2007), and *Exile and Revolution: José Dolores Poyo, Key West, and Cuban Independence* (University Press of Florida, 2014). He is also editor and coeditor of four books on Mexican American and Latino Catholic history.

ALLISON PROCHNOW is from Plano, Texas. She received her undergraduate degrees in Plan II and international business and her master's degree in Mexican American studies from the University of Texas at Austin. She recently served as interim Dallas Area director for Workers Defense Project, a nonprofit that seeks to achieve and enforce worker and immigrant rights through the education and empowerment of workers, when it opened its new Dallas location.

MAGGIE RIVAS-RODRIGUEZ, a former journalist, earned her Ph.D. in communications from the University of North Carolina at Chapel Hill. In 1999 she founded the multifaceted Voces Oral History Project at the University of Texas at Austin's School of Journalism, where she is an associate professor. She was on the committee that organized the National Association of Hispanic Journalists and has been active in establishing programs to promote inclusive and fairer journalism and academic research. She has coedited three books related to the World War II Latino experience. She is currently writing a book that addresses issues of civil rights advancements by, and the unique experiences of, the Latino World War II generation.

ANGÉLICA AGUILAR RODRÍGUEZ is a Ph.D. candidate in the Education Policy and Planning program at the University of Texas at Austin. She was previously a graduate research assistant with the Texas Education Research Center (ERC), a fellow at the Texas Center for Education Policy (TCEP), and a graduate research assistant at the UT Austin Public Policy Institute (PPI). Rodríguez also worked as a legislative assistant during the 81st Texas Legislative Session via the Senator Gregory Luna Fellow Program. Her dissertation will evaluate the effects of in-state resident tuition and Texas state financial aid on the persistence and graduation rates of undocumented college students.

Index

Numbers in italics refer to photographs.

CPSIA information can be obtained at www.ICGtesting.com
Printed in the USA
BVOW08s0404230816

459828BV00001B/45/P

DEC 28 2016